Cyber Law in Bulgaria

Cyber Law in Bulgaria

George Dimitrov
Martin Zahariev

This book was originally published as a monograph in the International Encyclopaedia of Laws/Cyber Law.

Founding Editor: Roger Blanpain
General Editor: Frank Hendrickx
Volume Editor: Jos Dumortier, Pieter Gryffroy, Ruben Roex & Yung Shin Van Der Sype

Wolters Kluwer

Published by:
Kluwer Law International B.V.
PO Box 316
2400 AH Alphen aan den Rijn
The Netherlands
E-mail: lrs-sales@wolterskluwer.com
Website: www.wolterskluwer.com/en/solutions/kluwerlawinternational

Sold and distributed by:
Wolters Kluwer Legal & Regulatory U.S.
7201 McKinney Circle
Frederick, MD 21704
United States of America
E-mail: customer.service@wolterskluwer.com

ISBN 978-94-035-4955-2

e-Book: ISBN 978-94-035-4605-6
web-PDF: ISBN 978-94-035-4615-5

The Authors

Prof. Dr George Dimitrov is a doctor of law of the Katholieke Universiteit Leuven, Belgium (PhD, 2008). He graduated cum laude from Sofia University, Bulgaria, Faculty of Law (LLM, 1995) and specialized at the Academy of American and International Law, Dallas, Texas (2002) as a holder of the prestigious Victor Folsom Fellowship. He also studied economics of the financial sector at the University of Delaware, Newark, US and microcomputer technology and programming at the Bulgarian Technical University. Currently, he is an associated professor in ICT Law at the University for Library Studies and Information Technologies and at the Sofia University 'St. Kliment Ohridski'.

Prof. Dimitrov is a founding partner of Dimitrov, Petrov & Co., a leading Bulgarian law firm, www.dpc.bg and head of its ICT & IPR Law Department. He is a panellist at the Czech Arbitration Court for the .eu domain ADR and at the International Arbitration Court at the Alliance for Legal Interaction. Prof. Dimitrov is also an expert at the Advisory Council to the Minister of Transport, Information Technologies and Communications and a member of the Scientific Council on ICT and the E-government Laboratory at the Bulgarian Academy of Sciences.

Being a Chairman of the Centre for Law of the Information and Communication Technologies in Bulgaria www.netlaw.bg, Prof. Dimitrov has served as an expert and head of numerous work groups that have drafted the contemporary Bulgarian legislation in the area of information and communications technology (ICT), *inter alia*, the Electronic Commerce Act (E-Commerce Act), the Electronic Governance Act (EGA), the Electronic Communications Act (ECA), the Commercial Register Act, the Electronic Document and Electronic Signature Act (EDESA), the state administration's corporate identity, laws, the cybercrimes section of the Criminal Code (CC), and many other acts of primary and secondary legislation. He has played a leading role in the elaboration of key strategies of national importance such as the Strategy for the Implementation of the E-healthcare in Bulgaria, the Strategy for E-government, the Strategy for Competitiveness of Bulgaria on the International ICT Markets, and so on.

Prof. Dimitrov was conferred the honour to be appointed as a Bulgarian national correspondent in a number of local and international projects of the European Commission (EC), the World Bank, the British Council, and other international institutions on the implementation of EU directives in the area of personal data protection, e-signature, e-documents, and e-governance. He is a member of the Scientific Board of the European Privacy Institute.

For a number of years, Prof. Dimitrov has trained attorneys-at-law, judges, prosecutors, investigators, in-house lawyers, and state officials in the legal aspects of the implementation of legislation in the areas of e-commerce, e-government, and cybercrimes and has authored a number of ICT articles and commentaries in Bulgarian and international specialized publications.

He is a member of various committees and professional legal organizations of local and international importance, such as: the International Bar Association (IBA) and the Information Technologies Law Association (ITechLaw), World IT Lawyers, Privacy Europe Network, and many others.

Assoc. Prof. Dr Martin Zahariev is a Senior Associate at Dimitrov, Petrov & Co. He is a promising young practitioner, specializing in the areas of privacy and data protection, intellectual property, life sciences, labour law, and commercial arbitration. Assoc. Prof. Zahariev graduated with honours from Sofia University 'St. Kliment Ohridski', Faculty of Law (LLM) and obtained his PhD degree from the University of Library Studies and Information Technologies (ULSIT), Sofia, with dissertation on automated data profiling and GDPR. Assoc. Prof. Zahariev is also a leading legal expert at the Law and Internet Foundation where he has participated as a researcher and trainer in several cross-border scientific projects, including as a data protection officer in one of them.

Assoc. Prof. Zahariev is the author of two monographs in the field of personal data protection – 'AUTOMATED PROFILING AND THE PERSONAL DATA PROTECTION. Analysis of GDPR' (2018), in Bulgarian – the first monograph on the topic in Bulgaria, and 'Data Protection in Commercial Arbitration: In the Light of GDPR' (2019), in English, the student book 'REGIME OF INFORMATION: Nature and significance of information. Personal data protection. Sample tests' (2020), in Bulgarian, as well as numerous articles, book chapters, and analyses in the field of personal data protection, ICT law, commercial arbitration, labour, and commercial law which are published in arbitration, data protection, and privacy blogs (including Kluwer Arbitration Blog), collections, local and international business and scientific journals.

His 292-pages scientific work 'Data Protection in Commercial Arbitration: In the Light of GDPR' represents his deep knowledge and understanding of the main roles in arbitration from data protection perspective and how compliance with the data protection legislation can be ensured in arbitration. It was ranked number 6 in the prestigious ranking *29 Best New GDPR Books To Read In 2020, 11 Best New GDPR Books To Read In 2021*, and included in the *64 Best GDPR Books of All Time* by BookAuthority.org – the world's leading site for nonfiction books.

Assoc. Prof. Zahariev is recommended by Who's Who Legal in the area of Data Privacy and Protection.

He is a university lecturer at ULSIT and Sofia University 'St. Kliment Ohridski' in different disciplines related to ICT law, data protection, and basics of law and a guest lecturer on Privacy & Data Protection in Stockholm University, the American University in Bulgaria, the Technical University of Sofia, and the University of Plovdiv 'Paisii Hilendarski'. Assoc. Prof. Zahariev is a contributor to the Austrian Yearbook on International Arbitration and co-organiser of various ICC Young Arbitration Forum events in the SEE region.

Assoc. Prof. Zahariev is also a member of the Sofia Bar Association, the International Moot Court Competitions Association, and the Bulgarian Society of Construction Law.

The Authors

Table of Contents

List of Abbreviations

ADR	Alternative Dispute Resolution
AECNPI	Act on the Electronic Communications Networks and Physical Infrastructure
APIA	Access to Public Information Act
ASANS	Act on the State Agency of National Security
ASDA	Access to Spatial Data Act
ATM	Automated Teller Machine
BEREC	Body of European Regulators for Electronic Communications
BNB	Bulgarian National Bank
BSD	Berkeley Software Distribution
BSI	Bulgarian Standardization Institute
BSS	Bulgarian State Standard
BTC	Bulgarian Telecommunications Company
CA	Commerce Act
CC	Criminal Code
ccTLD	Country Code Top-Level Domains
CEM	Council for Electronic Media
CEN	European Committee for Standardization
CENELEC	European Committee for Electrotechnical Standardization
CIA	Credit Institutions Act
ConsPA	Consumer Protection Act
CP	Certificate Policy
CPA	Competition Protection Act
CPC	Competition Protection Commission
CPDP	Commission for Personal Data Protection
CPS	Certification Practice Statement
CRC	Communications Regulation Commission
CRRA	Copyright and Related Rights Act
DNS	Domain Name System

List of Abbreviations

DPA	Data Processing Agreement
DPO	Data Protection Officer
DSFSA	Distance Supply of Financial Services Act
DSL	Digital Subscriber Lines
EC	European Commission
ECA	Electronic Communications Act
E-Commerce Act	Electronic Commerce Act
ECNIS	Electronic Communications Networks and Information Systems Agency
EDESA/EDETSA	Electronic Document and Electronic Signatures Act, new name: Electronic Document and Electronic Trust Services Act
EEAW	Extradition and European Arrest Warrant Act
eIDAS	Regulation (EU) No 910/2014 of the European Parliament and of the Council of 23 July 2014 on electronic identification and trust services for electronic transactions in the internal market and repealing Directive 1999/93/EC
EGA	Electronic Governance Act
EJN	European Judicial Network
ERP	Enterprise Resource Planning
ETSI	European Telecommunications Standards Institute
EU	European Union
GDP	Gross Domestic Product
GDPR	General Data Protection Regulation
gTLD	Generic Top-Level Domain
GNU	GNU's Not Unix
GPL	General Public Licence
GSM	Global System for Mobile Communications
IC	Insurance Code
ICAA	International Commercial Arbitration Act
ICANN	Internet Corporation for Assigned Names and Numbers
ICT	Information and Communications Technology
ICTA	Integrated Circuit Topology Act
IEC	International Electrotechnical Commission
IES	Intermediary to Electronic Statement
IFAA	Independent Financial Audit Act
IP	Internet Protocol
IPLC	International Private Law Code
ISO	International Organization for Standardization
ISSP	Information Society Service Provider

ITU	International Telecommunications Union
IVR	Interactive Voice Response
LAN	Local Area Network
MA	Mediation Act
MGIA	Marks and Geographic Indications Act
MTITC	Ministry of Transport, Information Technology and Communications
NGA	Access Networks from the Next Generation
NNP	National Numbering Plan
NSA	National Standardization Act
OCA	Obligations and Contracts Act
OCESPA	Ordinance on the Certificates for Electronic Signatures in the Public Administrations
OCG	Organized Criminal Group
OCSSP	Online Content-Sharing Service Provider
OLTATSP	Ordinance on the Liability and on the Termination of the Activity of Trust Service Providers
OJ	Official Journal
ORACVQES	Ordinance on the Requirements to the Algorithms for Qualified Electronic Signatures
PCIA	Protection of Classified Information Act
PDCDSSGA	Provision of Digital Content and Digital Services and Sale of Goods Act
PDPA	Personal Data Protection Act
PECL	Principles of European Contract Law
PETL	Principles of European Tort Law
PIN	Personal Identification Number
PIU	Passenger Information Unit
PLC	Power Line Communications
PNR	Passenger Name Records
PPA	Public Procurement Act
PPC	Public Procurement Contract
PRUMA	Patents and Registration of Utilities Models Act
PSPSA	Payment Services and Payment Systems Act
RIO	Reference Interconnection Offer
RTA	Radio and Television Act
SAC	Supreme Administrative Court
SANS	State Agency National Security
SCC	Standard Contractual Clauses
SG	State Gazette

List of Abbreviations

SMP	Significant Market Power
SMS	Short Message Service
SSL	Secure Sockets Layer
TA	Telecommunications Act
TRPA	Technical Requirements to the Products Act
TSP	Trust Service Provider
UNCITRAL	United Nations Commission on International Trade Law
VAT	Value Added Tax
WAP	Wireless Application Protocol
XML	eXtensible Markup Language

Preface

The development of the information and communication technologies drives the world into new dimensions. People communicate electronically in a virtual space without borders commonly referred to as cyberspace. The national jurisdictions are facing the challenge of finding a balance as to the need for enforcing a just legislation to secure protection for the lawful interests of the persons in the cyber world. Problematic issues could be found in personal data and privacy protection, in protection of intellectual property, in validity and formation of ICT contracts, in execution of electronic transactions, in investigating computer crimes, and so on. The monograph outlines the Bulgarian approach in regulating the above issues. Being a member of the EU, Bulgaria has transposed the European supranational legislation fairly well. The work aims at presenting the main legislative acts regulating the relations between people involving information and communication technologies, at outlining the market developments and at pointing out the way in which national regulatory authorities and courts apply and interpret the new rules. In a world of smart technologies and automation, the presence of sustainable legal framework that ensures the fundamental rights and freedoms of the citizens is of utmost importance. This is the only way to benefit from the technological progress and at the same time to develop our societies in harmony with the rule of law principles.

General Introduction

Chapter 1. General Background of the Country

§1. Geography

1. The Republic of Bulgaria is situated in south-east Europe and occupies the north-east part of the Balkan Peninsula. Bulgaria borders Romania to the north, Greece and Turkey to the south, and Serbia and the Republic of North Macedonia to the west. The coast of the Black Sea is the country's eastern border. The total territory of the country is 110,910 square kilometres. Despite its relatively small size, Bulgaria enjoys picturesque and diverse landscape with 38% of its territory covered with forests and woodlands. The country is rich in water resources such as rivers, lakes, and mineral springs. The climate is mixed: predominantly temperate in the north and Mediterranean-influenced in the south. There are four distinct seasons with cold snowy winters and hot summers.

§2. Demographic and Cultural Composition

2. Since ancient times, Bulgaria has been a place where many migration roads cross. Early settlement occurred mainly in fertile agricultural lands. Thus, the demographic composition of the country reflects in many ways the key historical events that took place on the Balkan Peninsula such as the Ottoman Empire presence for almost five centuries during the Middle Ages, the Crusades, the main migration paths of different nations, etc. Nowadays Bulgarian population comprises three main ethnic groups – Bulgarian (84.8%), Turk (8.8%), and Roma (4.9%); while other ethnicities comprise 1.5% of the population including Macedonian, Armenian, Tatar, Circassian, etc.[1]

3. Pursuant to Article 3 of the Bulgarian Constitution,[2] the official language in the country is Bulgarian. However, in practice, some minority languages that closely correspond to the ethnic breakdown (Turkish and Roma) are also used unofficially.

1. National Statistical Institute: Final Census 2011: http://www.nsi.bg/EPDOCS/Census2011final.pdf, accessed 16 Sept. 2013. Data to be taken with caution due to a high number of blank responses. In Sept.–Oct. 2021, a new 2021 census was conducted, but only its preliminary results are publicly available at the time of issuance of the present edition. Where possible, the present report contains up-to-date information about the latest census.
2. *State Gazette* (SG), issue 56 of 13 July 1991.

4. The Bulgarian Constitution guarantees the freedom of religious expression and separation of Church and state. Article 13(3) of the Bulgarian Constitution proclaims East Orthodox Christianity as traditional religion. It is estimated that around 76% of the Bulgarian population belong to the latter, whereas only a small percentage follow other religions such as Islam (10%), Roman Catholic (0.8%), Protestant (1.1%), and other 12% (Jewish, Gregorian-Armenian, atheists, undecided, etc.).[3]

5. After World War II, Bulgarian cities grew rapidly at the expense of the rural population. In 1990, nearly one-third of the population lived in the ten largest cities and two-thirds was urban. By the end of 1990, however, more than 6 million people lived in cities while fewer than 3 million lived in villages. Currently, 74.3% of the Bulgarian population (or 4,843,175 people) is urban and 25.7% is rural (or 1,677,139 people).[4]

§3. Political System

6. Bulgaria is a parliamentary republic. The national sovereignty belongs to the Bulgarian people who exercise the state power directly and through the bodies explicitly envisaged in the Constitution.[5]

The head of state is the president who symbolizes the unity of the nation and represents Bulgaria in international relations.[6] The presidential office is elective, and his powers are defined in the Bulgarian Constitution.

Bulgaria is a European Union (EU) Member State since 1 January 2007.

7. Article 8 of the Constitution regulates the separation of powers. The Bulgarian Parliament, a unicameral body, whose members are elected through universal, equal, free, direct, and secret suffrage, is invested with legislative power. The Parliament represents the Bulgarian people, and in addition to its legislative competences, it approves the state budget, sets state taxes, and exercises parliamentary control over government policies.

The executive power of the state is exercised by the Council of Ministers. The Council is approved by the Parliament upon a proposal of the Prime Minister who is directly elected (dismissed) by the Parliament. The government conducts domestic and foreign policy, civil and military administration, and the defence of the state in accordance with the Constitution and the laws.

The judicial power protects the interests and rights of natural persons, legal entities, and the state and is executed on behalf of the people.[7] Judges, jurists, prosecutors, and investigators shall be independent and shall be bound solely by the rule of

3. National Statistical Institute: Final Census 2011: http://www.nsi.bg/EPDOCS/Census2011final.pdf, accessed 16 Sept. 2013. Data to be taken with caution due to high number of blank responses.
4. National Statistical Institute, 'Preliminary estimation of the population of Bulgaria as of 7 Sept. 2021', https://www.nsi.bg/sites/default/files/files/pressreleases/Census2021_predvaritelna_ocenka.pdf, 2022, accessed 18 Jan. 2022.
5. Bulgarian Constitution, Art. 1(1) and (2).
6. *Ibid.*, at Art. 92.
7. Bulgarian Constitution, Art. 117.

law while exercising their functions. The Supreme Court of Cassation and Supreme Administrative Court (SAC) are the judicial bodies of highest rank except for constitutional issues where the Constitutional Court is competent. Their heads are appointed by the President of the state at the proposal of the Supreme Judicial Council.

The Constitutional Court comprises twelve members elected for five-year mandate:[8] one-third is elected by the Parliament, one-third is appointed by the President of the state, and one-third is elected by the General Assembly of the judges of the Supreme Court of Cassation and the SAC. The Constitutional Court is entitled, *inter alia*, to deliver mandatory interpretation of the Bulgarian Constitution, to hear cases concerning the unconstitutionality of parliamentary and presidential acts of the Parliament or President or the unconstitutionality of political parties or associations and to rule upon disputes on jurisdiction among the Parliament, Council of Ministers and President, as well as disputes on the legality of parliamentary or presidential elections.[9]

8. The Supreme Judicial Council is responsible for the appointment, promotion, demotion, relocation, dismissal and training of judges, prosecutors, and investigators. It sets the number of judicial districts and court seats and allocates the number of judges, prosecutors, and investigators per court, prosecutor office or investigation service. It, via its plenum, also reviews and adopts the draft budget of the judiciary and supervises its implementation.[10] The Supreme Judicial Council comprises twenty-five members elected for a term of five years. The Chairperson of the Supreme Court of Cassation, the Chairperson of the SAC and the Chief Prosecutor are members *ex lege*. The other members of the Supreme Judicial Court are elected jurists with high qualifications and moral values who have at least fifteen years of professional experience. Eleven of the Council's members are elected by the Parliament, and the judiciary elects another eleven.[11] With the constitutional amendments from 2015,[12] the Supreme Judicial Council was split into two panels – Judicial and Prosecutorial and all its members form the Plenum of the Council.[13] The Judicial Panel of the Supreme Judicial Council shall consist of fourteen members and shall include the chairmen of the Supreme Court of Cassation and the SAC, six members directly elected by the judges and six members elected by the National Assembly. The Prosecutorial Panel of the Supreme Judicial Council shall consist of eleven members and shall include the Chief Prosecutor, four members directly elected by the prosecutors, one member directly elected by the investigators and five members elected by the National Assembly. Each of the panels has competences in line with their professional orientation.[14] The Minister of Justice chairs the sessions of the Plenum of the Supreme Judicial Council. The Judicial Panel of the Supreme Judicial Council is chaired by the Chairperson of the Supreme Court of Cassation.

8. *Ibid.*, Art. 147.
9. *Ibid.*, Art. 149.
10. Bulgarian Constitution, Art. 130a(2), i. 1.
11. *Ibid.*, Art. 130.
12. SG, issue 100/2015.
13. *Ibid.*, Art. 130a(1).
14. *Ibid.*, Art. 130a(3)-(5).

The Prosecutorial Panel of the Supreme Judicial Council is chaired by the Chief Prosecutor. The Minister of Justice may attend the meetings without taking part in the voting. The Chief Inspector may attend the sittings of the plenum of the Supreme Judicial Council and the sittings of the Judicial and Prosecutorial Collegium of the Supreme Judicial Council, without participating in the voting.[15]

9. The state is organized territorially into 28 regions subdivided into 266 municipalities. Regions implement regional policies, represent the state at the local level and are responsible for reconciling state and local interests,[16] while municipalities constitute basic local administrative units that conduct local self-government.

The region is a local administrative unit that implements regional policy, represents the state at a local level, and reconciles national and local interests. A regional governor appointed by the Council of Ministers and assisted by the regional administration effects the government of the region. The regional governor ensures the implementation of national policy; he is responsible for the protection of national interests, of lawfulness and public order, and for exercising administrative control.[17]

The municipality is the basic local administrative unit, which conducts local self-government. The citizens participate in the municipality's government not only through the local self-government bodies elected by them, but also directly by referendum and general assembly of the population.[18] The mayors are the municipality's executive bodies. The population or the Municipality Council elects them for a four-year term pursuant to a procedure provided by law.[19]

§4. Population and Vital Statistics

10. In 2012, the population of Bulgaria was 7,282,041,[20] women being 51.3% and allowing 1,055 women for every 1,000 men. In comparison, in 2020 the population of Bulgaria was 6,916,548,[21] women being 51.56%. According to the latest 2021 census, the population in the country as of 7 September 2021 was 6,520,314 people, women being 52.1% and men – 47.9%. The households that participated in the census were 2,813, 847 and an average of 2.3 people were living in one household.[22]

---

15. *Ibid.*, Art. 130b.
16. Bulgarian Constitution, Art. 142.
17. *Ibid.*, Art. 143.
18. *Ibid.*, Art. 136.
19. *Ibid.*, Art. 139.
20. National Statistical Institute, 'Population and Demographic Processes in 2012', http://www.nsi.bg/EPDOCS/Population2012_IZXIDOM.pdf, 2013.
21. National Statistical Institute, 'Population by districts, municipalities, place of residence and sex', https://www.nsi.bg/bg/content/2975/население-по-области-общини-местоживеене-и-пол, 2020, accessed 9 Dec. 2021.
22. National Statistical Institute, 'Preliminary estimation of the population of Bulgaria as of 7 September 2021', https://www.nsi.bg/sites/default/files/files/pressreleases/Census2021_predvaritelna_ocenka.pdf, 2022, accessed 18 Jan. 2022.

In 2020, 4,139,056 people (58.39 % from the population in total) comprised the people in working age. The population over active working age was 1,713,457 (24.77%), and the population under the active working age – 1,064,035.[23]

The birth rate coefficient continuously decreases in the past six years, reaching from 9.2‰ for year 2015, 9.1‰ for year 2016, 9.0‰ for year 2017, 8.9‰ for year 2018, 8.8‰ for year 2019 to 8.5‰[24] or 59 440 children[25] in 2020.

Life expectancy for the period of 2010–2012 in the country was 74 years marking an increase of 2.1 years compared to the period of 2000–2002. It is 70.6 years for men and 77.6 years for women. For the period 2018-2020, life expectancy was 74.6 years – 71.1 years for men and 78.2 years for women. There is a decrease of 0.3 years in comparison to the earlier 2017–2019 period.[26]

People enrolled in universities for the academic 2012/2013 year counted up to 283,959,[27]of which bachelor and master's degree students were 278,588, men – 126,459 and women – 152,129.[28] For the academic 2020/2021 year, the total number of students was 219,791 men – 99,918 and women – 119,873.[29] The number of the graduated students in 2020 was 219,800.[30]

---

23. National Statistical Institute, 'Population under, in and over working age by districts, municipalities and place of residence', https://www.nsi.bg/bg/content/13038/население-под-във-и-над-трудоспособна-възраст-по-области-общини-и-место Живеене, 2020, accessed 9 Dec. 2021.
24. National Statistical Institute, 'Birth rate by statistical regions, districts and places of residence', https://www.nsi.bg/bg/content/2968/коефициент-на-раждаемост-по-статистически-рай они-области-и-местоживеене, 2020. accessed 9 Dec. 2021.
25. National Statistical Institute, 'Births by place of residence, statistical regions, districts and sex', https://www.nsi.bg/bg/content/2956/раждания-по-местоживеене-статистически-райони -области-и-пол , 2020, accessed 9 Dec. 2021.
26. National Statistical Institute, 'AVERAGE LIFE EXPECTANCY OF THE POPULATION DURING THE PERIOD 2018 – 2020', https://www.nsi.bg/sites/default/files/files/pressreleases/LifeExpectan cy_2018-2020_106QOF0.pdf, 2020, accessed 9 Dec. 2021.
27. National Statistical Institute, 'Enrolled students, levels breakdown, according to The International Standard Classification of Education (ISCE)-97, latest data', http://www.nsi.bg/otrasal.php?otr=23&a1=2226&a2=2228#cont, 2013.
28. National Statistical Institute, 'Students according to degree classification, citizenship, form of education, and gender in academic year 2012/2013, latest data', http://www.nsi.bg/otrasal.php?otr=23&a1=782&a2=783&a3=784#cont, 2013.
29. National Statistical Institute, 'Students in Educational Qualification, Citizenship, Form of Education and Sex, in Higher Education Institutions in The Form of Ownership, During the School Year 2020/2021', https://www.nsi.bg/bg/content/3390/студенти-по-образователно-квалификационна-степен-гражданство-форма-на-обучение-и-пол-във-висшите-училища-по-форма-на-собственост, 2020, accessed 9 Dec. 2021.
30. National Statistical Institute, 'The Education in the Republic of Bulgaria during the school year 2020/2021', https://www.nsi.bg/sites/default/files/files/pressreleases/Education2020_8POU0B1.pdf, 2020, accessed 9 Dec. 2021.

Chapter 2. Telecommunications Infrastructure

§1. General Statement

11. Bulgaria possesses an evolving telecoms market where the adoption of EU regulatory principles has created a stable regulatory environment, facilitating foreign investment. The years 2007 and 2008 showed the dynamic development of the telecommunications market. Since then, the economic crisis and M&A activity has determined a trend of decline. In 2012, the registered enterprises offering telecommunication services had decreased to 1,153, where 869 were active. In 2020, the numbers were 1,126 registered enterprises and 861 active ones, so the general tendency with regard to the operators on the market remained rather intact. The volume of the market was estimated at 3.6% of Gross Domestic Product (GDP) for 2012, at 2.3% of GDP for 2019 and at 2.4% for 2020 respectively. In 2020, for the first time there was a slight increase of 0.15% in comparison with a long period of constant decrease.[31]

In 2012, the voice telephony revenues dropped to BGN 1.840 billion – a steady trend visible through 2009 (2.614 billion in revenues), 2010 (2.323 billion in revenues), and 2011 (2.062 billion in revenues).[32] In 2013, fixed mobile substitution has led the fixed-line operators to focus on broadband and related services.[33] In 2020 the revenues from data transmission services and/or Internet access exceeded the revenues from voice services and with 41.8% share in the total market volume are the leaders on the market. The relative share of revenues from this market segment in the structure of the market increased compared to 2018 by 4.6%. In comparison, the revenues from voice telephone services (fixed, mobile and other voice services) continued to decline, both in absolute terms (by 1.9% over a one-year period), and in relative terms (by 3.5 %). In 2020, their share in the total volume of the public electronic communications market was 40.2%. Other three market segments also increased in 2020, namely (1) data transfer and/or Internet access services (reaching 19.8 %); (2) other services (7.4%) mainly due to the access to satellite systems service and the co-location and other forms of shared usage, including the provision of towers, masts, and others; (3) services for the transmission and/or distribution of radio and television programmes due to IPTV services (increase with 0.6%). Decrease for 2020 can be identified with regard to voice telephone services (with 1.9%) and leased line services (with 10.2%).[34] In connection with the provision of harmonized spectrum for wireless broadband networks and services, in 2020 the Communications Regulation Commission (CRC) held a public consultation on the prospects and conditions for the use of the free resource in radio

---

31. CRC Annual Report 2012, http://www.crc.bg/files/_bg/I._Sustoyanie,_razvitie_i_perspektivi_na_pazara_na_elektronnite_suobshteniq_GD2012.pdf.
    CRC. 'Annual Report 2020' https://crc.bg/files/AR_CRC_2020_22.06.2021.pdf, accessed 09 Dec. 2021.
32. CRC. 'Annual Report', http://www.crc.bg/files/_bg/I_GD2011.pdf, 2011, accessed 16 Sep. 2013.
33. CRC 'Annual Report': http://www.crc.bg/files/_bg/I%D0%86_Elektronni_syobshtitelni_mreji_i_uslugi_CRC_GD_2012.pdf, 2012, accessed 16 Sept. 2013.
34. CRC. 'Annual Report 2020' https://crc.bg/files/AR_CRC_2020_22.06.2021.pdf, accessed 09 Dec. 2021, pp. 10–11.

frequency 700 MHz band and launched such in terms of prospects and conditions of use of the free resource in the 26 GHz radio frequency band. The CRC also announced intentions to limit the number of spectrum authorizations in the bands 2.6 GHz and 3.6 GHz.[35] CRC in its report for 2020 recognized that the trend of growth in the number of subscribers to Internet access services in the country continued to be valid in 2020, although to a relatively lesser extent than in 2019. To 31 December 2020 the total number of subscribers of Internet retail services (fixed and mobile Internet access) was 8.630 million and marked an increase of 1.7% compared to the end of the previous year (5.4% growth in 2019 compared to 2018). Subscribers to bundled services (including fixed and/or mobile Internet access) were also growing, but unlike in previous periods, there had been some slowdown, with the last year increasing by only 0.6% in absolute terms to 6,123 million.[36]

Nevertheless, it should be pointed out that estimates and forecasts for the future of the sector's developments differ due to differences in methodologies and definitions applied by statistical and forecast research organizations.

§2. Fixed Communications

12. A factor of importance in the development of fixed communications were packaged services. The bundling of fixed and mobile voice services, sometimes including Internet and TV subscriptions, increased[37] to eighty-one in 2010. The relative market share of bundled services in 2011 was 8.1% (a five-point increase from 2010) and 11.01% in 2012, when revenues were up by 30.22%. There had been continuing development of the service, and thus subscribers started paying less and receiving better servicing by a single provider.[38] This growth trend was expected to continue through 2013 and beyond.

13. n 2020 the total number of enterprises authorized by the CRC for providing fixed communications service through the primary provided resource – geographical numbers and access to public telephone service through the service 'Selection of Operator' amounted to twenty-five. The total number of enterprises that declared provision activity of fixed telephone service through National Numbering Plan (NNP) numbers and/or wholesale interconnection services of public telephone networks amounted to twenty-eight. The main providers of fixed telephone service through NNP for end users (retail service) were Bulgarian Telecommunications

35. CRC. 'Annual Report 2020' https://crc.bg/files/AR_CRC_2020_22.06.2021.pdf, accessed 09 Dec. 2021, pp. 5–6.
36. *Ibid.*, p. 37.
37. European Commission, BULGARIA 2011: Telecommunication Market and Regulatory Developments, http://ec.europa.eu/digital-agenda/sites/digital-agenda/files/BG_Country_Chapter_17th_Report_0.pdf, 2012, accessed 16 Sept. 2013.
38. CRC, 'Annual Report', www.crc.bg/section.php?id=593&lang=bg, 2008, 27.

Company (BTC), A1 Bulgaria EAD (A1) and Telenor Bulgaria EAD (Telenor) with 98% from the volume of the market and 96% from the realized revenues from the market.[39]

§3. Mobile Communications

14. The Bulgarian mobile communications market is competitive: it had high infiltration in Bulgaria – 122.81% in October 2007. In 2007, cable operators served 1.66 million households, while those with satellite access reached 228,000.[40] In 2012, these numbers were as high as 148% mobile penetration. The CRC reported that towards the end of 2020 the penetration of the mobile telephone service in Bulgaria amounted to 114.9%, which represented a decrease of 2.1% compared to penetration for 2019 (117.0%). This decline indicated that in 2020 there was a slight slowdown in rate of decrease in the indicator 'mobile telephone density' compared to 2019, when, compared to 2018, a decrease of 2.8% was reported.[41]

15. Since 2008, three undertakings have operated commercially on the Bulgarian mobile cellular networks and services market. All of them operate under Global System for Mobile Communications (GSM) and Universal Mobile Telecommunications System (UMTS) standards.[42] In 2020 their number has increased compared to 2008, namely five enterprises had obtained an authorization by the CRC to provide mobile communications service in Bulgaria (meaning that they had permissions to use mobile numbers from the NNP and had obtained radiofrequencies to provide mobile services), with the number remaining unchanged in comparison to 2019. These were A1, BTC, Bulsatkom EAD (Bulsatkom), Telenor, and Ti.Kom AD, the latter had not yet commenced the effective provision of its service. The market share with regard to number of subscribers for 2020 was the highest for A1 (38.1% in comparison to 38.5% for 2019), followed by Telenor (33.4%, the same value as in 2019), BTC (28.5% in comparison to 28.1% for 2019), and Bulsatkom (0.02% in comparison to 0.01% for 2019). The market share with regard to revenues from provision of the services in the retail market was again the highest for Telenor (41.6% in comparison to 41.2% for 2019), followed by A1 (33.0% in comparison to 33.7% for 2019), BTC (25.4% in comparison to 25.2% for 2019), and Bulsatkom (0.002%, the same value as in 2019).[43]

---

39. CRC. 'Annual Report 2020' https://crc.bg/files/AR_CRC_2020_22.06.2021.pdf, accessed 09 Dec. 2021, pp. 17–19.
40. Commission of the European Communities, 'Progress Report on the Single European Electronic Communications Market (13th Report)' (COM(2008)153, 19 Mar. 2008), http://ec.europa.eu/information_society/policy/ecomm/library/communications_reports/annualreports/13th/index_en.htm, 89.
41. CRC. 'Annual Report 2020' https://crc.bg/files/AR_CRC_2020_22.06.2021.pdf, accessed 09 Dec. 2021, p. 25.
42. CRC, 'Annual Report', <www.crc.bg/section.php?id=593&lang=bg>, 2008, 45.
43. CRC. 'Annual Report 2020' https://crc.bg/files/AR_CRC_2020_22.06.2021.pdf, accessed 09 Dec. 2021, p. 23.

16. Again since 2008, the three digital mobile operators had continued to invest in their third-generation UMTS (3G) networks, which in 2012 already covered approximately 95% of the population. The court decision ruling a price drop of call termination (Decision 1362, CRC from the 31 May 2012) also had influence along with the growth of bundled services, which again has influenced the price downwards.[44] In September 2020 and November 2020 two mobile operators launched 5G services with temporary frequencies and one mobile operator was performing trials. In 2021 Bulgaria's telecommunications authority concluded its auction for 5G spectrum in the 3.6 GHz band and three mobile operators secured 100 MHz national licences each. By the end of 2021, these three mobile operators launched commercial 5G networks/services.

17. According to data provided by CRC's Annual Report,[45] the number of mobile communications users in 2008 was 10,780,732 equal to approximately 148% of the country's population, which is due to the fact that the number of users with more than one SIM card is constantly increasing. The bundled services and data transfer and Internet services continued to gain market, thus changing the market structure. In that respect, it is worth mentioning that according to CRC, the number of subscribers to bundled services at the end of 2020 increased as compared to the previous year by 0.2% to 6.526 million. In 2020, double packages covered 98.8% of the total subscribers to bundled services, with the number of subscribers to this type of bundle increasing by 0.2% compared to data from 2019. The CRC noted that as in the previous year, in 2020 the number of subscribers to triple packages significantly decreased (by 18.2%), mainly as a result of the decrease (by 55.6%) of the subscribers of the package 'fixed voice, television, and fixed Internet access' and the subscribers of the 'mobile voice, television, and mobile package Internet' (with 33%).[46]

18. Mobile services became increasingly popular with Bulgarian users causing smooth decline in the use of fixed services; as noted in previous paragraph, the number of subscribers reported by mobile operators was higher than the population of the country mainly due to the growing number of users having more than one SIM card, in particular for prepaid services.

19. At the end of 2012, there were fifty-six enterprises licensed for provision of telecommunications services through telecommunications networks related to the provision of the 'leased line' service, including international lines. Twelve new individual undertakings notified CRC of their intention to provide the 'leased line'

44. CRC 'Annual Report': http://www.crc.bg/files/_bg/I%D0%86_Elektronni_syobshtitelni_mreji_i_uslugi_CRC_GD_2012.pdf, 2012, accessed 16 Sept. 2013.
45. CRC 'Annual Report': http://www.crc.bg/files/_bg/I%D0%86_Elektronni_syobshtitelni_mreji_i_uslugi_CRC_GD_2012.pdf, 2012, accessed 16 Sept. 2013.
46. CRC. 'Annual Report 2020' https://crc.bg/files/AR_CRC_2020_22.06.2021.pdf, accessed 09 Dec. 2021, pp. 11–12.

service. The leased line services, including international lines for 2020 continued to decrease. Totally 24 enterprises provided these services actively on the market (from 113 which notified the CRC of their intention to commence its provision).[47]

47. CRC. 'Annual Report 2020' https://crc.bg/files/AR_CRC_2020_22.06.2021.pdf, accessed 09 Dec. 2021, pp. 31–32.

Chapter 3. The Information and Communications Technology Market

§1. General Statement

20. Between 2010 and 2012, the volume of the electronic communications market that comprises the market segments of voice telephone services (fixed and mobile services), leased lines, data transfer and Internet access, TV & Radio services (cable, fixed satellite networks, IPTV), bundled services, and other electronic communications networks and/or services amounted to respectively BGN 3,140.795 million, 2,944.427 million, and 2,821.664 million compared to BGN 3.532 billion or EUR 1.806 billion in 2008. The 2012 results represent a 4% decrease from 2011. As mentioned before, the downward trend has existed since 2008 following a trend of 10% yearly increase from 2005 to 2007. This market share accounted for about 3.6% of national GDP. In comparison, the share of the total volume of the public electronic communications market in the volume of Bulgaria's GDP in 2020 amounted to 2.4%. In that respect, the CRC notes that as for the first year after a long decline a growth in its share in GDP is determined, namely by 0.15% compared to 2019, when it amounted to 2.3%,[48]

21. In 2008, there were 90,000 people working in the information and communications technology (ICT) sector in Bulgaria, compared to 55,949 (20,328 in telecoms) in the second quarter of 2013. The number increased over the years and in 2020 96,400 people were engaged in the economic activity 'Creation and dissemination of information and creative products; telecommunications'.[49] The total expenditure in the information and communications sector – distribution of information and communications – was estimated at approximately BGN 7.5 million in 2011. The revenues were BGN 7.5 million.[50] In 2019 there were 15,193 enterprises with employed personnel operating in the sector 'Creation and dissemination of information and creative products; telecommunications'.[51] Their total turnover for the said period was BGN 12,976,227,000.[52]

Notable developments in the ICT market in 2020 according to the CRC Report were the following: the data transfer and Internet access services had revenues amounting in 2020 to BGN 1,196,047 million (an increase of 19.8% in comparison

48. CRC. 'Annual Report 2020' https://crc.bg/files/AR_CRC_2020_22.06.2021.pdf, accessed 09 Dec. 2021, p. 9.
49. National Statistical Institute, 'Employed persons and employment rates - national level; statistical regions; areas', https://www.nsi.bg/bg/content/4009/заети-лица-и-коефициенти-на-заетост-национално-ниво-статистически-райони-области , 2020, accessed 9 Dec. 2021.
50. National Statistical Institute, http://www.nsi.bg/otrasal.php?otr=70&a1=2461&a2=2462&a3=2467#cont, 2011, accessed 1 Oct. 2013.
51. National Statistical Institute, 'Creation and dissemination of information and creative products; telecommunications', https://www.nsi.bg/bg/content/7697/брой-на-предприятията, accessed 18 Jan. 2021.
52. National Statistical Institute, 'Turnover by sectors and by groups according to the number of persons employed in them for 2019', https://www.nsi.bg/bg/content/7699/Оборот, accessed 18 Jan. 2021.

to 2019)[53] and the transmission and/or distribution of radio and television programmes services had revenues amounting to BGN 427,294 million (an increase of 0.6% in comparison to 2019).[54] The following trends in 2020 are worth mentioning, with the CRC expecting them to continue in the following years:

(1) Growth in the consumption of mobile communications service and at the same time decline in the revenues from its provision.
(2) In 2021 it was not expected that the rate of decline in revenue from fixed and mobile phone service to be affected significantly, as Bulgarian enterprises were expected to apply comparatively equal to the currently applied wholesale prices for voice termination calls given the requirements of Commission Delegated Regulation (EU) 2021/654 of 18 December 2020 supplementing Directive (EU) 2018/1972 of the European Parliament and of the Council by setting a single maximum union-wide mobile voice termination rate and a single maximum union-wide fixed voice termination rate.[55]
(3) Increase in the number of mobile Internet subscribers using LTE technology, both due to strong competition among enterprises and due to their desire to provide new services. The CRC expected that in the following years the focus of mobile operators would be on building and deployment of fifth generation (5G) networks, whereas as the competition in the field of 5G would intensify in parallel with their more massive construction and development of the portfolio of services offered by operators.
(4) Increase in the number of subscribers using fixed high-speed and ultra-high-speed access due to the ongoing migration to the Access Networks from the Next Generation (NGA) networks.
(5) Upward development of IP TV both in terms of subscribers, as well as revenues from the provision of the service.
(6) Increase in the number of subscribers and revenues from bundled services, while maintaining the preference for bundled services formed by two electronic communications services (dual packages).
(7) Expected strengthening of the positions of BTC in the electronic communications market and a change in the structure of market segments, as a result of the planned and completed acquisitions of leading regional enterprises of national importance.[56]

§2. Retail Markets

22. While the overall theme of market analyses in 2008 highlighted the experienced growth of the electronic communications market in the past few years, in

53. CRC. 'Annual Report 2020' https://crc.bg/files/AR_CRC_2020_22.06.2021.pdf, accessed 09 Dec. 2021, p. 34.
54. *Ibid.*, p. 43.
55. *OJ L 137, 22 Apr. 2021, pp. 1–9.*
56. CRC. 'Annual Report 2020' https://crc.bg/files/AR_CRC_2020_22.06.2021.pdf, accessed 09 Dec. 2021, pp. 54–55.

2012 and 2013 the main subject was the development of bundled services, which shifted the market structure. According to the CRC, in the 2020 the Bulgarian electronic communications market demonstrated resilience against the background of the COVID-19 crisis, continuing its upward development. The key role of the providers of electronic communications services during the pandemic was emphasized, as they contributed to ensuring the functioning of a number of vital areas of social and economic life. Despite the force majeure circumstances, companies continued to invest in the deployment of next generation access networks (NGA networks) to provide high and ultra-high speeds Internet access and data transfer, connection quality and security, security of information and mobility of devices. New solutions going beyond the traditional communication services were also developed such as smart home, digital wallet, cloud services and ICT solutions.[57]

23. In 2012, there were more than 450 undertakings providing public electronic communications through cable networks for transmission and/or distribution of radio and TV programmes. Compared to the end of 2008, when there were thirty-four new operators, in 2012 there was an overall decrease in the new licences. According to the Annual Report of CRC, in 2012 the volume of total revenues stood at BGN 235.157 million – a 3.6% reduction from 2011. The main part of revenues still came from distribution of radio and television programmes, the share of which continued to decrease to 80.2%. In 2012, the penetration was 54.4% for paid TV with 826,522 subscribers of cable TV and 808,911 subscribers for satellite and IPTV, the latter showing remarkable growth compared to the previous year.

The CRC pointed out that in 2020 an increase was observed in the revenues from two services included in the segment transmission and/or distribution services of radio and television programmes: IPTV (by 13.4%) and services for distribution of radio and television programmes wholesale (by 13.5%), over the one-year period under review. Revenues from all other services in the segment decreased compared to 2019. A decrease was observed in the amount of revenues from cable TV – by 5% and satellite TV – by 4.7% compared to 2019. For another year the most significant decline compared to the previous year was registered in the revenues from wholesale services for transmission of radio and television programmes – 30.4%. According to the CRC, this was due to a decrease of over 35% in the revenues from wholesale services for satellite transmission, which account for a significant share in the total revenues from services for the transmission of wholesale radio and television programmes.[58]

In 2008, the volume of the market segment of data transfer and services for provision of Internet access was almost BGN 281 million, up by 33% from the previous year. In 2012, the volume was almost BGN 347 million with 9.78% growth year-on-year. The number of ADSL services subscribers had decreased and the most popular is the optical connectivity (FTTB/FTTN). According to CRC data from

57. *Ibid.*, p. 54.
58. CRC. 'Annual Report 2020' https://crc.bg/files/AR_CRC_2020_22.06.2021.pdf, accessed 09 Dec. 2021, pp. 43–44.

2012, the penetration rate of Internet access services in Bulgaria (based on population) was 26.2%. At the end of 2012, there were 874 (633 active) enterprises providing access to the Internet and the segment showed dynamic development with 1,904,934 Internet access subscribers including those who received telecommunications through public cable telecommunications networks for radio and TV programme distribution. Data indicated that the number of subscribers was up 18.7% from 2011.[59] There were 163 operators providing services through wireless point-to-multipoint WiMAX-based, RLAN, and HomeBox networks in 2012. The revenues from that segment accounted for a negligible share in total earnings from the electronic communications market but are expected to increase. Future development implied active searching for a market niche in the provision of mobile or fixed voice services and broadband Internet access. As far as broadband communications were concerned, Bulgaria ranked lowest within the EU – 7.6% in 2008,[60] with 716,000 broadband lines, only 28.3% of which were Digital Subscriber Lines (DSL).[61] The penetration of broadband communications reached 9.5% (still the lowest within the EU).[62] In the period 2018–2020 the penetration rate of fixed broadband Internet access and mobile Internet access by population was 27.2% (for 2018), 29.0% (for 2019), and 30.6% (for 2020) and 101.8% (for 2018), 106.3% (for 2019), and 106.9% (for 2020) respectively.[63] In 2008, 29% of the households in Bulgaria owned a computer, 25% of which were connected to the Internet.[64] Practically, this index was higher: there was a considerable improvement regarding the possibilities for broadband connection of households by using technologies other than DSL, for example, Cable TV, Fibre-To-The-Home/Building/Curb, Local Area Network (LAN), Power Line Communications, and wireless network access.[65] In 2021 83.5% of the households had access to the Internet,[66] while 17% of the population had never had access to the Internet.[67] The number of enterprises providing real services for Internet access and data transmission in 2020 was 69,335. This was a decrease of three enterprises compared to 2019. The number of enterprises providing retail services was 658, which was a decrease of 7 enterprises compared to the previous year, and the number of those providing wholesale services had

59. CRC 'Annual Report': http://www.crc.bg/files/_bg/I%D0%86_Elektronni_syobshtitelni_mreji_i_uslugi_CRC_GD_2012.pdf, 2012, accessed 16 Sept. 2013.
60. European Commission, 'EU: i2010 – Annual Information Society Report 2008', www. epractice.eu /en/library/292889#at, 16 Apr. 2008, 13.
61. EC, 'Progress Report on the Single European Electronic Communications Market' (13th Report), http://ec.europa.eu/information_society/policy/ecomm/library/communications_reports/annualreports/13th/index_en.htm, 87.
62. 'Broadband: Gap between Best and Worst Performing Countries in Europe', www.nieuwsbank.nl/en/2008/11/28/v018.htm, 28 Nov. 2008, 1.
63. CRC. 'Annual Report 2020' https://crc.bg/files/AR_CRC_2020_22.06.2021.pdf, accessed 09 Dec. 2021, p. 38.
64. EUROSTAT, http://epp.eurostat.ec.europa.eu/portal/page/portal/eurostat/home, 23 Feb. 2009.
65. Coordination Council for Information Society, 'National Broadband Programme of the Republic of Bulgaria', www.broadband-europe.eu/Pages/StrategyDetail.aspx?ItemID=28, Dec. 2008.
66. National Statistical Institute, 'Household Internet access', https://www.nsi.bg/bg/content/2808/достъп-на-домакинствата-до-интернет, 2021, accessed 18 Jan. 2022.
67. National Statistical Institute, 'People who have never used the Internet', https://www.nsi.bg/bg/content/2828/лица-които-никога-не-са-използвали-интернет, 2021, accessed 18 Jan. 2022

increased by 14 enterprises for the one-year period. Both in 2019 and 2020, the main providers of fixed Internet access for end users (retail service) were BTC, A1, and Bulsatcom.[68]

At the end of 2011, Bulgaria's fixed broadband penetration remained the second lowest in the EU. However, Bulgaria continued to be among the advanced EU Member States in terms of high-speed broadband – more than 20% of the lines being 30 Mbps and higher.[69] At the end of 2012, the broadband penetration in terms of households was 40.4% and in terms of population – 26.2% – closer to the EU average of 27.7%. In terms of mobile broadband, however, the situation was still lagging behind Europe – penetration rate was 14.4% in January 2012 (EU average of 43.1%). As regards dedicated data services, the EU average was 8.1% compared to 3.5% in Bulgaria. The fixed broadband penetration rate on the basis of population increased in the period 2018–2020 as follows: from 57.6% (2018) to 60.9% (2019) and 63.4% (2020). The mobile Internet access penetration rate on the basis of population increased in the period 2018-2020 as well: from 27.2% (2018) to 29.0% (2019) and 30.6% (2020).[70]

The general revenues from leased line services in 2020 amounted to BGN 19,156 million and a decrease of 10.2% in comparison to the revenues for 2019 was detected. The market share with regard to number of lines on the retail market for 2020 was the highest for BTC (77.6% in comparison to 76.8% for 2019), followed by A1 (11.1% in comparison to 12.6% for 2019), Sofia Communications EAD (Sofia Communications) (4.1% in comparison to 4.7% for 2019), and everybody else (7. 2% in comparison to 5.9% for 2019). The market share with regard to revenues from provision of the services on the retail market was the highest for BTC again (62.4% in comparison to 64.9% for 2019), followed by A1 (19.4% in comparison to 16.9% for 2019), Sofia Communications (6.6% in comparison to 7.7% for 2019), and everybody else (11.7% in comparison to 10.4% for 2019).[71]

The revenues from the retail market of transfer of data and Internet access services amounted in 2020 to BGN 1,061,964 million[72] and the revenues for the transmission and/or distribution of radio and television programmes services amounted in 2020 to BGN 391,719 million.[73]

§3. Wholesale Markets

24. The market share with regard to number of lines on the wholesale market regarding the leased line service for 2020 was the highest for Novatel EOOD

68. CRC. 'Annual Report 2020' https://crc.bg/files/AR_CRC_2020_22.06.2021.pdf, accessed 09 Dec. 2021, p. 35.
69. Bulgaria 2011Telecommunications market and regulatory developments, http://ec.europa.eu/digital-agenda/sites/digital-agenda/files/BG_Country_Chapter_17th_Report_0.pdf, accessed 16 Sep. 2013.
70. CRC. 'Annual Report 2020' https://crc.bg/files/AR_CRC_2020_22.06.2021.pdf, accessed 09 Dec. 2021, p. 38.
71. CRC. 'Annual Report 2020' https://crc.bg/files/AR_CRC_2020_22.06.2021.pdf, accessed 09 Dec. 2021, pp. 31–32.
72. *Ibid.*, p. 41.
73. *Ibid.*, p. 43.

(Novatel) (30.1% in comparison to 26.9% for 2019), followed by Sofia Communications (22.4% in comparison to 23.7% for 2019), BTC (12.5% in comparison to 13.8% for 2019), and everybody else (35.0% in comparison to 35.6% for 2019). The market share with regard to revenues from provision of the services on the wholesale market was the highest for Novatel again (43.0% in comparison to 49.5% for 2019), followed by BTC (21.3% in comparison to 21.2% for 2019), Sofia Communications (6.2% in comparison to 5.9% for 2019), and everybody else (29.4% in comparison to 23.3% for 2019).[74]

The revenues from the wholesale market in 2020 were as follows: the revenues from providing capacity for Internet connectivity (Peering and Transit) services amounted to BGN 28,124 million, the revenues from data transmission services were BGN 8,214 million; the revenues from providing wholesale access to Internet through next access networks generation (NGA) were BGN 9,234 million;[75] the revenues from the transmission of radio and television programmes services amounted to BGN 3,283 million; the revenues from distribution of radio and television programmes services, including IPTV, provided to other enterprises amounted to BGN 29,978 million and the revenues from TV wholesale service (via IPTV and/or DVB/C) provided to other enterprises with the purpose of resale amounted to BGN 2,315 million.[76]

74. CRC. 'Annual Report 2020' https://crc.bg/files/AR_CRC_2020_22.06.2021.pdf, accessed 09 Dec. 2021, p. 32.
75. *Ibid.*, p. 35.
76. *Ibid.*, p. 52.

Chapter 4. E-commerce: Facts and Figures

25. In 2021, the number of enterprises with Internet access could be divided as follows: small enterprises (with 10–49 employees) having such access were 95.4%, medium enterprises (with 50–249 employees) having such access were 99.3%, while large enterprises (over 250 employees) were 100%. In 2021, 95.5% of all enterprises had such access.[77] Generally, the number of employees accessing the Internet for work is on the rise. In 2012, an overall 22.5% of all employees had the opportunity to use the Internet and modern technologies,[78] whereas in 2021 these numbers were reaching 36.8%.[79]

26. In terms of household Internet use, its share in 2008 grew by 6% (up to 25% of the population). In 2012, the number of households using Internet is 1,393,681 (or 50.9%)[80] and the e-commerce users were 9.2% or 524,257 people. In 2021, 33% of the Bulgarian population purchased goods and services on the Internet over the entire year.[81] Internet access is a basic prerequisite for maintaining online communication and using information resources as well as for benefiting from e-services. More than half of Bulgaria's population browsed the Internet every day or at least once a week for various purposes. The most active age groups were 16-24 year-olds and 25-34 year-olds, 81.3% and 72%, respectively. Predictably, 85% of university graduates 'surfed' the Internet, while the number of high-school graduates going online reached 52.5%. As mentioned in paragraph 23 above, in 2021 78.9% of the households had access to the Internet.[82] The most active age groups remained 16-24 year-olds and 25-34 year-olds, 91.5% and 90.3%, respectively.[83]

27. E-commerce is undoubtedly attractive to customers because of its speedy registration, easy order tracking, and home delivery options. Statistics show that more and more Bulgarian enterprises developed their marketing and sales policies with the World Wide Web in mind. The number of enterprises receiving orders for goods and services through the Internet had been increasing since 2007 and counted up to 1,965 or 7.8% (compared to 4% in 2007). The same trend was visible in the

77. National Statistical Institute, 'Enterprises Internet Access', https://nsi.bg/bg/content/2848/предприятия-с-достъп-до-интернет, accessed 9 Dec. 2021.
78. National Statistical Institute, http://www.nsi.bg/otrasal.php?otr=17&a1=2422&a2=2423&a3=2426#cont, 2012, accessed 16 Sept. 2013.
79. National Statistical Institute, 'Employees in enterprises that use the Internet', https://nsi.bg/bg/content/2854/заети-лица-в-предприятията-които-използват-интернет, accessed 18 Jan. 2022.
80. National Statistical Institute, http://www.nsi.bg/otrasal.php?otr=17&a1=2405&a2=2406&a3=2407#cont, 2012, accessed 16 Sept. 2013.
81. National Statistical Institute, 'People who have purchased goods and services online for personal use in the last twelve months', https://nsi.bg/bg/content/2831/лица-които-са-купували-стоки-и-услуги-по-интернет-за-лични-цели-през-последните-12-месеца, accessed 18 Jan. 2022.
82. National Statistical Institute, 'Household Internet Access', https://nsi.bg/bg/content/2808/достъп-на-домакинствата-до-интернет, accessed 18 Jan. 2021.
83. National Statistical Institute, 'People who use the Internet regularly', https://nsi.bg/bg/content/2814/лица-регулярно-използващи-интернет, accessed 10 Dec. 2021.

number of undertakings ordering goods and services through the Internet – 7.3% in 2012.[84] In 2021, 51.9% of all undertakings had their own website.[85]

28. Even a cursory survey of Bulgarian online shops reveals a variety of goods on offer such as IT products, cosmetics and perfumery, jewellery, clothes, furniture, books, sport equipment, foods, etc. As far as services are concerned, it is also possible to pay online bills for electricity and water supply, mobile phones and Internet access, mp3 music and cable TV, or subscription to online issues. The COVID-19 pandemic outburst in March 2020 and the declared state of emergency from 13 March 2020 to 13 May 2020[86] further led to an increase of the usage of online services such as remote orders of food, goods, services, usage of electronic payment services, etc.

29. On the whole, however, the development of e-commerce and e-business in Bulgaria in 2012–2013 was still limited compared to the rest of the EU. According to the National Statistical Institute, almost 20% of all enterprises, 45.7% of large companies and 17.1% to 29.7% of the small and medium enterprises, have adopted integrated informational systems (Enterprise Resource Planning – (ERP)). In terms of CRM applications, the overall percentages are 17.9% and 28.2% (for large enterprises), 16.8% (for medium enterprises) and 21.7% (for small enterprises) respectively.[87] The numbers in 2021 were as follows: 21.8% of all enterprises used ERP[88] and 16.9% used CRM.[89] About 11.8% of the enterprises sold goods and services on the Internet in 2021.[90]

84. National Statistical Institute, Information Society data, http://www.nsi.bg/otrasal.php?otr=17&a1=2422&a2=2432&a3=2434#cont, 2012, accessed 16 Sept. 2013.
85. National Statistical Institute, 'Enterprises that have a website', https://nsi.bg/bg/content/2856/предприятия-които-имат-уебсайт, accessed 18 Jan. 2022.
86. Decision of the National Assembly of 13 Mar. 2020, promulgated SG 22/2020, prolonged until 13 May 2020 with Decision of the National Assembly, promulgated. SG 33/2020.
87. National Statistical Institute, Information Society data, http://www.nsi.bg/otrasal.php?otr=17&a1=2422&a2=2436&a3=2439#cont, 2012, accessed 16 Sept. 2013.
88. National Statistical Institute, 'Enterprises that use ERP', https://nsi.bg/bg/content/2885/предприятия-които-използват-софтуер-за-управление-на-ресурсите-erp, accessed 10 Dec. 2021.
89. National Statistical Institute, 'Enterprises that use CRM', https://nsi.bg/bg/content/2887/предприятия-които-използват-софтуер-за-управление-на-информацията-за-клиенти-crm, accessed 10 Dec. 2021.
90. National Statistical Institute, 'Enterprises selling goods and services on the Internet', https://nsi.bg/bg/content/2872/предприятия-които-продават-стоки-и-услуги-по-интернет, accessed 10 Dec. 2021.

Chapter 5. E-government Initiatives

30. Since 2010s the e-government has been ranked high on the priority list of the Bulgarian government. It includes delivering administrative services by electronic means, improving administrative processes, providing electronic information about public services, the institutions and the government as a whole. It is seen as an element of the transition from industrial to information society and for improving the competitiveness of the Bulgarian economy and the entire business climate.[91] The basic principles of e-government initiatives are accessibility, multilanguage services, security, personal data protection, and benefits from the advantages of the open source and multilateral relations:

– E-government includes four basic groups of relations: administration-citizens, administration-business, administration-administration, administration-officials. In 2008, Bulgaria ranked twenty-sixth in the EU with respect to the usage of electronic administrative services by citizens, twenty-fifth with respect to the usage of such services by businesses, and last by provision of entirely online accessible services.[92] There were several basic reasons for the insufficient development of e-government in Bulgaria: lack of interoperability of information systems in the administration, lack of electronic exchange on interdepartmental level, and presence of unsolved problem with data unification. The benchmarking results make it clear that the information society in Bulgaria is at a relatively early stage of development. In 2012, Bulgaria still ranked fairly low compared to the rest of the Member States. According to the latest Global E-Government Development Reports and Survey by the UN Public Administration Programme,[93] Bulgaria ranked forty-fourth in the world in 2010 and sixtieth in 2012. While Bulgaria's infrastructure, online service, and e-government index was above world average, the e-participation is ten times less than half of the existing countries. In 2012, 27% of Bulgarians aged 16-74 were using the Internet for interaction with public authorities, compared to 44% in the EU. The percentage of enterprises, however, is much closer to the EU level. In 2021 26.6% of the Bulgarian citizens used the Internet in order to interact with public authorities and 58.8% of them had high education and 22.2% – secondary education.[94] About 19.1% of the Bulgarian citizens used the Internet to obtain information from a public institution's website or

91. 'E-government Factsheets: E-government in Bulgaria', http://www.epractice.eu/files/eGovernmentBulgaria.pdf, 2011, 1, accessed 1 Oct. 2013.
92. EU: i2010 – Annual Information Society Report 2008, www.epractice.eu/en/library/292889#at, 16 Apr. 2008, 34, 44.
93. The survey presents a systemic assessment of how governments use Information and Communications Technology (ICT) to provide access and inclusion for all; Global E-Government Development Reports and Survey by the UN Public Administration Programme; http://unpan3.un.org/egovkb/datacenter/CountryView.aspx?reg=EUROPE%20~%20Eastern%20Europe, 2012, accessed 1 Oct. 2013.
94. National Statistical Institute, 'People using the Internet for the purpose of interaction with public institutions', https://nsi.bg/bg/content/2824/лица-използващи-интернет-с-цел-взаимодействие-с-публични-институции, accessed 10 Dec. 2021.

application, 13.4% – to download official documents, forms, declarations or reports and 15.5% – to submit completed documents, forms, declarations or reports online.[95]

31. The Minister of Transport, Information Technologies and Communications is empowered to implement the e-government policy in the country. The main objective of the Bulgarian e-government is to meet society's needs for high quality and easily accessible administrative services by launching initiatives such as:

(1) Operational Programme 'Administrative Capacity' is a strategic document for the modernization of the Bulgarian public administration and improvement of the work of judicial bodies and civil society structures for 2007–2013. It is part of the National Strategic Reference Framework and therefore contributes to the achievement of its main goals: strengthening the competitive power of the economy and ensuring employment, revenue, and social integration.[96]
(2) The National E-government Strategy, the National Framework for Interoperability of the Informational Systems in Executive Bodies followed by the implementation of the E-government Integrated System, the E-environment Integrated System, and the Integrated Administration and Public Services.[97]
(3) Consolidation of Bulgarian State Administration Capacity for Implementation of the E-government Strategy, a PHARE project.[98]
(4) 'Interchange of Data between Administrations (IDA)' Programme.[99]
(5) 'i-Bulgaria' initiative, which includes the projects 'i-Centre', 'i-University', 'i-Class', 'i-Net', and 'ESj@Centre'.[100]

32. Other objectives of the e-government initiatives include wider ICT penetration, growth of e-content and services delivered on the Internet, informational infrastructure development, and ICT access for all social groups. The basic principles regulating the e-government process are: one-time data collection and data creation, ex officio notification, automated submission based on interoperability, and information security. Bulgaria's e-Government strategy was broadly based on two pillars – the 'Concept of e-Government in Bulgaria 2010–2015' and the 'Common Strategy for e-Government in Bulgaria 2011–2015'. The 'Concept of e-Government' represented a vision for the e-Government in 2015 by the Ministry of Transport, Information Technology and Communications (MTITC) as well as the principles by

95. *Ibid.*
96. Ministry of State Administration and Administrative Reform, Draft Report on the State of the Administration, http://law.uni-sofia.bg/Kat/T/IP/T/EP/DocLib/Доклад%20за%20състоянието%20на%20администрацият, 2007, 83.
97. Ministry of State Administration and Administrative Reform, www.mdaar.government.bg/press.php.
98. BG2004/016-711.10.01 (Lot 1); EuropeAid/122540/D/SV/BG, http://idg.bg/events/event/2007/0301155359-Lirex_BTS.ppt#331,6,Релизация 2006 – 2007, 2007.
99. White Paper of the e-government in Bulgaria, www.jnn-marketing.com/index.php?p=egovernmentbg, 2005.
100. Ministry of State Administration and Administrative Reform, www.mdaar.government.bg/press.php.

which this is to be achieved. The document served as a basis for developing a national strategy and a roadmap for e-Government in Bulgaria until 2015. This 'Common Strategy for e-Government in Bulgaria 2011–2015', adopted in 2010, laid the foundation upon which sectorial policies, strategies, objectives, and activities of ministries and agencies were being deployed. The strategy aimed at establishing and developing electronic management in the country until 2015. A crucial step was the establishment of the e-Government Directorate, which aimed at improving horizontal communications and coordination between the institutions involved. It managed the then newly founded Electronic Communications Networks and Information Systems Agency, and oversaw all actors involved in the interoperability project.

Some developments in the area of e-Government may be noted. In July 2011, the MTITC initiated a project, which aimed to end up with the creation of an online register for the electronic identity (e-identity) of the users of government services and an identity management system (IDM). Previously the same year, the trade register Bulstat, the Cadastre and Property Register, the conviction status certificate, the national population database, the Register of Bulgarian IDs, electronic health records, centralized registers of the state and municipal property, local rates and taxes, and electronic deeds were announced to be digitized through the 'Development of the Administrative Services by Electronic Means' project. Since 2009, more than 455 public libraries participated in the 'Glob@l Libraries – Bulgaria' programme, enabling visitors to access information, knowledge, communication, e-Content and community services. Additionally, the National Computer Security Incidents Response Team (CERT Bulgaria) whose purpose is to provide information and assistance to its constituencies in taking proactive actions to eliminate cybersecurity risks, as well as to respond to incidents of this character, was officially accredited by the International Certifying Organisation 'Trusted Introducer'.

The current 'Updated Strategy for the Development of E-Governance in the Republic of Bulgaria 2019 – 2025' sets up the following perspectives for the development of e-governance in Bulgaria: to achieve an irreversible digital transformation in the public sector,

which includes:

– Transformation of the model of providing electronic administrative consumer-oriented services by changing technological and administrative processes behind them, resulting in a reduction of the administrative burden for citizens and businesses.

– Data-driven digital transformation of the public sector.

– Building a modern digital administration, including the implementation of online tools for civic participation.

– High level of network and information security.

– High-quality support of shared e-government resources.[101]

101. Available at: https://e-gov.bg/wps/wcm/connect/e-gov.bg-18083/1506d64e-0f16-4954-ba0b-dfd77ae58184/Стратегия+за+развитие+на+електронното+управление+2019-2025.pdf?MOD=AJPERES&CVID=nyx-ndJ&useDefaultText=0&useDefaultDesc=0, accessed 10 Dec. 2021, p. 35.

33. E-government regulation is the basis for the successful implementation of all activities mentioned above. The Electronic Governance Act (EGA, e-Government Act),[102] amended several times – in 2009, 2013, 2014, 2016, 2018, 2019, and 2020, is intended to govern the activity of the administrative bodies while handling electronic documents, the provision of electronic administrative services, and the circulation of electronic documents among various administrations. Its scope also extends to other entities that carry out public functions and to public service providers. Aiming to provide high-quality service to citizens, the scope of the EGA encompasses also the persons carrying out public functions and organizations providing public services, unless otherwise stated in a law. One of the act's main provisions is that administrative bodies and persons charged with public functions and the organizations providing public services cannot require from citizens and organizations to produce, or prove data, which have already been collected or created. Its last amendment abolished the need for certification of the information systems of the administration.

Other related normative acts are the Access to Public Information Act, Access to Spatial Data Act,[103] the Commercial Register Act,[104] the Regulation (EU) No 910/2014 of the European Parliament and of the Council of 23 July 2014 on electronic identification and trust services for electronic transactions in the internal market and repealing Directive 1999/93/EC (eIDAS)[105] and the Electronic Document and Trust Services Act (EDETSA),[106] the Regulation (EU) 2016/679 of the European Parliament and of the Council of 27 April 2016 on the protection of natural persons with regard to the processing of personal data and on the free movement of such data, and repealing Directive 95/46/EC (General Data Protection Regulation (GDPR))[107] and the Personal Data Protection Act (PDPA), the Electronic Communications Act (ECA), the Ordinance on the General Requirements for Information Systems, Registers and Electronic Administrative Services,[108] the Cybersecurity Act,[109] the Ordinance on the Certificates for Electronic Signatures in the Public Administration (OCESPA),[110] the Ordinance on the Internal Electronic and Paper-based Document Flow in the Administrations,[111] the Ordinance on the Minimum Requirements for Network and Information Security,[112] and the Ordinance on the General Requirements for Information Systems, Registers and Electronic Administrative Services.[113]

102. SG, issue 46 of 12 Jun. 2008.
103. SG, issue 19 of 9 Mar. 2010; amended, SG, issue 17 of 26 Feb. 2019.
104. SG, issue 34 of 25 Apr. 2006.
105. OJ, L 257, 28 Aug. 2014, pp. 73–114.
106. SG, issue 34 of 6 Apr. 2001.
107. OJ L 119, 4.5.2016, pp. 1–88.
108. Council of Ministers, SG, issue 5 of 17 Jan. 2017.
109. SG, issue 94 of 13 Nov. 2018.
110. Council of Ministers, SG, issue 48 of 23 May 2008.
111. Council of Ministers, SG, issue 48 of 23 May 2008.
112. Council of Ministers, SG, issue 59 of 26 Jul. 2019.
113. Council of Ministers, SG, issue 5 of 17 Jan. 2017.

Part I. Regulation of the ICT Market

Chapter 1. Regulatory Framework of the Telecommunications Sector

§1. Background

34. Until May 2007, the telecommunications sector in Bulgaria was regulated by the Telecommunications Act (TA)[114] from 2003, which implemented the old EU regulatory framework (*acquis* 1998/2000). Following the country's accession to the EU on 1 January 2007, a new ECA was adopted.[115] It transposes the current EU regulatory framework on electronic communications into the national law. By the end of 2009, Directive 2007/65/EC of the European Parliament and of the Council of 11 December 2007 amending Council Directive 89/552/EEC on the coordination of certain provisions laid down by law, directs that regulation or administrative action in Member States concerning the pursuit of television broadcasting activities[116] had to be transposed into Bulgarian law. In 2012, the following developments can be pointed out. In view of the optimal competition environment in the sector CRC, following a recommendation by the European Commission (EC), significantly alleviated the conditions for usage of BTC's underground cable network, thus improving competition and allowing alternative operators to develop their networks and provide services. At the end of 2011, the ECA was amended, implementing Directives 2009/136/EC and 2009/140/EC from the European Framework for electronic communication networks and services. There were also developments with regard to higher protection of consumers in procedures for number transfers – a reduced period of transfer in fixed networks and fewer obligations of the subscriber. As regards the switch to digital terrestrial TV distribution, the process finished successfully in 2013. Subsequent notable amendments in the ECA were made in 2021 to transpose the requirements of Directive (EU) 2018/1972 of the European Parliament and of the Council of 11 December 2018 establishing the European Electronic Communications Code.[117]

35. The ECA provides that the CRC identifies the relevant electronic communications markets, analyses them, and takes measures to promote competition on

114. SG, issue 88 of 7 Oct. 2003.
115. SG, issue 41 of 22 May 2007.
116. EU OJ, L 332, 18 Dec. 2007.
117. *OJ, L 321, 17 Dec. 2018, pp. 36–214.*

these markets after notifying the EC of these analyses and draft measures. The CRC has begun analysing the relevant markets because of the Commission Recommendation on relevant product and service markets within the electronic communications sector subject to *ex ante* regulation of 11 February 2003[118] and the updated Recommendation of 2007.[119]

§2. Scope of the Law

36. Bulgarian law adopts the term 'electronic communications' from the EU regulatory framework. The ECA does not provide a legal definition of the term, though Article 1(2) states that 'electronic communications are performed through transferring, delivery or reception of signs, signals, written text, pictures, voice or communications of any kind through a conductor, radio waves, optic or other electromagnetic medium'. On a constitutional level, Article 18 from the Bulgarian Constitution[120] provides that the state shall have supreme rights over the radiofrequency spectrum. By virtue of law, a state monopoly over the national post and telecommunications networks can be imposed. Thus the telecommunications sector is explicitly regulated, but nothing is said about the 'electronic communications' sector.

37. The terms 'electronic communications network', 'electronic communications services' and 'associated facilities' are defined in the Additional Provisions of the ECA closely following those of Article 2 of Directive 2002/21/EC of the European Parliament and of the Council of 7 March 2002 on a common regulatory framework for electronic communications networks and services (Framework Directive)[121] and subsequently were aligned with the rules of Directive (EU) 2018/1972 of the European Parliament and of the Council of 11 December 2018 establishing the European Electronic Communications Code (Recast) (the European Electronic Communications Code).[122] Thus, the scope of the law covers:

(1) internet access services as defined in point (2) of the second paragraph of Article 2 of Regulation (EU) 2015/2120;
(2) interpersonal communications service (number-based and number-independent); and;
(3) services consisting wholly or mainly in the conveyance of signals such as transmission services used for the provision of machine-to-machine services and for broadcasting;

118. OJ, L 036, 12 Feb. 2003.
119. OJ, L 344, 28 Dec. 2007.
120. SG, issue 56 of 13 July 1991.
121. OJ, L 108, 24 Apr. 2002.
122. *OJ, L 321, 17 Dec. 2018, pp. 36–214. The text below reflects the legal regime under the directives preceding the European Electronic Communications Code and the key legal provisions are updated in the analysis to properly reflect their current status as envisaged in the code. For a detailed comparison and correlation between the provisions under the old directives and their newer version in the code see ANNEX XIII CORRELATION TABLE to the code.*

Services providing, or exercising editorial control over, content transmitted using electronic communications networks and services, are explicitly excluded from the scope of the term 'electronic communications service'.[123,124,125]

§3. Policy Objectives and Regulatory Principles

38. Article 4 of the ECA specifies the main principles and objectives of regulating electronic communications:

(1) to create the conditions necessary for the promotion of competition in the provision of electronic communications and associated facilities, including effective infrastructure competition, as well as the provision of electronic communications and associated services;
(2) to create the necessary conditions for the development of connectivity and access to very high capacity networks, including fixed, mobile and wireless networks, as well as their use by all citizens and businesses;
(3) to contribute to the development of the internal market for electronic communications by:
   (a) removing obstacles and facilitating convergent conditions for, investment in and the provision of electronic communications networks and services, associated facilities and associated services;
   (b) establishing common rules and foreseeable regulatory approaches;
   (c) promoting the efficient, effective and coordinated use of spectrum, open innovation, the construction and development of pan-European networks, the provision, accessibility and interoperability of pan-European services and end-to-end connectivity, and ensuring connectivity, wide availability and use of very high capacity networks;
(4) to promote the interests of citizens by:
   (a) ensuring connectivity, accessibility and take up of very high capacity networks, including fixed, mobile and wireless networks, as well as electronic communications services;
   (b) providing the opportunity for maximum benefits in terms of choice, price and quality on the basis of effective competition;
   (c) maintaining that the security of networks and services is maintained;

---

123. ECA, Additional Provisions.
124. Framework Directive, Art. 2(a), (c), (e); European Electronic Communications Code, Art. 2(4) – (7)
125. The latest version of the definition for 'electronic communications networks' according to the ECA reads as follows: 'a set of transmission systems, whether based on fixed infrastructure or centralized administrative capacity, and, where applicable, switching or routing equipment and other resources, including inactive network elements, that allow the transmission of signals by wire, radio, optical or other electromagnetic means, including satellite networks, fixed (with circuit-switched and packet-switched, including the Internet) and mobile networks, electricity transmission systems, insofar as they are used for the transmission of signals, networks used for radio and television broadcasting, and cable networks for the distribution of radio and television programmes, regardless of the type of information transmitted' (§ 1., i. 15 of the Additional Provisions).

(d) ensuring a high and general level of protection for end-users through the necessary rules, including conditions for the provision of clear information, requirements for tariff transparency and conditions for the use of public electronic communications services and the use of applications and services choice;
(e) taking into account the needs of specific social groups, in particular people with disabilities, the elderly and people with special social needs, as well as the choice and equal access for people with disabilities.

These principles are in a complete accordance with the provisions of the Framework Directive[126] and the European Electronic Communications Code.[127]

§4. National Executive and Regulatory Authorities

39. Competence in the area of electronic communications is vested in the Council of Ministers, the National Radio Frequencies Spectrum Council, and the Minister of TITC. These are the decision – and policymaking – authorities, whereas the CRC is the national regulator responsible for supervising the compliance of electronic communications with the provisions of the applicable legislation.

The media sector is regulated by the Radio and Television Act (RTA)[128] from 1999 last amended in State Gazette (SG), issue 20 of 9 March 2021 and is generally harmonized with the EU framework. Broadcasting activities are regulated by the Council for Electronic Media (CEM).

40. The Council of Ministers, upon a motion by the Minister of TITC, adopts the national policy in the electronic communications sector and policy in the field of the information society and promulgates them in the SG. These policies should be updated at least once every four years subject to public discussions.[129]

The Council of Ministers also adopts upon a proposal of the National Radio Frequency Spectrum Council a policy on planning and distribution of the radio frequency spectrum and a national plan for the distribution of that spectrum and promulgates it in the SG.[130]

41. Both the CRC and the CEM are established as independent specialized authorities under ECA[131] and the RTA,[132] respectively. The CRC consists of five members, all Bulgarian citizens with 'master' high degree. The Chairman of the CRC is determined by a decision of the Council of Ministers and is appointed by the Prime Minister, the Vice-Chairman and two members of the Commission are elected and dismissed by the National Assembly. Finally, the president appoints (or

126. Framework Directive, Art. 8.
127. European Electronic Communications Code, Art. 3.
128. SG, issue 138 of 24 Nov. 1998.
129. ECA, Art. 7.
130. ECA, Art. 8.
131. ECA, Art. 22.
132. RTA, Art. 24.

dismisses) one of the members. The CEM consists of five members – three elected by the National Assembly and two appointed by the president. Both the ECA and the RTA provide for numerous requirements and limitations on the members of both authorities to ensure their independence and impartiality. The CRC's budget is based exclusively on fees and other monetary receivables *inter alia* administrative fees, annual fees for the use and temporary use of radio frequency spectrum, fees for the use of numbering resources, licence and registration fees under the Postal Services Act, the EDETSA, and the Electronic Communications Networks and Physical Infrastructure Act, the final tender price after the tender for the use of radio spectrum band and of position of the geostationary orbit, annual fees for the use of given radio spectrum band and of given position of the geostationary orbit and the stationary satellite system used by it, the one-time fee for the use of the additional frequency spectrum as well as the fines imposed under the ECA, interest upon delayed payments, and other sources.[133] Special provisions of ECA[134] and RTA stipulate the coordination procedure between the CEM and the CRC, mainly in the licence issuance procedures in the field of telecommunications and radio spectrum allocation.

42. Under the ECA, the functions of the CRC are:

(1) to define the relevant markets for electronic communications networks and/or services;
(2) to study, analyse, and prepare an assessment regarding the degree of competition in the relevant markets;
(3) to designate the undertakings, which have significant market power (SMP) on the relevant market;
(4) to impose, maintain, amend, or withdraw specific obligations on the undertakings designated as undertakings with SMP for the achievements of the purposes of the ECA;
(5) as an exception, to impose justified and proportionate provisional specific obligations;
(6) to impose, continue, amend or repeal measures and obligations with regard to the provision of universal service;
(7) to prepare, adopt, and update a regulatory policy for the use of numbering resources for the provision of electronic communications;
(8) to prepare and adopt general and statutory administrative acts related to the powers vested in the Commission as well as to execute, enact or submit for enactment by the competent state authorities the supplementary normative acts;
(9) prepare, adopt or submit for adoption by the competent state bodies the sub-legislative legislation in the cases provided for in the ECA;
(10) issue, amend, supplement, transfer, terminate or revoke permits for the use of limited resources;
(11) register and delete registrations for the use of radio frequency spectrum;

133. ECA, Art. 51.
134. ECA, Arts 46–49c.

(12) issue and terminate the effect of temporary permissions for usage of limited resource;
(13) issue, amend, supplement, transfer, terminate or revoke authorizations for the use of radio frequency spectrum from electronic communications networks for terrestrial analogue broadcasting following a decision of CEM;
(14) to conduct research and provide information to CEM on the technical parameters required for terrestrial analogue broadcasting, for a settlement, region or for the entire territory of the Republic of Bulgaria specified by CEM, including free radio frequencies, permissible transmission capacities, possible points of broadcasting, as well as other necessary technical information;
(15) prepare, adopt, and update the NNP;
(16) grant rights of use, reserve, and withdraw numbering resources;
(17) to control the use of national numbering resources;
(18) assist in the provision by international organizations of numbering resources for electronic communications in the Republic of Bulgaria;
(19) assist in the harmonization of certain numbers or numbering ranges within the EU in order to promote the functioning of the internal market and the development of pan-European services;
(20) represent the Republic of Bulgaria in the international organizations of the regulatory bodies in the field of electronic communications;
(21) participate in the work of the Body of European Regulators for Electronic Communications (BEREC) and promotes coordinated and consistent regulation;
(22) ensure compliance with the requirements for maintaining the integrity of public electronic communications networks and the security of public electronic communications networks and services and investigate cases of non-compliance with the requirements for ensuring the security of public electronic communications networks and services, as well as their impact on the security of networks and services, assisting the competent bodies under Article 244a(3) of ECA – the Ministry of Interior, the Ministry of Defense, the State Agency for National Security, the State Agency for Electronic Government, the competent bodies designated under Article 16 of the Cybersecurity Act, or the Commission for Personal Data Protection (CPDP);
(23) to perform the functions of a national standardization organization before the European Telecommunications Standards Institute (ETSI) and participates in the work of the technical committees for standardization in the Republic of Bulgaria, related to electronic communications;
(24) create and maintain the registers provided for in the ECA;
(25) conduct public discussions, consultations and polls in the cases and under the procedures provided for in the ECA;
(26) resolve disputes between enterprises, as well as disputes under the Electronic Communications Networks and Physical Infrastructure Act;
(27) contribute to the protection of the rights of end users in the electronic communications sector in coordination with other competent authorities and considers complaints of end users in the cases provided for in the ECA;

(28) determine the location of the end point of the network for the purposes of regulating electronic communications networks and services;

(29) approve for the purposes of application of Article 4 (4) of Regulation (EU) 2015/2120[135] mechanism for monitoring the performance of the Internet access service in terms of speed or other service quality parameters; the mechanism is developed and maintained by the CRC or a third party and enables end users to measure the performance of the Internet access service in terms of speed or other service quality parameters.[136]

These specific powers of CRC are furthermore detailed by the provisions of Articles 31–41 of the ECA.[137] A special section of the ECA (section IV, Articles 41a–43b) regulates the coordination and consultations that CRC should provide to the EC and the national regulatory authorities of the EU Member States. It mainly represents the general provisions of Articles 6 and 7 of the Framework Directive[138] on the consultation and transparency mechanism and consolidating the internal market for electronic communications procedure and the requirements of the European Electronic Communications Code.[139] Special procedures for coordinating the Competition Protection Commission (CPC) are also provided in the ECA and the Competition Protection Act (CPA).[140]

Under the Bulgarian legislation, the CPC is competent on competition matters; it supervises mergers, acquisitions, and joint ventures in the telecommunications and broadcasting sector. According to the CPA, the undertakings must inform the CPC in advance of their intention to make a concentration should the total turnover of the undertakings participating in the concentration in the territory of Bulgaria for the preceding financial year exceed BGN 25 million (approximately EUR 12.78 million) and at the same time either the total turnover of each of at least two of the undertakings participating in the concentration in the territory of Bulgaria for the preceding financial year exceeds BGN 3 million (approximately EUR 1.5 million), or the total turnover of the acquired undertaking within the territory of Bulgaria for the preceding financial year exceeds BGN 3 million (approximately EUR 1.5 million). By the date of submission of the notification, the parties should be aware of the parameters of the planned transaction since the permission is issued on the basis of the information provided by the undertakings.

135. Regulation (EU) 2015/2120 of the European Parliament and of the Council of 25 November 2015 laying down measures concerning open Internet access and amending Directive 2002/22/EC on universal service and users' rights relating to electronic communications networks and services and Regulation (EU) No 531/2012 on roaming on public mobile communications networks within the Union, OJ, L 310, 26.11.2015, pp. 1–18.
136. ECA, Art. 30.
137. ECA, Arts 31–41.
138. Framework Directive, Arts 6 and 7.
139. European Electronic Communications Code, Art. 10.
140. SG, issue 102 of 28 Nov. 2008.

After Bulgaria's accession to the EU on 1 January 2007, the provisions of Council Regulation (EC) 139/2004 on the control of concentrations between undertakings[141] are applicable directly. Regulation 139/2004 applies for notifications to the EC in the cases specified therein.

Provided that the concentration does not meet the Community's criteria as set forth in Regulation 139/2004, the Bulgarian national notification procedure shall apply. Besides the CPA, the procedure is described in the acts adopted or approved by the CPC on the implementation of the provisions of the CPA – Guidelines for Application of Chapter VI of the CPA issued under the repealed CPA but still applicable with regard to Chapter 10 of the new one and methods for investigation and definition of the market status of the undertakings on the relevant market. The CPC has also issued a standard form for notification of concentrations and guidelines, which can be useful to undertaking planning to conclude transactions subject to notification.[142], [143]

43. The Minister of Transport, Information Technologies and Communications is a high-rank executive authority who performs the state policy in the field of electronic communications and in the field of information society. The minister is vested with specific functions in all statutory procedures for the adoption of policies, strategies, investment programmes, projects, and secondary normative acts in the fields of electronic communications and information society. He also has some representative functions in international organizations and is responsible for performing Bulgaria's obligations before EU institutions. Among his particular duties, the minister coordinates the development and the implementation of standards and technical requirements, performs the international registration of radio frequencies and radio facilities, and performs the international coordination of all radio services of radio frequencies for national security purposes.[144] Certain competences were taken away from the minister and vested in the Chairman of the State Agency for Electronic Government such as the powers to: (1) create, operate, maintain and develop electronic communications network and physical infrastructure for its deployment and national security management points, which are serviced by personnel holding specific positions; (2) provide electronic communications for disaster management within the meaning of the Disaster Protection Act, in case of declaration of martial law, state of war or state of emergency within the meaning of the Act on Defence and the Armed Forces of the Republic of Bulgaria, as well as declaring a state of emergency within the meaning of the Counter-Terrorism Act; (3) use and develop the network under item 1 for the needs of the state administration.[145]

141. OJ, L 024, 29 Jan. 2004.
142. ECA, Arts 44–45.
143. CPA, Arts 78–90.
144. ECA, Art. 16.
145. ECA, Art. 17.

§5. Provision of Electronic Communications: Requirements, and Conditions

I. General Authorization of Electronic Communications Networks and Services

44. Because the general authorization regime applies in Bulgaria, a person willing to carry out public electronic communications should generally only notify (unless scarce resource would be used) the CRC so that the regulator enters it in a special register. This entry has to be performed within fourteen days of the date of submission of a complete notification.[146]

In accordance with the provision of Article 3 from Directive 2002/20/EC of the European Parliament and of the Council of 7 March 2002 on the authorization of electronic communications networks and services (Authorization Directive),[147] and Article 12 of the European Electronic Communications Code, Article 66 of the ECA states that public electronic communications are performed after the submission of a notification to CRC, whereas a permission or registration shall be necessary for use of scarce resources (numbers, spectrum). Notification is not required when: (1) number-independent interpersonal communication services are provided or (2) access to a public electronic communications network is provided via a local radio network by enterprises, public sector organizations, non-governmental organizations or end users for whom the provision of such access is not part of an economic activity or is in addition to an economic activity or public service dependent on the transmission of signals over these networks. The terms and the procedure for submitting notifications shall be determined by the CRC in the General Requirements adopted under Article 73(1) of the ECA.[148,149] The Commission shall take into account the guidelines of the BEREC on the model notification.

45. The procedure for obtaining permit for use of spectrum may take up to six weeks or up to eight months depending on the procedure to be performed and if international coordination is needed.[150] Where the provision of electronic communications services requires an individually assigned radio spectrum, permission is issued on a competitive basis following a tender or a competition procedure that may only be omitted in cases listed exhaustively in the ECA, namely[151]:

(1) for state authorities' own requirements;
(2) for foreign diplomatic missions;
(3) for providing electronic communication services for personal needs;
(4) if the number of candidates is smaller or equal to the number of persons that may be granted individual rights;

146. ECA, Arts 66 and 73.
147. OJ, L 108, 24 Apr. 2002.
148. ECA, Art. 66.
149. SG, issue 108 of 17 Dec. 2021
150. ECA, Art. 67 in relation to Arts 79–88.
151. ECA, Art. 81.

(5) for the provision of electronic communications through analogue terrestrial radio transmitters, following a decision by CEM with certain exceptions envisaged in ECA;[152]
(6) temporary permission (for a term not longer than six months); and
(7) for granting individual rights for use of radio frequency spectrum to radio and television operators, when necessary for achieving a goal of common interest, determined in accordance with the EU law, after conducting public consultations under Article 37 of ECA.

The CRC issues a permit for the use of numbering resources, without holding a competition or tender – the procedure for obtaining permission for use of numbers may take up to three weeks. The CRC issues a permit for the use of a geostationary orbit position with the respective radio frequency spectrum and of radio frequency spectrum used by a non-geostationary satellite system registered in international electronic communications organizations at the initiative of a person, without holding a competition or tender.

Individual rights may be reassigned to third parties but only upon permission of the CRC. According to the ECA, providers holding an individual permission for use of radio spectrum may assign it wholly or partially. The CRC permits assignment, provided this does not distort competition or lead to changes in the conditions for using the scarce resource. If analogue terrestrial transmitters are used, an additional requirement that the assignment should not result in a change to the broadcast programmes of providers governed by public law exists.

The conditions and the procedure for permission reassignment are subject to regulation by secondary legislation issued by the CRC.[153]

46. In accordance with Article 3.2 of the Authorization Directive and now Articles 12(2) and (3) of the European Electronic Communications Code, electronic communications are performed after the submission of a notification to CRC. Article 73 of the ECA does not require the provider to obtain an explicit decision or any other administrative act by the CRC before exercising the rights stemming from the authorization. These rights should be exercised in accordance with the General Requirements accepted through a CRC decision by virtue of Article 73(1) and (2) of the ECA. The rights stemming from the authorization arise from the moment of submission of the notification to the CRC.

II. Rights and Obligations Attached to the General Authorization

A. *Establishment of Rights and Obligations*

47. Under Bulgarian law, operators have the following main rights:

152. ECA, Arts 49a and 49b.
153. ECA, Arts 89–105.

(1) to provide electronic communications networks and/or services as of the date of submission of the notification except when individual rights are required to use a limited resource;
(2) to construct, deploy, use, and dispose with electronic communications networks and physical infrastructure for their deployment, as well as facilities in accordance with applicable law;
(3) to use radio frequency spectrum in connection with the electronic communications networks or services, observing the General Requirements under Article 73, the rules under Article 66a(3) and, where applicable, the conditions of a permit for the use of radio frequency spectrum issued in accordance with the ECA;
(4) its requests for granting the necessary rights for use of numbering resources to be considered under the conditions and by the order of the ECA;
(5) to negotiate interconnection and, where applicable, to gain access to or interconnection with networks of other undertakings providing public electronic communications networks or services, subject to the requirements of applicable law;
(4) to be given the opportunity to be determined to offer some or all of the services from the scope of the universal service in the whole territory of the country or on a part of it by the order of the ECA.[154]

Depending on the type of electronic communications network or service, the applicable General Requirements may include all or some of the following requirements:

(1) general conditions for:
  (a) payment of administrative fees according to Chapter Eight of the ECA;
  (b) ensuring the protection of personal data and the right to privacy in accordance with the requirements of Chapter Fifteen, sections II and III of the ECA;
  (C) providing the CRC with the information during the submission and consideration of a notification according to Article 75, as well as the information under Article 40 of the ECA;
  (d) creation of opportunities for interception of electronic communications on legal grounds by the competent authorities under the conditions of Articles 251b–251i of the ECA, the PDPA and Regulation (EU) 2016/679;
  (e) providing conditions for the use of the network or service in relation to communications from public authorities to the public to warn of imminent threats and to mitigate the effects of severe emergencies and disasters;
  (f) providing conditions for use of the network and its facilities in case of declared emergency within the meaning of the Disaster Protection Act, in case of declaration of war, martial law or state of emergency within

154. ECA, Art. 74.

the meaning of the Act on Defense and Armed Forces of the Republic Bulgaria, as well as when declaring a state of emergency within the meaning of the Counter-Terrorism Act, to ensure communications between the emergency services and state authorities;

(g) obligations for access beyond those provided for in Article 106(2) of the ECA and Article 107(2) of the ECA, as well as in Chapters X and XI of the ECA;

(h) application of existing standards or standardization documents in the field of electronic communications networks and services and associated facilities and services;

(i) transparency obligations in order to ensure end-to-end connectivity in accordance with the objectives and principles set out in Articles 4 and 5 of the ECA, and, where appropriate, in accordance with the principle of proportionality, in order to ensure access to the CRC to the information necessary to verify the accuracy of the disclosure;

(2) specific conditions for the provision of electronic communications networks for:

(a) interconnection of networks in accordance with Chapter X of the ECA;

(b) ‘mandatory carry-over’ obligations in accordance with Article 49c of the ECA;

(c) measures to protect public health from the harmful effects of electromagnetic fields resulting from the operation of electronic communications networks in accordance with EU law, taking into account as far as possible the requirements for limiting the exposure of the population to electromagnetic fields;

(d) maintaining the integrity of public electronic communications networks in accordance with the requirements of Chapter Fifteen, section I of the ECA, including conditions to prevent electromagnetic interference between electronic communications networks and services in accordance with the requirements of the Act on Technical Requirements for Products and its implementing acts;

(e) protection of public networks against unauthorized access to user data and personal data in accordance with the requirements of Chapter Fifteen, sections II and III of the ECA, and the PDPA;

(f) conditions for use of the radio frequency spectrum in accordance with Article 266 of the ECA, when the use is not subject to granting individual rights for use of radio frequency spectrum in accordance with Articles 67 and 79 of the ECA;

(3) specific conditions for the provision of electronic communications services, other than interpersonal communications services without numbers, for:

(a) interoperability of services in accordance with Chapter X of the ECA;

(b) accessibility for end users of the numbers from the NNP, of the numbers from the universal international toll-free numbers and, where technically and economically feasible, of the numbers from the numbering plans of other Member States of the EU, and the conditions accordingly Chapter VII of the ECA;

(c) consumer protection rules specific to the electronic communications sector;
(d) restrictions on the transmission of illegal content in accordance with the Electronic Commerce Act (E-Commerce Act) and restrictions on the transmission of harmful content in accordance with the RTA.[155]

The latest adopted General Requirements include additional rules on various reporting obligations, end-user rights, security of networks and services, requirements on national security obligations, etc.[156]

Finally, operators shall provide all the information required by CRC in the cases specified explicitly by the ECA. First of all, the Commission should give reasons justifying the request, as the request should be proportionate to the aims for which the information is requested. The undertakings should explicitly and in written form point out which part of the requested information represents a trade secret. The ECA specifies rules according to which this information may be presented to European authorities both to fully protect the rights of the national undertakings and to ensure cooperation with European institutions.[157]

B. Modification of the Obligations Related to the General Authorization

48. The General Requirements are secondary legislation and as such may be amended following public consultations where the proposed amendments are published for a period not less than thirty days on the website of the CRC and on a specific governmental website where all public consultations must be published.[158]

C. Provision of Services by Entities with Special or Exclusive Rights or by Public Administrations

49. The electronic communications market in Bulgaria is currently liberalized and no provider of electronic communications services benefits from any exclusive rights. On 1 January 2003, the monopoly of BTC over the provision of fixed voice telephone services and leased lines was lifted.

The ECA promulgated in 2007 does not provide for any specific conditions for special or exclusive rights. The only provision related to this matter is the one of Article 63 of the ECA regarding the obligation for accounting separation. According to the mentioned rule, undertakings providing public electronic communications networks and/or services, which have special or exclusive rights for providing services in other sectors, including in other EU Member States, keep separate accounting for that sector.

---

155. ECA, Art. 73(4).
156. SG, issue 108 of 17 Dec. 2021
157. ECA, Art. 40.
158. ECA, Art. 36.

50. The ECA does not provide for any specific rules for public administrations, which could have specific rights or obligations different from those for general authorization and the other measures provided within the act.

§6. Access and Interconnection

I. Definitions of Access and Interconnection

51. The ECA provides a definition of the term 'access' as 'the making available of facilities and/or services to another undertaking, under defined conditions, on either an exclusive or non-exclusive basis, for the purpose of providing electronic communications services, including when they are used for the delivery of information society services or radio and television content broadcasting services'. It covers access to network elements and associated facilities, which may involve the connection of equipment by fixed or non-fixed means (including access to the local loop and to facilities and services necessary for the provision of services over the local loop); access to physical infrastructure including buildings, ducts and masts; access to relevant software systems, including operational support systems; access to information systems or databases for pre-ordering, provisioning, ordering, maintaining, repair and billing requests; access to number translation systems or systems offering equivalent functionality; access to fixed and mobile networks, including for roaming; access to conditional access systems for digital television services; access to virtual network services.[159]

52. The definition for 'interconnection' reads:

a specific form of access implemented between public network operators through the physical and logical linking of public electronic communications networks used by one or different undertakings to enable users of one undertaking to exchange messages with users of the same or another undertaking or to gain access to services provided by another undertaking where such services are provided by participating countries or by other parties having access to the network.[160]

The definition is compliant with the European Electronic Communications Code and used to fully comply with Article 2 of Directive 2002/19/EC of the European Parliament and of the Council of 7 March 2002 on access to, and interconnection of, electronic communications networks and associated facilities (Access Directive).[161]

II. General Framework for Access and Interconnection

53. The ECA promotes the principle of free negotiation of interconnection arrangements between providers. Detailed rules for implementing interconnection

---

159. ECA, Additional Provisions, i. 8.
160. ECA, Additional Provisions, i. 4.
161. OJ, L 321, 17 Dec. 2018, pp. 36–214.

are provided by the CRC in December 2008 with the Ordinance for the Conditions and Order for Implementing Access and/or Interconnection,[162] which abolished the related Ordinance of 2004 issued under the repealed TA. If no agreement between the providers is reached, the CRC may impose an obligation for interconnection of networks to ensure end-to-end connectivity between end users, following the principles of objectivity, transparency, proportionality, and non-discrimination. The CRC may intervene in interconnection matters ex officio or upon any party's request if needed to develop competition or the internal market, or to promote the interests of end users. In conformity with EU legislation, the CRC may also impose specific obligations on undertakings with SMP related to access or interconnection listed exhaustively in the ECA: transparency, non-discrimination, separate, accounting, access to and use of specific network facilities as well as price control and cost accounting obligations. When an obligation for cost-oriented process for interconnection is imposed, the CRC may amend the offered prices to prevent price squeeze.[163]

54. If a transparency obligation is imposed together with a non-discrimination obligation, the CRC may oblige the respective provider to publish a reference interconnection offer (RIO) and may make amendments to it. Under the old TA repealed with the ECA, providers of fixed voice telephone services as well as providers of leased lines services enjoying a position of SMP were obliged to publish a RIO. In June 2004, the CRC approved the first RIO of the incumbent operator, BTC,[164] which was, however, repealed by the SAC. The CRC adopted a new decision approving the RIO in March 2006, confirmed with a final ruling by the SAC in February 2008 when the first Bulgarian RIO entered into force. The latest RIO (again imposed on BTC) was approved by the CRC in 2016 and amended in 2017.

In January 2009, the EC called on the Bulgarian authorities to introduce a faster reduction of mobile termination rates reiterating that in 2008 mobile termination rates in Bulgaria were, with over EUR 15 cents per minute, the highest in the EU. In March 2009, the CRC issued its final decision[165] for identifying the market for call origination on the public telephone network provided at a fixed location and the market for call termination on individual public telephone networks provided at a fixed location as relevant markets susceptible to *ex ante* regulation. With the decision, the CRC extends and amends BTC's obligations for publishing a RIO and setting cost-oriented prices with the obligation to amend the RIO in accordance with the decision in a month's term of its issuance. The decision also provides a glide path for call termination and generation prices until the calculation and implementation of cost-oriented prices is carried out. These are located in the appendix to the decision. In 2009, the CRC followed the EC recommendation regarding the approach to price regulation in the EU (2009/396/EC) based on the calculation of effective costs of an active operator or the Bottom-Up Long-Run Incremental Cost (BULRIC) model. In 2016, the market for call origination on the public telephone

162. SG, issue 5 of 20 Jan. 2009.
163. ECA, Arts 159–160d.
164. Presently Vivacom.
165. No. 237/17.03.2009.

network provided at a fixed location was deregulated and the wholesale market for call termination on individual public telephone networks provided at a fixed location (Market 1 as per Commission Recommendation (2014/710/EU) remained under ex ante regulation). The CRC imposed specific obligations on the undertakings with SMP to provide access and interconnection, as well as other specific obligations such as cost-oriented prices, transparency, etc.[166,167] The ex ante regulation of the latter market was further continued in 2020.[168] The wholesale market for voice call termination on individual mobile networks is also under ex ante regulation (Market 2 as per Commission Recommendation (2014/710/EU).[169]The price levels, until the adoption of Commission Regulation (EU) 2021/654 (adopted in accordance with Article 75 of the European Electronic Communications Code) for mobile and fixed termination services were as follows: BGN 0.0014 per minute, net Value Added Tax (VAT), respectively BGN 0.0015 per minute, net VAT.

III. Conditions Applicable to Access and Interconnection

55. The Bulgarian law imposes the obligation to negotiate access and/or interconnection on certain operators.[170] It does not impose the obligation to reach an agreement but as Recital 5 of the Access Directive suggests, operators who receive requests for access or interconnection should reach such agreement on a commercial basis and conclude a contract in a written form.[171] This is later acknowledged in Recital 143 of the European Electronic Communications Code, according to which in an open and competitive market, there should be no restrictions that prevent undertakings from negotiating access and interconnection arrangements between themselves, in particular on cross-border agreements, subject to the competition rules laid down in the TFEU. In the context of achieving a more efficient, truly pan-European market, with effective competition, more choice and competitive services to end users, undertakings which receive requests for access or interconnection from other undertakings that are subject to general authorization in order to provide electronic communications networks or services to the public should in principle conclude such agreements on a commercial basis, and negotiate in good faith.

Accordingly, the ECA provides several mechanisms to guarantee adequate access and interconnection in cases no agreement is reached (as described above). The CRC may intervene at its own initiative or at the request of either party so that end-to-end connectivity is ensured for users.

56. When operators are acquiring information from others during the process of negotiating access or interconnection agreements, they shall have the obligation to use this information solely for the purpose for which it was supplied and respect at

166. No. 356/23.06.2016.
167. No. 550/20.10.2016.
168. No. 265/23.07.2020.
169. No. 266/23.07.2020.
170. ECA, Arts 158–165.
171. Access Directive, Recital 5.

all times the confidentiality of the information transmitted or stored. ECA specifically provides that the operators shall comply with the requirements of confidentiality regarding the information provided or stored and use it only for the purposes for which it is intended. This information shall not be presented to any persons (third parties or internal structures) for which it may provide competitive advantage.[172] This provision is in compliance with the provision of the Access Directive[173] and the European Electronic Communications Code.[174]

§7. Numbering

I. General Statement

57. Recital 20 of the Framework Directive provided that 'access to numbering resources on the basis of transparent, objective, and non-discriminatory criteria is essential for undertakings to compete in the electronic communications sector'. Similarly, Recital (250) is contained in the European Electronic Communications Code, according to which 'Access to numbering resources on the basis of transparent, objective, and non-discriminatory criteria is essential for undertakings to compete in the electronic communications sector. Member States should be able to grant rights of use for numbering resources to undertakings other than providers of electronic communications networks or services in light of the increasing relevance of numbers for various Internet of Things services. All elements of national numbering plans should be managed by national regulatory or other competent authorities, including point codes used in network addressing. Where there is a need for harmonization of numbering resources in the union to support the development of pan-European services or cross-border services, in particular new machine-to-machine-based services such as connected cars, and where the demand could not be met on the basis of the existing numbering resources in place, the Commission can take implementing measures with the assistance of BEREC'. In accordance with that, the ECA ensures that the adequate numbers, names, and addresses are provided for all publicly available electronic communications services. However, Internet second and third-level domain names under the Bulgarian country code top-level domain (ccTLD) '.bg' are governed by the General Conditions of Register.BG.[175]

172. ECA, Art. 162.
173. Access Directive, Art. 4.3.
174. European Electronic Communications Code, Art. 60(2).
175. Register.BG Ltd, 'Terms and Conditions for Domain Name Registration and Support in the BG Zone and the Sub-zones' https://www.register.bg/user/static/rules/bg/index.html, 2011, accessed 16 Sept. 2013, latest version available at: https://www.register.bg/tld_user_reg/documents/en/terms_and_conditions-v4.9.pdf, accessed 12 Dec. 2021.

II. National Numbering Plans

58. The national numbering plan[176,177] is the regulatory mechanism for the designation of the numbers used in electronic communications networks for identification, routing, and imposing charges by undertakings providing public electronic communications services.

59. The national numbering plan is compiled in accordance with the regulatory policy and in observance of the regulatory policy under Article 30, i. 7 of the ECA. The national numbering plan is performed in compliance with any international law acts of international organizations or foreign competent authorities related to numbering resources so that effective use of numbers is ensured. The CRC shall determine a range of non-geographic numbers for the provision of electronic communications services, other than interpersonal communications services, throughout the EU, subject to the requirements and restrictions of Regulation (EU) No. 531/2012[178] and Article 132a(3) of the ECA. The CRC shall send to the BEREC the range of non-geographic numbers. The CRC may authorize these numbers to be used in the territory of countries outside the EU. Providers who use numbering resources with the Code of the Republic of Bulgaria in other Member States of the EU comply with consumer protection rules and other national regulations regarding the use of numbering resources applicable in countries where numbering resources are used. The rules for use, distribution, and the procedures for primary and secondary provision for use, reservation, and withdrawal of numbering resources shall be determined by an ordinance of the CRC after conducting a public discussion under Article 36 of the ECA, which is published in the SG. The CRC may conclude agreements for the use of interpersonal communication services with numbers between neighbouring settlements in the border areas with other EU Member States, including the use of a common numbering plan for all or specific categories of numbers. The CRC shall inform all undertakings and end users affected by the agreement in due time before the entry into force of the agreement.[179]

III. Numbering Management and Allocation

60. The rules for the numbering management and allocation were provided by Ordinance No. 7 for the Rules for Allocation and the Procedures for Primary and Secondary Providing for Use, Reservation, and Deprivation of Numbers, Addresses, and Names (Ordinance No. 7.)[180,181] and are now regulated in Ordinance No. 1 of

176. ECA, Art. 132.
177. CRC, 'National Numbering Plan', Annex to Decision No. 873, www.crc.bg/files/bg/n8.htm, 4 June 2007, latest version available at: https://crc.bg/files/_bg/NNP-2014.pdf, accessed 12 Dec. 2021.
178. Regulation (EU) No 531/2012 of the European Parliament and of the Council of 13 June 2012 on roaming on public mobile communications networks within the Union, OJ, L 172, 30.6.2012, pp. 10–35.
179. ECA, Arts 133–133b.
180. SG, issue 62 of 11 July 2008.
181. Ordinance No. 7, Art. 7.

22 July 2010 on the Rules for Distribution and the Procedures for Primary and Secondary Provision for Use, Reservation, and Revocation of Numbers, Addresses, and Names.[182] It states that upon the performance of the national numbering plan, the CRC carries out a public consultation as primarily provided in Article 36 of the ECA. The national numbering plan and its amendments are promulgated in the SG.[183]

IV. Number Portability

61. According to the ECA (Article 134), the undertakings providing public electronic communications services using numbers from the NNP should ensure number portability and shall ensure that their subscribers can keep their number for:

(1) their geographic number in case of change of the provider providing the respective service and/or in case of change of their address within the boundaries of one geographic national designation code;
(2) their non-geographic number for every location.

The ECA also provides that the functional specifications for number portability shall be determined by CRC after a public consultation and promulgation in the SG. These functional specifications are:

(1) technical conditions for implementation of portability;
(2) actions that the undertakings which are obligated to ensure portability must take, including time limits for implementation of such actions;
(3) method for implementation of portability;
(4) requirements regarding the database required to ensure the routing;
(5) obligations of the undertakings, which ensure the portability, and reasons for a refusal to provide the service to end users;
(6) procedure for implementation of portability;
(7) principles of pricing and apportioning the costs among undertakings;
(8) rules for compensating end users by providers in an easy and timely manner in the event of non-compliance with obligations under this section, including in the event of delays or abuses of number portability processes, as well as missed service and installation meetings;
(9) requirements for informing the end users during the transfer processes, as well as for the existence of the compensation rights referred to in (8).

The number portability procedure shall be carried out in the shortest possible period defined in the functional specifications mentioned above, if possible, on the date when such is explicitly agreed with the end user. The receiving provider activates the requested number for porting within one working day from the agreed

182. SG, issue 64 of 17 Aug. 2010.
183. SG, issue 14 of 20 Feb. 2009, latest amendment SG, issue 42 of 20 May 2014.

date, and the deprivation of service during the portability process does not exceed one working day. In cases where the end user does not exercise his right to agree on a specific date of portability, it is determined by the receiving and donating provider. When an end user terminates a contract, he reserves the right to carry a number to another supplier for a period of at least one month after the date of termination, unless he explicitly waives this right.[184] The host provider conducts the number portability process by cooperating in good faith with the donor provider. Providers are obliged not to delay, not to abuse the number porting process and not to port numbers without the explicit consent of the end users. End-user contracts with the donor provider are automatically terminated once the portability process is complete. Upon request, donor providers repay the remaining credit to consumers who use prepaid services. The donor may charge a fee for reimbursement that is proportionate and proportionate to the actual costs incurred by the donor only if this is provided for in the contract. In case of failure of the transfer process, the donor provider reactivates the number and services of the end user until the successful completion of the transfer. The donor provider continues to provide its services under the terms of the current contract with the end user until the activation of the services of the receiving provider. The obligations under the above sentence shall not apply in case of portability of numbers reserved for a period of at least one month after the date of termination, as described above. Undertakings whose access networks or facilities are used by the donor or host provider, or both, shall ensure that there is no deprivation of service which would delay number portability.[185]

§8. Radio Spectrum

I. Introduction

62. The ECA defines the 'radiofrequency spectrum' as comprising radio waves with frequencies under 3000 GHz and provides that radio waves are electromagnetic waves emitted in space without an artificial guide.[186]

II. Management of the Radiofrequency Spectrum

63. Where the provision of electronic communications services requires an individually assigned radio spectrum, permission has to be granted. Permission is issued on a competitive basis following a tender or a beauty contest procedure that may only be omitted in the following cases listed exhaustively in the ECA:

(1) for state authorities' own requirements;
(2) for foreign diplomatic missions;
(3) for carrying out of electronic communication services for personal needs;

184. ECA, Art. 134.
185. ECA, Arts 134a–134b.
186. ECA, Additional Provisions, i. 57.

(4) if the number of candidates is smaller or equal to the number of persons that may be granted individual rights;
(5) for the provision of electronic communications through analogue terrestrial radio transmitters, following a decision of the CEM with certain exceptions envisaged in ECA; and
(6) temporary permission (for a term not longer than six months) and
(7) for granting individual rights for use of radio frequency spectrum to radio and television operators, when necessary for achieving a goal of common interest, determined in accordance with the EU law, after conducting public consultations under Article 37 of ECA.

Individual rights may be reassigned to third parties but only upon permission of the CRC. According to the ECA, providers holding an individual permission for use of radio spectrum may assign wholly or partially. The CRC permits assignment, provided that it does not distort competition or lead to changes in the conditions for use of the scarce resource. If analogue terrestrial transmitters are used, there is an additional requirement whereby the assignment should not result in a change to the broadcast programmes of providers governed by public law.

The conditions and the procedure for permission reassignment are subject to regulation by secondary legislation.

64. Radio frequencies are an essential input for radio-based electronic communications services, and should therefore be allocated and assigned by national regulatory authorities according to a set of harmonized objectives and principles governing their action.

In accordance with the requirements of the European Electronic Communications Code, Article 124 of the ECA states that management and the effective use of the radio frequency spectrum without harmful interference is performed in accordance with the state policy on planning and the distribution of the spectrum, with the national plan for the distribution of the radio frequency spectrum, with the regulatory policy for the management of the radio frequency spectrum for urban needs, and with international agreements that are binding for the Republic of Bulgaria. Such management should be in accordance with guaranteeing the effective management of the radio frequency spectrum in accordance, applying objective, transparent, non-discriminatory and proportionate criteria. When all these conditions are met, the CRC issues permission for the use of radio frequencies.[187,188] Rules on allowing alternative use of all or part of the radio frequency band, on authorizing the use of a specific harmonized spectrum and on determining general aspects of the procedure for issuing a licence for the use of radio frequency spectrum together with a regulatory or other competent body of another Member State of the EU were envisaged in the ECA in line with the European Electronic Communications Code.[189]

---

187. ECA, Arts 124–125.
188. R. Cholakov, *Law of Radio and Television Organizations in Bulgaria* 113–121 (Sofia: Ciela – Soft and Publishing, 2000).
189. ECA, Arts 124a–124c.

If all national conditions related to the right of use of the radio frequencies are met in a case of a general choice procedure, the CRC should not impose other conditions or additional criteria or procedures that would limit, amend, or delay the proper use of the general appropriation of these radio frequencies.[190]

§9. Public Service Obligations and Other Public Rights and Obligations

I. General Statement

65. Chapter 11 and Chapters 14–19 of ECA provide the regulation concerning public services obligations, which refer to the universal service and other public service obligations aimed at protecting public interest. The expression 'other public rights and obligations' is used to address those aspects of the provision of electronic communications networks and services that are of public nature. Such cover *inter alia* the regulation of rights of way, co-location and facility sharing, personal data processing, protection of privacy, cryptography, and user rights.

II. Public Service Obligations

A. *Universal Service*

1. Concept and Scope

66. The ECA[191] provides that the universal service is a range of services with a specified quality, offered to all end users, irrespective of their geographic location in the territory of the country at an affordable price. The universal service includes (1) provision of voice messaging services by connecting in a certain location to a public electronic communications network, regardless of the technology used; (2) providing adequate broadband Internet access in a specific location, through which at least the following services can be supported: (a) e-mail; (b) search engines for searching and finding all kinds of information; (c) basic online tools for training and education; (d) online newspapers or news; (e) the purchase or order of goods or services online; (f) job search and job search tools; (g) professional networking communities; (h) Internet banking; (i) use of electronic administrative services; (j) social media and real-time communication via text messages; (k) voice and video calls; (3) provision of services, other than those specified under items 1 and 2, for which there are current obligations for the provision of universal service. Further regulation of the quality of the universal service is provided by an Ordinance issued by the Chairperson of the State Agency for Information Technologies and Communications (nowadays a competence of the Minister of Transport, Information Technologies and Communications).

190. ECA, Art. 125.
191. ECA, Art. 182.

67. The universal service obligations[192,193] shall be imposed after conducting a tender procedure, in compliance with the rules of Chapter Five of the ECA, in compliance with the principles of objectivity, transparency, equality, and in the interests of consumers, without precluding an undertaking from being able to be entrusted with the provision of universal service or part thereof.

2. Designation of Operators

68. The CRC imposes to one or more undertakings providing public electronic communications networks and/or services to provide universal service in the whole territory of the Republic of Bulgaria. The CRC notifies the EC for such appointed undertakings with imposed obligations.[194] Being the incumbent undertaking, BTC still has certain universal service obligations. Some of them, namely the obligations to provide public telephones and/or other points of public access to voice telephone services of a certain quality, to provide a telephone directory, and to provide telephone directory services were recently repealed by the CRC.[195]

3. Cost and Financing of Universal Service Obligations

69. According to Recitals 210 et seq. of the of European Electronic Communications Code, the universal service ensures that a set of at least the minimum services is available to all end users and at an affordable price to consumers, where a risk of social exclusion arising from the lack of such access prevents citizens from full social and economic participation in society. A fundamental requirement of the universal service is to ensure that all consumers have access at an affordable price to an available adequate broadband Internet access and voice communications services, at a fixed location. In the same time, the code requires Member States to establish mechanisms for financing the net cost of universal service obligations where it is demonstrated that the obligations can only be provided at a loss or at a net cost which falls outside normal commercial standards.

Therefore, Article 200 from the ECA[196] provides that the undertakings who were imposed with obligations with regard to the universal service, may request compensation for proved net expenses, whereas the provision of universal service represents an unfair burden for them. The existence of an unfair burden is determined on the basis of the net expenses and by taking into account the non-material advantages for the undertaking from the provision of the universal service or part thereof provided that the supply results in losses or is offered at prices below a reasonable

192. Directive 2002/22/EC (Universal Service Directive), OJ, L 108, 24 Apr. 2002, Arts 6–10 and subsequently replaced by the European Electronic Communications Code, OJ, L 321, 17 Dec. 2018, pp. 36–214.
193. ECA, Art. 191.
194. ECA, Arts 191–194.
195. No. 350/30.09.2021.
196. ECA, Arts 200–202.

rate of return. The compensation assets are provided by a specially determined Universal Service Recovery Fund. The recourses for recovery of the net costs of universal service provision are raised by the undertaking providing public telephone services and from other sources. The National Audit Office exercises control over the activity of the fund.

III. Other Public Rights and Obligations

A. Rights of Way

70. Chapter 17 of the ECA used to provide three general types of special rights to electronic communications operators – rights related to the construction of electronic communications infrastructure, easement, and use rights. In 2018, these provisions were removed from the ECA and moved in a special Act on the Electronic Communications Networks and Physical Infrastructure (AECNPI), which aimed to transpose Directive 2014/61/EU.[197],[198] According to AECNPI, the network operators shall provide to the operators of electronic communications networks access to and/or joint use of their physical infrastructure, including its elements and/or facilities, with a view to deployment and use of electronic communications networks, in the presence of justified request and under the conditions of this section and the acts on the application of the act. Network operators shall provide access to and/or sharing of their physical infrastructure with a written contract under transparent, proportionate, and fair general conditions, including price, published in advance on their website. If technically and physically feasible and upon a reasonable request, electronic communications network operators may provide network operators with access to and/or sharing their physical infrastructure for the purpose of building networks other than electronic communications networks. The operators of electronic communications networks shall provide with a written contract access to and/or joint use of their physical infrastructure under transparent, proportional, and fair conditions, including price. The operators of electronic communications networks may request from the network operators to be granted the right of passage and the right of special use under the Roads Act of elements and/or facilities of physical infrastructure of other network operators, including with regard to the easement zones of these elements. and/or facilities of natural water bodies. These rights are granted for: (1) construction, maintenance and use of physical infrastructure for electronic communications networks in accordance with the detailed development plans; (2) deployment, maintenance, and use of electronic communications networks and installation of facilities in the physical infrastructure. The granting of the rights shall be carried out in compliance with: (1) the rules and norms for structure and safe operation of the respective networks, whose physical infrastructure is used; (2) the requirements for the security and continuity of the supplies of other services; (3) the requirements for protection of the environment. The rights shall be granted on the basis of a written contract between the electronic communications

197. OJ L 155, 23 May 2014, pp. 1–14
198. SG, issue 21 of 09 Mar. 2018, in force as of 09 Mar. 2018.

network operator and the network operator managing the relevant physical infrastructure or a special road use permit. Upon transfer of ownership over electronic communications networks and the related physical infrastructure, which are built, respectively located, maintained, improved, and operated on the basis of a right granted as described above, this right shall be automatically transferred in favour of the new owner – acquirer. The operators of electronic communications networks, in favour of which the above-mentioned rights have been established, have the right to provide other network operators with access to and joint use of the physical infrastructure built on the basis of these rights, under the conditions of Article 15 and 16 of the act.[199] For the granted rights, the operator of electronic communications networks shall owe to the network operator a one-time indemnity, except for the cases where rights are granted on bridges, roads, streets, sidewalks, and other properties – public state or public municipal property, shall be provided free of charge in favour of the operators of electronic communications networks. Upon transfer of the rights the acquirer shall not owe remuneration or fee for these rights.[200] The AECNPI contains rules on obtaining rights on elements of physical infrastructure, state or municipal property, on the right to refuse granting such rights, on the right to access and transfer to properties for the activities of deployment, maintenance, and use of electronic communications networks and others.[201] Except in the cases under Article 15 and 17 of the AECNPI, the operators of electronic communications networks shall have the right to deploy electronic communications networks and to build the related physical infrastructure on the basis of a written contract, including a lease, contract or administrative act, on, above or below property: (1) public or private state or municipal property; (2) private property of natural or legal persons. For the physical infrastructure of transceiver stations of wireless electronic communications networks shall be required the conclusion of a written lease contract or another type of contract, granting a temporary right of use to the operator for a definite term. In the cases of condominium ownership, the above contracts shall be concluded on the basis of a decision of the general meeting of the owners. In the cases of co-ownership the contracts shall be concluded with the persons owning more than half of the property. When the property is state or municipal property, the rights shall be provided for a term of up to ten years by the order of Article 19 of the act.[202] AECNPI also contains rules on easements.[203]

B. User Rights

71. The ECA provides definitions of the terms ‘user’ and ‘end user’. As it is stated in the ECA, a ‘user’ is a natural person or legal entity, who is using or requesting a usage of publicly available electronic communications service, while an ‘end

199. AECNPI, Arts 15–17.
200. AECNPI, Art. 18.
201. AECNPI, Arts 19–30.
202. AECNPI, Art. 30.
203. Section II of Ch. IV of AECNPI.

user' is 'a user, not providing public communications networks or publicly available electronic communications services'. These definitions are in a complete compliance with the provisions of Article 2 of the European Electronic Communications Code. The term 'consumer' is also present and corresponds with the EU definition for any natural person who uses or requests a publicly available electronic communications service for purposes which are outside his or her trade, business, craft or profession.[204]

72. In respect to protection of end user interests, the ECA[205] stipulates the mandatory information that should be presented to the consumers before the latter are bound by contract or offer for the conclusion of a contract. The information includes, among other things, the identification data of the undertaking providing electronic communications services; contact data; types, description, and quality of services; terms and conditions for payment of offered services; maintenance of the offered services; special measures for disabled people; rights and obligations of the undertaking and end users; the presentation of information for prices, and new services, etc.; procedures for attending to and passing on appeals and requests by the end users, methods of dispute resolutions; the liability for breach of contract; conditions and order of seizing of the provision of the service upon non-payment or other breaches of contract, etc. The CRC has further clarified and detailed certain rules on end-user protection in Section V of the General Requirements[206] The law also stipulates the general rules on contract duration (e.g., that individual contracts cannot mandate a commitment period longer than twenty-four months; that the contracts can be terminated without sanction by consumers in certain cases of unilateral amendments of the contracts/general terms) and termination of contracts, availability of services, rules on access and choice for end users with disabilities, rules on switching between providers of Internet access services, specific rules on bundle of services or a bundle of services and terminal equipment, emergency communications, rules on transparency, public warning systems, comparison of offers, and publication of information etc.With minor deviations (considering the prescribed level of harmonization in Article 101 of the European Electronic Communications Code), the ECA transposes entirely and seemingly correct the rules of Part III, Title III of the European Electronic Communications Code.

73. The ECA introduces also explicit rules obliging the undertakings to take all necessary measures to ensure the integrity of the voice messaging and Internet access services provided through public electronic communications networks in cases of force majeure, as well as for the provision of an uninterrupted access to emergency calls services. These obligations of undertakings perceived as rights of the users are provided in the ECA Chapter establishing the rules for the protection of the interests of the end users.[207]

---

204. § 1., i. 48a of the Additional Provisions of the ECA and Art. 2, i. 15 of the European Electronic Communications Code.
205. ECA, Art. 226.
206. General Requirements, Art. 11 et seq.
207. ECA, Art. 237.

The obligation for ensuring access to the single European emergency call number 112 is provided as operators' obligation within the obligation for providing universal service (as described above).[208]

In respect to providing maximum protection of user interests, special provisions of the ECA concern the protection of the security of the electronic communications networks and services, the confidentiality of communications, and protection of users' personal data.[209]

§10. Administrative Charges

74. Currently, the issue about administrative charges and fees is regulated by two acts – the ECA, regulating the types of fees due, and the Tariff for Fees Collected by the CRC under the ECA[210] (the Tariff), regulating fee ranges. According to the ECA, the CRC is entitled to collect the following types of fees:

(1) one-off fee for issuance of a permit to use individually assigned scarce resource;
(2) one-off fee for amendment and supplement of the permit;
(3) annual fee for use of individually assigned scarce resource;
(4) fee for temporary use of individually assigned scarce resource;
(5) annual supervisory fee; and
(6) fees for different administrative services.

The ECA provides that the annual supervisory fee may not exceed 1.2% of the annual gross revenue from the provision of electronic communications networks or services, excluding VAT and after deduction of payments to other undertakings for access, interconnection, transit, roaming, value added services, as well as costs for settling of intellectual property rights over radio and television programmes. Gross revenues from the provision of electronic communications networks and services include all revenues arising from the use of scarce resources. The 2009 fee was set at 0.2% for undertakings with gross annual revenue exceeding BGN 100,000 (approximately EUR 51,130), and no fee was set for undertakings with gross annual revenue below this threshold.

The one-off fee for permission to use individually assigned scarce resource shall be cost oriented, that is, it will be equal to the administrative costs for the preparation and issuance of the permission.[211]

There is also a Tariff for Fees Collected by the CRC under the AECNPI.[212]

208. *See* Part I, Ch. 1, para. 68 *supra*.
209. ECA, Arts 243–262.
210. SG, issue 107 of 31 Dec. 2011.
211. *See* ECA, Arts 139–149.
212. SG, issue 96 of 20 Nov. 2018, in force as of 20 Nov. 2018.

Chapter 2. Regulation of Competition in the ICT Market

§1. General Statement

75. The authority competent for competition matters is the CPC. However, the CRC also enjoys certain powers with regard to competition protection in the communications sector such as determining undertakings with SMP, identifying markets, and assessing the competition level on the relevant markets. According to the ECA, the CPC and the CRC must collaborate through consultations, exchange of information and opinions, as well as through establishing joint workgroups.[213] The details are set in the Rules for Collaboration and Coordination between CPC and CRC[214] adopted jointly by the two commissions. Notwithstanding the above, in fact no legislative mechanism for avoiding conflict in the exercising of these commissions' powers in the field of competition exists.

As a result of the unprecedented changes in the global telecommunications industry, a wave of pro-competitive and deregulatory telecommunications policies swept the world. Those processes necessitated the interrelation of the topics of liberalization of telecommunications and free competition in the market of electronic communications services.

One of the most important measures for strengthening competition and further liberalization in the telecommunications sector is to develop the regulatory framework concerning:

(1) interconnection of networks, access and leased lines;
(2) co-location and local loop unbundling;
(3) universal service provision;
(4) obligations of the SMP operators.

76. With the implementation of the above-mentioned developments in the Bulgarian electronic communications legislation, the *ex ante* regulation of the sector was implemented. This regulation is based upon a previous analysis of the relevant markets with the aim to determine whether the level of competition on the particular market can be defined as effective. If effective competition is present, no *ex ante* regulation obligations are imposed. Nevertheless, if the competition on the particular market is considered ineffective, *ex ante* obligations may be imposed on undertakings having an SMP.[215]

213. ECA, Arts 44 and 45.
214. CPC, CRC, 'Rules for Collaboration and Coordination between CPC and CRC', www.crc.bg/files/_bg/PRAVILA_26.02.2008.pdf, 26 Feb. 2008.
215. ECA, Arts 150, 155–157c.

§2. Market Definition Procedure

77. In Bulgaria, the CRC is the national regulatory authority in charge of defining the relevant markets in terms of the provision of electronic communications networks and services. The ECA[216] provides that periodically the CRC will identify the relevant electronic communications markets, analyse the conditions and take measures to promote competition in those markets. The CRC has begun analysing the relevant markets because of the Commission Recommendation on relevant product and service markets within the electronic communications sector subject to *ex ante* regulation of 11 February 2003[217] and the updated Recommendation of 2007[218] and the updated Recommendation of 2014/710/EU.[219] Until 2020, the CRC has adopted more than fifteen final decisions as result of several (first-fourth) rounds of identification, analysis, and evaluation of the relevant electronic communications markets, as follows:

(1) From the first round the CRC adopted decisions for identification of retail lease market (Market No. 7 of EC Recommendation 2003/311/EC of 11 February 2003), market for wholesale terminating segments of leased lines (Market No. 14 of EC Recommendation 2003/311/EC, respectively No. 6 of EC Recommendation 2007/879/EC) and wholesale market for trunk segments of leased lines (Market *№* 13 of EC Recommendation 2003/311/EC), wholesale market for provision of (physical) access to network infrastructure (including stand-alone and unbundled access) at a fixed location and wholesale broadband market (Markets No. 4 and No. 5 of EC Recommendation 2007/879/EC), markets for access to a public telephone network provided at a fixed location and publicly available telephone services provided at a fixed location (Markets No. 1, 2, 3, 4, 5 and 6 of EC Recommendation 2003/311/EC), markets for call generation on public telephone networks at a fixed location and for call termination on individual public telephone networks at a fixed location (Markets No. 2 and 3 of EC Recommendation 2007/879/EC, respectively Markets No. 8 and 9 of the EC Recommendation 2003/311/EC), market for voice calls termination on individual mobile networks (Market No. 7 of the EC Recommendation 2007/879/EC, respectively market No. 16 of the EC Recommendation 2003/311/EC), and transit services market in public fixed telephone networks (Market No. 10 of EC Recommendation 2003/311/EC).[220]

(2) From the second round the CRC adopted decisions for identification of wholesale market of high-quality access at a fixed location (Market 4 of the EC Recommendation 2014/710/EU), wholesale market for local access at a fixed location and wholesale market for central access at a fixed location

216. ECA, Arts 151–152.
217. OJ, L 114, 8 May 2003.
218. OJ, L 344, 28 Dec. 2007.
219. OJ L 295, 11 Oct. 2014, p. 79–84.
220. All decisions from the first round of identifications, analysis, and evaluation can be found here: https://crc.bg/bg/rubriki/221/okonchatelni-reshenija-prieti-ot-krs-v-rezultat-ot-pyrvija-kryg-opredeljane-analiz-i-ocenka-na-syotvetnite-pazari-na-elektronni-syobshtenija, accessed 26 Dec. 2021.

(Markets 3a and 3b of EC Recommendation 2014/710/EU), wholesale market for voice call termination on individual mobile networks (Market 7 of the EC Recommendation 2007/879/EC), wholesale market for call generation on public telephone networks at a fixed location and wholesale market for call termination on individual public telephone networks at a fixed location (Markets 2 and 3 of EC Recommendation 2007/879/EC), market for access to a public telephone network for home and business users provided at a fixed location (Market No. 1 of EC Recommendation 2007/879/EC), market for publicly available national telephone services provided to home and business users provided at a fixed location and a market for publicly available international telephone services provided to home and business users at a fixed location (Markets No. 3-6 of EC Recommendation 2003/311/EC).[221]

(3) From the third round the CRC adopted decisions for identification of wholesale market for local access provided at a fixed location (Market 3a of Recommendation 2014/710/EC), market for access to a public telephone network at a fixed location for home and business users (Market No. 1 of EC Recommendation 2007/879/EC), market for publicly available national telephone services provided to home and business users at a fixed location, and a market for publicly available international telephone services provided to home and business users at a fixed location (Markets No. 3-6 of Recommendation EC 2003/311/EC), wholesale market for call origination on public telephone networks at a fixed location, wholesale market for call termination on individual public telephone networks at a fixed location (Market 2 of Recommendation 2007/879/EC and Market 1 of EC Recommendation 2014/710/EU), wholesale market for voice call termination in individual mobile networks (Market 2 of the EC Recommendation 2014/710/EU).[222]

(4) From the fourth round the CRC adopted decisions for identification of wholesale market for call termination on individual public telephone networks provided at a fixed location (Market 1 of European Commission Recommendation 2014/710/EU) and Wholesale market for voice call termination on individual mobile networks (Market 2 of European Commission Recommendation 2014/710/EU).[223]

221. All decisions from the second round of identifications, analysis, and evaluation can be found here: https://crc.bg/bg/rubriki/220/okonchatelni-reshenija-prieti-ot-krs-v-rezultat-ot-vtori-kryg-opredeljane-analiz-i-ocenka-na-syotvetnite-pazari-na-elektronni-syobshtenija, accessed 26 Dec. 2021.

222. All decisions from the third round of identifications, analysis and evaluation can be found here: https://crc.bg/bg/rubriki/219/okonchatelni-reshenija-prieti-ot-krs-v-rezultat-ot-treti-kryg-opredeljane-analiz-i-ocenka-na-syotvetnite-pazari-na-elektronni-syobshtenija, accessed 26 Dec. 2021.

223. All decisions from the fourth round of identifications, analysis, and evaluation can be found here: https://crc.bg/bg/rubriki/618/okonchatelni-resheniq-prieti-ot-krs-v-rezultat-ot-chetvyrti-kryg-na-opredelqne-analiz-i-ocenka-na-syotvetnite-pazari-na-elektronni-syobshteniq, accessed 26 Dec. 2021.

§3. Market Analysis Procedure

78. Following the definition of relevant markets, the CRC shall perform an analysis of the relevant markets for the purpose of determining how effective competition might affect them.[224] Thus, the CRC shall request and take into account the opinion of the national competition regulator. In the process of this procedure, the CRC shall present all relevant documentation and decisions for public consultation through publishing the information on their Internet site for a period of at least thirty days. The CPC shall present their opinion in a thirty-day term of the presentation of the project to the CRC. In a new thirty-day term, as from the later date, the CRC shall summarize the submitted opinions and proposals and shall publish them on the Internet except the parts that may be considered a trade secret. The CRC shall issue decisions on the analysis and the evaluations of the relevant markets and the specific obligations imposed on the undertakings with SMP. The CRC shall notify the EC, the BEREC and the Regulatory Authorities of the Member States of the EU about these decisions in accordance with the provisions of Articles 6, 7, and 16 of the Framework Directive.[225,226]

§4. Operators with SMP

I. Identification of the Operators with SMP

79. The term 'significant market power' was defined first in Directive 97/13/EC[227] (already repealed), then in Directive 2002/22/EC (as of 7 March 2002)[228] (also repealed by the European Electronic Communications Code). The basic wording from the current European legislation provides that a telecommunications operator shall be deemed to have SMP if, either individually or jointly with others enjoys a dominant position, that is, a position of economic strength providing it with the power to behave to an appreciable extent independently of competitors, customers, and ultimately consumers.[229] And the latest rule on the matter envisaged in the European Electronic Communications Code reads as follows: An undertaking shall be deemed to have SMP if, either individually or jointly with others, it enjoys a position equivalent to dominance, namely a position of economic strength affording it the power to behave to an appreciable extent independently of competitors, customers, and ultimately consumers. In particular, national regulatory authorities shall, when assessing whether two or more undertakings are in a joint dominant position in a market, act in accordance with Union law and take into the utmost account the

224. ECA, Art. 151.
225. Directive 2002/21/EC of the European Parliament and of the Council of 7 Mar. 2002, OJ, L 108, 24 Apr. 2002.
226. *See also* ECA, Art. 42.
227. OJ, L 107, 17 May 1997.
228. Universal Service Directive, Ch. III.
229. Framework Directive, Art. 14(2).

guidelines on market analysis and the assessment of SMP published by the Commission pursuant to Article 64 of the code.[230]

The ECA provides a definition of an 'undertaking with significant market power', which is in accordance with the definition given by the European Electronic Communications Code, namely that is, 'an undertaking that, alone or jointly with others, enjoys a position equivalent to a dominant one, i.e. a position of economic strength that allows it to behave substantially independently of competitors, users, and end users'.[231] Also, the ECA[232] in line with Article 63(3) of the European Electronic Communications Code envisages that where an undertaking has SMP on a specific market, it may also be designated as having SMP on a closely related market, where on the basis of market analysis it is established that the links between the two markets allow the market power held on the specific market to be leveraged into the closely related market, thereby strengthening the market power of the undertaking.

II. Legal Status of Operators with SMP

A. Introduction

80. The procedure for the identification of the operators with SMP states the principles for this identification and specifies that the conditions for defining, analysis, and evaluation of relevant markets, and the criteria for the determination of operators with SMP shall be provided within a methodology issued by the CRC and promulgated in the SG[233] (but not included within the ECA itself). The ECA also provides that upon the performance of its functions, the CRC shall respect the principles of objectivity, transparency, proportionality, and non-discrimination.[234]

As the basic issue in the procedure for determining operators with SMP is defining the markets of telecommunications products and services, the ECA provides that the national regulatory authorities analyse these markets in accordance with the methodology developed by the CRC. The methodology defines the principles that national regulatory bodies are expected to follow when evaluating the competition efficiency on the market or the presence of an SMP. Each market analysis by national regulatory authorities should be published. On the basis of the analysis conducted in accordance with the methodology mentioned above, the national regulatory authorities express their opinion whether the market in a given geographical region is competitive.

81. Nevertheless, the ECA explicitly states that in determining the relevant markets, different from the ones specified in the applicable act of the EC, the CRC shall be guided by competition law principles and the following criteria that must be cumulatively met:

230. European Electronic Communications Code, Art. 63(2).
231. ECA, Additional Provisions, i. 51.
232. ECA, Additional Provisions, Art. 156(6).
233. ECA, Art. 150(2).
234. ECA, Art. 166(5).

(1) high and intransient structure, legal, or regulatory barriers for entrance into the market;
(2) the structure of the market does not imply the achievement of effective competition within a relevant time horizon, taking into account the state of competition in terms of infrastructure and other sources of competition beyond barriers to entry;
(3) not sufficient effectiveness of the competition law for overcoming of the identified problems on the relevant market.[235]

82. When determining the specific obligations CRC may impose, prolong, amend, or abolish, it shall stick to the following principles:

(1) proportion of the imposed obligation considering the costs and benefits, where possible;
(2) proper motivation with regard to the purposes of the ECA;
(3) the obligations should be imposed after conducting the procedures in accordance with Articles 36 and 42 of the ECA;
(4) the obligations should be based on the nature of the problem, identified by the CRC in the market analysis, and, if appropriate, the determination of cross-border demand according to Article 157c of the ECA.[236]

B. Obligations with Regard to Access and Interconnection

1. General Statement

83. The obligations imposed on the telecommunications operators with SMP are defined in EU legislation with regard to ensuring universal service and interoperability through application of the principles of open network which are based on transparency, non-discrimination, separate accounting, access to network infrastructure; control over prices, including in terms of cost orientation and in terms of accounting systems.

84. Some of those obligations are provision of access at a fixed location, provision of special measures for disabled users, quality of service, among others.

85. In the ECA, the specific obligations that the CRC may impose on operators with SMP are specified within the ECA[237] as follows:

(1) transparency in providing interconnection and access making operators publicize specific information such as accounting information, technical specifications, network characteristics, terms and conditions for supply and use,

235. ECA, Art. 152(5).
236. ECA, Art. 157.
237. ECA, Art. 166(2).

and prices; in particular, the CRC may require from an operator having an obligation of non-discrimination to publish a reference offer;

(2) non-discrimination in ensuring that the operator provides equal conditions to other undertakings providing equivalent electronic communication services as well as providing services and information under the same conditions and of the same quality as those of the undertaking when it connects its networks and/or provides to related persons or undertakings;
(3) accounting separation when providing access or interconnection;
(4) access to and use of specific network facilities and associated facilities;
(5) price control, including obligations for cost orientation of prices and cost accounting systems, the purpose being to avoid price squeeze;
(6) access to physical infrastructure, buildings and physical infrastructure in buildings;
(7) compliance with the conditions under the proposals of the enterprises for undertaking commitments for cooperation agreements for joint investments in new very high-capacity networks or for effective and equal access of third parties in voluntary separation from a vertically integrated undertaking.

These rules follow closely the concept of specific obligations provided by the Framework Directive[238] and the European Electronic Communications Code.[239]

86. In exceptional circumstances, the CRC may decide that there is an urgent need to act to safeguard competition and protect users' interests. Thus, it may immediately adopt proportionate and provisional measures deviating from the general notification procedure to the EC set by Article 7(1)–(5) of the Framework Directive[240] and later by the European Electronic Communications Code. In such cases, CRC shall, without delay, communicate those measures with full justification to the Commission, the other national regulatory authorities and to BEREC.[241] A decision of the national regulatory authority to render such measures permanent or extend the time for which they are applicable shall be subject to the provisions for general notification to the EC, as described in Article 7 of the Framework Directive and later by the European Electronic Communications Code.[242]

---

238. Framework Directive, Arts 9–13.
239. European Electronic Communications Code, Arts 69–74.
240. Framework Directive, Art. 7.
241. European Electronic Communications Code, Art. 32(10).
242. ECA, Art. 42c(9).

Chapter 3. Regulation of Cryptography and Other Dual-Use Goods

§1. Regulation of Cryptography Related to Electronic Communications

I. General

87. No explicit general permit for use of encryption hardware and software for electronic communication services in the Bulgarian legislation exists.

Article 21(1) of the ECA[243] provides that the functions of regulation and control over carrying out electronic communications shall be performed by the CRC. It regulates and controls the implementation of electronic communications in compliance with this Act and the EU law.[244]

Furthermore, Article 274 of the ECA provides that radio equipment and electronic communication terminal equipment including hardware accessories to radio equipment or terminal equipment for encryption of electronic communications and using cryptographic keys more than 56 bits long, shall be manufactured or imported after registration in the State Agency for National Security.[245]

88. ECA gives the legal definitions of radio equipment and electronic communications terminal equipment in its Supplementary Provisions. Paragraph 1, i. 28 defines electronic communications terminal equipment as '(a) equipment for sending, processing or receiving information intended for direct or indirect connection to the interface of a public electronic communications network; in both cases, directly or indirectly, the connection can be made by wire, by optical fibres or by electromagnetic means; the connection is indirect if other equipment is placed between the terminal and the network interface; (b) equipment for satellite earth stations'. Pursuant to i. 56 of the same paragraph, radio equipment shall mean an 'electrical or electronic product designed to transmit and/or receive radio waves for radio communication and/or radio determination purposes, or an electrical or electronic product which must be equipped with an accessory, such as an antenna, so as to transmit and/or receive radio waves for the purposes of radio communication and/or radio determination'.

The definition of a 'cryptographic key' is provided in paragraph (1), i. 29, and it is described as 'a series of symbols that is used in an algorithm to generate cipher text (encryption) from plain text or vice versa – from cipher text into plain text (decryption)'.

243. SG, issue 41 of 22 May 2007.
244. ECA, Art. 21(4).
245. ECA, Art. 274.

II. Provisions Regarding Encryption of Electronic Communications

89. The registration of the equipment under Article 274(1)[246] of ECA shall be effected at the State Agency for National Security.

However, cryptographic devices for bank transactions protection, smart cards, scramblers for scrambling television signals, mobile phones without a built-in additional cryptographic module, and cryptographic devices used by representative offices or other organizations having a status of diplomatic missions shall not be subject to registration.

90. The public register shall contain identification data about the manufacturer or importer (full name and permanent address for natural persons; company name, headquarters, and registered address for legal entities) and name and type of the terminal equipment.[247]

The manufacturer or importer shall file an application to the State Agency for National Security in order to register radio equipment or electronic communication terminal equipment. The application shall contain:

(1) identification data on the manufacturer or the importer (the importer shall state data on the manufacturer as well):
   (a) in respect of natural persons: forename, patronymic and surname, standard public registry personal number and permanent address, and in respect of foreigners: personal number;
   (b) in respect of legal persons and sole trader natural persons: designation (business name), registered office, address of the place of management and unified identification code under BULSTAT and, in respect of non-resident persons: the respective identification code;
(2) full designation of the radio equipment or the electronic communications terminal equipment;
(3) short description of the radio equipment or the electronic communications terminal equipment, including the type of the cryptographic algorithms used and the length of the cryptographic keys.[248]

The application should be accompanied by a copy of the technical documentation of the radio equipment or the electronic communication terminal equipment, a description of the cryptographic algorithms (if they are not publicly accessible), the methods of their initialization, and working modes and formats of incoming and outgoing data – each attached separately.

The Directorate for Technical Operations under the State Agency for National Security enters the radio equipment or device in the public register within thirty days from the date of receipt of the application with the attachments, or from the date of correction of omissions if any.

246. Last amendment, SG, issue 93/2009.
247. ECA Art. 274(3) and (4), amended, SG, issue 43/2008 and SG, issue 20/2021.
248. ECA Art. 275(2).

Under Article 276 of the ECA the State Agency for National Security shall issue a certificate of entry in the register to the entity importing or producing radio equipment and/or electronic communication terminal equipment.[249]

Every entity carrying out transactions with radio equipment or electronic communication terminal equipment shall provide regularly and at least once every three months details in writing to the State Agency for National Security on any transaction with such equipment or device including name, type, serial number, and identification data on the person wherewith the transaction was effected.[250]

91. If the encryption technology is applied to classified information, the encryption devices and the encryption keys are subject to a special regulatory regime under the Protection of Classified Information Act (PCIA),[251] the Ministry of the Interior Act and the Ordinance on the Cryptographic Security of Classified Information. Pursuant to Article 1(3) of PCIA, classified information is defined as the information constituting state or official secret, as well as foreign-classified information. The definitions of state secret, official secret, and foreign-classified information are provided in Articles 25,[252] 26,[253] and 27[254] of the PCIA. Pursuant to these provisions, a List of the Categories of Information Subject to Classification as a State Secret is enacted.

§2. Regulation of Cryptography Related to Electronic Signatures

I. General

92. EIDAS, EDETSA[255] and its secondary normative acts regulate the usage of cryptography related to electronic signatures both in the private and public sectors.

249. For the issuance of the certificate a fee shall be paid to the amount fixed in the Rate Schedule of Fees Collected by the State Agency for National Security.
250. Article 277, last amendment, SG, issue 20/2021.
251. SG, issue 109 of 30 Apr. 2002.
252. Under Art. 25, a state secret shall be considered the information listed in Appendix No. 1 the unauthorized access to which would create danger or would damage the interests of the Republic of Bulgaria, or which is related to national security, defence, foreign policy, or the protection of the constitutionally established order.
253. Under Art. 26(1), an official secret shall be the information created or stored by state or local government bodies, which is not state secret, but the unauthorized access to which would influence unfavourably the interests of the state or would hinder other legally protected interests. The information subject to classification as official secret shall be defined in law. The chief of the respective organizational unit shall, within the law, provide a list of the categories of information from the sphere of activity of the organizational unit. The procedure for announcing the list shall be determined in an ordinance implementing the act.
254. Under Art. 27, foreign-classified information shall be the classified information conceded by another state or international organization by force of international agreement to which the Republic of Bulgaria is a party.
255. *See* Introduction, Ch. 5, para. 33 *supra*.

Article 3(12) of eIDAS defines the qualified electronic signature as an advanced electronic signature, which is: (i) created by a qualified electronic signature-creation device, and (ii) which is based on a qualified certificate for electronic signatures. The transformation shall be carried out through algorithms employing the use of the private key of an asymmetric cryptographic system.

The 'signature-creation device' is regulated by Article 3(2) of the eIDAS as configured software or hardware used to create an electronic signature. The requirements for qualified signature-creation devices are envisaged in Annex II of eIDAS: they shall ensure, by appropriate technical and procedural means, that at least:

(a) the confidentiality of the electronic signature creation data used for electronic signature creation is reasonably assured;

(b) the electronic signature creation data used for electronic signature creation can practically occur only once;

(c) the electronic signature creation data used for electronic signature creation cannot, with reasonable assurance, be derived and the electronic signature is reliably protected against forgery using currently available technology;

(d) the electronic signature creation data used for electronic signature creation can be reliably protected by the legitimate signatory against use by others. Signature-creation devices shall not alter the data to be signed or prevent such data from being presented to the signatory prior to signing. Generating or managing electronic signature creation data on behalf of the signatory may only be done by a qualified trust service provider (TSP). Without prejudice to point (d) above, qualified TSPs managing electronic signature creation data on behalf of the signatory may duplicate the electronic signature creation data only for backup purposes provided the following requirements are met:

(a) the security of the duplicated datasets must be at the same level as for the original datasets;

(b) the number of duplicated datasets shall not exceed the minimum needed to ensure continuity of the service.

93. 'Signature-creation data' refers to unique data which is used by the signatory to create an electronic signature (Article 3(13) of eIDAS).

94. In accordance with Article 16(2) of the old redaction of Electronic Document and Electronic Signatures Act (EDESA), the Council of Ministers adopted an Ordinance on the Requirements to the Algorithms for Creation and Verification of Qualified Electronic Signatures (ORACVQES). It was later repealed with the Ordinance on the Liability and Termination of the Activity of the TSPs of 2018.

II. Activity of the TSPs

95. Several rules in the Ordinance on the Liability and on the Termination of the Activity of Trust Service Providers (OLTATSP) regulates the responsibilities of the providers in the field of cryptography related to electronic signatures. According to Article 10 of OLTATSP, a provider of qualified trust services, which has taken over the activity of another provider of qualified trust services, shall be obliged to maintain the issued certificates within the term of their validity under the same conditions under which they are issued. The provider which has taken over the activity of another provider of qualified trust services shall be entitled to use the public key infrastructure of the transferred provider for the purpose of managing already issued certificates for a period not exceeding the validity of the last validly issued user certificate.

III. Regulation of Cryptography Related to Electronic Signatures for E-government Purposes

96. This specific sphere of the cryptography related to electronic signatures is regulated by the OCESPA.[256]

Article 17 of the OCESPA provides that administrations may use information systems allowing automatic signing of electronic documents in cases of processing applications for internal administrative services and in the cases of automatic generation of statements by administrations necessary for the electronic administrative services provided to citizens and organizations. In this sense, the automatic signing is done by the use of secure signature-creation device following minimum security requirements EAL 4 under the Common Criteria for Information Technology Security Evaluation – CC 2.1 adopted by the International Organization for Standardization (ISO) in its international standard ISO/IEC 15408:1999.

Administration heads assign to a highly qualified employee the responsibility for the maintenance of the technical equipment ensuring automatic signing. Setting, installing private keys and certificates for automatic signing is duly recorded and supervised by the head of the directorate or unit.[257]

Under Article 18, the issued electronic signature certificates shall be renewed in accordance with the procedure of the provider and the provision of Article 8, Article 9, respectively of the OCESPA. The issued certificates may be renewed by following a renewal policy only (but not re-key).

When the key or the security of its usage is compromised, or the key validity expires, the certificate is terminated under Articles 22 and 23 of the OCESPA. When documents encrypted by the public key of the respective employee are received, they must be submitted to the head of the directorate or of the unit in decrypted form. Upon expiration of the validity of the certificate, the employee submits[258] the signature-creation device and the Personal Identification Number (PIN), if it is in his/her keeping, in a sealed envelope, to the head of the directorate or of the unit responsible for human resources management. The latter encloses them to the personal file of the employee. In this case, a new electronic signature certificate with a new pair of keys for a new device is issued. The same procedure applies where employee's assignment is terminated.

256. *See* Introduction, Ch. 5, para. 33 *supra*.
257. Article 17(5) of the OCESPA.
258. The directorate or unit maintains a list of all types of issued electronic signature certificates.

§3. Regulation of Dual-Use Goods

97. A specific regulation on import and export of certain types of encryption of hardware and software is contained in the Bulgarian Defence-Related Products and Dual-Use Items and Technologies Export Control Act (the act).[259]

The act regulates the terms and procedures for export, import, transfer, transport, passage, carriage, and transit of defence-related products, brokering services with them and the control over such activities; the measures for implementing Council Regulation (EC) No. 428/2009 of 5 May 2009 on the introduction of a Community regime for the control of exports, transfer, brokering, and transit of dual-use items;[260] the terms and procedures for dual-use items import and brokering activities with them and the control over these activities; and technical assistance provision for military end-use pursuant to Council Joint Action 2000/401/CFSP.

The statutory control under the above paragraph shall be exercised for the purpose of protecting national security, the economic and foreign policy interests of the Republic of Bulgaria as well as for strengthening international peace and security and for implementing the Republic of Bulgaria's international obligations.

The Council of Ministers has adopted by its decree a list of defence-related products to which the statutory provisions shall apply and a list of dual-use items which shall be controlled on import (the list).[261] Particular interest to goods, related to information technologies and communications reveal sections ML11 – Electronic Equipment (part of the same category with, 'Spacecraft' and Components, not specified elsewhere in the EU Common Military List), ML21 21 – Software, ML 22 – Technologies, Category 3 of the Appendix 1 – Electronics, and Category 5 – Telecommunications and Information Security.

The dual-use items, the export, brokering, and transit of which shall be subject to control, are specified in Annex I of Regulation (EC) No. 428/2009 and the dual-use items, the transfer of which shall be subject to control, are specified in Annex IV of Regulation (EC) No. 428/2009.

The Council of Ministers may introduce restrictions and impose prohibitions on carrying out activities with defence-related products and dual-use items when the activities contradict the objectives and the obligations specified in the law; the products and items are intended or may be used for creating, manufacturing, processing, developing, managing, maintaining, storing, and distributing weapons for mass

259. Promulgated, SG No. 26/29.03.2011, effective 30 June 2012.

260. OJ, L 134/1 of 29 May 2009, subsequently amended several times with Regulation (EU) No 1232/2011, OJ, L 326, 8 Dec. 2011, pp. 26–44, Regulation (EU) No 388/2012, OJ, L 129, 16 May 2012, pp. 12–280, Regulation (EU) No 599/2014, OJ, L 173, 12 Jun. 2014, pp. 79–83, Commission Delegated Regulation (EU) No 1382/2014 OJ, L 371, 30 Dec. 2014, pp. 1–212, Commission Delegated Regulation (EU) 2015/2420, OJ, L 340, 24 Dec. 2015, pp. 1–302, Commission Delegated Regulation (EU) 2016/1969, OJ, L 307, 15 Nov. 2016, pp. 1–251, Commission Delegated Regulation (EU) 2017/2268, OJ, L 334, 15 Dec. 2017, pp. 1–252, Commission Delegated Regulation (EU) 2018/1922, OJ, L 319, 14 Dec. 2018, pp. 1–252, Commission Delegated Regulation (EU) 2019/2199, OJ, L 338, 30 Dec. 2019, pp. 1–254, Commission Delegated Regulation (EU) 2020/1749, OJ, L 421, 14 Dec. 2020, pp. 1–280, Regulation (EU) 2020/2171, OJ, L 432, 21 Dec. 2020, pp. 4–6, Commission Delegated Regulation (EU) 2021/1528, OJ, L 329, 17 Sep. 2021, pp. 6–6.

261. Decree of the Council of Ministers No. 204/19.09.2018.

destruction; there are restrictions or prohibitions ensuing from international agreements or from the Republic of Bulgaria's membership in international organizations; these activities affect substantive interests of the Republic of Bulgaria in the security field or there are considerations related to maintaining public order.[262]

98. Apart from some governmental bodies, export, import, and transfer of defence-related products may be done by natural and legal persons registered pursuant to the Commerce Act (CA). These persons engage in export or import of defence-related products after acquiring a licence issued by the Defence Industry and Supplies Security Interdepartmental Board at the Council of Ministers (Interdepartmental Board), and an export or import authorization issued by the Export Control and Non-Proliferation of Weapons of Mass Destruction Interdepartmental Commission under the Minister of Economy (Interdepartmental Commission).[263]

Export or import of defence-related products may be performed by certain governmental bodies without a licence after registering the import and/or export with the Minister of Economy.

Transfer of defence-related products from the territory of the Republic of Bulgaria to the territory of another Member State may be performed after obtaining a transfer registration certificate issued by the Interdepartmental Board and a general global or individual transfer authorization issued by the Interdepartmental Commission.

Transfer of defence-related products from the territory of the Republic of Bulgaria to the territory of another Member State may be performed after obtaining a transfer registration certificate issued by the Interdepartmental Board and after registering the transfer with the Minister of Economy when the recipient is a government organization in a Member State and when the transfer is carried out between structures of the EU, of NATO, of the International Atomic Energy Agency or between other intergovernmental organizations for the purpose of implementing their tasks.

The persons envisaged herein above may receive defence-related products specified in the general transfer authorization issued and published by the Member State of origin after obtaining a recipient certificate issued by the Interdepartmental Board and after declaring the transfer at the Ministry of Economy under a procedure specified in the by-laws on implementing the act. Receiving of defence-related products from a supplier who holds an individual or global authorization issued by the Member State of origin after receipt of a transfer registration certificate issued by the Interdepartmental Board and after registering the transfer with the Minister of Economy under a procedure specified in the by-laws on implementing the act.

Transportation of defence-related products from the territory of a third state to the territory of another third state without entry into the Republic of Bulgaria may be performed on the basis of a licence issued by the Interdepartmental Board.

---

262. The Bulgarian Defence-Related Products and Dual-Use Items and Technologies Export Control Act, Art. 4.
263. The Bulgarian Defence-Related Products and Dual-Use Items and Technologies Export Control Act, Arts 5–6.

No authorization is required for the transit of defence-related products through the territory of the Republic of Bulgaria when the state of the supplier has issued a transfer authorization or when the state of the supplier does not require a transfer authorization.

No authorization is also required for the entry into the territory of the Republic of Bulgaria of defence-related products when the state of the supplier has issued a transfer authorization or when the state of the supplier does not require a transfer authorization.

Carriage through the territory of the Republic of Bulgaria of defence-related products, which are exported or imported by a Member State different from the Republic of Bulgaria, to and from a third state respectively, shall be done on the basis of an authorization issued by the Interdepartmental Commission.

Transit of defence-related products shall be done on the basis of an authorization issued by the Interdepartmental Commission.[264]

---

264. The Bulgarian Defence-Related Products and Dual-Use Items and Technologies Export Control Act, Arts 6–9.

Chapter 4. Legal Status of Standardization

§1. General

99. For the purposes of determining the current state of the ICT market and forecasting its trends of development, the topic of standardization in the field of information and communication technologies should be taken into account. It refers to the possibility of fast and secure deployment and implementation of cutting-edge technologies and high-quality information and communication services. The basic arguments for the development of standards in the area of ICT are the necessity for clear technical criteria on legal issues and contracts, assessment criteria of products, processes or services, as well as for global recognition.

100. A standard is defined as a 'document compiled with consensus, which defines common and repeated application of rules, basic directions or characteristics of activities or their results so that optimal order in a given combination of circumstances is achieved'.[265] The National Standardization Act (NSA) provides for the implementation of national standardization and the order for establishing the structure and the activity of the Bulgarian Standardization Institute (BSI). Bulgarian standards are identified with alphabetical and numerical symbols. The alphabetical symbol consists of the letters Bulgarian State Standard[266] or a combination thereof and other alphabetical symbols in cases of introduction of European or national standards. The numerical symbol consists of the number of the standard and the year of approval or introduction.[267]

Nowadays, standardization should be considered as a voluntary process, based on consensus between economically and socially related subjects – manufacturers, users, public institutions, and other stakeholders. However, only standards complying with the provisions of Article 4 could enter into force and be considered as official Bulgarian standards.

101. Presently, the field of standardization in the area of electronic communications is regulated by the NSA and the Technical Requirements for Products Act,[268] as well as the provisions of Article 30(23[269]) of the ECA which appoints the CRC as 'a national organization for standardization before the ETSI and to participate in the work of technical standardization committees in the Republic of Bulgaria related to electronic communications'. The current legal regime is supplemented by a number of Ordinances and Procedures. Some of those acts are: the Functional Specifications for Implementing Portability of National Significant Numbers in the Event of Change of the Provider of Public Mobile Telephony Service,[270] the General

265. National Standardization Act, Additional Provisions, (1), i. 1, SG, issue 88 of 4 Nov. 2005.
266. Bulgarian State Standard (BSS), in Bulgarian '.Български държавен стандарт' (БДС)
267. NSA, Art. 4.
268. SG, issue 86 of 1 Oct. 1999.
269. Former item 19 – SG, issue 105/2011, in force as of 29 Dec. 2011 and former item 22 – SG, issue 20/2021.
270. SG, issue 8 of 25 Jan. 2008.

Requirements for Provision of Public Electronic Communications[271] in force as of 4 March 2008 issued by the CRC, the List of Radio Equipment using Frequency Bands Harmonized throughout the EU and Electronic Communications Terminal Equipment,[272] the Methodology for Measuring Intermodulation Products of type 'A1', during the Operation of Closely Situated VHF-FM Radio Broadcasting Stations,[273] the Ordinance on Specific Labelling for of Radio Equipment Identification,[274] etc.

§2. Bulgarian Standardization Institute

102. The standardization process in the field of information and communication technologies is an activity that is organized and managed by the BSI and the Technical Council for Standardization in the Field of Electrical Engineering, Electronics, Information Technologies and Telecommunications[275] to the BSI.

BSI is the national standardization body that represents the state before international and European Standardization Organizations.[276] Its powers are derived from Article 7(1) of the NSA. However, it should be emphasized that under the explicit provisions of Article 30, i. 23 of the ECA, CRC is the national standardization organization corresponding to the ETSI. Bulgarian law envisages the following competences of the BSI:

(1) develops, approves, and amends national standardization rules and procedures;
(2) develops methodical instructions for standards applied in institutions and enterprises;
(3) compiles, approves, and publishes the programme for standardization;
(4) develops, accepts, approves, and introduces Bulgarian standardization documents;
(5) disseminates Bulgarian standards, drafts of Bulgarian standards, and standardization documents;
(6) disseminates drafts of European standards, international standards, foreign national standards, and drafts of foreign national standards;
(7) sets up and maintains a fund of national, international, European, and foreign national standards and a specialized library;[277]
(8) exchanges standards;

271. SG, issue 24 of 4 Mar. 2008.
272. CRC, 'List of Radio Equipment using Frequency Bands Harmonised throughout the EU and Electronic Communications Terminal Equipment', www.crc.bg/files/_en/LIST_of_radio_ equipment1 .pdf, 20 Dec. 2007.
273. CRC, 'Methodology for Measuring Intermodulation Products of type "A1", during the Operation of Closely Situated VHF-FM Radio Broadcasting Stations (in conformity with i. 2.5 of Appendix 1 to the Technical Requirements for Electronic Communications Networks of Broadcasting Services and Related Equipment)', www.crc.bg/section.php?id=124&lang=en.
274. SG, issue 98 of 27 Nov. 2007.
275. NSA, Art. 28(1), i. 2.
276. NSA, Art. 34.
277. NSA, Art. 33.

(9) creates a conformity assessment system containing the requirements of Bulgarian standards; etc.

The management bodies of BSI are the Management Council and the Executive Director. There are also several technical councils and technical committees with specialized powers to implement the main BSI objectives.

103. The Management Council manages BSI.[278] It approves the conformity assessment system containing the requirements of Bulgarian standards, approves the standardization programme, etc. The Executive Director has the power to organize the operational management of *BSI*,[279] by approving national standards, national standardization documents, and procedures, among other things.'.

104. According to the provisions of Article 28(1), three councils have the power to manage standardization – the Technical Standardization Council in the Non-technical Field; the Technical Standardization Council for Electrical Engineering, Electronics, Information Technologies and Telecommunications; and the Technical Council for Conformity Assessment System Containing the Requirements of Bulgarian Standards.

Technical Standardization Committees are BSI working bodies, and they carry out duties for the defined fields of standardization. These are established and dismissed by the Technical Councils. The Technical Committees have the responsibility to develop and approve drafts of Bulgarian standards and standardization documents, to propose drafts of these documents to the Executive Director, and to participate in the development of the European and the international standards and standardization documents in the respective fields and in their introduction as Bulgarian standards.

The rules and procedures for the work of both the Technical Councils and Technical Committees are regulated in Article 7(1) NSA and Article 23, i. 6 of NSA, respectively.

§3. Standards Development Procedures

105. The NSA introduces two procedures for standards recognition. The procedure under Chapter III, section II of NSA regulates the development, the application, and approval of Bulgarian standards, while the procedure under Chapter III, section III of NSA regulates the process of introduction of international and European standards as Bulgarian standards.

106. All interested individuals and corporate bodies can apply before BSI for recognition of a standard by filing a justified proposal. The proposal should be supported by sound reasoning on: objectives that will be achieved with the adoption of

278. NSA, Art. 17.
279. NSA, Art. 23.

the proposed standard, economic factors, financial and expert justification, possibilities for applying the standard to meet the objectives of the conformity assessment, and the correlation of the proposed standard with other standards.

107. European and international standards are introduced in Bulgaria only as Bulgarian standards.[280] They become official if the procedure of the NSA is followed.

European standards can be introduced by following either of the two procedures. The first one entails accepting, approving, and publishing identical texts of the standard in Bulgarian or in the official languages of the European Standardization Organizations. The second one regulates the recognition of standards as Bulgarian.[281]

Such recognition takes place if the standards are published on the national site for confirmation, or if the standards are announced in the Official Bulletin of BSI. It is worth mentioning that the introduction of European standards repeals any contradicting Bulgarian standards.

The introduction of international standards could be initiated by the Technical Standardization Committees upon proposals by natural persons and/or legal entities.

§4. Specific Competences of the CRC

108. CRC has issued General Requirements for Providing Public E-communications that regulate the terms, rights, and obligations of enterprises who have notified CRC of their intention to provide e-communications. Article 15 of the General Requirements describes the standards to which enterprises providing public e-communications comply:

(1) Radio equipment and terminal e-communications equipment should comply with Bulgarian standards transposing harmonized European standards published in the Official Bulletin of the BSI reflecting those in the *Official Journal (OJ) of the EU.*

(2) To ensure interoperability of e-communications services and to expand the choice of users of e-communications services, the standards recommended by the EC and/or specifications included in a list published in the OJ of the EU shall apply.

When no published standards and/or specifications are present, the standards of the European Standardization Organizations such as the ETSI, European Committee for Standardization, European Committee for Electrotechnical Standardization shall apply. Otherwise, international standards or recommendations by International Telecommunications Union, ISO, International Electrotechnical Commission (IEC)

280. The specific order for the introduction of European and international standards in Bulgarian is provided in work rules and procedures for national standardization, NSA, Art. 46.
281. NSA, Art. 47(1).

shall apply. European and international standards or recommendations are introduced as Bulgarian standards and apply in accordance to the NSA. The Commission requires the application of standards/specifications only if they are defined as mandatory in the *Official Journal of the EU*.

§5. TECHNICAL REQUIREMENTS FOR PRODUCTS

109. The Technical Requirements to the Products Act[282] (TRPA) regulate the responsibilities of electronic communications enterprises regarding their products or equipment as well as the supervision of their conformity with technical requirements.

Putting products in operation, as defined in the Additional Provisions of the TRPA, is the time when the product passes into a stage of first use by the end user. Electronic communications operators' activities, connected with products for which essential requirements are determined, could be exercised lawfully only upon assessment of the product's conformity with these requirements. They are determined in ordinances issued by ministers upon delegation of the Council of Ministers and define the results to be achieved or the risks to be avoided in order to provide protection of the lives and the health of people, the safety of domestic animals, and the protection of the environment and belongings. Obligations of the electronic communication enterprises arise in relation to Article 4a(1) of TRPA, which provides that the obligation to assess the compliance of the products refers to those who put them in operation, such as producers, importers, or persons who assemble, instal, or carry out other activities that can affect the compliance of the product with essential requirements. Assessment of the essential requirements could be carried out by individuals who put products in operation or by persons who have obtained a permit to carry out conformity assessments. The only exception from the obligation for assessment is that of Article 5 of TRPA.

Electronic communications liberalization and globalization, technologies convergence, network migration to Automated Teller Machine (ATM) and Internet Protocol (IP), and the endeavour to an ever greater mobility of telecommunications lead to strengthening the role of standardization as a technical normative basis for regulation and provision of services in a competitive environment. That is why the introduction of standards for services and terminal and network equipment is of key importance in order to facilitate the commercial negotiations between the electronic communications operators and users of access and services.

282. SG, issue 86 of 1 Oct. 1999.

Chapter 5. Legal Status of Out-of-Court Dispute Settlement in the ICT Sector

§1. General Statement

110. The Bulgarian legislation provides for and regulates alternative methods for dispute settlement between legal entities and/or natural persons, but it does not introduce any specific regulation of out-of-court disputes in the ICT sector.

§2. Arbitration

111. The general principles regulating resolution of disputes via arbitration are provided in the Civil Procedure Code of the Republic of Bulgaria[283] and the International Commercial Arbitration Act (ICAA).[284]Article 19(1) of the Code explains that the parties in a property dispute can agree to have it resolved by arbitration unless the subject of the dispute has in rem rights or possesses a real estate, alimony, holds rights under employment relations or a dispute in which one of the parties is a consumer within the meaning of § 13, item 1 of the Additional Provisions of the Consumer Protection Act. [285] In addition, some special laws introduce additional limitations on the arbitrability (i.e., the possibility to have a dispute resolved by arbitration). According to the Concessions Act,[286] disputes related to a concession agreement whose value (of the concession agreement) is below the 'European threshold' cannot be resolved by arbitration, but by state courts, and only concessions above this threshold are arbitrable.[287] This threshold is currently set by the EC at EUR 5,350,000.[288] According to the ICAA, arbitral awards rendered under disputes the subject of which cannot be resolved by arbitration, are null and void.[289] In addition to that, any clause in a contract concluded between a trader and a consumer, by which the parties assign to an arbitration court the resolution of a dispute between them, outside the procedure for alternative settlement of consumer disputes within the meaning of the Consumer Protection Act (ConsPA),[290] shall be invalid.[291] The ICAA even provides for fines and property sanctions for arbitrators/arbitral institutions which consider consumer disputes – arbitrators could be punished by a fine of BGN 500 to 2,500 and legal entities – by property sanction in the amount of BGN 5,000. In case of repeated violation, the sanctions are three times

283. SG, issue 59 of 20 July 2007.
284. SG, issue 60 of 5 Aug. 1988.
285. The said provision defines a consumer as 'any natural person who acquires goods or uses services which are not intended for carrying out commercial or professional activity, and any natural person who, as a party to a contract under this law, acts outside his commercial or professional activity'.
286. SG, issue 96 of 01 Dec. 2017, in force as of 03 Jan. 2018.
287. Art. 154(2) and (3).
288. *See* the National Concession Register, https://nkr.government.bg/Information/GetPage/09cdd63b-386a-4851-9564-51aa10de24d3, accessed 03 Oct. 2021.
289. Art. 47 (2).
290. SG, issue 99 of 9 Dec. 2005, in force as of 10 June 2006.
291. Art. 3(4) of the Consumer Protection Act.

the said amount.[292] The above provisions related to consumer disputes aim to protect consumers from unfair practices and limitation of the possibility to protect their rights before court but deviate from the general tendency among EU to have consumer disputes resolved preferably out of court, i.e., via alternative dispute resolution (ADR) mechanisms.

112. Considering the above legislative peculiarities, out-of-court disputes in the field of information and communication technologies shall follow general provisions unless otherwise provided in the relevant legislative act regulating specific relations in this sphere. Arbitration agreements are regulated by the ICAA.

The ICAA explains the general and specific principles of arbitration agreements. Arbitration agreement shall be the agreement of parties to refer to arbitration all or some disputes that may arise between them in the future or have already arisen in respect of contractual relations. It shall also mean an arbitration clause in a contract or a separate agreement.[293]

The international commercial arbitration could be employed to resolve civil property disputes arising from international commercial relations, as well as disputes over gaps in contracts or over the adjustment thereof because of new circumstances, if the place of residence or head office of at least one of the parties is not in the Republic of Bulgaria.[294] The rules of the ICAA also apply to arbitration between parties with place of residence or head office in Bulgaria, with certain minor exceptions.[295]

In the light of the above, it could be concluded that dispute settlement in the ICT sector is admissible insofar as arbitrable civil property disputes are concerned.

---

292. Art. 53(1) and (2).

293. The ICAA regulates the arbitration agreement as follows:

> Art. 7. (1) Arbitration agreement shall be the agreement of the parties to refer to arbitration all or some disputes that may arise between them in the future or have already arisen in respect of contractual or non-contractual legal relations. It shall be an arbitration clause in another contract or a separate agreement. (2) The arbitration agreement shall be in writing. The agreement shall be considered written when it is evidenced by a document signed by the parties, or by exchange of letters, telex, telegrams, or other communication means. (3) The arbitration agreement shall also be considered evidenced in writing when the defendant accepts in writing or by declaration recorded in the minutes of the arbitration hearing that the dispute shall be settled by arbitration or in case the defendant participates in the arbitration proceedings via filing a written response, presenting evidence, filing a counterclaim or appearing in an arbitration hearing without challenging the competence of the arbitration.

294. ICAA, Art. 1(2):

> Article 1(2) (prom. SG, issue 93 of 1993). The International Commercial Arbitration resolves civil property disputes arising from international commercial relations, as well as disputes over gaps in contracts or the adjustment thereof because of new circumstances, if the place of residence or head office of at least one of the parties is not in the Republic of Bulgaria.

295. *See* § 3 of the Transitional and Final Provisions of the ICAA.

§3. Mediation

113. Article 140(3) of the Civil Procedure Code provides for another alternative method for dispute settlement: the court can advise mediation (as regulated by the Mediation Act (MA)) or another voluntary settlement method of the dispute between parties.

The MA[296] regulates relations in mediation as an alternative means of disputes settlement. The subject of mediation may be disputes of civil, commercial, employment, family, and administrative matters related to consumer rights, and other disputes between natural persons and/or legal entities, including cross-border disputes. Article 3(2) of the MA provides that mediation can also be carried out in some cases under the Criminal Procedure Code.[297] Article 3(3) of the MA observes that mediation shall not be carried out in cases where a legislative act provides for a different procedure for conclusion of a settlement agreement.

In practice, mediation is applicable to almost all kinds of disputes.[298] Judgment as to the relevance of mediation for a particular dispute is based on the following factors: whether a prompt dispute settlement is needed; whether the parties prefer to avoid formal, expensive, and long procedures; whether they insist on preserving confidentiality; whether the preservation of relations is important to them; whether the dispute is a result of failure in communication between parties; whether the conflict cannot be avoided, because the parties work or live together; whether only one or more issues have to be resolved; whether the parties argue on facts; or whether there is a legislation gap – the ICT sector. The statute of limitations does not run during the mediation procedure.[299]

§4. ICT Disputes Involving Consumers

114. As explained in paragraph 120 above, consumer disputes are excluded from the type of disputes that can be resolved via arbitration. Nonetheless, the legislation presently in force provides a significant institutional framework for resolving disputes, especially pertaining to consumer protection *inter alia* in the ICT sector. Article 178(1) of the ConsPA explains that upon violation of consumer rights under this Act,[300] consumers and consumer associations shall be entitled to file complaints, signals and petitions with consumer protection supervisory authorities. State

---

296. SG, issue 110 of 17 Dec. 2004.
297. SG, issue 86 of 28 Oct. 2005.
298. Article 3(1) of the MA: 'Article 3(1) The subject of mediation may be civil, commercial, labour, family, and administrative disputes related to rights of consumers and other disputes between natural and/or legal persons.'
299. Article 11a of the MA.
300. Consumer Protection Act, Art. 1 reads that the act shall regulate consumer protection, state authorities' powers and consumer associations' activity in this sphere. The act aims to ensure protection of the following key consumer rights: (1) right of information regarding goods and services; (2) right of protection from risks of acquiring goods and services that can endanger their life, health, and property; (3) (in force as of 1 Jan. 2022) right of protection of their economic interests upon acquisition of goods and services in case of unfair commercial practices and sale methods, unfair contractual provisions; (4) right of compensation for damages incurred because of defective goods; (5)

authorities are obliged to register the complaints, signals and petitions received from consumers, and initiate proceedings for examining these documents.[301] Article 180(1) of the ConsPA stipulates that if an inspection regarding a complaint, a signal or a petition is not required, the competent authority is obliged to examine the case and resolve the issue within fourteen days, or otherwise within a month as of the date of receipt of the complaint, signal or petition. A ruling of great social significance can be announced by the press or by other appropriate means at the discretion of the authority that has made it.

115. Article 181a–Article181v (in Bulgarian 181ц) of the ConsPA provide for a special method for out-of-court settlement of consumer disputes – via ADR bodies. This method applies to national and cross-border disputes relating to obligations arising from contracts of sale or the provision of services (including online contracts and contracts for the sale of digital content or its provision for consideration) between a trader established in the territory of the EU and a consumer residing in the territory of the EU. The cross-border disputes between consumers and traders in connection with obligations arising from concluded contracts for online sales or services are resolved via the usage of platform for online dispute resolution according to the requirements of Regulation (EU) No 524/2013 of the European Parliament and of the Council of 21 May 2013 on online dispute resolution for consumer disputes and amending Regulation (EC) No 2006/2004 and Directive 2009/22/EC (Regulation on consumer ODR).[302] The following outcomes are possible when a dispute is settled via ADR bodies: proposing a decision, imposing a decision or gathering the parties to the dispute in order to assist in finding a decision by mutual agreement. The ADR bodies can be individual or collegial and the ones recognized for the territory of the Republic of Bulgaria are included in a special list issued by the Minister of Economy.[303] The rules on ADR bodies do not apply to: (i) procedures before dispute settlement bodies, in which the natural persons, responsible or participating in the settlement of disputes, are employed or receive remuneration entirely from a certain trader; (ii) procedures for consideration of consumer complaints under rules developed by the trader; (iii) services of general interest, provided by the state or on behalf of the state, which are not of economic character; (iv) disputes between traders; (v) direct negotiations between a consumer and a trader for resolving a dispute between them; (vi) initiated court proceedings, in the course of which a voluntary settlement of the dispute has started; (vii) procedures initiated by a trader against a consumer; (viii) health services provided by health

---

right of access to court and out-of-court procedures for settling consumers disputes; (6) right of education on issues concerning their protection; (7) right of association for the purpose of protection of their interests; (8) right of representation before state authorities ruling on consumer-related issues.

301. Consumer Protection Act, under Art. 178(1) upon violation of their rights, as provided by this act, consumers and associations of consumers shall be entitled to file complaints, signals and petitions with consumers' protection supervisory authorities. Copies of complaints, signals, and petitions can be sent to superior authorities as well.

302. OJ, L 165, 18.6.2013, pp. 1–12.

303. The list is accessible at the following URL: https://www.mi.government.bg/files/useruploads/files/zashtita_na_potrebitelite/spisuk_adr_2018.pdf, accessed 03 Oct. 2021.

specialists to patients with a view to assessing, maintaining or restoring their health condition, including the prescribing, the implementation of medical prescriptions, and the provision of medicinal products and medical devices; (iv) state higher schools or state schools after completed secondary education. Special requirements are provided with regard to the procedure under which the ADR bodies operate, the natural persons who compose the ADR body, the transparency of the ADR bodies regarding their activity, their accountability, etc. Where the parties use an ADR procedure which does not provide for the imposition of a decision, the limitation periods for judicial protection shall not run until the procedure is completed.[304]

116. An interesting solution is provided in Article 182. This rule grants powers to the Minister of Economy, Energy and Tourism to establish general and sectoral reconciliation committees to resolve disputes between consumers and traders.[305] The general reconciliation committees assist in resolving national and cross-border disputes between consumers and traders in connection with (i) contracts for the provision of digital content and digital services, (ii) contracts for the sale of goods, including of goods containing digital elements, (iii) contracts for the provision of services, including in relation to warranty liability, (iv) the right of reclamation for goods or services, (v) unfair terms in contracts, (vi) unfair commercial practices, (vii) provision of essential information, (viii) travel services, and (ix) contracts concluded with consumers. The general reconciliation committees also deal with disputes between consumers and traders in sectors of the economy in which there is no ADR body. The sectoral conciliation committees consider national and cross-border disputes between consumers and traders in the following sectors of the economy: energy, water supply and sewerage services, electronic communications and postal services, transport and financial services.

117. Special rules are provided for alternative dispute of resolution concerning payment services, usage of electronic money and the application of the relevant EU regulation concerning payment services. In particular, disputes between payment service providers and payment service users, as well as between electronic money issuers and their customers, concerning the application of the Payment Services and Payment Systems Act,[306] its implementing regulations, Regulation (EC) No 924/2009 of the European Parliament and of the Council of 16 September 2009 on cross-border payments in the Community and repealing Regulation (EC) No 2560/2001,[307] of Regulation (EU) No 260/2012 of the European Parliament and of the Council of 14 March 2012 establishing technical and business requirements for credit transfers and direct debits in euro and amending Regulation (EC) No 924/

304. According to § 12g (in Bulgarian § 12Ж) of the Additional Provision to the ConsPA, however, this provision does not affect the provisions on limitation periods in international agreements to which the Member States of the European Union are parties.
305. More about the different conciliation committees can be found on the website of the Commission for Consumer Protection at the following URL: https://kzp.bg/koi-sa-vidovete-pomiritelni-komisii, accessed 3 Oct. 2021.
306. SG, issue 20 of 6 Mar. 2018, in force as of 6 Mar. 2018.
307. OJ, L 266, 9 Oct.2009, pp. 11–18.

2009[308] and of Regulation (EU) 2015/751 of the European Parliament and of the Council of 29 April 2015 on interchange fees for card-based payment transactions[309] are considered by the Conciliation Committee for Payment Disputes in accordance with Chapter 10, section II of the Payment Services and Payment Systems Act.[310]

118. In addition to the reconciliation committees, alternative out-of-court dispute settlement can be achieved via specially designated mediators. According to the ConsPA, the Chairman of the Commission for Consumer Protection appoints by order mediators who are employees of the Commission and who assist in resolving disputes between consumers and traders. The assistance is provided at the request of a consumer by submitting an application to the Commission for Consumer Protection, and the proceedings before a mediator are conducted in an inhabited place indicated among the inhabited places in which the Commission for Consumer Protection has territorial divisions.[311] The proceedings before general and sectoral conciliation committees and a mediator are not a mandatory precondition for bringing an action in court. The statute of limitations shall cease to run when proceedings have been instituted before the general and sectoral conciliation commissions or a mediator.[312]

§5. Out-of-Court Agreements

119. Another general provision for settlement of out-of-court disputes is regulated by the Obligations and Contracts Act (OCA).[313] It stipulates that by concluding a settlement agreement the parties can terminate an existing dispute or avoid a possible dispute by mutual concessions. Thus, certain legal relations can be established, amended, or terminated.[314] In such a case, the transfer of rights shall be performed in the respective statutory form.[315]

In addition, Article 366 of the OCA announces that a settlement on an illegal contract shall be null and void even though the parties have agreed on its nullity. A settlement reached on the basis of documents subsequently recognized as forged shall be subject to invalidation.

Article 9 of the OCA designates the content of the contract (respectively, the settlement agreement) to be 'unrestricted', insofar as it does not contravene the mandatory provisions of both the law and good morals. Persons who are parties in

308. OJ, L 94, 30 Mar. 2012, pp. 22–37.
309. OJ, L 123, 19 May 2015, pp. 1–15.
310. Part of these rules shall enter into force as of 1 Jan. 2022.
311. Article 181.
312. Article 184a.
313. SG, issue 275 of 22 Nov. 1950.
314. OCA, Art. 365.
315. The parties to the settlement agreement may agree on the method of settling the dispute. However, should a special form for the performance of certain activities agreed is required by law, it must be observed.

a settlement agreement shall be entitled to exercise their rights to satisfy their interests, but shall not be entitled to exercise these rights to the detriment of public interests. That is what makes the settlement agreement valid with regard to legal relations in the ICT sector as well, unless it contradicts the provisions of another legislative act applicable to the particular subject matter.

§6. Out-of-Court Disputes Settlement with Regard to Electronic Communications

120. The ECA[316] empowers the CRC with special obligations to regulate the electronic communications market and the relations between providers of public electronic communications services, as well as to settle disputes between providers, disputes under the Electronic Communications Networks and Physical Infrastructure Act[317] and to contribute to the protection of the rights of end users in the electronic communications sector in coordination with the other competent authorities and to examine consumers' complaints.[318] The actions taken by the Commission shall always be reasonable with a view to providing the necessary conditions for stimulating competition in electronic communications, facilitation of the development of the internal electronic communications market, and support of citizens' interests (i.e., ensuring connectivity, accessibility, and use of very high capacity networks, including fixed, mobile, and wireless networks, as well as electronic communications services; ensuring the opportunity for maximum benefits in terms of choice, price, and quality on the basis of effective competition; ensuring that the security of networks and services is maintained; ensuring a high and general level of protection for end users through the necessary rules, including conditions for the provision of clear information, by setting requirements for transparency of tariffs and conditions for the use of public electronic communications services and the use of applications and services upon their choice; taking into account the needs of specific social groups, in particular people with disabilities, the elderly and people with special social needs, as well as the choices and equal access for people with disabilities).[319] The CRC is obliged to observe the principles of legality, impartiality, objectivity, predictability, transparency, publicity, consultancy, equality, proportionality, and neutrality in respect to networks and services, and reducing the regulatory participation to the necessary minimum, as stipulated by Article 5 of the ECA.

Section 8 of Chapter 4 of the ECA regulates dispute settlement between undertakings providing public electronic networks and/or services or between such undertakings and undertakings benefiting from imposed access or interconnection obligations, or between undertakings providing electronic communications networks or services and providers of associated facilities, where one of the parties

316. SG, issue 41 of 22 May 2007.
317. ECA, Art. 30, i. 26 (former item 22 – SG, issue 105/2011, in force as of 29 Dec. 2011, former item 25 – SG, issue 20/2021).
318. ECA, Art. 30, i. 27 (former item 23 – SG, issue 105/2011, in force as of 29 Dec. 2011, former item 26 – SG, issue 20/2021).
319. ECA, Art. 4(1).

concerned has made a written request, and specifies in detail the order and conditions for applying the procedure. In case of default under the ECA, any affected party can file a written application with the Commission for assistance in reaching consent or by giving mandatory instructions.[320] The chapter also provides the time limits applicable for response of CRC in the different cases.

Chapter 10 of the act regulates rights and obligations for provision of public electronic communications services and ensures interoperability between services provided by two undertakings. Article 163 stipulates that the CRC is entitled to intervene on matters of access and/or interconnection on its own initiative, where justified, in view of attaining the purposes set out in Article 4 and adhering to the principles set out in Article 5, as well as the requirements of this Act, including the procedure under Article 37 of the ECA (conducting public consultations on important issues of public importance for the development of electronic communications).

320. ECA, Arts 54 and 55.

Part II. Protection of Intellectual Property in the ICT Sector

Chapter 1. Application of Copyright in the Area of ICT

121. In the information age, it is virtually possible for a great number of works subject to copyright to be digitalized and become available in digital form. This refers to movies, music, design, photographs, sketches, novels, etc. As access to digital information through electronic networks from anywhere in the world and by an unlimited number of persons at the same time becomes popular, the issue of strengthening the protection of holders of intellectual property rights is brought to different jurisdictions with unusual urgency.

The main legal framework of intellectual property protection in Bulgaria is composed of several normative acts: the Copyright and Related Rights Act (CRRA),[321] the Patents and Registration of Utility Models Act (PRUMA),[322] the Marks and Geographic Indications Act (MGIA),[323] the Integrated Circuit Topology Act (ICTA),[324] and the Industrial Design Act.[325]

The provision of Article 67 of the European Association Agreement obligates Bulgaria to harmonize its legislation with EU *acquis*; Bulgaria achieved a lot to bring it in line with Community Law in the area of intellectual property. In the table below, there can be seen the EU regulations forming the main framework regarding intellectual property in ICT.

Main EU intellectual property laws in ICT
Directive 2009/24/EC of the European Parliament and of the Council of 23 April 2009 on the Legal Protection of Computer Programmes (Codified version) (2009)

321. SG, issue 56 of 29 Jun. 1993.
322. SG, issue 27 of 2 Apr. 1993.
323. SG, issue 98 of 13 Dec. 2019.
324. *Ibid.*
325. *Ibid.*

Main EU intellectual property laws in ICT
Council Regulation (EC) No. 207/2009 of 26 February 2009 on the Community trade mark (Codified version)(Text with EEA relevance) (2009), later repealed and replaced by Regulation (EU) 2017/1001 of the European Parliament and of the Council of 14 June 2017 on the European Union trade mark (Text with EEA relevance) (2017)
Directive 2008/95/EC of the European Parliament and the Council of 22 October 2008 to approximate the laws of the Member States relating to trade marks (Codified version) (2008), later repealed and replaced by Directive (EU) 2015/2436 of the European Parliament and of the Council of 16 December 2015 to approximate the laws of the Member States relating to trade marks (Text with EEA relevance) (2015)
Council Regulation No. 1891/2006 of 18 December 2006 amending regulation (EC) No. 6/2002 and (EC) No. 40/94 to give effect to the accession to Hague Agreement concerning the international registration of industrial designs (OJ EC No L 386 of 29 December 2006, p. 14) (2006))
Directive 2004/48/EC of the European Parliament and of the Council of 29 April 2004 on the enforcement of Intellectual Property Rights (2004)
Council Regulation (EC) No 1992/2003 of 27 October 2003 amending Regulation (EC) No 40/94 on the Community trade mark to give effect to the accession of the European Community to the Protocol relating to the Madrid Agreement concerning the international registration of marks adopted at Madrid on 27 June 1989 (2003), later implicitly repealed by Council Regulation (EC) No 207/2009 of 26 February 2009 on the Community trade mark (codified version) (Text with EEA relevance) (2009), the latter subsequently repealed and replaced by Regulation (EU) 2017/1001 of the European Parliament and of the Council of 14 June 2017 on the European Union trade mark (Text with EEA relevance) (2017)
Council Regulation(EC) No 6/2002 of 12 December 2001 on Community designs (2002), amended by Council Regulation (EC) No 1891/2006 of 18 December 2006 amending Regulations (EC) No 6/2002 and (EC) No 40/94 to give effect to the accession of the European Community to the Geneva Act of the Hague Agreement concerning the international registration of industrial designs (2006)

Main EU intellectual property laws in ICT
Directive No. 2001/29/EC of the European Parliament and of the Council of 22 May 2001 on the Harmonisation of Certain Aspects of Copyright and Related Rights in the Information Society (2001), amended by Directive (EU) 2017/1564 of the European Parliament and of the Council of 13 September 2017 on certain permitted uses of certain works and other subject matter protected by copyright and related rights for the benefit of persons who are blind, visually impaired or otherwise print-disabled and amending Directive 2001/29/EC on the harmonization of certain aspects of copyright and related rights in the information society (2017) and Directive (EU) 2019/790 of the European Parliament and of the Council of 17 April 2019 on copyright and related rights in the Digital Single Market and amending Directives 96/9/EC and 2001/29/EC (Text with EEA relevance) (2019)
Directive 98/84/EC of the European Parliament and of the Council of 20 November 1998 on the legal protection of services based on, or consisting of, conditional access. (1998)
Directive No. 98/71/EC of the European Parliament and of the Council of 13 October 1998 on the Legal Protection of Designs (1998)
Directive No. 98/6/EC of the European Parliament and of the Council, of 16 February 1998 on the Protection of consumers (1998)
Directive No. 96/9/EC of the European Parliament and of the Council, of 11 March 1996 on the legal protection of databases (1996), amended by Directive (EU) 2019/790 of the European Parliament and of the Council of 17 April 2019 on copyright and related rights in the Digital Single Market and amending Directives 96/9/EC and 2001/29/EC (Text with EEA relevance) (2019)
Council Decision of 22 December 1994 on the extension of the legal protection of topographies of semiconductor products to persons from a Member of the World Trade Organization (94/824/EC) (1994)
Council Directive No. 93/83/EEC of 27 September 1993 on the Coordination of Certain Rules Concerning Copyright and Rights Related to Copyright applicable to Satellite Broadcasting and Cable Retransmission (1993), amended by Directive (EU) 2019/789 of the European Parliament and of the Council of 17 April 2019 laying down rules on the exercise of copyright and related rights applicable to certain online transmissions of broadcasting organizations and retransmissions of television and radio programmes, and amending Council Directive 93/83/EEC (Text with EEA relevance) (2019)
Council Decision of 21 December 1992 amending Decision 90/510/EEC on the extension of the legal protection of topographies of semiconductor products to persons from certain countries and territories (93/17/EEC) (1992)
Council Resolution of 14 May 1992 on increased protection for copyright and neighbouring rights (92/C 138/01) (1992)

Main EU intellectual property laws in ICT
First Council Decision of 9 October 1990 on the extension of the legal protection of topographies of semiconductor products to persons from certain countries and territories (90/510/EEC) (1990), later repealed by Council Decision of 22 December 1994 on the extension of the legal protection of topographies of semiconductor products to persons from a Member of the World Trade Organization (94/824/EC) (1994)
Agreement 89/695/EEC of 15 December 1989 relating to Community Patents (1989)
Council Directive of 16 December 1986 on the legal protection of topographies of semiconductor products (87/54/EEC) (1986)
Regulation (EU) No 1257/2012 of the European Parliament and of the Council of 17 December 2012 implementing enhanced cooperation in the area of the creation of unitary patent protection (2012)

At present, the basic regulations of the European directives have been transposed: Directive 96/9/EC of the European Parliament and of the Council of 11 March 1996 on the legal protection of databases,[326] Directive 2001/29/EC of the European Parliament and of the Council of 22 May 2001 on the harmonization of certain aspects of copyright and related rights in the information society,[327] Directive (EU) 2017/1564 of the European Parliament and of the Council of 13 September 2017 on certain permitted uses of certain works and other subject matter protected by copyright and related rights for the benefit of persons who are blind, visually impaired or otherwise print-disabled,[328] and Directive 93/83/EEC of 27 September 1993 on the coordination of certain rules concerning copyright and rights related to copyright applicable to satellite broadcasting and cable retransmission.[329] Key EU legislative acts regulating the IP protection that are pending to be transposed in Bulgarian legislation[330] are Directive (EU) 2019/789 of the European Parliament and of the Council of 17 April 2019 laying down rules on the exercise of copyright and related rights applicable to certain online transmissions of broadcasting organizations and retransmissions of television and radio programmes, and amending Council Directive 93/83/EEC (Text with EEA relevance)[331] and Directive (EU) 2019/790 of the European Parliament and of the Council of 17 April 2019 on copyright and related rights in the Digital Single Market and amending Directives 96/9/EC and 2001/29/EC (Text with EEA relevance).[332]

326. OJ, L 077, 27 Mar. 1996.
327. OJ, L 167, 22 Jun. 2001.
328. OJ, *L 242, 20 Sept. 2017.*
329. OJ, L 248, 6 Oct. 1993.
330. Given the fact that the latest elections for National Assembly in Bulgaria are scheduled for 14 Nov. 2021, it could reasonably be expected that the legislative amendments will most likely take place in 2022.
331. OJ, L 130, 17 May 2019.
332. OJ, L 130, 17 May 2019.

122. The basic function of copyright as a legal concept is to provide protection to copyright holders against unauthorized use of their works by third parties. Such protection involves regulation as illegal any reproduction, public presentation, transmission, and distribution of the work including on the Internet without the consent of the copyright holder.[333] The policy of the EU relevant to this area sees copyright and related rights as providing an incentive for the creation of (and investment in) products such as music, films, print media, software, performances, broadcasts, etc., and contributing to improved competitiveness, employment, and innovation. The field of copyright is associated with important cultural, social, and technological aspects.

Pursuant to the definition given in Article 3(1) of the CRRA, any work of literature, art, and science that is a result of creative activity and is expressed in any way and any objective form whatsoever is deemed subject to copyright. Thus, it becomes clear that any work should have an element of originality objectified in any form, including digital, in order to benefit from copyright protection.

123. Pursuant to Article 18 of the CRRA, the author has the exclusive right to use his/her own work and to authorize its use by other persons, unless otherwise prescribed by law. In Article 18(2), the actions classified as use and constituting material rights of the author are enumerated. The most significant among them with regard to electronic commerce and online service providers are:

(1) reproduction of the work;
(2) distribution of the original or copies of the work among unlimited number of persons;
(3) broadcasting by wireless means or cable retransmission, by making the work available to the public in such a way that members of the public may access it from a place and at a time of their own choosing;
(4) import or export in third countries of production specimens in commercial quantity regardless of whether manufactured legally or in violation of the right;
(5) revision and synchronization of the work, as well as the use of the work to create a new derivative work.

124. The definitions of reproduction and distribution are set out in paragraph 2, i. 3 and i. 4 of the Additional Provisions of the CRRA. Pursuant to the latest wording of the first definition, last amendment in SG, issue 77/2002 and in force since 1 January 2003, respectively, 'reproduction of a work' means 'the direct or indirect duplication in one or more copies of the work or part of it by any means and in any form, permanent or temporary, including saving it in a digital form on an electronic carrier'. Pursuant to the latest wording of the second definition, last amendment in SG, issue 99/2005 and in force since 11 January 2006, 'distribution of a work' means 'the sale, exchange, donation, rental, as well as storage in commercial quantities and also the proposal for sale or rental of originals and copies of the work'.

---

333. R. Apostolova, *Protection of the Distribution of Movies and Entertainment Software on the Internet*, 6 Ownership L. Mag. 64 (2002).

'Broadcasting by wireless means' is defined in paragraph 2, i. 5 as radio or television broadcasting over ground as well as its inclusion in a continuing communications chain leading to a satellite and back to Earth by the means of signals of programmes controlled by the broadcaster and under its responsibility in order to be received, directly or individually by the public, or through the intermediation of an organization different from the broadcaster.

125. The work may be used with the prior consent of the author unless otherwise provided by law. Authors are entitled to a compensation for all types of use of their work and for each successive use of the same type of work.[334] Hence, the use of such works as computer programs, multimedia products, music, movies, databases, etc., including their reproduction on a magnetic, optic or other carrier, uploading on the Internet or storage in the computer hard disk, as well as their subsequent distribution or providing access to an unlimited number of persons ought to be done only after the consent of the copyright holder has been obtained. This consent may be given by concluding an agreement with the author for use of the created work (licence agreement) through which the author concedes to the user the exclusive or non-exclusive right to use the work the former has created under specific conditions. With the 2011 amendments,[335] the definition of users of works in paragraph 2, i. 6 of the Additional Provisions of CRRA was expanded to explicitly specify that these are 'the natural or legal persons, such as ... Internet content providers and others who bring the work to the attention of readers, viewers, and listeners directly or through … distributors'. This text introduces the legal term 'Internet content providers' in Bulgarian legislation (it covers online media, Internet portals, resource, and information sites, etc.). Implementing legal regulation governing the status of these subjects is of crucial importance given that in the digital age in the traditional chain of providing intellectual products to end users, in particular author → publisher (producer) → distributor, the part of distributor (and often of publisher as well) is played increasingly by Internet content providers, in particular. Without having their rights and obligations clearly defined through legal and contractual instruments, a genuine risk exists of depriving copyright holders of the opportunity to manage their material rights, including the right to receive compensation for every use of their works.

126. The amendments of the CRRA from 2000, subsequently re-amended in 2005, introduced a new material right for authors to authorize or prohibit the use of their work or parts thereof by wireless or cable retransmission of access from an unlimited number of persons in a way that allows it to become accessible from a place and time individually chosen by each of them.[336] Thus, an emphasis on the right of authors to authorize or prohibit the publication of their work on the Internet is made. The very presence of musical works, movies, software, or games subject to copyright on a publicly accessible website maintained by an Internet content provider without the consent of the copyright holder is considered a breach of existing

334. CRRA, Arts 19 and 35.
335. SG, issue 25/2011, in force as of 25 Mar. 2011.
336. CRRA, Art. 18(2), i. 10.

legislation and is subject to respective civil, administrative, or criminal liability. If the content has been published by that very online service provider or if the provider has been notified of the violation and has failed to take any actions for its termination, the provider will be held liable. Liability should also be borne in case of unauthorized distribution of a copyrighted work when a copy thereof could be ordered from a website of the online service provider using a catalogue, where the catalogue has been prepared by the provider and no consent has been obtained by the copyright holder.

127. Without authors' consent and compensation, the free use of works is admissible only in cases stipulated by law under the condition that the normal use of the work is not obstructed and the legal interests of the copyright holder are not violated. Article 24 of the CRRA[337] states that temporary reproduction of works is admissible, if it has a transitional or incidental nature, has no significance on its own, constitutes an inseparable and essential part of the technical process, and is performed with the sole purpose of allowing transmission to a network through an intermediary. This exception includes actions during Internet transmission like browsing or caching under the condition that the intermediary does not alter the information. Thus, in electronic commerce, Internet access providers are given the opportunity to mediate in transmitting items subject to copyright without the consent of the copyright holder for each reproduction of the work. These permissions do not, however, apply to software.

128. Pursuant to Article 25 of the CRRA without the consent of the copyright holder but upon payment of fair compensation, reproduction of works is admissible on whatsoever carrier by a natural person for his/her personal use under the condition that it is not done for commercial purposes. The compensation is paid not directly by the natural persons reproducing the works for their personal use, but by the persons who produce or import media and devices, designed for recording and reproduction of video and music. This compensation is paid under the terms defined in Article 26 of the CRRA. The authors of works, performers, producers of sound recordings, and the producers of the initial recording of recorded films or other audiovisual recordings, as well as the authors and the publishers of all types of printed works (when these works are reproduced in a reprographic manner for personal use) are entitled to receive compensation. Moreover, any renouncement of the compensation right by the holders of rights is considered invalid. The compensation is due from the persons who produce or import blank data media from third countries and with reference to the executed sales, on the territory of Bulgaria, of such media addressed to reproduction of works for personal use. The amount of the compensation may not be lower than 1% and higher than 1.5% of the delivery price in compliance with the accounting standard for stock report with reference to the respective blank data media. It is paid to two separate categories of associations that represent the different right holders categories with reference to their compensation rights and have a mechanism for individual distribution of these compensations among their members. Prior to the distribution, 30% of the collected sum is

337. SG, issue 99 of 9 Dec. 2005.

deducted and transferred to the account of the National Culture Fund. The distribution of the collected sums among the different categories of right holders is done as follows:

(1) The authors of works, performers, producers of sound recordings and the producers of the initial recording of recorded films or other audio-visual recordings:
   (a) one-half to the authors;
   (b) one-fourth to the performers;
   (c) one-fourth to the producers.
(2) The authors and the publishers of all types of printed works:
   (a) 50% to the authors;
   (b) 50% to the publishers.

129. Article 25a of the CRRA (in force as of 1 January 2003) stipulates that in case of use of works under Article 24 and Article 25 without the consent of the copyright holder, this use cannot be performed in a way presupposing obliteration, damage, destruction, or disarrangement of technical protection means without the consent of the copyright holder. This provision attempts to implement in national legislation the provision of Article 6 of Directive 2001/29/EC obliging EU Member States to create conditions for effective protection against performing actions aiming to evade in any way the technological measures for protection against irregular use of items subject to copyright.[338]

It should be noted that both specified exceptions do not refer to software for which the special rules of Articles 70 and 71 of the CRRA apply.

338. OJ, L 167, 22 Jun. 2001.

Chapter 2. Legal Protection of Software

§1. General Statement

130. Bulgarian law provides a legal definition of a computer program. Under Article 93, i. 26 of the Bulgarian Criminal Code (CC),[339] 'any set of machine instructions capable of making an information system perform given functions' shall be deemed a computer program.

Computer software as a subject of copyright is equalized to literary works, but their use is specifically regulated in section VII of the CRRA.[340]

§2. Subject Matter of Protection: Conditions and Limitations

131. The protection of computer programs reveals certain specificity in comparison to the protection of other literary works. A special exception is made for the free use of computer programs according to Article 71, i. 1 of the CRRA, that is, the person who has legally acquired the right to use a computer program can, without the author's consent and without paying any additional fee, make a backup copy of the program if it is necessary for the specific use of the program. At the same time, the general rule of the CRRA prohibits reproducing copyright-protected works on any carrier by a natural person for the purpose of his/her personal use even when they are not used for commercial purposes.[341] If the exception of Article 71 of the CRRA had not been introduced for the usage of computer programs, we would have faced a copyright infringement in the form of reproduction of works unauthorized by the author for purposes beyond those stated by law.

132. Article 70 of the CRRA outlines the limits within which legitimate users of the computer program can use it. They can run the program, visualize its results on a screen, execute it, transmit it over a distance, store it in the computer memory, translate it, process it, and make other changes in it if it is necessary for the accomplishment of the purpose for which the right of use of the program is acquired including error elimination. In fact, these are the property rights over the computer program, which, unless otherwise agreed between the parties, users acquire from authors under a licence agreement.

133. Two specificities of the computer program as a subject of copyright protection should be pointed out. First, the program could be seen as an algorithm. This means that some features of the algorithm are typical of this program. At the same time, the program may be considered a method for the realization of the algorithm, and as such, it is characterized by specific features. From that point of view, for the purposes of analysing the program in terms of legal protection, it should be mentioned that while the algorithm should be considered a sequence of logical and

339. SG, issue 26 of 2 Apr. 1968, last amended SG, issue 101/2017.
340. CRRA, Arts 70–71.
341. CRRA, Art. 25(2).

mathematical operations for transforming information, the program contains a sequence of commands describing a process of realization of the algorithm and securing the control of this process.

An objective form of the program expression is the record of formalized language. In fact, this expression appears to be the subject matter of copyright protection. Ideas implemented in the computer program expressed therein and described thereby are not copyright protected. Their protection can be achieved in some cases by other means – by those provided by patent law.

134. According to Article 6 of PRUMA,[342] patents are issued for inventions that are novel, innovative, and practical for industry in all technical spheres. It is expressly stated that computer programs are not considered inventions.[343] It is pointed out that the exclusion of the above works is applied as far as legal protection is requested per se. This regulation follows the wording of Article 52(2) of the European Patent Convention[344] to which Bulgaria is a party, and should refer to the interpretation by the European Patent Office.

This means that a computer program by itself is not a subject matter of patent law, unless it meets all requirements of Article 6 of PRUMA and possesses the quality of a 'technical contribution' in which case the program shall be considered 'a computer-implemented invention'. Computer-implemented inventions may include devices such as mobile phones, intelligent household appliances, engine control devices, and inventions concerning computer programs.

135. The dual mode of protection of computer programs should be analysed when it comes to whether they are considered a subject of copyright protection or should be protected as patent inventions.

Even though computer programs per se are not eligible for protection under PRUMA, this does not mean that they are subject to copyright automatically. As mentioned above, copyright protects programs as literary works taking into account the form, the code strings written by the programmer, and offers the possibility of prohibiting copying or commercializing the code by third parties. At the same time, copyright does not protect the ideas behind the software, how the software affects the functionality of the machine or how the machine communicates with the environment controlled by the software. If such a process includes solving a technical problem in an innovative way (i.e., a novel and non-obvious way), then it could be formally considered a patentable invention. In fact, this is meant by the legislator when regulating computer-implemented inventions. Granting such a patent is completely compatible with the principles of European Patent Law. In the course of time, the practice in the European Patent Office has been liberalized concerning the patentable criteria and, as a result, current patents are granted to computer-implemented inventions provided that they have a 'technical contribution'.

---

342. *See* Part II, Ch. 1, para. 121 *supra*.
343. PRUMA, Art. 6(2), i. 3.
344. 'Convention on the Grant of European Patents', www.epo.org/patents/law/legal-texts/html/epc/1973/e/ma1.html, 5 Oct. 1973.

136. The concept of protection of computer programs by a patent has both supporters and opponents. The following practical obstacles arise in patenting computer programs:

(1) The patenting procedure is very long – from two to five years, and the lifespan of the program might be shorter. It is well known that computer programs become obsolete very fast.
(2) A register of programs is unavailable; therefore, no possibility exists for finding out those analogues and prototypes that could serve for comparison with the new solution at the time of patent examination.
(3) Because of the difficulty in discovering the infringement of rights in such works, the complete publication of the description of works as defined in the patent documentation is inexpedient, on the one hand, and it might prove extremely bulky to include in a patent application that fits more to a scientific publication than to a patent description, on the other hand.

Therefore, even in its present state, copyright protection is capable of securing the interests of authors of computer programs.

137. Considering the booming software development and the easy spread of pirate programs on the Internet, less bureaucratic methods for protection are deemed effective. In this respect, the most effective method for protection of computer programs is considered the copyright one, whilst it lacks an inspection procedure and has practically no special formal requirements. The harmonization of the national protection regimes on copyrights as a result of a number of already enforced international treaties and conventions also contributes to achieving effective legal protection on the international level.

§3. Ownership and Scope of Exclusive Rights

138. While computer programs are considered a kind of literary work,[345] the natural person whose activity results in the creation of the computer program shall be deemed their author. Other natural persons or legal entities can be copyright holders only in cases explicitly regulated by the CRRA, Article 3(1), i.1.[346]

Article 8 of the CRRA regulates joint rights and co-rights in case of joint authorship of works, including, computer programs. In case of two or more authors, the latter shall be considered joint holders of the copyright over their work irrespective of whether the work is an integral whole or consists of individual parts. Hence, the consent of all authors is required for any particular use or transformation of the work. Once consent has been granted for use of the work in a certain manner or a decision thereon has been adopted by the court, none of the co-authors can, without any reasonable grounds, oppose its future use in this manner.

345. *See* Part II, Ch. 2, para. 131 *supra.*
346. CRRA, Art. 5.

The CRRA stipulates that payments due to co-authors for use of the work shall be allocated among them in shares as determined by their mutual consent. In case of lack of such consent, the authors shall be deemed to have equal shares.

It is expressly stated that in case the work created by co-authors comprises individual parts each co-author can allow the individual use of his or her part unless otherwise agreed between the co-authors and unless that hinders the use of the work as a whole.

139. The general provision concerning works created under an employment contract states that the author holds the copyright unless otherwise provided by CRRA.[347] In case of works created under employment contract, the employer has the exclusive right, without the author's consent and without payment of any compensation unless otherwise stipulated in the employment contract, to use the created work for its own purposes. The employer is entitled to exercise this right within the scope of his/her usual activity. In practice, if the employer aims to ensure the possibility to use the created works for purposes outside the scope of his/her usual activity, this should be explicitly agreed between the parties.

The legal regime of creation of computer programs under employment relations is specifically regulated by Article 14 of the CRRA. Unlike the general regime of the works created under employment contract, the employer holds the copyright over computer programs unless explicitly provided otherwise.

In case the works are created under civil (assignment) contract, the author holds the copyright unless otherwise agreed in the contract. Unless otherwise agreed, the assignor has the right to use the work without the permission of the author for the purpose for which it was ordered.[348] There is relatively little court practice interpreting the said provision. It is generally accepted that the parties are entitled 'to agree otherwise', but within the boundaries set by the mandatory rules of the legislation. Some of the key decisions of the Supreme Court of Cassation on the said provision make the following interpretations: (i) the parties can agree on exclusive licence of the artistic project that can be granted by its author to the assignor of the project for a term determined between them in the assignment agreement or in other contract which rearranges the relations between the parties regarding the assignment;[349] and (ii) the possibility 'to agree otherwise' does not include the possibility to agree on the transfer from the author to the assignor the non-property (moral) rights of the author that the CRRA declares as non-transferable by virtue of Article 15 (1), item 2 and 4, namely the right to demand recognition of the author's authorship over the work and the right to request that his/her name, pseudonym or other identifying author's mark be marked accordingly in each use of the work.[350]

347. CRRA, Art. 41.
348. CRRA, Art. 42.
349. Decision No. 214 of 13.05.2016 under case No. 3088/2014 of the Supreme Court of Cassation, 1st Commercial Division.
350. Decision No. 45 of 09.07.2020 on commercial case No. 1437/2019 of the Supreme Court of Cassation.

§4. DURATION OF THE PROTECTION

140. The general provision regulating the copyright protection states that copyright shall be protected throughout the author's life and seventy years after his/her death.[351] In case of two or more co-authors, the said term shall be counted as from the moment of the death of the last co-author.

Article 28a enforced in 2000 amends the general provision by specifying that the copyright over a computer program arising under employment relations continues seventy years after making the work available to the public.

351. CRRA, Art. 27.

Chapter 3. Legal Protection of Databases

§1. General Statement

141. Article 3(2) of the CRRA reads that along with other collective works (encyclopedias, digests, etc.) databases are also subject to legal protection. What is specific about them is that the elements of the database may but do not need to be individual works – subject to copyright.

142. The CRRA gives a legal definition of 'database'. Pursuant to i. 13 of paragraph 2 of the Additional Provisions of the CRRA, it shall mean a 'collection of independent works, data or other materials arranged systematically or methodically and individually accessible in electronic or other way'. The CRRA explicitly declares that the computer programs used for the creation or operation of databases, the recordings of a separate audiovisual, literary or musical work, as well as the collection of sound recordings with musical performances on a CD are not a database within the meaning of this law.

§2. Subject Matter of Protection: Conditions and Limitations

143. With regard to databases, Bulgarian law protects two kinds of intellectual property rights. First, this is the copyright, which belongs to the person who performed the selection and arrangement of included works and/or materials unless otherwise provided by CRRA.[352] The copyright over each separate element included in the database, which could be a piece of literature, art, or science, belongs to their authors. The inclusion of works or parts thereof in such a product requires the consent of their authors unless otherwise provided by law.

The amendments[353] to the CRRA stipulate the creation of a new so-called special (sui generis) right of the database maker. A database maker is defined as a 'natural person or legal entity who has taken the initiative and the risk to invest in collecting, verifying or using the database contents if this investment is significant in qualitative or quantitative terms'.[354]

§3. Ownership and Scope of Exclusive Rights

144. In 2002 (in force as of 1 January 2003), a new chapter 11 'a' to the CRRA was introduced. It regulates the rights of database makers as owners of rights regulated by the CCRA.

---

352. CRRA, Art. 11.
353. SG, issue 77 of 9 Aug. 2002.
354. CRRA, Art. 93b(2).

The right of a database maker is not a copyright *strictu sensu*. It consists of the right to demand from every third person abstention from extracting of a part of the database or its reutilization in another form, including distribution of copies without his/her consent.

Introducing this new kind of right is due to the development of digital recording technologies that allow the electronic copying and rearrangement of database contents without constituting a violation of any copyright whatsoever. This right applies regardless of whether the databases or parts thereof enjoy the protection of copyright or related rights.[355] The specificity of the indicated rights of the database maker refers to the fact that they are not based on creativity (the way the copyrights enjoy protection), but on the investment made.[356]

145. Pursuant to Article 93c of the CRRA, a database maker shall have the right to prohibit permanent or temporary extraction of the contents of the database or its substantial part in quantitative or qualitative terms with respect to another carrier by any means or in any form. This also applies to reutilization of the contents of the database or a substantial part thereof in quantitative or qualitative terms by making it available to the public by any means or in any form, including by distribution of copies, renting, or providing contents in an electronic way. The right under Article 93c arises regardless of whether the database or parts of the contents thereof enjoy the protection of copyright or related rights.

The first sale on the territory of an EU Member State of a material copy of a database by the owner of the right referred to in Article 93c or with their consent precludes their right to control the further selling of copies on the respective territory. Where a database is transferred digitally including in a communication network, the right of Article 93c shall not be terminated regarding the materialized copies of the database made by the recipient with the consent of the right holder.

146. The copyright over database created under employment relationship belongs to the employer unless otherwise indicated by CRRA.

147. A person who has legally acquired the right to use a database or a copy thereof, may freely perform the actions of representation, distribution among unlimited number of persons of the original or copies thereof, public presentation, broadcasting of the work by wireless means, cable transmission and retransmission, translation into another language, and remodelling (adaptation and introduction of any changes as well as use of the work for creating a new one, a derivative thereof) of it, as well as actions concerning the results possibly reached through the translation, remodelling, processing, and any other changes made to it, where it is necessary to access the contents of the database for common use. When this person has the right to use only a part of the database, this provision applies only with respect to this particular part.

355. CRRA, Art. 93e.

356. Tsv. Kamenova, *Copyright: International and National* 416 (Sofia: ILS – BAS, 1999).

The legal user of a database, which has been made public by any means, may without the consent of its maker: (i) extract or reutilize a significant part of its contents when this is done for personal use of the database contents that is not in electronic form, (ii) extract contents of the database with no commercial purpose for teaching or scientific research in a volume justified by the purpose, and (iii) extract or reutilize it in administrative or legal proceedings.

§4. Duration of the Protection

148. The rights of a database maker expire in a fifteen-year term. This term is counted from the 1 January of the year following the year of creation of the database. In case the database was made public in any way before the expiry of the fifteen-year term, the period of protection shall be counted as from 1 January of the year following the year in which it was made public.

The law allows for every new significant investment in the database that entails a significant change in its contents to start a new term of protection with regard to the part resulting from the investment.

Chapter 4. Legal Protection of Computer Chips

§1. General Statement

149. The topology of integrated circuits is regulated by the ICTA.[357] This Act transposes in Bulgarian legislation the provisions of Council Directive 87/54/EEC of 16 December 1986 on the legal protection of topographies and semiconductor products.[358]

The act provides for the conditions and procedures for registration of the topology of integrated circuits (referred to hereinafter as 'topology'), the rights ensuing from this registration and their protection. The act applies to Bulgarian as well as foreign[359] natural persons and legal entities.

150. The Patent Office (PO) is in charge of the state Topology Register,[360] which contains data for all registered topologies and their subsequent amendments. The state Register is open to the public and excerpts from its records may be requested.

The PO keeps a record of each topology, including all registration documentation and subsequent entries. Prior to registration, only the applicant, the owner, their representative, or a person authorized by the applicant/the owner may access that record. After registration, the PO provides access to the record, without the right to copy it, according to the rules set by its Chairperson.

§2. Subject Matter of Protection Conditions and Limitations

151. Paragraph 1, i. 1 of ICTA's Additional Provisions defines 'integrated circuit' as 'a product in a final or an intermediate stage of its production designed to perform functions such as generating, transmitting, receiving, processing, and/or storing information, whose elements and some or all of its connections are integrally joined into, and/or onto a shared base'. Section i. 2 of the same paragraph defines the 'topology on integrated circuit' as a 'three-dimensional random pattern of the elements and the connections between them on the integrated circuit or such a pattern produced for an integrated circuit designed for manufacturing'.

152. Under ICTA, an original topology that is a result of its creator's own intellectual efforts and is not known among topology creators and integrated circuit manufacturers at the time of its creation is subject to legal protection. Other topologies representing a combination of known elements and connections between them

357. SG, issue 81 of 14 Sept. 1999.
358. OJ, L 024, 27 Jan. 1987, pp. 36–40.
359. Provided these foreign nationals and firms come from states, which are parties to international agreements with the Republic of Bulgaria. ICTA is applied with regard to foreign entities under conditions of mutuality assessed by the Patent Office of the Republic of Bulgaria.
360. ICTA, Art. 7.

are protected by law as well, but only when they meet the requirements of the previous sentence. The legal protection of the topology under ICTA does not cover the manufacturing technology of the integrated circuit in which the topology is used or the information stored therein.

§3. Ownership and Scope of Exclusive Rights

153. According to Article 10 of ICTA, the right over a topology is exclusive and is acquired in the moment of its registration with the PO. That right encompasses the options of the holder to use it, to dispose of it, and to forbid third persons to use it in their commercial activities without his/her consent.[361] The exclusive right is valid with respect to conscientious third persons as of the date of publishing the topology registration in the PO's Official Bulletin.

154. The right of applying for topology registration rests with the creator of the topology. When the right of application belongs to several persons, they exercise it jointly; the refusal of one or more of them to participate in the application process does not hinder the other holders. The refusal should be submitted in writing.

When the topology is produced under conditions of employment or upon assignment,[362] in accordance with Article 11(2), the right to apply belongs to the employer or assignor. If three months after the creation of the typology, provided the employer or assignor has been informed in writing of the creation, the topology has not been registered, the right of application for registration passes on to the creator of the topology, unless otherwise agreed.[363]

155. The right over a topology can be owned by two or more persons. In this case, each co-owner can use the topology without the consent of the others and without reporting that use to them unless otherwise agreed in writing.

156. The owner's right does not apply to: reproducing the whole or part of the registered topology by including it in an integrated circuit or in any other way (with the exception of the parts that are not original) if this is done only for personal use, assessment, analysis, research or training; the commercial use of topology created by a third person as a result of assessment or analysis when the new topology is original; actions of reproducing, selling, exchanging, lending, importing, or exporting or any other way of commercial distribution performed or assigned by a person who does not know, or does not have any other reason to believe, that the registered topology is used unlawfully in the given integrated circuit or in a product containing such integrated circuit.[364]

---

361. ICTA, Art. 15.
362. Conditions set out in Art. 12(1) of ICTA.
363. ICTA, Art. 11(3).
364. ICTA, Art. 17.

§4. Duration of Protection

157. The legal protection over the topology is effective as of:

(1) the date of the applicant's first commercial use of the topology anywhere in the world, if an application is filed at the PO within a two-year term of that date; or
(2) the date of filing the application at the PO, if the topology has not been used commercially or has been used, but only secretly.

The legal protection is terminated in a ten-year term.

Chapter 5. Other Intellectual Property Rights in the ICT Sector

§1. General Statement

158. According to Article 3(1) of the CRRA, an object of copyright is any literary, artistic, or scientific work, which is a result of creative effort and is expressed in any way and in any tangible form whatsoever. With the development of information technologies, almost every work subject to copyright protection may be presented in digital form through some generally accepted standard for transforming and presenting information. In other words, literary works including works from the scientific and technical literature, journalism, computer software, musical works, stage works – drama, musical drama, pantomime, choreographies, etc., motion pictures and other audiovisual works, works of fine arts (including design; photography and the like), projects, maps, schemes, blueprints, works pertaining to architecture, spatial planning, geography, topography, museum and other scientific or technologic exhibits, cadastral and topographic maps, etc., even when presented in digital format can be subject to copyright.

Yet, with the development of the Internet, the possibility for such works to be distributed unlimitedly for free has brought about a boom in copyright violations. There are various technologies for direct exchange (peer-to-peer) of files (torrent sites, eMule, etc.) and huge volumes of content subject to copyright is available for free download from free hosting servers. Thus, the issue of how Bulgarian legislation protects such copyright content on the Internet, and what are the specifics of legal protection becomes increasingly popular.

§2. Literary Works

159. Books, pamphlets, articles, and other written works fall in the category of literary works.[365] There is no legal definition for a literary work in the CRRA specifying which works may be classified as 'works of scientific and technical literature, journalism and computer software'. At the same time, a great part of the materials available on the Internet are exactly literary works – e-books, catalogues, dictionaries, texts published on websites, messages distributed through e-mail lists and discussion groups, etc. – all of them being literary works within the meaning of copyright.

§3. Photographs and Other Static Works

160. Photographic and other images may be visualized or created through a variety of software applications – programs intended for editing or viewing photos and images, Internet browsers, etc.

365. CRRA, Art. 3(1), i. 1.

Digitalized photos and images are subject to copyright even when they are part of the interface of programs or the design of web pages. This refers to all types of images irrespective of the way they are created – digitally or through transformation from paper-based forms (scanning).[366]

§4. Musical Works and Records

161. Musical works, whether including text or not, are traditionally protected by copyright. It is of key importance to make the distinction between the terms 'musical work' and 'phonogram'. The latter is a result of creative work as well, but it represents a secondary result of fixing the performance into material form. The rights over the musical work belong to its author, the rights over the performance – to the performer, and over the phonogram – to its producer. The last two groups of subjective rights are called related rights in the continental law countries, such as Bulgaria, and in their nature, they are analogous to copyright.

Bulgarian law follows the provisions of the Convention of 1971 for the Protection of Producers of Phonograms against Unauthorized Duplication of their Recordings. It provides that a phonogram is 'any exclusively aural fixation of sounds of a performance or other sounds'.[367] CRRA defines the 'phonogram' as a 'product of audio recording'[368] and 'audio recording' as a 'fixing on a durable material medium of a sequence of sounds in such a manner as would allow their listening, reproduction, broadcasting by wireless, cable or other technical means'.[369]

Therefore, a phonogram may be an audio recording of not only musical, but also of other works – oral, dramatic, musical dramatic, choreographic, as well as of all sounds – which are subject to recording.

The popularity of Internet distribution of phonograms may be due to the fact that in this form of distribution it is no longer necessary to supply the traditional physical carriers containing the phonogram (records, tapes, CDs, etc.), which used to significantly complicate the process of delivering phonograms to the audience and make their use more expensive.

§5. Audiovisual Works

162. With the development of cinema, motion pictures fell within the scope of copyright. Other audiovisual works were also included eventually in the process of development of new technologies. Bulgarian law defines this category as 'motion pictures and other audiovisual works'.[370]

---

366. CRRA, Art. 3(1), i. 7.
367. Convention for the Protection of Producers of Phonograms against Unauthorized Duplication of their Phonograms of 29 Oct. 1971, Art. 1(a), www.wipo.int/treaties/en/ip/phonograms/trtdocs_wo023.html#P41_2094, 29 Oct. 1971.
368. CRRA, Additional Provisions, para. 2, i. 8.
369. *Ibid.*, para. 2, i. 7.
370. CRRA, Art. 3(1), i.4.

By 'audiovisual work', it usually means a work consisting of a series of interconnected images that may contain audio accompaniment designed for reproduction exclusively and only by specific technical means. To audiovisual works belong cinematographic works, as well as works 'expressed in a manner, analogous to the cinematographic'.[371]

Audiovisual works, especially those, stored in digital form and their versions like video motion pictures, video conferences, commercial videos, musical videos and cartoons are extremely widely spread on the Internet.

§6. Derivative Works

163. Works resulting from creative adaptation of other works in any of the above-mentioned categories are protected by copyright as derivative works in the same way as works on whose grounds they have been created insofar as there has not been a violation of the rights of the author(s) of the source works.

The following derivative works are protected under Bulgarian law:

(1) translations and adaptations of pre-existing works and folklore works;
(2) arrangements of musical works and folklore works.

There are a lot of translations, picture reproductions, new versions of computer programs, etc. on the Internet. However, many of the works published on the Internet are derivative by virtue of the sole fact that original works cannot be published online.

The majority of works in view of their very nature and form of expression are not subject to direct publishing on the Internet since it acknowledges a single form of fixing – the digital one. This concerns works of oral art, drama, choreography, pantomime, fine arts (pictures, drawings, engravings, sculptures, etc.), architecture, science, and applied arts.

However, most literary, musical, audiovisual, and photographic works (including computer programs), after being stored digitally or transformed by other technical means, can be published on the Internet. Fixing them in traditional two- or three-dimensional forms, makes them available to Internet users only by virtue of their photographing, capturing on a cinema or video reel, or scanning. Only these works can be seen as derivative works.

Furthermore, if the obtained photo, cinema, or video materials have not been stored digitally, then the result of the transformation of these materials into digital form may also be considered as derivative works on condition that they meet the originality criterion. The originality of the derivative works may come from digital transformation of other images or creative processing of the image, such as correcting the defects of the original or colouring as in the restoration of old photographs and motion pictures.

371. Berne Convention for the Protection of Literary and Artistic Works of (Paris Act, 1971), Art. 2(1), www.wipo.int/treaties/en/ip/berne/trtdocs_wo001.html, 9 Sept. 1886.

§7. COLLECTIONS AND OTHER COMPILATIONS

164. The collections of works belonging to the above-mentioned categories, including derivative works provided they meet the originality criterion, are subject to copyright protection without prejudice to the copyright of each of the works forming part of such collections.[372] The originality of collections shall be recognized where these are a result of creative efforts of selection, coordination, and arrangement of the included materials.

According to Bulgarian law, this category of works includes periodicals, encyclopedias, collections, anthologies, bibliographies, databases, and other similar subject matter including two or more works or materials.[373]

As evident from the quoted provisions of the copyright laws, collections are protected by copyright irrespective of whether the materials included therein are subject to legal protection. In other words, the materials within a compilation may be protected works as well as non-protected objects, including mere data.

165. Websites and multimedia works belong to compilations as well and could be protected as such. However, insofar as the interface of the website is an essential element aimed at 'consuming' the information on this site, the graphic design per se and the elements thereof can be protected on separate grounds. In addition, the software by virtue of which a respective website functions is subject to separate copyright protection on its own grounds as a separate copyright work. This is also the case with photos, videos, texts such as articles, analyses, etc. that are displayed on the website. Thus, in practice the website can also be seen as a combination of separate works eligible for copyright protection. As a result, contracts for 'sale' of websites actually consist of the combination of (i) the transfer of the domain name[374] for the website which can have the elements of a sale contract and (ii) a licence contract for granting the right to use (to licence) to the maximum extent permitted by the law – in terms of scope of the licensed rights and the duration of the licence – of the respective objects of copyright forming the website. The second part is necessary, as under Bulgarian law, once the copyright has arisen, it cannot be subsequently fully assigned (transferred), but only licensed for certain periods by its original author(s).

166. Multimedia works are works resulting from the compilation of two or more categories of works in a digital form. Although the possibility of protection of multimedia works under copyright is beyond doubt, the determination of the scope of this protection is extremely complicated. The problem is that multimedia works originate as a result from a process of convergence of various items, subject to copyright protection, into only one work in digital form, which can be 'consumed' by using contemporary information technology tools.

Traditionally, several groups of protected objects are distinguished in copyright, each of them consisting of several kinds of works, according to different scopes of

372. Berne Convention, Art. 2(5).
373. CRRA, Art. 3(2), i. 3.
374. *See* Part II, Ch. 6 below.

protection. The significance of such distinction rests in allowing that all peculiarities and qualitative differences among categories of protected works are taken into account.

The development of digital technologies has made possible the digital transformation of all copyright-protected objects and their incorporation into digital compilations.

The copyright protection in the digital environment is expected to be strengthened via the transposition in the Member States' national law, including in Bulgarian legislation, of the rules of Directive (EU) 2019/790 of the European Parliament and of the Council of 17 April 2019 on copyright and related rights in the Digital Single Market and amending Directives 96/9/EC and 2001/29/EC (Text with EEA relevance).

Chapter 6. Internet Domain Name Registration

§1. Background

167. The Internet as an open public network is constructed in a manner that makes it possible to provide in real time an opportunity for unlimited number of users to access an unlimited number of devices or resources. For the purpose of identification of individual devices and resources, a technical system has been constructed to provide each device or resource with a unique identification number during the time of connectivity.[375] The number is called an IP address.[376] As it proves quite inconvenient to memorize and use the IP address, a system of their association with alphanumeric expressions akin to the human language has been created in order to facilitate Internet users. This system is known as Domain Name System.[377]

The term 'domain' or 'domain name' is defined as the alphanumeric association of a certain IP address providing each device or resource on the Internet with a unique identification number (address), which identifies it during connectivity. Hence, from a technical point of view, the domain name is assumed to be an alphanumeric association of a particular IP address, which is established by a registering organization (the so-called Registrar).

In contrast to the absolute technical clarity of the matter, no serious doctrinaire study has been developed so far to provide a precise answer to the question of the nature of the domain name from a legal point of view. In Bulgaria, there is neither a relevant legal definition, nor any applicable court practice.

§2. The Legal Nature of Domain Names

168. The legal nature of domain names still brings difficulties to jurisdictions. Some scholars find that the domain name is used as a form of 'intangible intellectual property'.[378] Other authors find the domain name economically similar to real estate, and for this reason, the efficient protection for them is somewhere closer to real property law than traditional trademark law.[379]

---

375. For example, 192.168.0.254.
376. G. Dimitrov, *Legal Nature and Protection of Domains*, Mk. L. Mag. 69 (Feb. 2002).
377. The DNS protocol was developed and defined in the early 1980s and published by the Internet Engineering Task Force.
378. *Umbro International, Inc. v. 3263851 Canada Inc.*, 1999 Va. Cir. LEXIS 1; 50 U.S.P.Q.2D (BNA) 1786 (Circuit Court of Fairfax County, Virginia) of 3 Feb. 1999.
379. K. Yee, *location.location.location: A Snapshot of Internet Addresses as Evolving Property*, J. Info. L. Tech. 1 (1997). J. Lipton, *What's in a (Domain) Name? Web Addresses as Loan Collateral*, J. Info. L. Tech. 2 (1999).

Courts in jurisdictions within the so-called continental legal systems, like France, Germany, Italy, etc. have also approached the problem.[380] The Bulgarian legal system falls within this family. In such systems, the answer should be in the contractual nature of the relationship.

169. Under Bulgarian doctrine, the subjective right is considered a legally recognized and guaranteed possibility of the legal subject to demand the same behaviour or result from the legally obliged person(s).[381] On the other hand, the doctrine recognizes the division of subjective rights into two main types: absolute and relative.

Any subjective right shall be considered absolute, provided the obligation towards the right holder falls upon unlimited number of liable persons. For example, the property right holder shall be entitled to demand from any third person not to hinder or force him/her to exercise his/her property rights and to derive benefits from the usage of that property. The copyright is such an absolute right.

The rights of relative right holders arise from contractual relationships, torts, etc. The buyer as a right holder under a purchase contract shall be entitled to demand the transfer of the title and handing over of the property – subject to the contract only from the seller and not from anybody else.

The domain name is not an absolute right. As mentioned above, legal protection of any absolute right over intangible goods depends on the law – whether there is a legal attribution of the goods to a certain person in such a way that s/he can enjoin any other person from using it. While there is no explicit legal provision under Bulgarian law for creating, protecting, and regulating such a right over a domain name in a way that the right holder can oppose it to any third party, it shall not be considered an absolute right and cannot be protected as such.

According to Bulgarian law, the right over a domain name shall be considered a relative right. This deduction is based on the analyses of the relationships between the actors on the Internet market.

If somebody is willing to register a domain name, he or she should enter into an agreement with an organization accredited by the Internet Corporation for Assigned Names and Numbers (ICANN) for the generic top-level domains (gTLD) like.com,.org,.net, respectively, by an accredited organizations ('registers') for country code TLDs (ccTLD) like.bg,.de,.fr, etc. Such accredited Registrars also act through authorized agents ('Registrars'). Customers who register domain names are referred to as 'Registrants'.

The main obligations under this agreement are:

(1) for the applicant – payment of registration and/or annual fee; and
(2) for the Registrar – to approve the registered domain name to the Registrant; to administer the domain name server; to administer and keep up-to-date the 'who is' database; to associate the domain name with a certain IP address –

380. *See* examples of court decisions on domain name dispute cases available at www.online-recht.de, www.netlaw.de, www.legalis.net, www.dominiuris.es, http://arbiter.wipo. int/domains/decisions/ index.html.
381. M. Pavlova, *General Civil Law* 67 (Sofia: Sofi-R, 1997).

all these coming to provide the Registrant with the possibility to use the registered domain name. Each Registrar has its own contractual terms of service and the registers (at least in Bulgaria) also act as official Registrars.

Considering the above, it could be stated that under Bulgarian law, the registration of a domain name is based on the contractual relationship between the applicant and the Registrar.[382] The Registrars explicitly envisage this fact.[383]

Under Bulgarian law, this contract shall be considered valid as far as its object, terms, legal, and agreed consequences do not contradict the law. There is a special provision in the Bulgarian OCA providing freedom of contracting. As a contract for specific result, the contract shall be classified as a service contract.[384] Other doctrinal definitions regarding the domain name emphasize not only on its contractual (relative) nature, but also on the fact that (i) it is a proprietary right (i.e., capable of being evaluated in money), (ii) it is a transferable right (i.e., can be transferred by one Registrant to another via contract), and that (iii) it gives limited, transferable, renewable exclusive right to the Registrant to use the domain for the time of its registration and maintenance.[385]

§3. The Assigning Authorities and the Registrars

170. ccTLD names with the 'bg' domain extension are administered by a local register (manager) of names.

Since 2002 in Bulgaria, this function has been performed by Register.BG OOD (Register.BG) – the successor of Digital Systems OOD, a company performing this function since 1991. Register.BG OOD was established after its split from Digital Systems OOD in 2001 having as its main scope of activity registration and support of domain names in the.bg zone and other subzones within admissible zones.[386]

Register.BG has developed requirements and procedures of registration to serve as a source of information to applicants, Internet service providers (ISP), and the staff of Register.BG, so that each application for registration of a domain name in

382. P. Hourigan, *Domain Names and Trade Marks: Disputes from an Australian Perspective, Going Digital: Legal Issues for Electronic Commerce, Multimedia and the Internet*, in 77 (C. Cifuentes et al. ed., New South Wales: Prospect Media, 1998).
383. For example, terms of the contracts with Network Solutions, Inc. www.networksolutions.com/en_US/legal/service-agreement.jhtml, with DIGSYS www.register.bg, with Nominet www.nic. uk/ref/terms.html, with DeNIC www.denic.de/doc/DENIC/agb.en.html.
384. Of the same opinion: I. Bubert & M. Buening, *Domain Name Issues – European Jurisdiction*, ESPRIT Project 27028 (Electronic Commerce Legal Issues Platform, 2000).
385. M. Zahariev & D. Krusteva, 'The Legal Nature of Domain Names' *TITA Taxes Magazine* Issue 132 (Sept. 2020), https://www.tita.bg/free/commercial-law/706?fbclid=IwAR0xEfA--qWa7hS_SWL20NXMYGGa3b7HDmPg-qewzh4ly_wJzm9BhXNHrOA, accessed 16 Dec. 2021.
386. Admissible zones are zones where registration of names is implemented by Register.BG – a first-level zone (.bg) and second-level zones (*.bg, where * takes values a-z /0–9). All zones from the list of admissible zones are functionally equivalent. Since 5 Sept. 2009, Register.BG extends its services of registration of domains in the.bg zone and the subzones by providing the possibility of registering domain names in Cyrillic. The registration of such domains requires that the Internet name be written only in Cyrillic and contain at least one letter that can be visually distinguished from the Latin alphabet.

the.bg zone can be processed in a predictable and uniform manner without any delay. Since their entering into force, the rules have been amended several times, whereas the latest amendments are valid as of 23 May 2018.

As set forth in the preceding paragraph, Register.BG's rules are the general terms and conditions of the contract with persons that have entered into contractual relations and have registered a domain name in the.bg zone. That is, in fact, a contract for provision of services (a kind of civil contract) under which Register.BG undertakes to enable the applicant meeting certain requirements to use the particular Internet address for a certain period of time; on the grounds of this contract, no intellectual property rights are established or transferred, but only contractual rights arise between the parties.[387]

171. On 03 June 2016 the company IMENA.BG AD (IMENA.BG) officially received from ICANN the right to administer the registration of domain names in the new '.бг' ccTLD (i.e. '.bg' in Cyrillic). As per IMENA.BG's website, shareholders therein are the Bulgarian Library and Information Association (BLIA), Register.BG OOD, Association for Sectoral Electronic Communications, Digital Systems OOD, Digital Systems Limited OOD, Global Libraries – Bulgaria Foundation. IMENA.BG operates in a similar manner to Register.BG, namely conducts registration of domain names in the zone '.бг' under its terms and conditions, their last amendment valid as of 23 May 2018.[388] Therefore, the analysis below will be focused on the registration procedure as defined in Register.BG's general terms and conditions as the organization operating for longer time in Bulgaria, and only certain peculiarities introduced in the terms and conditions of IMENA.BG shall be highlighted (Register.BG and IMENA.BG shall be separately referred as the 'respective register' and jointly – as the "registers").

172. In accordance with the rules of Register.BG, several groups of persons have the right to apply for registration of a '.bg' ccTLD:[389]

(1) Persons (private persons or legal entities) with a court or commercial registration in Bulgaria or in another EU Member State, or with articles of incorporation issued by a Bulgarian state authority.
(2) Subjects created pursuant to an agreement between the Republic of Bulgaria and other countries, companies, and organizations registered abroad which have their own branches or commercial representative offices in Bulgaria.
(3) Persons with full legal capacity, citizens of the Republic of Bulgaria, foreigners permanently residing in the territory of the Republic of Bulgaria or citizens of an EU Member State.

387. G. Dimitrov, *Legal Nature and Protection of Domains*, 69.
388. IMENA.BG EAD 'TERMS AND CONDITIONS FOR DOMAIN NAME REGISTRATION AND SUPPORT IN THE .бг ZONE' https://www.imena.bg/tld_user_nam/app.pl?action_key=ac_c1p3d1_to_general_terms&frame_key=fr_c1p3_main_frame&lang=en 2018, accessed 17 Oct. 2021.
389. Register.BG Ltd, 'Terms and Conditions for Domain Name Registration and Support in the BG Zone and the Sub-zones' https://www.register.bg/tld_user_reg/app.pl?action_key=ac_c1p3d1_to_general_terms&frame_key=fr_c1p3_main_frame&lang=en, 2018, accessed 17 Oct. 2021.

(4) Companies and organizations registered abroad which have authorized a third person to register a '.bg' ccTLD. That third authorized person has to meet the requirements under the two items above.

Approximately the same are also the requirements imposed by IMENA.BG for registration of a '.бг' ccTLD in Cyrillic.

§4. Registration Procedure

I. Registration Documentation

173. The subject who wishes to register a '.bg' domain name shall submit an application for registration and documents of identification to the naming authority.

The application for registration of a domain shall be filled in online (in English or Bulgarian) through the interface of the selected Registrar or Register.BG when acting as an official Registrar.

The set of required identification documents depends on whether an electronic signature is used when filing the application. In case an electronic signature is used, the identification of the Registrant is verified by the electronic signature certificate, and no additional documents are required. In case an electronic signature is not used, upon filing the application certain additional documents shall be submitted depending on the category of the Registrant. Legal entities file the original application signed by the Registrant's representative(s), and a certificate of good standing issued by the court or the commercial Register, respectively, a copy of the articles of incorporation issued by the Bulgarian state authority or the international agreement (a copy of the publication in the SG, if possible). Foreign companies and commercial representative offices in the Republic of Bulgaria shall present a certificate of registration of their representative office issued by the Bulgarian Chamber of Commerce and Industry. If the Registrant is an embassy or a consulate of another state in the Republic of Bulgaria, the application shall be filed in original, signed by the representative of the embassy or consulate, and shall be accompanied by an official cover letter.

In regards to applicants that are natural persons, an application with a notary certification of the signature is required or the proof of identity in person through an ID card or a certificate of permanent residence of a foreigner.

Companies and organizations registered abroad shall submit their applications in original signed by an authorized person and shall present documents verifying their registration. The authorized person shall present respective identification documents.

Upon registering a domain in the.bg zone, Registrants can additionally file documents verifying the grounds (if any) for use of the Internet name by which the domain has been created. The provision of these documents prior to the registration of the domain will favour the Registrant in case of an arbitration procedure, i.e., in case of dispute, they can 'lose' the domain name registration on a very limited number of grounds.

In any case, the Registrant shall present a power of attorney – certified by a notary public – when the application is filled in by a proxy.

The application shall be accompanied by a declaration that the Registrant accepts the general terms and conditions of Register.BG.

All documents required for registration of a domain shall be presented in one of the working languages of Register.BG – in Bulgarian or in English – or as an official translation into one of these.

For each Registrant, contact persons for administrative issues, for financial issues, and for technical issues shall be designated.

II. Requirements in Respect to Names

174. The rules contain certain requirements in respect to the names the applicants wish to register. The following characters may be used in the domain name for the '.bg' ccTLD: letters of the Latin or Cyrillic alphabet, regardless of whether these are small or capital, numbers, and hyphens. For the '.бг' ccTLD in Cyrillic the eligible characters are the letters only of the Cyrillic alphabet, numbers, and hyphens. The domain name has to contain at least three characters, and no more than sixty-three characters. It is recommended that the first character be a letter, though it can also be a number. The Internet name shall be different from the existing reserved names.[390]

In accordance with the rules of Register.BG and IMENA.BG, a domain name in the first-level zone .bg or Бг can be registered as protected, if the applicant has used and provided grounds to use the name – e.g., if it is formed by the name of the applicant, the name of a registered trademark, etc.[391]

The names of towns and villages are reserved for municipalities and the regions. When the requested name may, according to the opinion of the naming authority, lead to confusion or misunderstanding, the applicant has to choose another name.

Registrants may not choose Internet names containing obscene and/or offensive words or phrases in contradiction to the public interest and good manners.

---

390. ICANN, Reserved Domain Names, http://res-dom.iana.org.

391. The chosen Internet name shall fall within one of the following categories to be considered protected: the name of the Registrant; the name of a registered trademark or a geographical indication of the Registrant or such that are in process of registration (provided that they are valid for Bulgarian territory); a registered name of a publication (e.g., with an ISSN or ISBN); a name of a programme or a project of the state, regional or municipal administrations and institutions of an EU Member State, or an EU body; a name acquired by the Registrant in accordance with licences valid on the territory of the Republic of Bulgaria; a name of a consortium or of a non-personalized civil partnership; a name of a media programme or a show; a name of a cultural, sports, scientific event, etc.; a name of a coalition, an initiative committee, or a name used by a candidate for his or her participation in the parliamentary, presidential, or local elections campaign; a name that is allowed to use under a franchise agreement; a name of an artistic group registered under Art. 83 of the CRRA; a name of a classified tourist site; a name of a construction; or a name of a vessel.

The term 'protected domain name' was introduced in 2008.[392] In the course of arbitration, the domain name shall be deemed protected if for its formation the Registrant has used and provided Register.BG with grounds for the use of an Internet name. Registrants that have obtained grounds for use of the Internet name have been provided with the opportunity to file an application for changing the registration of the domain name into a protected domain name after the registration of the domain name.

III. Registration Procedure

175. Applications for registration of domain names shall be filled in online through the interface of the Registrar selected by the customer. The very registration application shall be confirmed by the Registrant by means of the electronic signature (automatic confirmation) or by confirmation of the information sent by the respective register to the e-mail address stated in the application. The application shall be confirmed within 24 hours.

After confirmation of the application, its term of validity shall last thirty calendar days. Within this period, the Registrant shall perform all actions required for the registration of the domain name. The Registrant shall undertake to remove any inconsistencies in the documents and effect the payment within the validity term of the application. If after expiry of the term the application does not meet the requirements of registration yet, the respective register terminates the registration procedure and vacates the domain name for registration by other Registrants.

The Registrant has the opportunity to make the configuration of the domain name by himself/herself; the configuration includes a record of information about: servers of names, contact persons for technical issues, and a contact person for financial issues.

In case the documents are accurate, the applicant receives a pro forma invoice and is obliged to pay a fee for the first year within the validity term (published in section 15 – Prices and Payments – of the Terms and Conditions of the respective register). In 2021, there is no domain name registration fee for both .bg and Бг zones, but only annual support fees.

With reference to domain names that have been registered unconditionally in the .bg ccTLD, not later than thirty calendar days before the expiry of the term of the domain name maintenance, the Registrant shall select services through the web interface of the Registrar for this domain name, prepare a pro forma invoice stating the selected services and their prices, and pay the value thereof.

With reference to domain names that have been registered under certain conditions in the .bg ccTLD, not later than thirty calendar days before the expiry of the

392. Domain name in the.bg or Бг zone upon registration of which the Registrant has submitted documents verifying the grounds for use of the Internet name pursuant to the Terms and Conditions of the respective register (the grounds that give such protection are the same for both Register.BG and IMENA.BG), or according to Register.BG's Terms and Conditions, the domain name has been registered and continuously supported for more than five years.

term of the domain name support, the Registrant shall, through the selected Registrar, present to Register.BG evidence of fulfilment of the condition for the domain name support to be carried on, and afterwards shall undertake the necessary actions for the payment of the selected services.

Within three working days, Registrars shall examine the validity and availability of the full set of documents submitted by the Registrant, and shall send the documents to Register.BG. After ascertaining all facts: accuracy of the documents, valid configuration, and due payment of the services related to the domain name, the register effects the registration.

IV. Limitation of Liability of the Naming Authority

176. The registers and Registrars explicitly limit their liability in connection with the domain name registration. Pursuant to the rules of Register.BG, the applicant is required to enclose a signed declaration upon applying for registration of a domain name stating that:

(1) The applicant is liable before third parties in connection with the choice of the name that the applicant wishes to register.
(2) The owner of a domain name shall hold Register.BG and the respective Registrar, their employees and agents, as well as the members of the arbitration commission harmless from and against any losses, damages, liability, claims, or expenses resulting from a claim or claims asserted by third parties regarding the ownership or the right of use of the domain name.
(3) Register.BG and the Registrar of the Registrant, as well as their employees and agents shall not bear any liability for any losses or damages suffered by the applicant or the ISP resulting from the activity or inactivity of Register.BG and the Registrar of the Registrant, or their employees and agents during the performance of their duties as a Register and a Registrar beyond the provision of services under a particular application from the Registrant .
(4) Register.BG and the Registrar shall not be liable for the accuracy of the data filled in by the applicant where the applicant uses electronic updating of the information that already exists in the register for the applicant's domain name.
(5) Register.BG shall not be liable for the actions or omissions of Registrars, except for the official Registrar.
(6) Register.BG and Registrars shall be liable only for actions and omissions performed with intent or gross negligence.
(7) Register.BG and Registrars shall not be liable for any consequences of the registration of a domain that has not been protected pursuant to the general terms and conditions.

Approximately the same rules on limitation of liability are also introduced in the terms and conditions of IMENA.BG.

§5. Cancellation of Domain Name Registration

177. The domain name registration is terminated when the respective register, through the Registrar providing services to the Registrant, receives a written request for termination from the representative of the applicant. In such a case, the registration is terminated within five working days.

The registers are empowered to terminate the registration when the domain ceases to meet the requirements for accessibility of the domain name. Contact persons are notified and given the opportunity to correct the deficiency. If relevant measures are not duly taken within one month, the naming authority has the right to terminate the registration without any further notice.

The registration in both .bg and Бг zone shall be also terminated in the following cases:

(1) The annual support fee has not been paid within the designated terms.
(2) The respective register finds that the Registrant has provided documents with false content.
(3) The respective register finds that the Registrant has registered a domain with an Internet name, not observing the requirements of the registration procedure.
(4) A decision of the arbitration commission or a decision entered into force adopted by a competent court is enforced.

The registers do not undertake to keep domain names of Registrants who have terminated the support of their domains.

§6. Dispute Resolution Procedure

178. All disputes concerning domain name registration are examined in accordance with the Terms and Conditions (TaC) of Register.BG, and the specific procedure regarding disputes is laid down in section 11 of said Terms.

Disputes can be opened for every current domain name registration in the.bg zone. The applicant for a dispute can request termination of the domain name registration only if the label of the registered domain is identical with the full name of which he or she has grounds to use. If:

(a) the domain name is unprotected and the applicant has grounds to use the label with an earlier priority than the entity, which registered it;
(b) the domain name has been registered with providing grounds to use the label, but there are preconditions indicated in i.9.4. and i.9.5. of the TaC, a registered domain name can be transferred in favour of the applicant who has raised the dispute.
  - Before the beginning of a dispute, the applicant shall create an application for registration of the domain name in the.bg zone, which will become subject of the dispute. The application for the dispute is created online through

www.register.bg and all documents and payment are due as specified by the TaC. The Registrant is informed and allowed to provide an answer within a thirty-day period.

– After this period, the dispute committee makes a decision, again within a thirty-day period, in a closed session, based on the documents from both sides. Both sides in the dispute are informed of this decision via e-mail. If the decision is in favour of the applicant, the latter has the opportunity to go on with the registration procedure of the domain name. Provided all fees have been duly paid, the Registrant will lose the domain name within fifteen days, unless within this period the registry receives a protective order by a Bulgarian competent court, by which the 'stop the domain name termination' protective order has been applied to the Registrant.

The procedure is substantially the same for disputes under the terms and conditions of IMENA.BG, but based on the information available on their website, currently there is no Arbitration Court for Dispute Resolution concerning Domains, so any such disputes regarding domain names in the '.бг' ccTLD need to be referred directly to court.[393]

It must be noted that the ADR procedure established under the terms and conditions of Register.BG for arbitration proceedings within the true sense of the word, i.e. as a procedure established under the Bulgarian ICAA.[394] The decisions of Register.BG regarding a dispute concerning a domain name do not have the same legal effect as a court decision or an arbitral award (e.g., res judicata, enforceability, etc.) and are not subject to set aside proceedings under Article 47 of the ICAA.[395]

§7. Conflicts Between Domain Names and Trademarks

I. Legal Instruments for Protection of Domain Names

179. While the right over a domain name is a contractual relative right stemming out of a contractual relationship, the right holder is entitled only to demand from the Registrar to fulfil its obligations and nothing else from third parties except for hindering the fulfilment of the obligations of the parties.[396]

Therefore, protection of the domain name towards third parties should be searched in several directions.

It is undisputable that the domain name is a wording sign. Under Bulgarian law, as such, it could benefit from protection that is granted to the right holders of signs considered an absolute right: for example, copyright, trade or service mark right, right to a personal or trade name, etc.

393. *See* https://www.imena.bg/tld_user_nam/app.pl?action_key=ac_c1p13d1_to_dispute&frame_key=fr_c1p13_main_frame, accessed 17 Oct. 2021.
394. *See* Part II, Ch. 5, § 2 *supra*.
395. *See* in that respect M. Zahariev & D., Krusteva, 'The Legal Nature of Domain Names' *TITA Taxes Magazine* Issue 132 (Sept. 2020) and the court practice quoted therein.
396. OCA, Art. 21(2).

On the other hand, protection could be sought in tort or unfair competition law.

II. Registration as a Trade or Service Mark

180. In Bulgaria, no legal obstacle exists for registering a domain name as a trade or service mark at the PO before or after its registration as a domain name,[397] unless it fails to meet the requirements of the MGIA.

Bulgarian law provides that any sign (including the domain name) could be registered as trademark, if it could lead to distinguishing the goods or services of the sign holder from those of other persons and can be represented in the State Register of Trademarks in a manner which enables accurately and precisely to determine the subject of the protection granted by the registration. As a sign consisting of words, including the names of persons, or letters, numbers, etc., the domain name would be capable for registration as a mark.

The PO may refuse to register the full domain name as URL with prefixes like 'ftp://', 'http://', 'www' due to lack of distinctive quality of these elements and suffixes having the country code like '.bg', '.uk', '.de', etc., because they represent geographical origin. This approach is followed by almost all EU jurisdictions.[398] The PO permits registering a mark with the suffix '.bg', '.eu'.

Second, under Article 11 of the MGIA, the PO would not register the domain as a mark, provided that it consists exclusively of signs or indications that:

- have become customary in the current language or established practices of the trade in Bulgaria;
- consist exclusively of signs or indications designating the kind, quality, quantity, intended purpose, value, geographical origin, time or process of production of the goods or the manner of rendering the services, or other characteristics of goods or services;
- are contrary to public order and the accepted principles of morality;
- may mislead users as to the nature, quality, or geographical origin of the goods or services;
- consist of, or include armorial bearings, flags or other emblems (or imitations thereof) of any states parties to the Paris Convention or international intergovernmental organizations;
- consist of, or include official control and warranty signs where such are used to mark identical goods; emblems or coat of arms different from those declared or being of particular public interest (Paris Convention, Article 6); names or representations of cultural value;

397. For example, Orbitel™ registered in the Bulgarian PO as a trademark three years after the registration of the domain name orbitel.bg with the local Registrar.

398. M. Viefhues, *Kennzeichenrecht in: Hoeren, Thomas, Sieber, Ulrich*, Ch. 6 (München: Handbuch Multimedia-Recht, 1999), *see also* Cruquenaire, *Internet: la proplématique des noms de domaine* 222 (Revue de droit intellectual L'ingeniear – Conseil 1997).

– violates the Bulgarian and EU legislation or international agreements to which Bulgaria or the EU are a party and which grant legal protection to geographical indications.[399]

181. The legal requirements are almost the same in other jurisdictions of the continental law family and almost the same as the ones provided in the old Marks and Geographical Indications Act.[400]

'Dressed' like a trade or service mark, the domain name would be considered an absolute right, and would benefit from all legal means for protection of trademark provided by law against any third party. 'Any usage of the domain name by another person in his/her business activity, without the consent of the holder, shall be considered an infringement (Article 11 of the First Council Directive 89/104/EEC of 21 December 1988 to approximate the laws of the Member States relating to trade marks).[401] The holder of a mark is entitled to bring an infringement action against any third infringing party. Apart from the above, some infringements are subject to administrative and even criminal liability.[402]

It is important to consider what particular usage of the domain name registered as a trade or service mark shall be considered infringement by usage 'in business activity without the consent of the holder'. Obviously, usage of a domain by a third party for associate goods or service on a website accredited to the domain name shall be considered infringement, but the mere use of the domain name in a URL or as an e-mail address shall be excluded. This view is also supported by the practice of Bulgarian Supreme Court of Cassation, according to which 'A domain by its characteristic is an Internet address containing certain information for Internet users. Therefore, the registration by the Registrar/in the case of "R" OOD/of a domain with a certain name identical or similar to an already registered trademark does not constitute a commercial activity, respectively illegal use of a trademark within the meaning of Article 13 para. Article 13, paragraph 1, item 2 of the MGIA [revoked – note of the authors]'.[403] It can be concluded that a case-by-case assessment is necessary to assess whether a registration of a domain name identical/similar to an already registered trademark owned by third party different from the Registrant amounts to trademark infringement.

Needless to say, the trade-/service mark protection of the domain name would shield its holder only for the classes of goods and/or services covered by mark registration by the PO. In addition, registration in the zones .bg and Бг of domain names which consist of trademarks with effect for the territory of the Republic of Bulgaria would amount to registering the domain names as protected.[404]

In divergence to some other jurisdictions' approach, Bulgarian law cannot create an absolute right to the domain name user as an unregistered trademark prior to submission of the registration application to the PO.

399. MGIA, Art. 11.
400. SG, issue 81 of 14 Sept. 1999, repealed SG issue 98 of 13 Dec. 2019.
401. OJ, L 040, 11 Feb. 1989.
402. MGIA, Art. 127, Criminal Code Art. 172b.
403. Decision No. 53 of 06.04.2009 under commercial case No. 605/2006, II Commercial Division of the Supreme Court of Cassation.
404. *See* Part II, Ch. 6, § 4, II Requirements in Respect to Names *supra*.

III. Protection Against Registered Marks

182. Under Bulgarian law, it is very difficult to protect the domain name holder against rightful user of an already registered trade- or service mark.

This is due to the fact that the MGIA does not protect the user of a mark or sign against registered user of such, provided the former has used it in a business way prior to the latter. In this respect, the Bulgarian MGIA differs from the legislative solutions in other jurisdictions,[405] but is in conformity with Article 4 (4) 'b' of the Trademark Directive.

An exception to this rule constitutes protection of domain names used as marks and registered as such with no coverage in the territory of the Republic of Bulgaria, but would be regarded as well known or 'famous' under the meaning of Article 6(b) of the Paris Convention. Further successful protection could be reached against registered marks, if they are identical or similar to a domain name and the protection is intended for goods or services that are not identical or similar to those sold by the website with the said domain name in the case when that domain name is well known in the territory of Bulgaria as a mark and when use without due cause of the applied mark would take unfair advantage of, or be detrimental to, the distinctive character or reputation of the domain as an earlier mark.

In jurisdictions where such rights of the prior user are granted, a successful protection could be achieved.[406]

IV. Protection Against Other Domains

183. A very interesting question is whether domain names could be defended against similar domains, subdomains or if there is a conflict of similarity between gTLD and ccTLD.

Under Bulgarian law, a domain name cannot be protected and opposed against a similar one on general grounds.

An opportunity for protection of the absolute rights of their legitimate holders is provided by the CPA,[407] namely its provisions forbidding unfair competition (Chapter VII, Article 29–37).

Article 35(3) of the CPA prohibits the use of domain names or an interface of a website that are identical or similar to those of other persons in a manner that can result in error and/or harm competitors' interests. That is the first provision of Bulgarian legislation that officially regulates domain names and their usage. Thus even an online service provider who has registered a certain domain name for the purpose of providing its services (e.g., www.marr.bg) containing a word that cannot be registered as a trademark,[408] would be entitled to submit to the CPC a subsequent

405. For example, Greek Trademark Act, Art. 4(3), French Copyright Act, Art. L 711-4, Finnish Trademark Act s. 14(1), i. 4, 12 German Trademark Act s. 11.
406. Décision – Tribunal de grande instance de Paris, 3ème chambre – 2ème section – 13 Novembre 1998, *AGAPHONE c/COTTIN, SARL BURODAFER et C.T.S, see also Microcaz c/Oceanet et S.F.D.I.*, TGI Mans, 29 June 1999.
407. *See* Part I, Ch. I, para. 42 *supra.*
408. MGIA, Art. 11.

registration similar to www.marr.bg provided that all conditions as required by competition law are present. Practice of the CPC on this text is already available.[409]

In such a case, the CPC has the authority to fully investigate, decide on whether a violation of the prohibition of unfair competition is present, impose a fine on the competitor in breach (up to 10% of annual turnover of the infringer for the preceding financial year), and rule a prohibition of the domain usage. However, it cannot order transfer of the domain name or termination of the contract between the unfair competitor and the respective Register (Register.BG or IMENA.BG).

This provision superseded the preceding provision of former Article 33(2) of the CPA[410] (now Article 35(2) in the new CPA), which used to prohibit the 'use of firm names, marks or distinctive signs identical or similar to those of other persons in a manner which might lead to damage of the interests of the competitors and/or consumers'. In the CPC's practice, this provision is used in the cases of unauthorized use of similar domain names as far as it is widely accepted that domain names are distinctive signs (in the sense that they are used to identify particular goods and services provided by a particular online provider).[411] Therefore, Article 35(2) of the CPA extends its scope of application to the traders holding domain names, who could use it to protect their right against the illegitimate actions of their competitors. The SAC of Bulgaria has developed its practice regarding Article 35 of the CPA accepting that 'imitation' in the sense of the article can be done only by the producer of a good or the provider of a service. For the *actus reus* of Article 35 to be complete, two elements are necessary: using of a firm, brand, or distinctive characteristic, identical to those belonging to another entity; and the possibility of such using to be harmful to the interests of a competitor. According to Article 13(3) MGIA (revoked, now Article 10(4) of the new MGIA – note of the authors), the moment of creation of a right on a brand or a design is the very moment of its registration. Hence, if identification of the holders of such right is missing, it is not possible to claim unlawful or unconscientious behaviour of third parties before registration.[412] Another necessary precondition for a breach of Article 35(1) to be found is for the brand, object of the alleged imitation, to hold a stable position and be well-known in the market so that the alleged imitator may have certain benefits from imitating. Moreover, it is necessary that the imitating actions by the competitor be intended to (potentially) mislead the consumers, while it is not necessary that actual harm be caused. Consumers are assumed not to have any special knowledge or skills to ascertain similarity.[413] Finally, a theoretical example of a breach of Article 35(2), under the current court practice, would be the following case. The two brands Example-bg and Example.bg would be considered identical and, as such,

409. CPC, Ruling No. 747 of 23 Jul. 2009 on Art. 35(3), http://reg.cpc.bg/AllResolutions. aspx?dt=1&ot=2.
410. SG, revoked, issue 102 of 28 Nov. 2008.
411. CPC, Ruling No. 501 of 24 Jun. 2008 on Art. 33(2) under the revoked CPA, http://reg.cpc.bg/AllResolutions.aspx?dt=1&ot=2.
412. Decision No. 1003 from 14 Aug. 2013 by the CPC (in No CPC- 431/2013).
413. Decision by No. 1590/2010 by the CPC, confirmed by the SAC in decision No. 7523/2011; decision No. 866/2012 by CPC, confirmed by SAC in decision No. 4264/2013, etc.

confusing and misleading the consumers as to the identity of the service provider, allowing the imitating competitor an unfair advantage.[414]

184. Last, it should be acknowledged that owners of registered trademarks cannot seek special protection against bad faith registration of domain names (so-called cybersquatting), at least for the zones .bg and.бгPotential redress against such bad faith behaviour could be the initiation of the respective dispute resolution procedures envisaged in the general terms and conditions of the respective registers, but specific procedures such as the Uniform Domain-Name Dispute-Resolution Policy (UDRP) and the Uniform Rapid Suspension System (URS) of ICANN are not available for .bg and бгccTLD.[415,.416]

414. Decision No. 1059 from 4 Sept. 2013 by the CPC (in No CPC-206/2013).

415. More about the UDRP and the URS procedures can be found in M. Zahariev, Protection of trademark against bad faith registration of domain name, *Computerworld*, 14 Feb. 2017.

416. See a list of ccTLDs that adopted UDRP as per WIPO https://www.wipo.int/amc/en/domains/cctld/, accessed 23 Oct. 2021.

Part III. ICT Contracts

Chapter 1. Hardware Contracts

185. In Bulgaria, the relationships that could arise, develop, and end under the so-called hardware contracts could fall under the regulation of the general contractual rules stipulated by the OCA and the CA.[417]

A hardware contract may provide for the hardware to be sold directly to the client. In this case, it will possess many of the features of a standard contract for sale.

Sold hardware is very often accompanied by software necessary for its operation – either embedded (e.g., BIOS), pre-installed (e.g., operating systems, software applications operating different peripherals), or stored on media installation packages (e.g., bundled utilities). In such cases, more complicated relationships involving intellectual property rights will arise.[418] The choice of software best suited to the purchased hardware equipment, as well as their compatibility and interoperability, is of great importance. Therefore, some hardware contracts incorporate a clause obliging the provider to achieve specific results in order to meet the client's criteria.

Some of the typical provisions of hardware contracts are those related to the delivery of the product, consumer guarantees, damages and indemnification, etc.

Hardware contracts may include provisions for installation and maintenance or may be accompanied by separate maintenance contracts. Some hardware providers outsource the maintenance provision; therefore, the maintenance contract may be concluded with a different entity. Due to the significance of computer system support, providers may guarantee that the maintenance will be performed timely, onsite, and by qualified personnel within specified terms and conditions.

---

417. SG, issue 4 of 18 Jun. 1991.
418. *See* Part III, Ch. 2 *infra*.

Chapter 2. Software Contracts

186. In Europe, the need to foster the computer software industry, the growing role of computer programs in a broad range of industrial sectors, and the perceived lack of adequate harmonization among the copyright laws of the Member States with respect to such software, motivated the creation of the 91/250/EEC Directive. This Council Directive was formally replaced by Directive 2009/24/EC, which consolidated the various minor amendments introduced over the years. Under it, computer programs and any associated design material are protected under copyright as literary works within the sense of the Berne Convention for the Protection of Literary and Artistic Works (Article 1). For the purposes of protection of the rights of authors and other right holders, delimiting the scope of the transfer of rights over the computer program is of paramount importance. The protection applies to:

- the expression in any form of a computer program. Not included remaining ideas and principles, which underlie a computer program or any elements thereof;
- a computer program when it is original – the author's own intellectual creation;
- computer programs created before 1 January 1993.

'Author' of a computer program is considered the natural person (or a group of natural persons), who has created the program or, where the legislation of the Member State permits, a legal person. The exclusive rights are held jointly by these persons when there are multiple authors and by the employer when an employee creates a computer program following an assignment. Permanent or temporary reproduction (or a part thereof), translation, adaptation, arrangement, and any other alteration, as well as distribution of the program are included in the scope of the rights held by the author.

However, these rights are subject to certain limitations. The legal owner of a program is assumed to have a licence to create any copies necessary to use the program and to observe, study, or test the functioning of the program in order to determine the ideas and principles which underlie any element of the program without the agreement of the right holder. The results of these actions, however, may not be used for any other purpose without infringing the copyright in the program.

The duration of the copyright was originally fixed at fifty years after the death of the author, in accordance with the Berne Convention standard for literary works (Article 7.1 Berne Convention), but it has since been prolonged to the life of the author plus seventy years by the Directive harmonizing the term of protection of copyright and certain related rights.

In Bulgaria, software contracts are subject to the general provisions of the OCA, the CA and the CRRA.[419] The subject of the software contract is the computer program and the adjacent documentation including technical literature and user manuals. When concluding such a contract, the client shall have the assurance that the possession and use of the software do not infringe any third party's intellectual property rights. In addition, the provider may undertake to indemnify the client and

419. *See* Part II, Ch. 1, para. 122 *supra.*

ensure their protection against any expenses, losses, damages, and claims arising from the use or possession of the software.[420]

The CRRA does not provide for particular rights and obligations with regard to contracts for use of computer programs. Thus, its general provisions concerning the use of works apply, and so do the specific provisions of Articles 70 and 71 regulating the use of computer programs. According to Article 36 of the CRRA, the author may transfer to the user an exclusive or non-exclusive right to use the work. In the first case, the author can neither use the program in the way, during the period, or in the territory agreed in the contract, nor transfer such a right to third parties. In the second case, the author is entitled to perform such actions. The transfer of an exclusive right of use must be explicit and in writing. In case the parties do not specify the duration and territorial scope of the transfer, it is valid in the country of citizenship of the user (the country of its headquarters in case of a legal entity) and for a period of three years. The maximum permitted length of such contracts is ten years. If a period longer than ten years is agreed, the right to use is considered granted for ten years.

When a computer program is created as under an employment relationship, the copyright thereof belongs to the employer, unless otherwise agreed between the parties. When a computer program is created upon an assignment by the assignor of the creator, the copyright belongs to the author and the assignor is entitled to use the work without the author's permission for the purposes for which it is intended, unless parties agree otherwise.[421] Finally, Article 70 of the CRRA lists the actions that can be performed by a person who has obtained the right to use the software. These include translating, loading the program, storing it, etc., unless a specific agreement between the parties stipulates otherwise.

In accordance with Council Directive 2009/24/EO, Article 71 of CRRA provides for restrictions concerning the copyright holder. Pursuant to its mandatory requirements, the legal software user is entitled to make a backup copy of the software, to study and test it, to translate the source code for the purposes specified without the author's consent, and not owing additional remuneration.[422,423]

187. Software contracts could be theoretically divided into two categories according to the transferred rights – those for software provision and those for its maintenance (although is not uncommon for both to be combined into one contract). Software provision contracts subdivide into two categories: contacts for provision of an existing software package, and contracts for development of a new software product, tailored to the requirements of a particular client. Standard software contracts commonly include abusive clauses with regard to making copies, updates, decompiling, liability, and access to the source code, i.e., strict prohibitions to perform such actions without authorization and penalties or other forms of contractual liability therefor.

420. J. de Otaola Zamora, *Monograph Spain in Cyber Law*, in *International Encyclopedia of Law*, suppl. 4, 124 (R. Blanpain ed., The Hague: Kluwer Law International, 2004).
421. CRRA, Art. 42.
422. Tsv. Kamenova, *Copyright: International and National*, 224–225.
423. CRRA, Art. 71.

Depending on the scope of the granted rights, all main kinds of software contracts completed online (also known as 'licence agreements') are enforceable under Bulgarian law.

The shareware[424] contract in Bulgaria is seen as a kind of software contract by way of which the author grants non-exclusive and non-transferable licence to use the software for a limited term for evaluation purposes. After expiration of the stipulated term, the users are required to pay the due remuneration, or otherwise to discontinue its usage. It is feasible to include clauses whereby the user shall be bound to destroy all the copies of software upon expiration of the evaluation term and to issue a certificate attesting that fact.

188. The trial contract, similar to the shareware contract, is also seen under the Bulgarian law doctrine as a software contract granting non-exclusive and non-transferrable licence to the user to test the software for evaluation purposes for a given period of time. Unlike the shareware contract however, after expiration of the contractual term the software automatically discontinues its operation, if the user has failed to pay the due remuneration to the author. Introducing further binding conditions is also feasible.

The demo software contract also exists under Bulgarian law. This contract reveals its own *differentia specifica*. Similar to the above software contracts, it is meant to grant the user a non-exclusive right for testing the main functionalities of a software for a given period of time. With rare exceptions, the software used under demo licence has limited functionalities. Under this licence, the user is usually granted the right to freely distribute copies of the software.

189. In Bulgaria, many software applications are distributed under the Creative Commons (CC) licence concept.[425] Under the terms and conditions of this software contract, the author grants the user a worldwide, royalty-free, non-exclusive licence to use and distribute copies of the software. The users, under this concept, are neither allowed to distribute the software in any way controlling the access to its use, nor to exercise any of the rights granted in a manner that is intended for, or directed towards commercial advantage or private monetary compensation.

190. Under all of the above contracts, the users are not entitled to introduce any changes into the source code. However, widely distributed software could be found in Bulgaria under the GNU's Not Unix General Public Licence (GNU GPL).[426] Under this licence, the author grants the user the right to freely distribute and change the software and any of its derivatives, while the derived works are to be available under the same copyright.[427] This is the difference from permissive free software licences (like the Berkeley Software Distribution (BSD) licences). The software contracts under GNU GPL are considered fully enforceable in Bulgaria.

424. 'Shareware', http://en.wikipedia.org/wiki/Shareware.
425. Creative Commons International, Bulgaria, http://creativecommons.org/international/bg.
426. 'GNU General Public Licence', www.gnu.org/licences/gpl.html.
427. 'GNU General Public Licence', http://en.wikipedia.org/wiki/GNU_General_Public_License.

191. Freeware software contracts are among the most common software contracts nowadays. They can be enforced in Bulgaria under different modifications depending on the scope of the rights granted in them. Typically, these are the right to use given software free of charge and to distribute it, as long as the copyright of the holder is preserved. Among the freeware licences, the most popular seem to be BSD licences. Apart from the typical clause allowing unlimited redistribution for any purpose of the software as long as its copyright notices and the licence's disclaimers of warranty are maintained, the BSD licence also contains a clause restricting use of the names of contributors for endorsement of a derived work without specific permission.[428]

192. In respect of the actions required of the user to conclude the contract, the software contracts reveal divergent particularities, which may lead to their further classification.

Shrinkwrap software contracts are licence agreements which can only be read and accepted by the consumer after opening the product.[429] In other words, such actions on the part of the consumer are seen to be a manifestation of his/her consent to enter into a contractual relationship. Bulgarian law does not regard shrinkwrap contracts in particular, and there is no court practice so far either. Considering that the general principle of civil law rests on the idea that parties should be aware and agree beforehand on all the essential issues of the contract, the enforcing of a shrinkwrap agreement seems disputable – one of the parties (the user) learns the essential scope of the terms of the contract only after opening the product package, hence it is conceivable that the latter might not have agreed, had he or she been aware of these terms.[430,431]

193. The clickwrap software contract (also known as a 'clickthrough' contract or a 'clickwrap licence') is a common type of agreement mostly used in connection with software licences.[432] Such forms of contracts could easily be found on the Internet, where agreement is sought using electronic media. Clickwrap is the electronic equivalent of the shrinkwrap method that allows users to read the terms of the agreement before accepting them.[433] Since the manifestation of the consent is made after the consumer has become aware of the terms of the contractual relationship, these contracts seem more easily enforced under Bulgarian law.

---

428. 'BSD Licences', http://en.wikipedia.org/wiki/BSD_licences.
429. The term describes the shrinkwrap plastic wrapping used to coat software boxes, though these contracts are not limited to the software industry. *See* 'Shrink Wrap Contract', http://en. wikipedia.org /wiki/Shrink_wrap_contract.
430. D. Halbert, *The Open Source Alternative: Shrink-Wrap, Open Source and Copyright*, Murdoch U. Elec. J.L., www.murdoch.edu.au/elaw/issues/v10n4/halbert104_text.html, Dec. 2003.
431. T. Finkelstein & D.C. Wyatt, 'Shrinkwrap Licences: Consequences of Breaking the Seal', *St. John's Law Review*, http://findarticles.com/p/articles/mi_qa3735/is_199710/ai_n8778077.
432. Examples of clickwrap agreements – signing up for software usage by MN https://accountservices.passport.net/reg.srf?id=2&sl=1&lc=1033); selling online phones by T-Mobile www.t-mobile.com.
433. R. Kunkel JD, *Recent Developments in Shrinkwrap, Clickwrap and Browsewrap Licences in the United States*, 9 Murdoch U. Elec. J.L., www.murdoch.edu. au/elaw/issues/v9n3/kunkel93_ text.html#Shrinkwrap%20Licence%20Cases_T, Sept. 2002.

194. A browse-wrap contract is a part of a website and it is concluded if users agree to the contract, before entering a particular area or doing something specific on the website.[434] This contract differs from other types of software contracts analysed above. Usually, only if a user has scrolled down the page to the end of the contractual terms, would the user have been granted the functionality to click a hyperlinked button to express consent and thus proceed with concluding the contract. Similarly to the clickwrap software contracts, the validity of the browse-wrap agreements seems feasible under Bulgarian law.

434. 'Browse-wrap', http://en.wikipedia.org/wiki/Browse_wrap.

Chapter 3. Turnkey Contracts

195. The term 'turnkey' is often used in the technology industry, most commonly to describe pre-built computer, or other bundled technology 'packages' in which everything needed to perform a certain type of task (e.g., audio editing) is put together by the provider and sold as a ready-to-use facility. This often relates to delivery of computers with pre-installed software, hardware, and its peripherals (modems, printers, scanners), as well as other accessories.[435]

Under Bulgarian law, the turnkey contract is enforceable insofar as the action of the client can be considered an expression of will (*facta concludentia*)[436] of the latter to enter into a contractual relationship, whereby the action of the provider is meant to execute multiple functionalities of a set of equipment and/or software to deliver a result expected by the client. Thus, upon entering into a turnkey contract, the provider undertakes to ensure the provision of the results which might encompass provision of equipment, performing of software installations, etc. The turnkey contract may also incorporate a clause obliging the provider to perform additional actions, such as testing, training, logistical, and operational support, etc. Due to the fact that the provider is responsible for a wide range of risks regarding the project, he or she shall obtain and consider all the relevant information before concluding such a contract. By way of turnkey contracts, some of the companies adapt to the changing market environment through outsourcing manufacturing functions to specialized providers. In such a case, they can also reduce the costs and risks regarding their business.

A typical feature of a turnkey contract is that the provider shall prove the reliability of performance of the equipment. Therefore, special attention is given to the so-called tests on completion used for determining whether the offered technical solution can meet the requirements of the client. Generally, contractually stipulating the methods and criteria for the acceptance tests is to the provider's interest. So is the obtaining of a written notice of the acceptance. The turnkey contract often regulates a possible failure of the provider to pass the acceptance tests. In such cases, the provider usually makes the necessary changes to the system and runs the acceptance test again free of extra charge. Should the provider fail to pass the acceptance test within a specified term, the client may be entitled to terminate the contract.[437]

Turnkey contracts may also stipulate the provision of support services, and specify the features of the relevant training in the use, administration, and maintenance of the system including its time, location, maximum number of participants, etc. In addition, the client shall be entitled to use the solution, materials, and data provided.

---

435. 'Turnkey', http://en.wikipedia.org/wiki/Turnkey.
436. Pavlova, *Civil Law*, 92.
437. Zamora, *Monograph Spain in Cyber Law*, 127.

Chapter 4. Distribution Agreements

196. In Bulgaria, as well as in most European countries, there is no specific regulation concerning distribution agreements. Therefore, the parties are free to determine their rights and obligations while observing mandatory legal requirements – in Bulgaria those of the OCA and the CA. Distribution agreements usually relate to the distribution of machinery and mechanical goods – automobiles, trucks, farm and construction equipment, etc., but they are widely used in the ICT sector as well – distribution agreements are widely used e.g., for distribution of mobile phones, desktop computers, laptops, tablets, smart watches and other smart devices, smoke-free devices used as alternatives to the traditional tobacco cigarettes and many more.

197. The distributor is a trader having an exclusive or non-exclusive right of sale. Distributors obtain the right to commercialize the goods and/or services at their own cost and risk in a predetermined territory (the manufacturer is usually not entitled to sell the products in the same territory); otherwise, under Bulgarian law, they are considered as agents and the agreement is governed by the CA. The distributor enters into two types of legal relations – the first one is with manufacturers, and the second one is with clients. Thus, a distributor's subject of activity is usually limited to the purchase of products for the purpose of their resale,[438] but they may in certain occasions also conclude with clients other types of agreements (e.g., renting agreements). They are obliged not to perform distribution activities for another manufacturer in the same territory, as well as to keep the trade secret of their contractor. With regard to the main obligation of distributors to commercialize the products of the supplier, including using sub-distributors, they undertake additional obligations, such as to perform advertising activities, to sell the products at minimum prices, etc. While performing their activity, distributors are entitled to use the manufacturer's trademarks, and logos, but not as their own. In case of bad faith actions of distributors aiming to register the manufacturer's trademarks without their consent for the respective territory where the trademark is used by the distributor, Bulgarian MIGA provides for tool for protection, namely for an explicit ground for filing opposition against the registration or cancellation of the registration already made. Article 12, Paragraph 6 of the MIGA stipulates that in the case of opposition filed by the actual proprietor of a trademark, a trademark shall not be registered when it is applied for on behalf of an agent or a representative of the actual proprietor without its consent. 'Agent or representative' is a term defined in the Additional Provisions of the MIGA as a person who acts or must act in the interests of the actual proprietor of a trademark on the basis of a legal or factual connection with it in respect of the goods or services covered by the trademark.[439] The requirement for having 'legal or factual connection' with the actual proprietor of the trademark in any case could encompass situations where the distributor uses the trademark of the manufacturer on the basis of distribution agreement. This is reaffirmed by the court practice on the similar provision contained in the old MIGA

---

438. O. Gerdjikov, *Comment on the Commercial Act*, Book 1, 204–206 (Sofia: Sofi-R, 2007).
439. § 1., item 7.

from 1999, Article 26, paragraph 3, item 3, where such actions were a ground for cancellation of the already registered trademark. According to the Bulgarian SAC, in such cases 'the narrow interpretation of the terms "representative" and "agent" cannot be accepted; moreover, the fact that the very norm of Art. 26, Para. 3 item 3 of the MIGA (old – note of the authors) does not speak of commercial representation in order to apply the definition of representative given in the commercial law. The purpose of the law and in particular of the rule of Art. 26, Para. 3, item 3 of the MIGA (old – note of the authors) is not to allow an agent or representative, who has learned as a result of commercial legal relations with its proprietors, to benefit and register the mark in its own name without the consent of its proprietor'.[440] Similarly to the old regime, such registration can be cancelled by the actual proprietor by virtue of the provision Article 36, paragraph 3, item 3 of the new MIGA. The MIGA provides for two exceptions in the above-mentioned scenario, namely the registration shall not be refused or the trademark registration shall not be cancelled when: (i) the agent or the representative justifies its actions, or (ii) the application (for the registration of the trademark – note of the authors) is transferred to the actual proprietor at its request.[441] In the light of the above, it is recommendable for distributors to refrain from unfair actions aiming to obtain the rights over manufacturer's trademark without its consent, as it could lead to complicated legal proceedings, loss of time, efforts, and money and ultimately to refusal/cancellation of the trademark registration.

Due to the fact that commercial activity requires serious investment, distributors share this burden with the manufacturer, providing them with the opportunity to use their capital for production purposes. The manufacturer often organizes marketing and technical training programmes for distributors. The manufacturer may also provide common methods for display and inventory management, offer incentives, etc. However, the distributor is an independent entity, and as such not under the direct management supervision of the manufacturer.

198. In case intellectual property rights issues arise, i.e., in case the agreement includes the usage of work(s) subject to copyright protection, the agreement is subject to the CRRA.[442] The transfer of an exclusive right of use must be explicit and in writing. In case the parties do not specify the duration and territorial scope of the transfer, it is valid in the country of citizenship of the user/the country of seat (in case of a legal entity) and for a period of three years.[443] The distribution agreement must include provisions specifying the sublicensing process, as well as those concerning the transfer of distribution rights to third parties.

Distributors are required to act with due care to avoid causing any damage to the commercial image of manufacturers. In order to prevent any fraudulent use of the products or services, they may be entitled to discontinue the supply and perform the respective actions.

---

440. Decision No. 4184 of 31 Mar. 2009 of the SAC under Adm. Case 13857/2008.
441. Article 12, para. 9 and Art. 36, para. 9.
442. *See* Part II, Ch. 1, para. 122 *supra*.
443. CRRA, Art. 36.

The parties determine the remuneration of the manufacturer at their discretion, and the payment is a responsibility of the distributor. The distributor's remuneration is based on the difference between purchase and sale price of the product. The supplier may recommend, but not impose, the price that the distributor charges for the products. Furthermore, the distribution agreement often provides for an obligation of distributors to make periodical reports on their activities to the manufacturer.[444]

If one of the parties is an author of a copyrighted work, and distribution rights are transferred for a certain sum paid only once, Article 38 of the CRRA stipulates increase of the remuneration in case the one-off compensation is obviously inadequate in comparison with the profits of the transferee, that is, the distributor. If agreement is not reached, the parties can refer to the competent court.

Although distribution agreements have lost their importance due to Internet developments and increase of business-to-business selling practices, they are still used by market agents for commercial purposes.

444. Zamora, *Monograph Spain in Cyber Law*, 128.

Chapter 5. Maintenance Contracts

199. In times of fast development of the information and communication technologies, maintenance contracts play a significant role. Due to the fact that proper functioning of computer systems is of great importance not only to the day-to-day business activities, but also to information and data storage, a clause regarding maintenance of equipment, software, communication devices, and networks is often included in various types of contracts or may be agreed separately.

A maintenance contract is a contract under which a service provider undertakes to perform maintenance services. Contracts vary and may include clauses regarding the costs of service and/or materials. Services may refer to diagnosing problems, phone support, on-site repairs, provision of spare parts, supplementary equipment, preventive measures, etc.[445] Maintenance contracts are aimed at reinforcing pre-emptive security and ensuring safe working environment by way of regular, pre-defined visits of qualified personnel, who checks and reports on equipment, as well as performs repair works within scheduled maintenance periods. The main advantage of this type of contracts is that the client is provided with a wide range of services by virtue of a single contract – from configuration and ensuring compatibility to repairs and software installation.

200. The main types of maintenance contracts can be divided into corrective, preventive, adaptive, and perfective maintenance contracts, all of them depending on the modification of a certain product performed after delivery. Other authors distinguish three types of maintenance contracts only.[446] The most widely used among them are corrective maintenance contracts related to fixing failures of the equipment and systems when such occur and restoring their normal functioning. However, it is preferable to combine corrective maintenance with preventive maintenance, which aims at avoiding any errors through performing tests and taking various other preventive measures, such as antivirus and malware protection and recommendations regarding the optimal functioning of systems. Adaptive maintenance deals with keeping systems and equipment up to date so as to meet the changing needs and requirements of clients and the ICT environment itself. Perfective maintenance, also defined as proactive maintenance, aims at achieving the optimal performance of key facilities. The key equipment and systems, such as data backup, internal and external component cleaning, and software updates, is administered on a scheduled basis. By following a few basic procedures, clients can greatly reduce the risk of data loss or hardware failure.[447]

201. The equipment and software subject to maintenance are usually explicitly specified in the contract but they can also be prepared on the basis of fees per user.

---

445. *See* US Legal Definitions, 'Contractual Maintenance Agreement', http://definitions.uslegal. com/c /contractual-maintenance-agreement.
446. Zamora, *Monograph Spain in Cyber Law*, 130.
447. *Ibid.*

In the majority of cases the client is entitled to modify or upgrade equipment, software, and systems as long as this does not significantly alter the scope of the contract. The issues of service level, response times, and availability of providers are among the ones that need to be explicitly specified in a maintenance contract.

Maintenance may be either remote or in the premises of the client but it is usually a combination of both. Most maintenance contracts are on-site ones under which a qualified technician comes to the client's premises to fix the problems occurred and the client is then obliged to provide access to equipment, software, and systems. However, some contracts still operate on a return-to-depot basis whereby the client must return the equipment to the manufacturer for repair. Costs vary considerably depending on the minimum response time and working hours needed for the service provision. While performing obligations under the maintenance contract, the provider undertakes to comply with the relevant security and health and safety conditions. In addition, the parties agree to prevent unauthorized access to the systems and equipment.

In case the provider has access to personal data, the provisions of the GDPR[448] and the PDPA[449] apply. In such kind of contracts, the provider usually acts as a data processor within the meaning of the applicable data protection legislation and the data processing operations related to the maintenance need to be regulated by virtue of data processing agreement (DPA) with the minimum content prescribed by Article 28 of the GDPR. This includes obligations: to processes the personal data only on documented instructions from the controller; to impose confidentiality obligations to the personnel accessing personal data on behalf of the provider; to apply appropriate security measures and preferably explicitly enlist them as an attachment to the DPA; to delete or return all the personal data to the controller after the end of the provision of services relating to processing, and to delete existing copies unless EU or Member State law requires storage of the personal data; to respect the conditions for including further sub-processor as agreed between the parties and as prescribed by the rules of the GDPR; to cooperate with the data controller, etc. The EC adopted standard contractual clauses (SCC) between controllers and processors under Article 28(7) of the GDPR[450] which could serve as orientation and be used as a basis to draft DPAs to the maintenance contracts.

448. Regulation (EU) 2016/679 of the European Parliament and of the Council of 27 April 2016 on the protection of natural persons with regard to the processing of personal data and on the free movement of such data, and repealing Directive 95/46/EC (General Data Protection Regulation), *OJ, L 119, 4 May 2016, pp. 1–88.*

449. SG, issue 1 of 4 Jan. 2002, last amended in SGNo. 93 of 26 Nov. 2019 with Decision No. 8 of 15 Nov. 2019 of the Constitutional Court of the Republic of Bulgaria under constitutional case No. 4/2019.

450. *See* Commission Implementing Decision (EU) 2021/915 of 4 June 2021 on standard contractual clauses between controllers and processors under Art. 28(7) of Regulation (EU) 2016/679 of the European Parliament and of the Council and Art. 29(7) of Regulation (EU) 2018/1725 of the European Parliament and of the Council, *OJ, L 199, 7 June 2021, pp. 18–30.*

Chapter 6. Facilities Management

202. Facilities management demands specific expertise and covers non-core or supporting services regarding the primary business of the client aimed at optimizing maintenance resources and results and improving equipment and staff productivity. By signing a facilities management contract, one undertakes to professionally consult, collaborate, supervise, and technically support client's facilities. Therefore, facility management relates to coordinating and overseeing the safe and proper operation and maintenance of assets in a cost-effective manner for the purpose of the long-term preservation of their value. In addition, it represents service provision supporting the client's core business where improvement is performed on a continuous basis and may be considered as an integral part of a coordinated and controlled process of design, engineering, maintenance, and operation.

Facilities management is conceptualized as a specific type of outsourcing where the client concludes a contract for provision of certain services with external experts instead of using in-house persons having relevant qualifications. The reasons for this can vary, including lack of in-house resources or expertise; necessity for reducing costs; making the use of labour, capital, and information technology more efficient, etc. However, the two terms are not synonymous due to the fact that outsourcing represents one of the means used for providing facility-related services to the client's company.[451]

When entering into a facility management contract, the client usually remains in control of facilities management. The provider may provide housing for all facilities or subcontract a part of them to a third party, but it is an obligation of the former to guarantee that they are maintained under optimal conditions. When concluding a housing contract, clients are entitled to instal in the provider's premises their facilities, including but not limited to equipment, cables, and connections necessary for the normal functioning of facilities. It is an obligation of the provider to maintain such installations, infrastructures, etc. in an appropriate condition and to inform the client in due course of any issue related to them. The term for which the facilities are fitted and placed needs to be specified in the contract. The provider is obliged to keep in strict confidentiality all information regarding the contract and its execution and neither to disclose it to other clients, nor to allow unauthorized access to the client's equipment. Access is usually limited to clients' employees and persons explicitly authorized by the latter. In addition, providers guarantee that the facilities meet all security standards required.[452]

Facilities management contracts in the majority of cases include clauses settling issues of conflicts of interests, confidentiality, and liability – the latter usually being limited to certain amounts and cases (direct damages). The liability clause does not usually include indirect consequential damages; anticipated savings or profits; damages for loss of revenue, business, or contracts. Insurance of the facilities and civil liability are generally taken by the parties.[453]

451. *See* Wikipedia, 'Facility Management', http://en.wikipedia.org/wiki/Facility_management.
452. Zamora, *Monograph Spain in Cyber Law*, 132.
453. *Ibid.*

Chapter 7. Network Services

203. The subject of network services contracts is a provision of services regarding operating network-related resources or resources accessible through the provider's network. These services are regarded as the foundation of networked computing environment. E-mail, printing, and network file-sharing services are also network services used in the LAN environment for the purpose of streamlining data transfer within the network.[454] Individual network services contracts are usually concluded on the basis of the general terms and conditions of providers applicable to all their clients, as well as in compliance with the relevant provisions of the ECA,[455] mainly with regard to providers' obligations. Providers are obliged to observe the requirements of the CRC and must take the necessary and proportional technical and organizational measures in order to maintain the network in proper condition, guarantee the confidential character of traffic and consumers' data, notify the Commission for Electronic Communications about security incidents, etc.[456]

A typical network services contract incorporates a clause obliging the client to perform certain actions aiming at ensuring the effective provision of services. Clients usually undertake to cover the expenses necessary for equipment, such as computer hardware and software. All devices and cables delivered by the provider and used for connection purposes remain his/her exclusive ownership, and the client is obliged to refrain from any modifications regarding them. In addition, network capacity of the provider is of great importance to the quality of service. When concluding a network services contract, the client usually undertakes neither to transfer his/her rights of using the services to any party by virtue of selling, leasing, etc. without having the advance written consent of the provider, nor to perform actions not mentioned in the contract or causing damages to the provider or his/her clients. In this respect, indemnification in case of fraudulent, unlawful, or abusive use of the service should be stipulated. Such contracts usually state that the provider cannot guarantee the stability, safety, and security of the network, and he/she is not to be held liable for any loss of profit or data incurred by the client.[457]

As far as usage fees are concerned, they may be charged on an hourly basis, but it is also possible to establish monthly or annual flat fees. The client usually undertakes to pay a service activation fee as well. In contrast to the main principle of contractual law, these contracts are modified upon mutual agreement of the parties. Due to technological developments network services, contracts can be automatically amended. Among the clauses typical for such contracts are those regarding payment, warranties, indemnification, liability, etc.[458]

---

454. 'Network Service', http://en.wikipedia.org/wiki/Network_service.
455. *See* Part I, Ch. 1, para. 36 *supra.*
456. ECA, Art. 243, Art. 243b, Art. 243c.
457. Zamora, *Monograph Spain in Cyber Law*, 134.
458. *Ibid.*

Chapter 8. Government Contracts

§1. General Information

204. Government contracts are governed by the Public Procurement Act (PPA).[459]

Although the contracting parties must meet the specific requirements of public authorities, such contracts are often concluded because providers have guaranteed that they will be paid in due term. Furthermore, market agents and potential clients rely on service providers contracting with public authorities due to the special selection procedures performed before the conclusion of the contract.

In Bulgaria, the state policy in the public procurement sector is implemented by the Minister of Finance (Article 227, PPA) through the Public Procurement Agency (Article 228, PPA). The notices and other decisions concerning the public procurement process are individual administrative acts created as electronic documents through a special electronic platform (Article 39a). The assignor adopts a decision for procedure opening and sanctions the notice, as well as the documentation needed for participation. Pursuant to Article 31 of the PPA, the contract documentation for participation in a public procurement award procedure includes technical specifications; the investment and other projects, when they are required for the preparation of the offer; the methodology for determining the complex evaluation of the offer, when applicable; samples of documents, as well as instructions for their preparation; draft contract except when the contract is concluded under general conditions or a normative act determines its obligatory content, etc. In order to participate in such procedures, candidates submit documents proving that their economic and financial standing, as well as technical capabilities and/or qualifications correspond to assignor's requirements. Public procurement is performed by means of an open procedure, restricted procedure, competitive procedure with negotiation, negotiation with a preliminary invitation for participation, negotiation with publication of a procurement notice, competitive dialogue, innovation partnership, negotiation without prior notice, negotiation without prior invitation to participate, negotiation without publication of a contract notice, competition for project, public competition, and direct negotiation. Article 18(8) of the PPA provides for a competition for project – a procedure in which the contracting authority acquires mainly in the fields of urban and urban planning, architecture, engineering or data processing, a plan or conceptual design selected by an independent jury on the basis of a competition with/without prizes.[460] Contracting authorities may use electronic auctions, framework agreements, and dynamic purchasing systems as well.

---

459. SG, issue 13 of 16 Feb. 2016, in force as of 15 Apr. 2016, last amended and supplemented in SG, issue 107/2020, in force as of 1 Jan. 2021.

460. *See* regarding the similar provision in the old PPA (revoked SG, No. 13 from 16.02.2016, in force as of 15 Apr. 2016) M. Krivachka & M. Markov, *New Conditions in the Public Procurement Act*, Lab. L. 169–176 (2006).

§2. Hardware, Software, and Maintenance Contracts

205. Article 151 of the PPA and Appendix No. 14 thereto regulate public information technologies and related services contracts as well as the maintenance and repair services contracts. Their subject could deal with provision of equipment, computer programs, or systems. As public procurement contracts (PPCs), they are bilateral, consensual, *intuitu personae*, and formal (written form is required). The PPC is the final element of the assignment process. It also includes the decision for procedure opening, the act for appointing a commission for procedure management, the tender, as well as the assignor's decision for announcing the classification and determination of an assignee.

The PPC is concluded on the basis of the assignor's decision for announcing the classification and selection of an assignee. First, by means of the public procurement notice, the assignor makes a public offer for negotiations and the contract may not include clauses that significantly differ from the conditions announced. The candidates' tenders are an important element of the pre-contractual relations. They are not offers within the meaning of Article 13 of the OCA due to the fact that their acceptance is not enough for the occurrence of contractual relations. The contents of the PPC depend on the assignee's tender. A contract having contents different from the ones, specified in the tender documents or proves to be concluded with a person who has not participated in the tender procedure is invalid. The provisions of the CA and the OCA are applied where no specific rules are envisaged in PPC, for example in respect to reaching consent or any other issue concerning the conclusion, performance, or termination of PPCs. The contract shall be deemed concluded in case the document offered and signed by the assignor is signed by the selected assignee. The PPA provides for some pre-contractual obligations of the provider, such as to pay in a guarantee for performance and to submit a document proving this fact when signing the contract. Pursuant to Article 112(6) of the PPA, the contract shall be concluded in one month as of the date of the enforcement of the resolution for appointment of a contractor or the ruling allowing the preliminary execution of that decision, but not before the expiration of the fourteen-day term as of the notification to the interested applicants. The signed contract shall be entered into the Public Procurement Register.

Being an administrative contract, the PPC includes exclusive clauses in the interest of the public authority – it organizes and directs procedure management, it determines the amount of the guarantee paid by the assignee, and finally it is the only party entitled to amend the contract under certain circumstances (Article 116).[461]

Pursuant to Article 35 of the PPA, in the OJ of the EU shall be published information regarding the awarding and performance of public procurements with the value specified in Article 20 of the PPA and for the establishment of qualification systems through: (i) the preliminary notices under Article 23 (1) of the PPA, including when they are used for announcing the opening of a procedure; (ii) the announcements for public procurements; (iii) the announcements for amendment or additional information; (iv) the announcements for awarding procurements; (v) the

461. *See* Part III, Ch. 8, §1 *supra.*

announcements in case of project competition; (vi) the announcements for amendment of PPCs and framework agreements in the cases under Article 116 (1), items 2 and 3 of the PPA; (vii) the announcements for voluntary transparency; (viii) the announcements for qualification systems. These announcements are prepared according to samples, approved by an act of the EC, and shall contain at least the information prescribed in the PPA (Article 35(2)). These announcements shall be sent to the Publications Office of the EU through the electronic platform created under Article 39a (1) of the PPA, maintained by the Public Procurement Agency. The date of sending the announcements is the date certified by the platform by electronic time stamp. Public procurement notices not subject to the publication requirement may be published in the OJ of the EU, provided that such notices are sent to the Publications Office of the EU in accordance with above requirements and procedure.

The selection criteria shall be determined by the assignor and specified in the public procurement notice, in the invitation for confirmation of interest, or in the invitation for participation in negotiations – depending of the type of procedure.[462] The public procurements are assigned on the basis of the most economically advantageous offer which is determined on the basis of one of the following criteria for awarding: lowest price; level of costs, taking into account the cost efficiency, including the costs for the whole life cycle; optimal quality/price ratio, which is assessed on the basis of the price or the level of the expenses, as well as on indicators, including qualitative, ecological and/or social aspects, related to the subject of the public procurement.[463]

§3. Electronic Communications Contracts

206. Electronic communications contracts relate to services such as fixed and mobile telephone services, circuit leasing, data transmission, Internet access, and where necessary, accompanying services as well (wiring). The PPA does not include provisions regarding electronic communications contracts. Thus, the general rules specified in the preceding paragraph apply.

Providers of electronic communications services are subject to the relevant provisions of the ECA.[464] They are obliged to observe the requirements of the CRC and take the necessary technical and organizational measures in order to maintain the electronic networks in proper condition, guarantee the confidential character of communications, of traffic and consumers' data, etc. Electronic communications contracts specify parameters for quality of services, conditions for services maintenance, liability and indemnification, as well as dispute settlement. They may also incorporate a clause empowering the parties to modify the initial conditions due to technical or economic amendments.

462. PPA, Arts 59, 60, 61, 62 and 63.
463. PPA, Art. 70.
464. *See* Part I, Ch. 1, para. 34 *supra*.

207. In compliance with Directive 2014/25/EU,[465] the PPA includes specific provisions with regard to public procurements awarded by sectoral assignors. PPA defines sectoral activities as activities related to natural gas and heat energy; electricity; water supply; transport services; operation of a geographical area; postal services.[466] The PPA shall not be applied in respect of public procurements and competitions for project, intended to create conditions for the realization of sectoral activity, if the activity is directly exposed to competition and is realized in the conditions of a market, the access to which is not limited.[467] The procedure for exclusion of a sectoral activity shall be conducted under rules of the EC.[468] In addition, sectoral assignors possess more operative independence than the other ones and are entitled to select freely one of the following public procurement procedures to use – open and restricted procedure, negotiation with a preliminary invitation to participate and competitive dialogue.[469] Other forms of procedures include partnership for innovations (Article 137) and negotiated procedure without prior invitation to participate (Article 138).

465. Directive 2014/25/EU of the European Parliament and of the Council of 26 Feb. 2014 on procurement by entities operating in the water, energy, transport, and postal services sectors and repealing Directive 2004/17/EC Text with EEA relevance, *OJ, L 94, 28 Mar. 2014, pp. 243–374.*
466. PPA, Arts 123, 124, 125, 126, 127, 128 and 129.
467. PPA, Article 130.
468. PPA, Article 131.
469. PPA, Article 132.

Part IV. Electronic Transactions

Chapter 1. Legal Status of Electronic Transactions

§1. Legal Framework

208. The basic rules regarding e-contracting on a supranational level are contained in Chapter II, section 3 'Contracts Concluded by Electronic Means' of Directive 2000/31/EC of the European Parliament and of the Council of 8 June 2000 on certain legal aspects of information society services, in particular, electronic commerce, in the internal market[470] (hereinafter 'E-commerce Directive'). The Model Law on Electronic Commerce adopted by the United Nations Commission on International Trade Law on 12 June 1996[471] (hereinafter 'the UNCITRAL's Model Law') is also a model of legal regulation regarding general rules on electronic statements, electronic documents, their transmission, etc. Pursuant to Article 9 of the E-commerce Directive, 'Member States shall ensure that their legal system allows contracts to be concluded by electronic means'.

The act that specifically regulates e-commerce in Bulgaria is the E-commerce Act.[472] The E-commerce Act was adopted in June 2006 to implement the Directive on Electronic Commerce, and entered into force on 24 December 2006. Further, the CA,[473] the OCA,[474] the EDETSA,[475] the Consumer Protection Act,[476] and the ECA[477] are also applicable to electronic transactions. Other related acts containing relevant provisions are the GDPR and the PDPA,[478] the Provision of Distance Financial Services Act (DPFSA),[479] the CRRA,[480] the CC,[481] some of the tax laws, etc.

470. OJ, L 178, 17 Jul. 2000.
471. UNCITRAL's Model Law for Electronic Commerce, www.uncitral.org/uncitral/en/uncitral_ texts/electronic_commerce/1996Model.html, 12 Jun. 1996.
472. SG, issue 51 of 23 Jun. 2006.
473. *See* Part III, Ch. 1, para. 185 *supra.*
474. *See* Part III, Ch. 1, para. 185 *supra.*
475. *See* Introduction, Ch. 5, para. 33 *supra.*
476. *See* Part I, Ch. 5, paras 114–115 *supra.*
477. *See* Part I, Ch. 1, para. 34 *supra.*
478. *See* Part III, Ch. 5, para. 334 *supra.*
479. SG, issue 105 of 22 Dec. 2006.
480. *See* Part II, Ch. I, para. 121 *supra.*
481. *See* Part II, Ch. 2, para. 361 *supra.*

209. The state body exercising powers in the area of e-commerce in Bulgaria is the Consumer Protection Commission. Certain powers with regard to interaction and cooperation with the relevant EU authorities are vested in the Minister of Transport, Information Technologies and Communications.

Where privacy issues are concerned, the CPDP and its Chairperson have competences as well. Depending on the relevant case, other authorities may also have certain powers.

§2. Electronic Commerce the E-commerce Act and EDETSA

I. Legal Concept of an Electronic Contract and Formal Requirements

210. Prior to the adoption of EDESA (now EDETSA), the legal basis for e-contracting in Bulgaria was the provision of Article 293(4) of the CA. It reads that 'The written form shall be deemed complied with if the statement has been technically recorded in a way that permits it to be reproduced.' However, this norm only refers to commercial transactions as defined in the CA. Thus, in civil transactions, the possibility of concluding contracts by electronic means was based solely on Article 9 of the OCA (the freedom of contracting principle), and e-contracting was only possible for informal contracts. Furthermore, before EDESA's entry into force, the electronic form was seen as a valid form for transactions, but it was rarely used in practice. The reason for this was the lack of clear rules regarding the moment of sending and receiving the electronic statement. The above-mentioned facts combined with the lack of adequate procedures for proving e-contracts were hampering the willingness of market agents to use electronic means for entering into contractual relationships.

211. EDESA (now EDETSA) proved to be a decisive step towards eliminating the insecurity related to e-contracting and towards putting the legal consequences of electronic and written statements on an equal basis. Pursuant to Article 2(1) of EDETSA, the electronic statement is 'a verbal statement, represented in digital form through a common standard for conversion, reading and visual presentation of information'. It may also contain a non-verbal information. Article 3 of EDETSA in connection with Article 3, item 35 of the eIDAS Regulation give a legal definition of the term 'electronic document'. As such shall be considered any content stored in electronic form, in particular text or sound, visual or audiovisual recording. The written form of the document is considered met if an electronic document is created that contains electronic statement. The latter is a special rule introduced in the Bulgarian legislation which further narrows the scope of the concept of electronic document under the eIDAS Regulation. EDETSA has thus created the possibility of concluding formal contracts for which the written form is a validity prerequisite not only in commercial (under CA), but also in civil transactions. EDETSA does not elaborate on the legal consequences of making, sending, receiving, and confirming electronic statements. The act only defines technical rules for pinpointing the exact moment of sending, receiving, and confirmation of the statement. Therefore, for contracts concluded by electronic means all general legal rules of the OCA, CA, and ECA for conclusion of contracts and those of EDETSA holding special provisions for electronic statements apply.

212. The rules regarding the signatory and owner of the electronic statement, the addressee of the statement, and the possible errors in transmitting electronic statements are provided in EDETSA. In defining the signatory, EDETSA does not adopt literally the UNCITRAL's Model Law concept, which refers only to originator and addressee of the electronic statement.

As a signatory of an electronic statement is considered the natural person that is named in the statement as its performer, while the principal (titular) is the person on behalf of whom the electronic statement has been performed.[482] While the signatory may be only a natural person, the principal can be either a natural person, or a legal entity.[483]

Bulgarian law defines the figure of the addressee of the electronic statement in Article 5 EDETSA. Such can be a person who by virtue of law is obliged to receive electronic statements or who, under unambiguous circumstances, may be considered to have agreed to receive a statement in an electronic form.[484] Thus, the law establishes the principle of freedom of using electronic form established by law.[485] No one can be forced to receive electronic statements, unless explicitly required by law.[486] An addressee should give his or her consent.

II. Scope of the E-commerce Act

213. Article 1 of the E-commerce Act regulates certain legal aspects of electronic commerce, particularly the relations related to provision of information society services. Pursuant to Article 1(3), information society services are those, including provision of commercial messages, which are normally reimbursable and are provided at a distance by using electronic means after an explicit statement on behalf of the recipient of the service. Moreover, the latest amendments in the E-commerce Act (Article 1(4)) from November 2020 explicitly declare one additional specific type of service as information society services, namely the online intermediation services[487] under the meaning of Regulation (EU) 2019/1150 of the European Parliament and of the Council of 20 June 2019 on promoting fairness and

482. EDETSA, Art. 4.
483. G. Dimitrov et al., *Electronic Document and Electronic Signature. Legal Regime* 46 (Sofia: Ciela Publishing/CSD, 2004).
484. EDETSA, Art. 5.
485. Dimitrov et al., *Electronic Document and Electronic Signature. Legal Regime*, 46.
486. Such addressees are all state bodies in their capacity of providers of electronic administrative services by virtue of Art. 11 of the EGA. They are obliged to receive electronic statements from citizen.
487. Online intermediation services are defined by Art. 2, item 2 of Regulation 2019/1150 as 'services which meet all of the following requirements:

(a) they constitute information society services within the meaning of point (b) of Art. 1(1) of Directive (EU) 2015/1535 of the European Parliament and of the Council;

transparency for business users of online intermediation services (Regulation 2019/1150). Thus, the scope of the E-commerce Act stays close to the one of the E-commerce Directive.

The E-commerce Act excludes from its scope the following cases (Article 1(5)): establishment and collection of public receivables, gambling, regulation of electronic commerce transactions related to personal data protection, notary activity, and other professional activities involving the exercise of public functions, litigation and 'the agreements, decisions, and coordinated practices under Article 9 of the Competition Protection Act'.[488] Those cases are treated by specialized legal acts.

III. Validity and Effectiveness of Contracts Concluded by Electronic Means

214. The E-commerce Directive adopts the same principle as one of Article 11(1), i. 2 of the UNCITRAL's Model Law not to limit the validity and effectiveness of e-contracts on the sole ground that they are concluded by electronic means. There are several exceptions to this rule. Article 9(2) of E-commerce Directive enumerates the contracts that allow the introduction of the above-mentioned limitation (but it is not obligatory). The Bulgarian legislator establishes two exceptions whereby e-contracting is inadmissible – transactions requiring a qualified written form as a mandatory validity requirement, and those transactions where the retention of the document is deemed legally relevant (promissory notes, letters of consignment, bearer shares, etc.). The analysis of the contracts under Article 1(2) of EDETSA leads to the conclusion that in this respect the Bulgarian Act complies with the E-commerce Directive.

IV. Evidential Value of Electronic Contracts

A. The Electronic Contract and Its Evidential Value

215. The definition of an electronic document is based on the concept of a written document. The written document is a chattel on which written symbols conduct a statement. The law treats the electronic document the same way as the written document.[489] This means that in all cases when the legislator requires a written form, the legal requirement as regards the form will be considered met if an electronic document is created.[490]

(b) they allow business users to offer goods or services to consumers, with a view to facilitating the initiating of direct transactions between those business users and consumers, irrespective of where those transactions are ultimately concluded;

they are provided to business users on the basis of contractual relationships between the provider of those services and business users which offer goods or services to consumers'.

488. *See* Part I, Ch. 1, para. 43 *supra*.
489. EDETSA, Art. 3(2).
490. Dimitrov et al., *Electronic Document and Electronic Signature. Legal Regime*, 46.

B. Intermediaries

216. According to Article 6(2), i. 3 of EDETSA when the electronic statement is transmitted, received, copied, or kept by an intermediary, the intermediary must ensure the determination of the time and source of the transmitted electronic statement. Further, the intermediary must maintain secure systems for keeping this information, and retain it for a period of one year. If the intermediary fails to perform any of these obligations, it shall be liable for damages incurred as a result of non-performance. In addition, where an intermediary does not retain the information for the one-year term, the natural persons responsible may bear criminal liability in accordance with the CC.[491]

V. Formation of the Contract

217. A number of cases in the field of electronic commerce contracts are concluded without individual contracting based on general terms and conditions only. As a general rule, this type of contracting excludes the possibility of one party influencing the clauses of the contract as they are already predetermined by the other contracting party.

On a European level, these issues are treated in Articles 10 and 11 of the E-commerce Directive. In Bulgarian internal law, similar provisions can be found in Article 16 of the OCA, Article 298 of the CA, and Chapter 6 of the Consumer Protection Act (regarding unequal provisions in contracts). However, unlike the rules of the E-commerce Directive, the provisions of the OCA and the Consumer Protection Act are rather broad – they refer to all contracts concluded under the general terms and conditions. The special regulation of e-contracts under general terms and conditions could be found in the E-commerce Act.

The E-commerce Act creates a different regime depending on whether one of the parties is a consumer or not. The only imperative norm applicable to any contract under general terms and conditions regardless of the parties' capacity is contained in Article 9: 'The service provider must provide to the service recipient the conditions and general content of the contract in a way that allows the latter to store and reproduce them.' This rule is of extreme importance as far as general terms and conditions in electronic commerce are concerned. Considering the specifics of e-commerce, the text of the general terms and conditions has to be made available for the whole period of validity of the contract. Apart from Article 9, the E-commerce Act does not establish other imperative rules for concluding e-contracts under general terms and conditions between parties none of which is a consumer. The provisions of Articles 8 and 10 of the E-commerce Act are set out by the Bulgarian legislator primarily with the purpose of protecting consumers' rights. Deviations are admissible in cases where the parties conclude contracts during the course of commercial or professional activity, that is, they do not act as consumers.

491. *See* Part II, Ch. 2, para. 390 *supra.*

Pursuant to Articles 8, 10, and 11 of the E-commerce Act, the service provider has three main obligations in relation to the conclusion of an e-contract under general terms and conditions.

A. *Provision of Information*

218. Among other information requirements, Article 8 of the E-commerce Act establishes the obligation of the service provider to provide the recipient of the service with the following information, when making an offer for concluding a contract by electronic means:[492]

(1) the technical steps for concluding the contract and their legal effect;
(2) whether the contract shall be kept by the service provider and how it may be accessed;
(3) the technical means for identifying and correcting errors made during the course of entry of information before the statement for concluding the contract is made;
(4) the languages of the contract.

219. In addition, the service provider shall indicate any relevant codes of conduct to which the provider abides and information on how those codes can be accessed electronically.

This information must be submitted to the recipient of the service before the 'latter has placed the order', that is, before they have accepted the general terms and conditions. The information shall be presented in a clear, understandable, and accessible way.

B. *Placing the Order*

220. Another obligation of the service providers is to confirm the order without undue delay, that is, in a reasonable term after its receipt. The 'order' consists of the electronic statement of the recipient of the service by which the latter objectifies his or her will to conclude the contract, and his or her consent to the contents of the general terms and conditions. Both European and Bulgarian legislators establish the presumption that the order and its confirmation are considered received, if the parties whom they are addressed to, have the possibility to access them.[493] In this sense, the provider would fulfil the obligation of guaranteeing access to the statements, if an accessible technology is available that does not create undue obstacles for the reception and confirmation of the order (e.g., web interface).

492. E-commerce Directive, Art. 10.
493. E-commerce Directive, Art. 11 and the E-commerce Act, Art. 11.

In cases falling outside the scope of the E-commerce Act, the general rule of Article 10(1) of EDETSA is applicable – the electronic statement shall be considered received upon (i) its receipt in the information system indicated by the addressee, and (ii) if the addressee has not specified a specific information system, the statement shall be considered received by entering it in any information system of the addressee, and (iii) if the addressee does not have an information system – by downloading it from the addressee from the information system in which the statement was received. Only if confirmation has been agreed, the electronic statement shall be considered received by sending a confirmation by the addressee for its receipt (Article 10 (2) of EDETSA).

VI. Time and Place of Conclusion of the Contract

A. Moment of Conclusion of the Contract

221. The theory of receipt determines the moment of conclusion of the contract – 'it is considered concluded when the acceptance reaches the offeror'.[494] The rules of EDETSA do not alter this model. EDETSA only establishes general rules for establishing the exact moment and place of sending and receiving electronic statements in the cyberworld. Under Articles 8 and 10 of EDETSA, the electronic statement is considered received with its entering into the information system, specified by the addressee (or if none exists or has been specified – into any of the information systems of the addressee or with its retrieving by the addressee from the information system the electronic statement has entered into), and a confirmation of receipt is not necessary in order to consider that it is received by the addressee, unless the parties have agreed otherwise. Such receipt does not evidence the content of the electronic statement. The original rules of Articles 8 and 10 of EDESA used to require explicit confirmation of the receipt from the addressee, unless otherwise agreed. This was contrary to the solution adopted in Article 14 of UNCITRAL's Model Law, which does not require confirmation of receipt unless agreed otherwise. The Bulgarian legislator's original idea was clear – to make the electronic document flow safer at this initial stage of introduction of electronic means of communication in Bulgaria. Such differences in regulation, however, were capable of impeding the electronic document flow and could be viewed as contradicting the EU requirement for speed and simplicity of the electronic document exchange. The latter conclusion may be inferred from the Preamble of the E-commerce Directive. The purpose of the Directive is to create equal conditions for e-commerce by ensuring speed and simplicity in the process of providing services and concluding contracts by electronic means. States may not create divergent legislation by introducing additional requirements concerning the legal consequences of electronic statements. Therefore, as mentioned above, the current rules of Articles 8 and 10 of EDETSA do not require explicit confirmation to consider the electronic statement received, unless otherwise agreed. In addition, with the

494. OCA, Art. 14(1).

adoption of the E-commerce Act the burden of electronic flow of contracts concluded by electronic means is removed through the introduction of the rule under Article 11 of the E-commerce Act that 'the statement for concluding a contract and the confirmation of its receipt are considered received when their addressees gain access to them'. This is also the moment of concluding the contact.

As the default rule of Articles 8 and 10 of EDETSA provides that confirmation of the receipt of the electronic statement is not necessary, then the question on how the exact time of sending and receiving the electronic statement arises. EDETSA gives an answer to this question. Under Article 9, the statement shall be considered sent upon its entry in the information system, which is not under the control of the signatory. The term 'information system' is not legally defined in Bulgarian law. Its definition can be derived from Article 2(f) of the UNCITRAL's Model Law. Under that provision, an 'information system' is a system for generating, sending, receiving, storing, or other forms of processing electronic statements. This definition of e-commerce is designed to cover all types of technical means used for sending, receiving, or storing information. That is why an information system is seen to include one or more computers, but not as a *conditio sine qua non*. Communication systems whose elements are a mobile phone or a fax shall be considered information systems as well. The wide scope of the definition of UNCITRAL's Model Law is an important advantage for its introduction in Bulgaria.[495]

Concerning the moment of receipt, as mentioned above, three rules are applicable. The first one reads that the electronic statement shall be considered received upon its entry in the information system indicated by the addressee. 'Indication' is the explicit identification by the addressee of the information system in which he or she is willing to receive e-statements. It is not obligatory for such an indication to be addressed to the signatory. It can be general and addressed to all or several legal subjects.[496] The way of indication is irrelevant – oral, written, or electronic. This rule is established for the purpose of protecting the interests of the addressee. Regardless of the fact that an addressee has requested to receive electronic statements or is bound by law to receive such, the addressee may have various means of doing so – e-mail servers, mobile phones to receive Short Message Service (SMS), servers hosting discussion forums on the Internet, etc.[497] For example, if an addressee indicates that she or he wishes to receive statements on her or his e-mail address, for instance, name-of-addressee@name-ofdomain.com, this will be considered an indication of the information system maintaining the name-of-domain.com.

The second rule envisages that when the addressee has not indicated an information system, the statement shall be considered received upon its entry into the information system of the addressee – e.g., the one that the addressee uses de facto without the necessity of announcing it to third persons. Usually, such usage refers to the addressee's rights and obligations related to the information system.[498] An illustration of the argument above are applications for online chat such as Skype

495. Dimitrov et al., Electronic Document and Electronic Signature. Legal Regime, 56.
496. *Ibid.*, 58.
497. *Ibid.*, 59.
498. *Ibid.*, 59.

chat, Facebook chat, etc. The addressee's information system shall be the one used to log into the respective application – at home, at the Internet club, via the mobile phone, etc.

Where the addressee has neither indicated nor uses de facto an information system for receiving electronic statements, these shall be considered received upon their downloading by the addressee from the information system where they have been entered. This is the case of posting messages on discussion forums on the Internet, sending private messages in Facebook, etc. In these cases, it will be considered that the addressee has received the message when the latter is downloaded in the browser and visualized before the addressee.[499]

Apart from the cases of entering into a contract under the E-commerce Act, the time of conclusion of an electronic contract is determined in accordance with general civil legislation. Unless otherwise agreed, the contract is deemed concluded in the moment when the statement holding the acceptance of the offer reaches the offeror.[500]

B. Place of Conclusion of Contracts Entered into by Electronic Means

222. E-contracts are distance contacts. Having in mind their specific characteristics, pinpointing the place of conclusion of such contracts is not an easy task.

The place of sending/receiving an electronic statement is of significant legal importance as this may determine applicable law. For example, if the statement is a proposal for concluding/accepting a contract, the place where the offer is made determines the place of conclusion of the contract[501] and thus the applicable law thereto. The electronic statement is deemed sent at the place of activity of its owner (titular).[502] If the electronic statement is an offer for concluding a contract, the place of activity of the owner is the place of conclusion of the contract.[503]

The electronic statement is considered received at the place of activity of its addressee.[504] If the owner or the addressee has more than one place of activity, the place of activity is the one that is most tightly related to the statement and its performance, bearing in mind the circumstances that were known to the owner and the addressee or that were considered by them at any time before or during the offer.[505]

If the offeror is a natural person, the offer is deemed made at the place of his or her permanent residence.[506] The term 'permanent residence' is not defined by law. It should be interpreted as a durable factual relation between the person and the respective place.[507]

499. *Ibid.*, 59.
500. OCA, Art. 14.
501. OCA, Art. 14.
502. EDETSA, Art. 12(1).
503. Dimitrov et al., *Electronic Document and Electronic Signature. Legal Regime*, 61.
504. EDESTA, Art. 12(2).
505. EDETSA, Art. 12(3).
506. *Ibid.*, Art. 12(4).
507. Dimitrov et al., *Electronic Document and Electronic Signature. Legal Regime*, 62.

VII. Applicable Law and Jurisdiction

223. The rules related to the determination of jurisdiction are provided in the International Private Law Code (IPLC)[508] and, of course, in the applicable EU legislation such as Council Regulation (EC) No 2201/2003 of 27 November 2003 concerning jurisdiction and the recognition and enforcement of judgments in matrimonial matters and the matters of parental responsibility, repealing Regulation (EC) No 1347/2000.[509] No specific regulations related to Internet-based transactions are provided for in Bulgarian national legislation. Thus, the general provisions of the IPLC shall apply.

However, in respect to provision of information society services, the E-commerce Act provides for special rules regarding applicable law. Article 19(1) provides that the requirements regarding providing information society services shall be governed by the law of the state in which the place of activity of the service provider is located, provided that it is within the territory of an EU Member State.

A place of activity under the meaning of the act shall be considered the place from which the service provider carries out business activity for an indefinite period of time. The presence and use of the technical means and technologies required to provide the information society service is not sufficient, in itself, to determine the place of activity of the service provider.

The rules of the E-commerce Act governing applicable law shall not apply with regard to:

(1) the requirements concerning the properties of the goods and the delivery thereof, and those services that are not provided by electronic means;
(2) copyright and neighbouring rights, industrial property rights, rights over databases, and rights over the topology of integrated circuits;
(3) the emissions of electronic money issued by issuers of instruments for electronic money, which are exempt from the General Requirements regarding licensing;
(4) the legal regulations, concerning the advertising of shares of collective investment schemes, of the country where these securities are traded;
(5) insurance contracts;
(6) freedom of the parties to choose the law applicable to a contract;
(7) contractual obligations under consumer contracts;
(8) requirements regarding the form of validity of those contracts that establish or transfer proprietary rights governed by the law of the state of the geographic location of the real estate;
(9) the permissibility of sending unsolicited commercial communications by electronic mail.

508. SG, issue 42 of 17 May 2005.
509. OJ, L 338, 23 Dec. 2003, pp. 1–29.

§3. Distance Contracts

I. General

224. Contracts concluded by electronic means are considered by definition distance contracts. The E-commerce Act and EDETSA are the acts complementing other civil and commercial acts whose analysis falls outside the scope of the current work. Only the most relevant provisions from these acts shall be examined.

II. Law on the Regulation of Distance Contracting

A. Introduction

225. The regulation of distance contracts on a national level is contained in the OCA and the Consumer Protection Act. Articles 13 and 14 of the OCA set out only the general rules about issuing an offer for the conclusion of a contract with and accepting the offer by an absent person. These rules apply to all distance contracts and therefore to all contracts concluded by electronic means. The special regulation of distance contracts and more precisely the special rules regarding the protection of consumers involved with these types of contracts are found in Chapter 4, section II of the Consumer Protection Act.

On a European level, the regulation of distance contracts is introduced in a separate normative act – Directive on Consumer Rights 2011/83/EU of the European Parliament and of the Council of 25 October 2011 (repealing the previous Directive 97/7/EC) on consumer protection with regard to Distance Contracts[510] (Directive on Distance Contracts), which will apply to contracts concluded after 13 June 2014. The new Directive contains common definitions such as 'consumer' and 'trader', and provides for a common set of rules applicable in all Member States, only allowing them to diverge from these rules in a few specific cases. It regulates core information to be provided by traders prior to the conclusion of all consumer contracts, specific information requirements and the right of withdrawal for distance and off-premises contracts, rules on delivery and passing of risk applicable to contracts for the sale of goods as well as certain rules applicable to all types of consumer contracts. The main new elements strengthening consumer protection are elimination of hidden charges and costs on the Internet (paying for 'free' services, such as horoscopes or recipes), increased price transparency, banning of pre-ticked boxes on websites, period of fourteen days for consumers to change their mind on a purchase, better refund rights, elimination of surcharges for the use of credit cards and hotlines, better consumer protection in relation to digital products, a single set of core rules for distance contracts (sales by phone, post or Internet) and off-premises

510. OJ, L 144, 4 June 1997. Amended with Directive (EU) 2015/2302 of the European Parliament and of the Council of 25 Nov. 2015 on package travel and linked travel arrangements, amending Regulation (EC) No 2006/2004 and Directive 2011/83/EU of the European Parliament and of the Council and repealing Council Directive 90/314/EEC OJ, L 326, 11 Dec. 2015, pp. 1–33.

contracts (sales away from a company's premises, such as in the street or the doorstep) in the EU, creating a level playing field and reducing transaction costs for cross-border traders, especially for sales by Internet, etc.

The Bulgarian Consumer Protection Act, though less elaborate on the rules about distance contracts, generally stood close to the previous Directive on Distance Contracts (Directive 97/7/EC). The remainder of the chapter will refer to the Directive previously in force and duly transposed in Bulgarian law. The Directive itself and the corresponding provisions implemented in Chapter 4, section II of the Consumer Protection Act also offered legal definitions of the terms 'distance contract' and 'means of distance communication'. These exclude from the field of application of the law certain types of contracts and determine the minimum information to be contained in the offer for concluding a contract. The said rules also established the consumers' right to withdraw from the contract. Still, there are some weaknesses and inconsistencies of the Bulgarian regulation with that of the currently transposed Directive on Distance Contracts.

226. Article 46 of the Consumer Protection Act enumerates types of contracts to which the provisions regarding distance contracts do not apply. Those contracts coincide to a large extent with the contracts excluded from the field of application of the Directive on Distance Contracts, currently transposed into Bulgarian law.

Pursuant to this Directive, the contracts for regular deliveries of foods are not completely excluded from its scope. The provisions of the Directive are applicable concerning the information to be contained in the offer for concluding a contract, the obligation for written confirmation of the information, the right of withdrawal from the contract and the trader's obligation to execute the order within thirty days from the date of the order. The provisions of the Consumer Protection Act, on the other hand, do not apply to contracts for regular deliveries of foods, beverages, and other goods for daily usage which are delivered by the merchant in case of frequent and regular deliveries to the consumer's home, place of accommodation or workplace. Apart from the above-mentioned rules, both the Directive 97/7/EC and the Consumer Protection Act exclude from their field of application not only contracts for periodic performance for delivery of foods, but also other types of contracts (*see* Article 46 of the Consumer Protection Act).

B. Prior Information

227. Under the Directive 97/7/EC and Article 48 in connection with Article 47(1) of the Consumer Protection Act, the information in an offer for concluding a contract should include detailed information such as the following data categories:

(1) the main characteristics of the goods/services according to the means of communication used and the nature of the goods or services;
(2) name, address and other contact data of the provider;
(2) main characteristics of goods or services;
(3) price of goods or services, taxes and fees included;

(4) cost of postal or transportation (delivery-related) expenses that are not included in the price of goods or services;
(5) cost for using the means of remote communication when this cost is calculated in a different manner from the one specified in the main tariff;
(6) way of payment, delivery and performance of the contract;
(7) consumer's right of withdrawal from the contract and the conditions under which the commodity may be returned/the service denied;
(8) period for which the offer/price remain in force;
(9) minimal duration of the contract – for contracts for permanent or periodic delivery of goods or services, etc.

Article 5 of Directive 97/7/EC and the Consumer Protection Act's corresponding rule obligated the trader to confirm in writing the minimal amount of information to be included in an offer for concluding a contract, except for the additional categories of data.[511] In the written confirmation, the trader must also indicate information on guarantees and support (if present). In cases when the contract's duration exceeds one year, the written confirmation shall designate the means of preliminary termination of the contract.

Independently from the consumer's right to withdraw from a contract within fourteen days of its conclusion or receipt of the commodity (Article 50(1) of the Consumer Protection Act), the Directive on Distance Contracts, and the Consumer Protection Act accordingly, establish an additional term of 1 year and 14 days for exercising the right of withdrawal if the trader has not fulfilled his or her obligation for providing the information about the right to withdrawal (Article 51).

C. Right of Withdrawal

228. Under Article 50(1) of the Consumer Protection Act, the consumer may, without owing compensation and without giving a reason, withdraw from a distance contract within fourteen days as of the date of:

(1) receipt of the goods by the consumer or by a third person other than the carrier and specified by the consumer, or (a) where the consumer has ordered many goods in a single order, which are delivered separately, from the date on which the consumer or a third party other than the carrier and specified by the consumer accepts the last goods; (b) in the case of a supply of goods consisting of several lots or parts, from the date on which the consumer or a third party other than the carrier and specified by the consumer accepts the last lot or part; (c) in the case of contracts for the regular supply of goods carried out over a period of time from the date on which the consumer or a third party other than the carrier and specified by the consumer accepts the first goods;

511. The cost of using the means of remote communication when this cost is calculated in a different manner from the one specified in the main tariff; the period of validity of the announced price and minimal duration of contracts for permanent performance.

(2) conclusion of the contract – for contracts for provision of services and contracts for the supply of water, gas or electricity, where they are not offered for sale, packaged in a limited volume or quantity, and in the case of contracts for the supply of central heating and digital content which is not supplied in a tangible medium.

The Bulgarian legislator, in conformity with the Directive on Distance Contracts, currently introduces several cases where the consumer cannot exercise their right of withdrawal from the contract:

(1) for the provision of services in which the service is fully provided and its performance has begun with the explicit prior consent of the consumer and confirmation by him/her that he/she knows that he/she will lose the right of withdrawal after the contract is performed in full by the trader;
(2) if the object of the contract are goods or services whose price depends on the fluctuations of financial markets, which cannot be controlled by the provider, and which may occur during the term for exercising the right of withdrawal;
(3) if the object of the contract are goods created according to the requirements of the consumer or as a result of an individual order;
(4) for delivery of goods, which due to their nature may deteriorate their quality or have a short shelf life;
(5) for delivery of sealed goods, which are unsealed after their delivery and cannot be returned due to reasons related to hygiene or health protection;
(6) for delivery of goods, which after they have been delivered and due to their nature have mixed with other goods, from which they cannot be separated;
(7) for delivery of alcoholic beverages, the price of which has been agreed upon at the conclusion of the contract of sale, in which case the delivery may be made not earlier than thirty days from the conclusion of the contract, and the actual value of which depends on the fluctuations of the market, which cannot be controlled by the trader;
(8) where the consumer has explicitly asked the trader to visit him/her in his/her home for the purpose of carrying out urgent activities for repair or maintenance; where, on such a visit, the trader provides other services in addition to those requested by the consumer or delivers goods other than the spare parts needed to carry out the repair or maintenance, the right of withdrawal shall apply to those additional services or goods;
(9) for delivery of sealed sound recordings or video recordings or sealed computer software, which are unsealed after the delivery;
(10) for delivery of newspapers, periodicals or magazines with the exception of subscription contracts for the delivery of such editions;
(11) concluded during a public auction;
(12) for the provision of accommodation services, which are not for the purpose of living, transport of goods, car rental, catering services or provision of services related to entertainment activities, if the contract provides for a specific date or term for implementation;

(13) for the provision of digital content, which is not delivered on a material medium, when the execution has started with the explicit consent of the user, who has confirmed that he/she knows that in this way he will lose his right of withdrawal.

229. The Bulgarian legal framework follows the European one as to the establishment of special rules for the cases when, in connection with the contract, for which the consumer uses their right of withdrawal, a credit contract has been concluded.

In this respect, Article 6(4) of the Directive on Distance Contracts, and respectively Article 56(1) and (2) of the Consumer Protection Act, stipulates that when exercising their right of withdrawal, any additional contract shall be considered automatically terminated without the consumer being liable for any costs, benefits and / or penalties other than certain costs explicitly envisaged by the Consumer Protection Act (Article 54(3) and 55). This rule does not apply to certain cases concerning credit contracts.

D. Payment by Card

230. The Directive on Distance Contracts regulates the cases of unauthorized usage of payment cards in connection with distance contracts. These cases are not treated in the present regulation of distance contracts so they need to be included in Bulgarian law.

E. Inertia Selling

231. As far as inertia selling is concerned, the Consumer Protection Act transposes the prerequisites stipulated in the Directive. Article 9 of the Directive, respectively Article 62(1) of the Consumer Protection Act, define inertia selling as supply of goods as well as water, gas, electricity, central heating, digital content or provision of services without a preliminary request from the consumer.

The provisions of Article 9 of the Directive on Distance Contracts, respectively Article 62(3) of the Consumer Protection Act, explicitly prohibit interpretation of consumer's silence as an act of consent in cases of unclaimed deliveries.

Chapter 2. Regulation of Electronic Signatures and Trust Services

§1. Introduction

232. Contemporary EU and Bulgarian laws provide a thorough regulation of electronic signatures[512] by a set of EU regulations as well as national primary and secondary legislative acts. EU Regulation 910/2014 (eIDAS/eIDAS Regulation/ Regulation 910/2014)[513] together with the national EDETSA (previously known as EDESA)[514] are the main legislative instruments, which regulate the legal regime of electronic documents and electronic signatures, the status of TSPs[515] and the rules for provision of trust services.

These acts regulate the usage of e-signatures in both private and public sectors. Usage of e-signatures in the judicial system, by the National Bank, by the Parliament and some other state bodies should be regulated by separate acts. In the private sector, the EDETSA does not apply to contracts for which other laws require qualified written form,[516] or to cases in which keeping a document or a copy has a specific legal meaning, such as for bills of exchange, securities and bills of lading. The law was originally elaborated on the basis of EU Directive 1999/93/EC of the European Parliament and of the Council of 13 December 1999 on a Community Framework for Electronic Signatures (E-signatures Directive)[517] and UNCITRAL's Model Law and subsequently amended in 2017 (including the very title of the act was changed from Electronic Documents and Electronic Signature Act to EDETSA) to reflect the leading role of the EU eIDAS Regulation.[518] Thus, currently EDETSA has a complementary role to eIDAS.

The regulation of particular usage of e-signatures and e-documents could also be found in other primary acts such as the Labour Code[519] and the related secondary legislation,[520] the Tax Procedure Code,[521] the PPA,[522] among others. Certain acts of secondary legislation contain rules for the implementation of EDETSA.

---

512. In view of the real necessity of a contemporary legislative framework for the development of electronic commerce, on the one hand, and the strategic emphasis on the harmonization of Bulgarian legislation with that of the European Union, on the other, the Bulgarian Council of Ministers adopted, by its Decision 679 of 29 Oct. 1999, a Strategy for the Development of the Information Society and a National Programme for the Information Society. One of the most important elements in this strategy is the development of electronic signatures and the security of information exchange and data protection.
513. OJ, L 257, 28 Aug. 2014, pp. 73–114.
514. *See* Introduction, Ch. 5, para. 33 *supra*.
515. *See* Part I, Ch. 3, para. 92 *supra*.
516. The expression 'qualified written form' is defined in the Additional Provisions of EDETSA.
517. OJ, L 013, 19 Jan. 2000.
518. *See* Part IV, Ch. 1, para. 210 *supra*.
519. SG, issue 26 of 1 Apr. 1986.
520. *See* e.g., Ordinance on the Type and Requirements for the Creation and Storage of Electronic Documents in the Employment File of the Employee, SG, issue 40 of 15 May 2018.
521. SG, issue 105 of 29 Dec. 2005.
522. *See* Part III, Ch. 8, para. 204 *supra*.

The eIDAS together with national secondary legislation (OSCPA[523] in the past and now the OLTATSP[524]) establish the legal framework of the activity of the TSPs and the order and manner of terminating their activity; the requirements to qualified certificates profiles; the requirements relating to the information storage for the purposes of provision of services by the TSPs; the requirements to the content, the format, and the sources related to data disclosure by the TSPs; the order and manner of directory keeping; the requirements to the certification bodies and auditors and the procedure for accreditation of such persons by the CRC.

The eIDAS lays down the order and the conditions, pursuant to which the TSPs are subject to supervision, the procedure for initiation of a qualified trust service, the way to be included in Member State trusted lists, the possibility to use EU trust mark for qualified trust services after being included in these trusted lists and the requirements which TSPs must meet.

233. eIDAS and EDETSA regulate the electronic document and electronic signature, as well as the conditions and procedure for providing trust services.

eIDAS and EDETSA regulate the applicability of the electronic document and the electronic signature, not only in the field of obligations and contracts but also in other legal areas. The regulation of the legal significance of the electronic document and the electronic signature is based on the regulation of the written document and the personal signature in civil and administrative law taking into consideration all specificities of the electronic form. Thus, in the application of these acts, all achievements of the doctrine and court practice in the field of proving, contesting, and recognizing written documents and personal signatures can be used.[525]

EDETSA, to the extent these matters are not primarily regulated by eIDAS Regulation, regulates three types of relations. The first type encompasses the relations regarding the electronic document – the concepts of electronic statement and electronic document, the concepts of 'signatory', 'owner', and 'addressee' of the electronic statement, the regime of sending and receiving electronic statements, etc. The second group of relations regulated by EDETSA together with eIDAS includes the relations pertaining to the electronic signature, types of electronic signatures, their field of application, etc. The third type of relations regulated by EDETSA together with eIDAS covers the provision of trust services and other related services, the regime of certificates for qualified electronic signature, competences of the supervisory body, etc.[526]

523. *See* Part I, Ch. 3, para. 95 *supra.*
524. SG, issue 70 of 24 Aug. 2018, in force of 24 Aug. 2018.
525. Dimitrov et al., *Electronic Document and Electronic Signature. Legal Regime*, 35.
526. *Ibid.*, 42.

§2. LEGAL EFFECTS OF ELECTRONIC SIGNATURES

I. General Statement

234. eIDAS and EDETSA have introduced a number of terms unfamiliar to the Bulgarian legal system so far. The equivalence of 'electronic document' to written document is achieved through the term 'electronic statement'. Under the EDETSA, an electronic statement is any verbal statement, or a statement containing also non-verbal information presented in a digital form through a generally accepted standard for the transformation, deciphering, and visualization of information. An electronic document under eIDAS shall be any content stored in electronic form, in particular text or sound, visual or audiovisual recording. The written form according to EDETSA shall be considered observed if an electronic document containing electronic statement has been created. Thus, the national EDETSA currently introduces narrower concept for electronic document in comparison to the one established via the EU regulation.

The eIDAS and EDETSA define three main types of electronic signatures 'basic', 'advanced', and 'qualified'.

Under Article 13(1) of the Bulgarian act in connection with Article 3, item 10 of the eIDAS Regulation, an electronic signature (basic) shall be considered any 'electronic signature' means data in electronic form which is attached to or logically associated with other data in electronic form and which is used by the signatory to sign. The advanced e-signature is defined by Article 13(2) of EDETSA in connection with Article 3, item 11 and Article 26 of the eIDAS Regulation as an electronic signature, which complies with the following requirements: it shall be uniquely linked to the signatory; it shall be capable of identifying of the signatory; it shall be created by using electronic signature creation data that the signatory can, with a high level of confidence, use under his sole control; and it shall be linked to the data signed therewith in such a way that any subsequent change in the data is detectable.

235. In addition to the requirements for the advanced e-signature, pursuant to Article 13(3) of EDETSA in connection with Article 3, item 12 of the eIDAS Regulation, the qualified one should also meet the following requirements: it shall be created by a qualified electronic signature-creation device, and it shall be based on a qualified certificate for electronic signatures. Although trying to stay technologically neutral, in fact the EU and Bulgarian law refer to a particular technology when regulating qualified e-signatures – use of PKI and asymmetric encryption system.[527]eIDAS (Article 25(1)) stipulates that an electronic signature shall not be

527. Under the old redaction of EDESA (now EDETSA), i.e., prior to its amendments introduced to align it the eIDAS, i. 2 of the Additional Provisions used to define 'an asymmetric encryption system' as a system for the encryption of information allowing the creation of cryptographic key pairs that employs a private key and an algorithmically related public key having the following characteristics: (a) the content of the electronic statement can be encrypted with one of the keys, while the decryption can be carried out with the other; (b) through the use of the public key, it can be undoubtedly determined whether the transformation of the original electronic statement has been made by using the corresponding private key and whether the electronic statement has been altered after its transformation; (c) if one of the keys is revealed, it is practically impossible to compute

denied legal effect and admissibility as evidence in legal proceedings solely on the grounds that it is in an electronic form or that it does not meet the requirements for qualified electronic signatures. In addition, as per eIDAS explicit rule of Article 25(2), qualified electronic signature shall have the equivalent legal effect of a handwritten signature. Moreover, a qualified electronic signature based on a qualified certificate issued in one Member State shall be recognized as a qualified electronic signature in all other Member States (Article 26(3) of eIDAS). Recital 49 of the eIDAS Regulation stipulates that it is for the national law to define the legal effect of basic and advanced electronic signature.

In line with that possibility granted by the EU law, national EDETSA defines that both main types ('basic' and 'advanced') shall be equal to a handwritten signature if the parties have agreed so (Article 13(3)).

The Bulgarian legislator's approach concerning the actors involved with electronic signatures was to provide two definitions that are relevant to electronic statements – owner and signatory.[528]

The owner of the electronic statement shall be considered the person on behalf of whom the electronic statement has been performed. This owner could be either a legal entity or a natural person.[529]

The signatory is the person who is authorized to make electronic statements on behalf of the owner of the electronic statement. The signatory could be a natural person only.[530]

II. Use of Electronic Signatures by the State and Municipalities

236. The EGA introduces some rules that explicitly regulate usage of qualified e-signatures for e-government purposes. The act envisages that the integrity and authorship of electronic statements in connection with electronic administrative services is established by electronic signature created according to the legislation applicable in that area (namely eIDAS and EDETSA) unless the law provides otherwise. For the use of electronic administrative services, the EGA requires that certificates of electronic signatures to be issued with accurate indication of the full name of the signatory and when the certificate contains data about the owner – its full name. To use electronic administrative services through a proxy, the principal must authorize him/her under the Electronic Identification Act.[531]

Pursuant to the EGA, a special ordinance is enacted to regulate the rules for obtaining, use, renewal, and termination of electronic signature certificates by the administrative bodies.[532]

---

the other. Currently this provision is revoked, but the very same PKI and asymmetric encryption system still remain the solid foundation on which the qualified e-signature concept is based.

528. *Ibid.*, Art. 4.

529. G. Dimitrov, *Liability of Certification Service Providers* 245 (Saarbruecken: VDM Verlag Dr Mueller 2008).

530. *Ibid.*

531. SG, issue 38 of 20 May 2016, in force as of 22 Nov. 2016.

532. Ordinance on the Certificates for Electronic Signatures in the Public Administration, SG, issue 48 of 23 May 2008.

§3. TRUST SERVICES AND PRODUCTS

I. Introduction

237. The mere use of a private key for signing documents electronically and the corresponding verification with the public key does not guarantee the identity of the signatory. A link is missing between the signature-verification data and the signatory. The role of a trusted third party that could guarantee and certify the link between the public key and the particular person (the signatory) proves to be of utmost importance for the use of electronic signatures in public key infrastructures. This third party is defined in the EU and therefrom in Bulgarian legislation as a TSP.[533] The requirements for its activities are thoroughly regulated by the law.[534]

II. Signature-Creation Devices

238. As specified in paragraph 234, a qualified electronic signature is an advanced e-signature that is created by a qualified electronic signature-creation device, and which is based on a qualified certificate for electronic signatures.[535] For the creation of the qualified signature, the signatory shall use the so-called electronic signature-creation data, which is 'unique data which is used by the signatory to create an electronic signature'.[536] Pursuant to the eIDAS 'an electronic signature-creation device' means 'configured software or hardware used to create an electronic signature'. eIDAS defines also 'qualified electronic signature-creation device' as 'an electronic signature-creation device that meets the requirements laid down in Annex II'. Thus, the special requirements which an electronic signature-creation device must meet to be 'qualified' are determined in Annex II to eIDAS

Furthermore, Article 18 of the EDETSA establishes the so-called secrecy of the data in the trust services, according to which a person other than the owner, respectively the creator, shall not have the right of access to: (1) the data for creation of the electronic signature, the electronic seal and the electronic time stamp; (2) the data for website authentication, and (3) the data related to electronic registered delivery service.

III. Certificates

239. As already mentioned above, the link between the signatory and the signature-verification data is established by means of an electronic document called qualified certificate for electronic signatures. Pursuant to Annex I of the eIDAS Regulation, the qualified certificate shall be an electronic document issued and signed by a TSP that contains the following data:

533. Article 3, item 19 of eIDAS.
534. *See* Ch. III of eIDAS and Ch. 3 of EDETSA.
535. eIDAS, Art. 3, item 12.
536. eIDAS, Art. 3, item 13.

(1) an indication, at least in a form suitable for automated processing, that the certificate has been issued as a qualified certificate for electronic signature;
(2) a set of data unambiguously representing the qualified TSP issuing the qualified certificates including at least, the Member State in which that provider is established and:
   - for a legal person: the name and, where applicable, registration number as stated in the official records;
   - for a natural person: the person's name;
(3) at least the name of the signatory, or a pseudonym; if a pseudonym is used, it shall be clearly indicated;
(4) electronic signature validation data that corresponds to the electronic signature creation data;
(5) details of the beginning and end of the certificate's period of validity;
(6) the certificate identity code, which must be unique for the qualified TSP;
(7) the advanced electronic signature or advanced electronic seal of the issuing qualified TSP;
(8) the location where the certificate supporting the advanced electronic signature or advanced electronic seal referred to in point (7) is available free of charge;
(9) the location of the services that can be used to enquire about the validity status of the qualified certificate;
(10) where the electronic signature creation data related to the electronic signature validation data is located in a qualified electronic signature-creation device, an appropriate indication of this, at least in a form suitable for automated processing.

Strict requirements are provided in respect of the organization and maintenance of the registers of the certificates issued by TSPs.

When issuing a qualified certificate for a trust service, a qualified TSP shall verify, by appropriate means and in accordance with national law, the identity and, if applicable, any specific attributes of the natural or legal person to whom the qualified certificate is issued. This information shall be verified by the qualified TSP either directly or by relying on a third party in accordance with national law:

(1) by the physical presence of the natural person or of an authorized representative of the legal person; or
(2) remotely, using electronic identification means, for which prior to the issuance of the qualified certificate, a physical presence of the natural person or of an authorized representative of the legal person was ensured and which meets the requirements set out in Article 8 of the eIDAS Regulation with regard to the assurance levels 'substantial' or 'high'; or
(3) by means of a certificate of a qualified electronic signature or of a qualified electronic seal issued in compliance with (1) or (2); or
(4) by using other identification methods recognized at national level which provide equivalent assurance in terms of reliability to physical presence. The equivalent assurance shall be confirmed by a conformity assessment body.

The provider must gather information on the facts regarding the identity of the signatory 'with appropriate means'. Such could be: presentation and review by the provider of the identity documents or other documents issued by the respective state or other authorities depending on the nationality of the signatory; visual assurance through comparison with the photographic identifier on these documents; comparison of the personal signature on the documents with a signature made in front of a representative of the provider, etc. Except for identity information, the law requires the verification of other specific attributes about the signatory to be included in the certificate.[537] For instance, data about the empowerment of the signatory, powers of attorney, mandate contracts with direct authorization, minutes with decisions of managing bodies, etc.

Article 26 of EDETSA provides the conditions under which a TSP shall suspend the validity of electronic certificates for a certain period of time depending on the circumstances, but for no longer than 48 hours: First, if there is a reasonable doubt that the activity of the certificate shall be terminated. Second, if any of the following is present:

(1) upon request of the owner, without being obliged to establish the identity or their representative powers;
(2) upon request of a person for whom, according to the circumstances, it is obvious that she or he might be aware of security breaches of the private key, such as a representative, partner, employee, member of the family, etc.;
(3) upon request of the CRC;
(4) in the case of an immediate risk for the interests of third parties or in the case of enough information for violation of the law, the Chairperson of the CRC can obligate the respective TSP to suspend the validity of the certificate.

In addition, certificates shall lose their validity *ex nunc* upon:

(1) expiration of the certificate's validity term;
(2) death or placing under judicial disability of the natural person –TSP;
(3) termination of the legal entity of the TSP without transferring the activity to another TSP.
(4) death or placing under judicial disability of the owner;
(5) termination of the owner's legal entity;
(6) request from the owner after asserting their identity;
(7) termination of the representative power of the signatory in respect to the owner;
(8) establishing that the certificate is issued on the grounds of false information.[538]

537. Dimitrov et al., *Electronic Document and Electronic Signature. Legal Regime*, 163. *See also* eIDAS, Art. 24.
538. EDETSA, Art. 27.

IV. Trust Service Providers

240. Chapter II of EDETSA together with Article 19 and Article 24 of eIDAS regulate in details the requirements, activities, rights, and obligations of TSPs in issuing certificates, providing access to published certificates, and the provision of services for the creation of private and public keys for qualified electronic signatures.

The TSPs shall submit to the supervisory body (for Bulgaria this is the CRC) a notification of their intention together with a conformity assessment report issued by a conformity assessment body. The supervisory body shall verify whether the TSP and the trust services provided by it comply with the requirements laid down in eIDAS Regulation, and in particular, with the requirements for qualified TSPs and for the qualified trust services they provide. If the verification is successful, the TSP is granted qualified status and is included in the respective trusted list.

EDETSA provides that the Council of Ministers shall adopt regulations on the requirements for the activities of TSPs regarding the following: maintaining sufficient funds for securing their activities in compliance with the requirements of the eIDAS and/or insurance requirements, etc.[539]

V. Legal Status of TSPs

A. General Obligations of the TSPs

241. EU and Bulgarian legislation aim at ensuring reliable and trustworthy electronic communication infrastructure, particularly with regard to trust services. Their main obligations and the requirements to their activity are envisaged in Article 19 and 24 of eIDAS as well as in Chapter 3, section II of EDETSA. In addition, Article 21(4) and (4) stipulate that (i) TSPs shall collect and retain all relevant information concerning data issued and received by the qualified TSP, in particular, for the purpose of providing evidence in legal proceedings and for the purpose of ensuring continuity of the service for the term of ten years, whereas such recording may be done electronically, and (ii) TSPs cannot use the collected and stored information for purposes incompatible with those related to their activity.

B. Termination of Activity

242. The procedure for the termination of the activity of TSPs is contained in the OLTATST in connection with eIDAS. The TSP shall have an up-to-date termination plan to ensure continuity of service in accordance with provisions verified by the supervisory body (Article 24(2), item i) of the eIDAS in connection with Article

539. *See* OLTATSP, Part IV, Ch. 3, para. 242 *supra*.

6 of the OLTATSP. The main rule related to the termination of the activity of a registered TSP reads that all certificates together with all documentation may be transferred to another trust service provider.[540] Otherwise, upon the termination of activity of the TSP, the certificates lose their validity and the documentation should be retained by the TSP for ten years.[541] In the latter case, the TSP is obliged to pay indemnification to the users for the termination of the effect of their valid qualified certificates. A TSP having accepted the certificates of a TSP who has terminated his or her activity, shall maintain the certificates until the expiration of their term of validity under the same conditions as upon their issue.[542] A qualified TSP which has taken over the activity of another qualified TSP shall have the right to use the public key infrastructure of the TSP who transferred its activity for the purpose of managing already issued certificates for a period not longer than validity of the last validly issued user certificate.[543]

A TSP wishing to terminate their activity is obliged to notify their users and the CRC four months prior to the termination date at the latest.[544] The TSP shall be obliged to notify the CRC immediately in case of initiation of proceedings for declaring it bankrupt, liquidation proceedings, other proceedings for termination of the TSP's activity or other unplanned termination of a qualified trust service and to publish information on its website, as well as to appropriately inform its users, contractual parties, and other interested parties within the above-mentioned period.[545]

§4. Supervision and Control

243. The eIDAS and the Bulgarian Act put in place an adequate supervisory scheme for provision of trust services. The state body authorized to perform supervision on the activities of the TSPs in Bulgaria is the CRC.[546]

The CRC is an independent specialized state authority, a legal entity with its head office in Sofia and its own budget. The CRC consists of five members and has its own administration. It implements the telecommunications sector policy and the postal sector policy adopted by the Council of Ministers protecting public interests, state sovereignty, and national security. The CRC regulates and supervises telecommunication activities under the terms of the ECA, and postal services under the terms of the Postal Services Act.[547]

540. OLTATSP, Article 9(1).
541. OLTATSP, Article 9(2). .
542. OLTATSP, Art. 10(1).
543. OLTATSP, Art. 10(2).
544. OLTATSP, Art. 7(1).
545. OLTATSP, Art. 7(2) and Art. 8.
546. The scope of CRC powers and responsibilities as national supervisory body for Bulgaria in the area of trust services could be found in Ch. III, ss 2 and 3 of eIDAS and Ch. V of EDETSA.
547. SG, issue 64 of 4 Aug. 2000.

The TSPs that operate and provide services on the territory of the Republic of Bulgaria despite their nationality or place of establishment are also subject to supervision.[548] Control activities constitute regular or incidental supervisions and audits. A supervising procedure could be initiated by the Commission itself at any time despite the submission of complaints. The controls could be carried out by CRC's officials or by designated external auditors, bodies, and laboratories.

244. To ensure compliance with the provisions of the eIDAS and the EDETSA, certain administrative fines and pecuniary sanctions are introduced. For natural persons, these fines range from BGN 1000 (ca EUR 500) to BGN 50,000 (ca EUR 25,000), provided that an act does not constitute a crime. Legal entities are subject to pecuniary sanctions ranging from BGN 5,000 (ca EUR 2,500) to BGN 100,000 (ca EUR 50,000).

548. 'Place of establishment' means jurisdiction under which the entity is registered or established and recognized as such.

Chapter 3. Legal Aspects of Electronic Banking

§1. General Notes

245. This chapter presents a review of the existing legal framework on the national level regulating the bank activity, bank transactions, and transactions carried out by electronic means and the use of electronic money. The effective provisions regulating these matters are contained in: the Credit Institutions Act (CIA),[549] the Payment Services and Payment Systems Act (PSPSA),[550] the DPFSA,[551] EDETSA,[552] the OLTATSP,[553] the ORACVQES,[554] Ordinance on the Procedure for Registration of Certification Service Providers,[555] Ordinance No. 3 of Bulgarian National Bank (BNB) on Terms and Procedure for Opening Payment Accounts, Carrying Out Payment Transactions and the Use of Payment Instruments[556] (Ordinance No. 3), Ordinance No. 16 of 29 March 2018 on Issuing Licences and Approvals for Entry in the register under Article 19 of the Payment Services and Payment Systems Act and on the Requirements for the Activity of Payment System Operators with Finality of Settlement (Ordinance No. 16),[557] Ordinance No. 10 on the Organisation, Management and Internal Control in the Banks (Ordinance No. 10),[558] the Measures against Money Laundering Act,[559] the Measures against Terrorism Financing Act,[560] the regulations for their implementation and for the implementation of the special acts regulating the specific relations regarding electronic banking in the EU legislation such as Directive 2009/110/EC of the European Parliament and of the Council of 16 September 2009 on the taking up, pursuit, and prudential supervision of the business of electronic money institutions, amended with Directive (EU) 2015/2366 of the European Parliament and of the Council of 25 November 2015 on payment services in the internal market, amending Directives 2002/65/EC, 2009/110/EC and 2013/36/EU and Regulation (EU) No 1093/2010, and repealing Directive 2007/64/EC – the E-money Directive.[561]

246. Electronic banking is a term that does not lack ambiguity in the theory of law and economy in Bulgaria. As there is no legal definition of the term, the harmonization of the regulatory framework of Bulgaria with EU legislation with respect to electronic banking depends on the content of the concept of 'electronic

549. SG, issue 59 of 21 July 2006.
550. SG, issue 20 of 06 Mar. 2018.
551. *See* Part IV, Ch. 1, para. 208 *supra.*
552. *See* Part IV, Ch. 2, para. 232 *supra.*
553. *See* Part I, Ch. 3, para. 95 *supra.*
554. *See* Part I, Ch. 3, para. 94 *supra.*
555. SG, issue 15 of 8 Feb. 2002.
556. SG, issue 37 of 4 May 2018.
557. SG, issue 32 of 13 Apr. 2018.
558. SG, issue 40 of 17 May 2019.
559. SG, issue 27 of 27 Mar. 2018.
560. SG, issue 16 of 18 Feb. 2003.
561. OJ, L 267, 10 Oct. 2009, P. 0007 – 0017; repealing Directive 2000/46/EC, OJ, L 275, 27 Oct. 2000.

banking'. In general, the term denotes two main things: electronic payment instruments (electronic money) and the use of information and communication technologies to facilitate customers' access to bank services.

§2. Electronic Money

I. Legal Regime

247. After Bulgaria's accession to the EU, the development of the regulatory framework of the country in the area of electronic money (having been delayed till that time) was optimized, and following the increasing popularity of such payment instruments and of payment by electronic means, a large body of legislative regulation of the governing legal relations was elaborated. As a result of the efforts of the Bulgarian legislator to create legal regulation of the relations in this matter, the following acts were adopted: the CIA, the E-commerce Act,[562] the PSPSA, and the DPFSA. The adopted legislative acts implement the main principles and some of the key legal provisions elaborated in the basic legislative acts of EU law – the E-money Directive, and the E-commerce Directive.[563]

248. Electronic money is an electronic analogue of banknotes and coins, and represents an alternative to the use of bank cards. Therefore, the legal provisions regulating the emission of electronic money and the relations regarding payment by this instrument are to a large extent predetermined by the existing legal framework regulating bank activity and bank transactions. The reason is that payments carried out by electronic money are not a different kind of payment, but a payment carried out in a different medium.

249. The role of banknotes and coins as a common equivalent and measure of the value of all other things rests at the core of the idea of electronic money. The latter is assumed to have all the features of money as a payment instrument: in electronic environment, it can play the role of a universal payment instrument, as it is characterized by anonymity, and does not require any procedures of authentication, identification, and authorization, as required by non-cash payments. The payment itself is effected by 'delivering' the money, and thus transaction expenses are reduced.

250. The established legal framework increases the public confidence in electronic money as a payment instrument that is complied with the specific features of electronic environment. Since electronic money meets turnover needs, their advantages are indisputably appreciated.

251. In this sense, through harmonizing electronic money with the general provisions concerning the bank system, the *acquis communautaire* regulates certain

562. *See* Part IV, Ch. 1, para. 213 *supra.*
563. *Ibid.*

specific issues related to their application, mainly with the purpose of allowing the development of their advantages and avoiding any obstacles to the development of new technologies.

252. The E-money Directive aims to enable the design of new, innovative, and secure electronic money services; to provide market access to new companies; and to foster real and effective competition between all market participants. It focuses on modernizing EU legal rules on electronic money, and especially on bringing the prudential regime for electronic money institutions in line with the requirements for payment institutions of the Payment Services Directive. The Directive distinguishes the normative regulation of computer-based monetary quantities from the ones based on bank cards. Its legal definition of electronic money is 'electronically, including magnetically, stored monetary value as represented by a claim on the issuer which is issued on receipt of funds for the purpose of making payment transactions … [and] accepted by a natural or legal person other than the electronic money issuer'. Payment transactions are defined by Directive (EU) 2015/2366 of the European Parliament and of the Council of 25 November 2015 on payment services in the internal market, amending Directives 2002/65/EC, 2009/110/EC and 2013/36/EU and Regulation (EU) No 1093/2010, and repealing Directive 2007/64/EC as acts, initiated by the payer or on his behalf or by the payee, of placing, transferring or withdrawing funds, irrespective of any underlying obligations between the payer and the payee. The example provided is the 'electronic purse', where users store relatively small amounts of money for making small payments on their payment card or other smart card.

253. The E-money Directive requires Member States to recognize the following categories of electronic money issuer (Article 1(1)):

(a) credit institutions[564] and their branches, where such are located within the Community and the head office is located outside the Community;
(b) electronic money institutions (legal entities that have been granted authorization to issue electronic money)[565] and their branches;
(c) post office giro institutions entitled to issue electronic money;
(d) the European Central Bank and national central banks when not acting in their capacity as monetary authority or other public authorities;
(e) Member States or their regional or local authorities when acting in their capacity as public authorities.

The Member States shall prohibit persons or undertakings that are not electronic money issuers[566] from carrying on the business of issuing electronic money. In spite of this prohibition, electronic money institutions are submitted to a comparatively simpler regime. The legal regulation of electronic money and electronic money

564. Defined in i. 1 of Art. 4 of Directive 2006/48/EC, and their branches – in i. 3 of Art. 4 of the same Directive, and in accordance with Art. 38 of that Directive.
565. Under Title II, E-money Directive.
566. As defined in Art. 2, i. 3 of the E-money Directive.

institutions pursuant to the Directive is subject to requirements differing from the ones of credit institutions, and therefore to some extent it falls beyond the security and strict regulation of social relations within the bank and financial systems. In order to simultaneously meet the requirements for bearer security and protection, and incorporate the specific features of electronic money, the E-money Directive introduces certain amendments to the Consolidated Bank Directive explicitly defining financial institutions exchanging and carrying out other transactions by electronic money as credit institutions. It is emphasized that the traditional means of payment received in exchange for electronic money are not deposits within the meaning of Directive 2006/48/EC, and therefore institutions issuing electronic money are not subject to all the requirements imposed on banks. The European legislator's approach is explained by the fact that the E-money Directive aims at providing a regulatory framework allowing payment by electronic money in compliance with the requirements for bearer security and protection, and at the same time avoiding any obstacles to technological innovations. For this reason, the Commission includes electronic money in bank activity, and at the same time offers regulatory decisions having regard to their specific features and providing a simplified regime.

254. The E-money Directive restricts the business activity of electronic money institutions to the issuing of electronic money and the provision of closely related financial and non-financial services such as administering of electronic money, and the issuing and administering of other means of payment, but excluding the granting of any form of credit. Another type of activity that can be carried out by such institutions is the storing of data on electronic devices on behalf of other undertakings or public institutions. Electronic money institutions shall not have any holdings in other undertakings, except where these undertakings perform operational or other ancillary functions related to the institution concerned. Electronic money institutions are required to have initial capital maintained at the amount of no less than EUR 350,000 (Article 4). The Directive introduces further limitations concerning own funds, the amount and kind of investment that can be made by electronic money institutions. Through prudential supervision, all these limitations aim at ensuring bearer security and confidence to stimulate wider use of this means of electronic payment.

255. Despite strict requirements to the institutions concerned, the Directive points out that banks are not the only possible electronic money institutions.. Therefore, the E-money Directive expressly excludes some of the provisions applicable to bank institutions. For instance, electronic money institutions are comparable to credit institutions, but the provision of funds for the issuance of electronic money is explicitly excluded from the concept of deposit if the funds received are immediately exchanged for electronic money.

256. Regardless of the advantages, and the technological developments enabling electronic money, there are still several issues in their regulation. One example is the legal regime applicable in cross-border transactions. It is usually dependent on the parties' agreement, according to the freedom of contract principle in contracting.. According to the Rome Convention of 1980, it could be the regime of the country of any of the parties to the contract or any other country agreed (Article 2). If nothing is agreed (Article 4), the applicable regime will be that of the party owing the consideration under the agreement. Similar resolutions can be found in the newer Regulation (EC) No 593/2008 of the European Parliament and of the Council of 17 June 2008 on the Law Applicable to Contractual Obligations (Rome I) (Article 3 and 4).

For the purpose of the present study, the following distinction shall be made: payments by electronic money based on electronic money transfers shall be distinguished from payment systems based on certification and debiting of contractual accounts (bank cards) and from payment orders to banks for effecting electronic payment. The latter requires that transactions should be carried out by banks and include by necessity a bank settlement, and prohibit micropayments. In contrast, electronic money overcomes the disadvantages of the aforesaid transactions and can be carried out by other financial institutions as well.

II. Trends of Development of the Legal Framework in Bulgaria

257. The electronic money enterprises are regulated as one of the five categories of payment services providers regulated by the new PSPSA in 2018.[567] There are also several other statutes, listed in the introduction, that form the legal framework of electronic money under Bulgarian law.

258. The CIA regulates the conditions and procedure for licensing, conduct of the business activity, and supervision and winding up of credit institutions, in order to ensure a sound, reliable, and secure banking system and safeguard the interests of depositors, as well as the requirements for disclosure of information by the BNB in the field of prudential regulation and supervision of banks (Article 1, CIA). As defined by the act, credit institutions cover banks and financial institutions. The credit institution (bank) may perform issuance of electronic money if this is included in its licence. The financial institution is a person different from credit institution and investment intermediary whose main activity includes certain exclusively enumerated in the CIA activities, among which is the issuance of electronic money. With regards to electronic money, the chapter of the act has been repealed in 2011,[568] and it is only stipulated that banks and financial institutions can issue electronic money (Article 2(2), i.13 and Article 3(1), i.1), and the BNB creates and maintains an information system about the monetary liabilities of clients towards banks and financial institutions, as well as towards payment institutions and electronic money companies lending credits.

567. SG, issue 20/06.03.2018, in force as of 06.03.2018, last amendment and supplement – SG, issue 12/12.02.2021, in force as of 12.02.2021.

568. SG, issue 101/2010, in force as of 30 Apr. 2011.

259. In Article 1 of the recently adopted PSPSA[569] (in force as from 2018 and last amended in 2021), it is said that the act regulates the requirements for the activities of payment services (PS) providers and the types of PS; the terms and conditions for granting authorization for such activities; the requirements for the provision of information; the rights and obligations of the parties to the PS; the terms and conditions for granting authorization for carrying out activities by electronic money institutions, the payment supervision and so on.

260. Chapter 3 of the act legally establishes the term 'electronic money' as a legal means of payment – an official means of payment in electronic environment. Electronic money is defined in section I of the Chapter, as 'electronically, including magnetically, stored monetary value as represented by a claim on the issuer, which is issued on receipt of funds for the purpose of making payment transactions, and which is accepted by a natural person or a legal entity other than the electronic money issuer', which is in accordance with the definition by the E-money Directive (Article 2, i.2). An individual who intends to issue electronic money as an electronic money institution must, in advance, be granted a licence for it (Article 36(1)), and must have an initial capital of no less than BGN 700,000. It is stipulated, that electronic money can be issued only following the prior receipt of funds of an amount not less in value than the monetary value issued. The receipt of funds against the issuance of electronic money does not represent receipt of deposits or other reimbursable funds, if the funds received are immediately exchanged for electronic money. Electronic money is issued on the grounds of a contract for issuance of electronic money. The contract for issuance of electronic money is concluded in writing, and on the grounds thereof the issuing institution shall emit against payment of a certain amount of money enabling the bearer to effect payments up to the monetary value issued, and the bearer shall pay the issuing institution remuneration for this service.

261. The legislator has also regulated the possibility of buying back electronic money (Article 35). Throughout the whole validity term of the electronic money instrument, the issuing institution is obliged at the request of the authorized bearer to buy back electronic money against cash or by wire transfer to a bank account. Upon buying back, the issuing institution shall be entitled to charge costs only if this is agreed in the contract in accordance with paragraph 3 and if there is at least one of the following conditions: (1) when the buying back is requested before the expiration of the contract; (2) when the contract provides for an expiration date and the electronic money holder terminates the contract before that date; (3) when the buying back is requested more than one year after the date of expiration of the contract. The fee should be proportional to the actual costs incurred by the issuer of electronic money.

262. Payment instruments are used for the purpose of payment transactions carried out by electronic money. A payment instrument within the meaning of the PSPSA (Additional Provisions, §1, i.30) is a personalized device or devices and/or

569. PSPSA, Additional Provisions, Arts 1; 4; 74–75; 77; 112(1), i. 16.

a set of procedures agreed between the PS user and the PS provider and used by the user for the purpose of submitting a payment order. As regards payment instruments, the law provides for obligations of the provider as well as the user of PS. The liability of both user and provider for unauthorized payment transactions is also regulated.

With regard to the funds that have been received in exchange for electronic money, the electronic money institution applies the safeguard measures as specified in Article 23, but funds received in the form of payment by a payment instrument are not subject to these safeguards until they are made available to the electronic money institution in accordance with the execution time requirements or no later than five business days after the issuance of the electronic money (Article 41(2)).

263. Electronic money institutions are payment service providers within the meaning of the PSPSA. PS are exhaustively listed in Article 4 of the PSPSA: services relating to depositing cash money on transactional accounts and related service operations; services relating to drawing cash money from transactional accounts and related service operations; payment transactions, including the transfer of funds to a transactional account of the user at the payment service provider or another payment service provider; payment transactions where funds are part of a credit granted to the payment service user; issuance of payment instruments and/or acceptance of payments carried out by payment instruments; cash money transfers; payment initiation services and account information services.

264. With regard to the legitimate execution of PS and transactions, the BNB is authorized to exercise supervision over payment institutions and other payment service providers with respect to payment service provision, payment systems operating companies and participators, and systems of securities settlement operators with respect to their activity related to payment transactions.

§3. Electronic Banking

265. In contrast to electronic money, the second component of electronic banking has gained a wider popularity in Bulgaria. It traditionally covers card payments and the four distribution channels of e-services: distance banking by means of a personal computer/smart mobile device, Internet (web) banking, as well as telephony (Interactive Voice Response), and GSM Wireless Application Protocol/SMS banking. Two forms of banking services, though not clearly defined, can be distinguished: provision of up-to-date information regarding the account status and payment orders.

266. Regarding the first form (provision of up-to-date information), due to the obligation of banks, pursuant to the CIA and Ordinance No. 3 of the BNB, to provide customers with a certain kind of information, each bank with an e-banking option provides at least information regarding account movements and balance. Electronic banking does not require any special regulation with respect to this particular banking activity. Instead, the general provision of the effective legislation pertaining to information security, customer's identification, and bank privacy when they refer to electronic environment applies. The second component of electronic banking (use of information and communication technologies to facilitate customers' access to banking services) is characterized by the fact that the performed activity falls within bank transactions as stated in effective law, and is therefore governed by the strict requirements imposed on them. After entering in force of the PSPSA, services provided by electronic banking already have the meaning of a main activity, but not of ancillary services and a means of facilitating and stimulating business transactions.[570]

267. Along with the provision of individual customer information, banks also provide the possibility of performing transactions where a distance order of a bank transaction is made by the customer to the bank. However, if the execution of the latter requires conclusion of transactions in electronic environment, specific requirements to the relations between issuing institution and bearer of an electronic payment instrument imposed at EU level need to be observed. On local legal level, this matter is regulated by the Distance Supply of Financial Services Act.[571] This Act regulates the regime of contracts for distance provision of financial services concluded between provider and user. Ordinance No. 3[572] introduces the requirement to conclude a framework agreement for provision of PS between provider and user in compliance with the requirements established by the PSPSA, before opening a payment account.

268. Traditionally, the contract between bank and customer is concluded offline, and the presence of the customer is obligatory. Therefore, 'transfer' refers to an electronic payment order but not to the bank transaction of a contract for bank transfer. Hence, examining that issue, we shall deem the bank transaction 'transfer' to be a service, an operation as represented by the filling of a payment order in electronic form and the sending thereof, thus establishing the grounds of effecting a certain payment by the bank. It should be noted that Bulgarian legislation does not provide for a prohibition of distance ordering of any bank operations by the customer to the bank. However, such an activity should be performed in compliance with certain requirements. Article 2(2) of Ordinance No. 3 requires that 'Payment from bank accounts should be effected only by order of or with the prior consent of the account holder within the amounts and conditions stipulated by the account holder.' On such grounds, in the contract to the customer the bank can stipulate different forms (including in electronic form) for giving a consent or order. Where written form is required pursuant to Article 3(2) of EDETSA,[573] the written form of the document is considered met, if the document is submitted electronically. Should a particular operation require a 'payment document' within the meaning of banking legislation, Ordinance No. 3 provides for the possibility of drafting such a document in electronic form by the provision of Article 8(2): 'The payment order may be provided

570. PSPSA, Art 4.
571. DSFSA, Art. 3.
572. Ordinance No. 3, Arts 2 and 13.
573. EDETSA, Arts 3; 13, Ch. 3, ss 1 and 2.

in written on paper medium or electronically, if agreed between the parties.' Hence, upon active banking, payment documents drafted in electronic form as a result of the use of the electronic banking service shall contain the prerequisites as provided in the sample documents, and correspond to the definition of the term 'electronic document' pursuant to EDETSA and Regulation 910/2014.

269. In order to be binding with the bank, the payment order should be valid – i.e., the payment document should be drafted so that it can serve as payment grounds. As regards to services provided by electronic banking systems, the bank shall use a system having such characteristics that can ensure valid declaration and subsequent establishment of the declarer's consent. Ordinance No. 3 does not provide for any requirements to the kind of document, and in this respect, there are no obstacles to using a document in electronic form. However, the ordinance envisages requirements to the prerequisites of payment documents, among which is the signature of the client. On the grounds of the provision of Article 8(2) of Ordinance No. 3, the requirement that the payment document should be signed by the client's handwritten signature can be met by using electronic signature. This could be qualified electronic signature that is equal by virtue of law to handwritten signature (Article 25(2) of Regulation 910/2014) or (in theory) basic and advanced electronic signatures, which can be equal to handwritten signature if agreed by the parties (Article 13(4) of EDETSA). Fulfilment of the condition for signing of a payment document in electronic form by an electronic signature is necessary, because it is not expressly stipulated in a legislative act that the pressing of a virtual button or another equivalent operation has the legal meaning of a declaration of intention. It must be noted that in certain cases Ordinance No. 3 explicitly requires the usage only of qualified electronic signature, hence, excluding the possibility to use the other two types of electronic signatures. This is the case upon concluding a framework contract for the provision of distance payment services and drawing up a power of attorney (if the party is represented by proxy), when the payment account is available only for initiating electronic payment transactions from a distance. In this situation, a qualified electronic signature may be used in accordance with the requirements of EDETSA and Regulation 910/2014 and a specimen of the signature of the account holder may not be required (Article 5(7) of Ordinance No. 3).

270. Actually, under certain conditions, the use of Secure Sockets Layer (SSL) connection protocol combined with identification before the electronic banking system used by the bank by means of a username and password can be deemed a basic electronic signature within the meaning of EDETSA. These conditions will be present if in the contract for use of the electronic banking system, the parties agree on the following: (1) that the described manner of identification is secure enough for the needs of the relations between the bank and the customer under the contract concluded between them; (2) that the encryption of declarations by a session key, as performed in an SSL session, shall be also deemed a signature; and (3) that the use of a username and password discloses the customer's identity and his or her consent with the declaration.

Even under these conditions, however, due to the lack of any established practice, upon arising of a possible in-court dispute, the bank will find considerable difficulty in proving that the document has been signed by a standard electronic signature. Such difficulties would be overcome if a qualified or advanced electronic signature is used on the grounds of the mechanisms and legal warranties established by Regulation 910/2014 and EDETSA. In fact, most banks have presently established practices to accept electronic orders only where qualified or advanced e-signatures are used.

271. Furthermore, it should be noted that electronic banking is related to exchange of signed electronic information. In order such a signed piece of information to be recognized as a signed electronic document, it should represent a verbal declaration of intention (expressed in words) objectified in electronic form by a common standard for transformation deciphering and visual presentation of information. This means that for the purpose of electronic banking, signed electronic documents exchanged between the bank and the customer shall be in a comprehensible (verbal) form, and be signed by an electronic signature insofar as some problems pertaining to proving and stability of legal consequences from the particular transaction are thus avoided. If these conditions are not fulfilled, upon sending the information signed by an electronic signature an extract from the margins of a filled-in web-form, there is the risk that law enforcement authorities will not recognize the declaration as a signed electronic document. Although at present the sending and processing of information over the Internet is carried out in this manner only, Bulgarian law does not acknowledge it as an electronic document. For this reason, along with the solutions providing the possibility of processing, sending, and storing of such information in databases, parallel functionality for signing and sending of a legible electronic document shall be maintained in the electronic banking system. Alternatively, usage of a secure reader should be provided where signed documents holding structured information are used (e.g., eXtensible Markup Language documents). At the same time, the requirements of Regulation 910/2014 and EDETSA should be observed for acknowledging receipt and storing the electronic document containing a payment order together with the electronic signature, as executed, with a view to preservation of its legal value and thus ensuring the possibility of future reproduction and proof. It should also be noted that, pursuant to Article 2 of EDETSA, the verbal declaration should be presented by a common standard for transformation, deciphering, and visualization of information. If the bank develops a standard of its own, the legislative requirement for acknowledging the verbal declaration as an electronic document will not be satisfied.

272. The next point of significance to banks providing electronic banking services is the customer's identification. It shall be studied in the light of specific features of electronic environment which requires that communications with customers is as limited as possible, and should be carried out from a distance. Security concerning customer's identification in the electronic document flow is ensured by the provisions of Regulation 910/2014 and EDETSA. Technical security is achieved by the establishment of certain legal requirements for generating and signing electronic documents. For instance, with regard to the qualified electronic signature,

Regulation 910/2014 and EDETSA introduce the requirement for the use of asymmetrical encryption system operating by a pair of private and public keys as the most effective algorithmic technical solution for achieving a high level of security. For the purpose of securing the authenticity and integrity of signed electronic documents, the law provides for a scheme of certification verifying the ownership of a particular person over the public key, through the issuing of special electronic certificates by confidential third persons – TSPs.

273. With regard to legal security, Regulation 910/2014 and EDETSA regulate in detail the requirements to the business activity, rights, and obligations of TSPs. Strict rules of issuance of certificates, of provision of any third persons with access to published certificates, etc. are established. In the secondary legislation implementing EDETSA, requirements to the activity of TSPs are specified: maintenance of available means at hand which enable the performing of activities in compliance with the requirements of law; insurance for the term of activity against any damages resulting from any default; availability of technical and technological equipment ensuring the security of operating systems; technical and cryptographic security of processes, etc.

274. On the grounds of the system for guaranteeing the security of electronic document flow as established by Regulation 910/2014 and EDETSA, it can be assumed that 'adequate' identification measures include the examination of electronic signature certificate issued by TSPs. Arguments in this regard can be found again in Regulation 910/2014 and EDETSA which stipulate that a certificate shall be issued only after TSPs ascertain the authenticity of information regarding the key bearer and the grounds of representation.

When using payment instruments (payment orders) because of the prerequisites provided in sample documents, effective legislation provides for minimal means. The reason is that the pursuit of business by using electronic devices is not another kind of activity; it is just carried out in another, non-traditional medium.

275. Relations between bank institutions and users of the service, and above all, the trader's liability for default in payment or unauthorized use of an instrument for distance access are regulated by law. It is provided that in case of unauthorized payment transaction, the payment service provider shall reimburse the payer with the value of that transaction, and, if necessary, restore the balance of the transactional account of the payer in the same condition as before the unauthorized payment transaction. This provision of Article 79(1)–(4) of the PSPSA also refers to electronic money transactions unless the payment service provider of the payer is unable to block the transactional account on which the electronic money or the payment instrument are stored. Besides, the payer is entitled to demand from the payment service provider reimbursement of all the amount of an allowed payment transaction that has already been carried out, if the latter has been ordered by or through the recipient, and the following conditions stipulated by law have been fulfilled: if at the moment of authorizing the execution of the payment transaction the exact amount is not specified, and if the value of the payment transaction exceeds the value expected by the payer with a view to his or her preceding expenses on similar operations, the terms of the framework contract and other circumstances specific for the situation. With regard to the last scenario, the law (Article 82(6) of PSPSA) explicitly provides for the possibility to be exempted from the obligation to reimburse the payer in the following situation: if in the framework contract between the payer and his/her payment service provider it was agreed that the payer will not have the right to refund under, when the payer has given his/her consent for execution of the payment transaction directly to his/her payment service provider and, if applicable the payment service provider or the payee has provided or has made available to the payer information about the forthcoming payment transaction in an agreed manner at least twenty-eight days before the date of execution of the payment transaction. Payment service providers are liable to respective users for reimbursement of all fees paid by the latter and all interests charged as a result of default or inaccurate execution of the payment transaction. Payment service users are also entitled to indemnity of up to the full amount of damages incurred pursuant to the legislation applicable to the contract concluded with the payment service provider.

Chapter 4. Protection of Users of Electronic Services

§1. Protection of Users of Information Society Services

I. General

276. As already mentioned above, the E-commerce Act[574] regulates certain aspects of the electronic commerce, in particular – the provision of information society services. The E-commerce Act is a supplementary instrument to other general legislative measures on consumer protection that specifically apply to electronic services.

Information society services are those services that are usually provided for remuneration, at a distance, by electronic means and at the individual request of the recipient of the service.[575] This definition is in accordance with the definition in the Directive 98/34/EC of the European Parliament and of the Council of 22 June 1998 laying down a Procedure for the Provision of Information in the Field of Technical Standards and Regulations and Rules on Information Society Services[576] and the E-commerce Directive.[577] The online intermediation services within the meaning of Regulation (EU) 2019/1150 are explicitly defined as information society services.[578]

II. Protection in Respect to Commercial Communications

277. The E-commerce Act ensures protection of users of electronic communications by establishing certain requirements for information society service providers. Thus, it protects users against unsolicited, excessive, and unfair direct marketing. Article 5(1) of the E-commerce Act defines commercial communications as 'advertisements or other communications presenting directly or indirectly the goods, services or reputation of the person exercising a commercial or artisanal activity or having a regulated profession'. Under Article 5(2), the independent usage of information giving direct access to the activity of the person (such as the name of their domain or e-mail address), as well as a communication about goods, services, and reputation of the person, information which is gathered by independent and unpaid means, is not a commercial communication.

The information requirements that commercial communications constituting or being a part of an information society service must meet are the following (Article 5(3)):

574. *See* Part IV, Ch. 1, para. 213 *supra*.
575. E-commerce Act, Art. 1(3).
576. OJ, L 204, 21 July 2008.
577. *See* Part IV, Ch. 1, para. 213 *supra*.
578. E-commerce Act, Art. 1(4).

(1) be clearly identifiable as such;
(2) clearly identify the natural person or legal entity on whose behalf the commercial communication is made;
(3) clearly and unambiguously present conditions, if any, for promotional offers, such as discounts, premiums, and gifts;
(4) clearly identify and present promotional competitions or games, and provide easy access to the conditions for participation; and
(5) finally, the commercial communications must comply with other laws regulating information provision.

These conditions have to be observed along with all General Requirements about giving information when procuring services in the information society. In this sense, the content of the commercial communication has to be consistent with the norms on dishonest and deceiving publicity establishing prices and their reduction, etc.

III. Protection in Respect to Unsolicited Commercial Communications

278. Commercial communications may be qualified as solicited or unsolicited. The solicited communications usually pertain to explicit requests of consumers to service providers for information or offers for particular goods or services. The unsolicited commercial communications, on the contrary, are never related to explicit requests for information. Depending on the intensity of legal protection of the users against unsolicited communications, these can be subdivided further into two other types: wanted and unwanted. In all cases of unsolicited commercial communications, the consumer is seen as a passive recipient – he or she receives information for given goods or services that are not specifically requested, but are sent at the sole discretion of the service provider. However, in some cases, the user may have consented beforehand to receive information from the provider for new goods or services by 'subscribing' to monthly letters, new promotions list, etc. Unwanted unsolicited commercial communications are the ones for which the addressee has not given his or her consent to receive in any form whatsoever.

Article 7 of the E-commerce Directive and Article 13 of the E-privacy Directive,[579] are reflected in the content of Article 6 of the E-commerce Act and Article 261 of the ECA,[580] and contain the provisions regarding unsolicited commercial communication.

The E-commerce Act prohibits sending unsolicited commercial communications to users (natural persons) without their prior consent (opt-in regime).[581] Later on, after the transposition of the E-privacy Directive in Bulgarian legislation, the ECA in its Article 261(1) introduces the rule that calls, messages, or electronic mail for the purposes of direct marketing shall be allowed only when a prior consent of the

579. Directive 2002/58/EC on processing of personal data and the protection of privacy in the electronic communications sector, OJ, L 201, 31 July 2002.
580. *See* Part I, Ch. 1, para. 34 *supra*.
581. E-commerce Act, Art. 6(4).

user has been obtained (applies for natural persons). Additionally, this article provides that when prior consent is not required or obtained 'any person who sends messages for marketing purposes, shall provide each user with the option to express their refusal to receive messages' and those persons shall be obliged to comply with that refusal. Finally, sending messages for marketing purposes shall be prohibited when the identity of the sender cannot be established, or the message has an invalid address to which the recipient is unable to send a refusal to receive messages.[582]

Since the ECA was enforced after the E-commerce Act, the former's provisions in respect to protection of natural persons against SPAM shall prevail. Thus, the protection regime of the E-commerce Act shall remain in place to protect legal entities only. In this respect, Recital 45 of the E-privacy Directive rules that the Directive is without prejudice to the arrangements that Member States make to protect the legitimate interests of legal entities with regard to unsolicited communications for direct marketing purposes. Where Member States establish an opt-out register for such communications to legal entities, mostly business users, the provisions of Article 7 of the E-commerce Directive are fully applicable.

Thus in respect to legal entities the Bulgarian E-commerce Act shall apply. Under Article 6(2) of the E-commerce Act, there is no prohibition for sending unsolicited commercial communications (wanted and unwanted) to legal entities, unless they have registered their e-mail addresses in special registries of the legal entities refusing to receive unsolicited commercial communications (opt-out regime). Therefore, sending unsolicited commercial communications via e-mail to legal entities that are not registered is admissible. The registry is public and kept by the Consumer Protection Commission. The providers of services to the information society have to inform themselves regularly about the registered persons. Sending SPAM to registered legal entities is penalized with a fine of BGN 250–1,500 (or approx. EUR 125–750) for natural persons and BGN 500–2,000 (or approx. EUR 250–1,000) for legal entities. In any case, however, under Article 6(1) of the E-commerce Act, the service provider sending unsolicited commercial communications has to make sure the message is unambiguously identified as unrequested immediately upon reception.

IV. Protection in Respect to Concluding of Contracts by Electronic Means

279. By imposing a number of obligations on the information society service providers, the E-commerce Act protects consumers in case of concluding contracts under general terms and conditions by using electronic means.

First, Article 9 of the E-commerce Act stipulates that contract terms and general terms must be provided by the service provider to the recipient in a way that allows the recipient to store and reproduce them.[583]

582. The opt-in regime for natural persons implemented in Bulgarian legislation is pursuant to the E-privacy Directive.

583. This provision is in compliance with Art. 10(3) of the E-commerce Directive.

Second, pursuant to Article 8(1) of the E-commerce Act, the following information must be provided by the service provider clearly, unambiguously and in full prior to the order being placed by the recipient of the service:

(1) the technical steps to follow to conclude the contract;
(2) whether or not the concluded contract will be filed by the service provider;
(3) the technical means for identifying and correcting input errors prior to placing the order;
(4) the languages offered for the conclusion of the contract.[584]

Article 8(2) requires that the service provider must indicate any relevant codes of conduct to which the service provider subscribes and how those codes can be accessed.

Third, the service provider shall make available to the recipient of the service appropriate, effective, and accessible technical means allowing the recipient to identify and correct input errors prior to the placing of the order.

The final step in protecting users is the requirement of information society service provider to acknowledge the receipt of the recipient's order without undue delay and by electronic means.

V. Supervision and Control

280. Pursuant to Article 4 of the E-commerce Directive, taking up and pursuit of the activity of an information society service provider may not be made subject to prior authorization or any other requirement having equivalent effect. In compliance with European legislation, Article 2 of the E-commerce Act guarantees the freedom to provide information society services.

However, supervision and control of information service providers after the commencement of their economic activity is not excluded, and such control ensures higher level of user protection. In addition to the control and supervision powers conferred on the Consumer Protection Commission[585] provided in the Consumer Protection Act,[586] Chapter 6 of the E-commerce Act explicitly stipulates the rights and obligations of the Consumer Protection Commission in relation to e-commerce. Without prejudice to the administrative penalties provided in the Consumer Protection Act pursuant to Article 24a of the E-commerce Act, for non-fulfilment of an order by the Consumer Protection Commission the guilty persons shall incur a penalty of BGN 250–1,000 (ca EUR 125–500), and sole traders and legal entities – a proprictary sanction for thc amount of BGN 500–2,000 (ca EUR 250–1,000); for repeated infringements the penalties double in amount.

584. Pursuant to Art. 10(1) of the E-commerce Directive.
585. *See* Part IV, Ch. 4, §4, 284 *infra.*
586. *See* Part I, Ch. 5, para. 114 *supra.*

In addition, the Consumer Protection Commission's officials are entitled to:

(1) access all documents regardless of their form, directly or indirectly related to any infringement of the E-commerce Act, or the legislation of the EU Member States implementing the requirements of the E-commerce Directive;
(2) order any person to provide information on such infringements known to them;
(3) perform on-the-spot checks.

Additionally, the Chairperson of the Consumer Protection Commission has the right to:

(1) order in writing to the offender to suspend the infraction;
(2) require from the offender to declare that they shall suspend the infraction and, if necessary, to obligate them to make that declaration public;
(3) order the termination or prohibition of any infraction and, if necessary, publicize the order for termination or prohibition of the infraction.

§2. Protection of Users of Trust Services

281. With respect to protecting users by increasing the legal confidence in electronic signatures, Regulation 910/2014 and EDETSA[587] lay down a number of rules.

First, these Acts provide for several statutory duties for TSPs. Under Article 21 of EDETSA in connection with Articles 19 and 24 of Regulation 910/2014, they are obliged to take appropriate technical and organizational measures to manage the risks posed to the security of the trust services they provide, to maintain sufficient financial resources or have an insurance, to use trustworthy systems, to employ qualified personnel, to provide measures against forgery of certificates and theft of data, to use trustworthy systems and products that are protected against modification and ensure the technical security and reliability of the processes supported by them, etc. The TSPs have also the following obligations:

(1) when issuing a qualified certificate for a trust service, a qualified TSP shall verify, by appropriate means and in accordance with national law, the identity and, if applicable, any specific attributes of the natural or legal person to whom the qualified certificate is issued. This information shall be verified by the qualified TSP either directly or by relying on a third party in accordance with national law: by the physical presence of the natural person or of an authorized representative of the legal person; or remotely, using electronic identification means, for which prior to the issuance of the qualified certificate, a physical presence of the natural person or of an authorized representative of the legal person was ensured and which meets the requirements set out in Article 8 of Regulation 910/2014 with regard to the assurance levels

587. *See* Introduction, Ch. 5, para. 33 *supra*.

'substantial' or 'high'; or by means of a certificate of a qualified electronic signature or of a qualified electronic seal issued; or by using other identification methods recognized at national level which provide equivalent assurance in terms of reliability to physical presence. The equivalent assurance shall be confirmed by a conformity assessment body;
(2) before entering into a contractual relationship, inform, in a clear and comprehensive manner, any person seeking to use a qualified trust service of the precise terms and conditions regarding the use of that service, including any limitations on its use;
(3) record and keep accessible for an appropriate period of time, including after the activities of the qualified TSP have ceased, all relevant information concerning data issued and received by the qualified TSP, in particular, for the purpose of providing evidence in legal proceedings and for the purpose of ensuring continuity of the service. Such recording may be done electronically, etc.

In any case, the relations between the TSP and the owner of the certificate shall be settled by a written contract.

Second, the TSP is liable before the signatory as well as before all third parties for damages caused intentionally or negligently as a result of failure to meet the requirements of Regulation 910/2014 (Article 29 of EDETSA in connection with Article 13 of the Regulation). The burden of proving intention or negligence of a non-qualified TSP shall lie with the natural or legal person claiming the damage, whereas the intention or negligence of a qualified TSP shall be presumed unless that qualified TSP proves that the damage occurred without the intention or negligence of that qualified TSP.

Similar to the approaches of other jurisdictions, under national liability rules the TSP shall not be held liable for damages caused by the certificate usage and for the value of transactions exceeding the indicated limits of the certificate. Where TSPs duly inform their customers in advance of the limitations on the use of the services they provide and where those limitations are recognizable to third parties, TSPs shall not be liable for damages arising from the use of services exceeding the indicated limitations (Article 13(2) of Regulation 910/2014). The rule is imperative.

The above rules shall be applied in accordance with national rules of the respective Member States on liability.

Regarding the types of fault within the limits of liability exposure, under general Bulgarian civil law and similarly to other jurisdictions' legislation, exemption of liability can be agreed upon between parties by contract. Releasing or limiting liability for intention or gross negligence cannot be agreed upon (Article 94 of the OCA). In compliance with this general rule and the above-mentioned rules of Regulation 910/2014 on the liability, agreements that exempt or restrict the liability of the TSP for any type of negligence are rendered null and void.

Maintaining available resources, or having an insurance which enables them to meet liability risks is obligatory for a trusts service provider established in or operating in any EU Member State, including Bulgaria (Article 24(2), i. c of Regulation

910/2014). Pursuant to Article 2(2) of OLTATSP,[588] TSP must keep minimum insurance coverage for damages of BGN 600,000 (ca EUR 300,000) or if they have not concluded an insurance contract, they are obliged to maintain available financial resources (cash or cash equivalents) during their activity in the said amounts (Article 2(3) of OLTATSP).

§3. Protection of Users of Electronic Communications Services

282. Under the E-communications Act (ECA), consumers are protected in relation to the provision of electronic communications services. According to i. 17 of the Additional Provisions of the act, electronic communications service means a service normally provided for remuneration, which includes the following types of services: Internet access service; interpersonal communication services and services consisting wholly or mainly of signal transmission, such as transmission services used for the provision of machine-to-machine and broadcasting services. The electronic communications service does not include services providing or exercising editorial control over content transmitted through electronic communications networks and services. From the scope of electronic communication services are excluded information society services that do not consist wholly or mainly in the conveyance of signals over electronic communications networks.[589]

The objectives and principles laid down in the ECA (Article 4(1), i. 4) include, *inter alia*, ensuring of protection of citizens, by:

(a) ensuring connectivity, accessibility and use of very high capacity networks, including fixed, mobile and wireless networks, as well as electronic communications services;
(b) providing the opportunity for maximum benefits in terms of choice, price and quality on the basis of effective competition;
(c) ensuring that the security of networks and services is maintained;
(d) ensuring a high and general level of protection for end-users through the necessary rules, including conditions for the provision of clear information, by setting requirements for tariff transparency and conditions for the use of public electronic communications services and the use of applications and services choice;
(e) taking into account the needs of specific social groups, in particular people with disabilities, the elderly and people with special social needs, as well as the choices and equal access for people with disabilities.

It should be noted that the ECA distinguishes between the terms ‘consumer’ and ‘end user’. Thus, ‘consumer’ (user) means a legal entity or a natural person who uses or requests to use a publicly available electronic communications service,

588. *See* Part I, Ch. 3, para. 95 *supra*.
589. This definition follows the wording of the Framework Directive. *See* Part 1, Ch. 1, para. 36-37 *supra*.

whereas an 'end user' is a consumer who does not provide publicly available communications networks or publicly available electronic communications services. On the other hand, the Framework Directive defines only the term 'consumer' which means any natural person who uses or requests a publicly available electronic communications service for purposes which are outside his or her trade, business or profession.

283. Chapter 14 of the ECA sets out the general rules regarding the protection of end users of electronic communications services. Article 225 of the ECA stipulates that undertakings providing electronic communications networks and/or services to end users must respect the principles of transparency and equality, conforming to the type of technology used, the categories of end users, the traffic volume and the method of payment, and do not allow advantages for certain types of end users or group of users of the same services.

Pursuant to Article 226 of the ECA, undertakings providing public electronic communications services different from machine-to-machine transmission services, provide the following information relevant to the requested service must provide to the consumer, before the latter being bound by contract or an offer for conclusion of contract, the following relevant:

(1) name, seat, and address of management, telephone number, as well as e-mail address and website, if any;
(2) type, description, and main characteristics of the services, including:
  (a) all obstacles to access to emergency call services or information on the location of the calling end user due to lack of technical feasibility, insofar as the service allows end users to generate calls to a number in national or international numbering plan;
  (b) proposed minimum levels of service quality:
    (aa) (aa) for Internet access services: at least information on delays, delay fluctuations, and packet loss;
    (ab) (bb) for interpersonal communications services, where they exerdcise control over certain elements of the network, directly or by virtue dof a service level agreement with undertakings providing access to the dnetwork: connection time, probability of failure, signalling delay;
    (ac) (cc) information that no minimum levels of service quality are doffered, where applicable;
    (ad) (dd) for the providers of Internet access services and the infordmadtion required under Article 4(1) of Regulation (EU) 2015/2120;
  (c) deadlines for activation of the electronic communications service;
(3) conditions and terms for payment of the offered services; the existence of deposits or other financial guarantees paid or given by the end user at the request of the undertaking and the conditions thereof;
(4) detailed information about the products and services, intended for users with disabilities, and the ways for receiving updates of this information;

(5) procedures for consideration and ruling on complaints, requests, and proposals of the end users, as well as means for initiating procedures for resolving disputes, including national and cross-border disputes, in accordance with the Consumer Protection Act;
(6) conditions and procedure for negotiation, determination of the amount and payment of compensations and refund of amounts applicable in case of non-fulfilment of agreed levels of service quality, including, where applicable, explicit indication of the rights of the consumers, which are applied in case of non-fulfilment of agreed levels of service quality, or if the provider has not taken appropriate action in the event of an incident, threat or vulnerability related to network security;
(7) the right of the end users to decide whether to include their personal data in a directory and the types of data, subject to inclusion according to Article 258 of ECA;
(8) actions that the enterprise may take in case of threat or in response to incidents related to vulnerabilities or network security;
(9) information about what personal data are provided before the provision of the service or are collected during the provision of the service, without prejudice to the obligation under Article 13 of Regulation (EU) 2016/679;
(10) maintenance of services for monitoring and control of the costs of the services for access to the Internet and the interpersonal communication services by the consumer, when such have been agreed or such obligation has been imposed, including a notice before reaching the limit volume included in the consumer's tariff plan and when the service included in the plan is fully utilized;
(11) term of the contract and conditions for renewal and termination of the services and of the contract, amounts due for termination, if such are provided, including:
  (a) all requirements for minimum consumption or minimum duration for taking advantage of promotional conditions;
  (b) amounts due in connection with a change of supplier and arrangements for compensation and reimbursement in the event of delay or abuse of a change of supplier, as well as information on the relevant procedures;
  (c) penalties and indemnities related to the early termination of the contract, including reimbursement of costs incurred in respect of terminal equipment and information on the unlocking and reimbursement of terminal equipment;
  (d) information on the right of consumers using prepaid services to a refund upon request of the remaining credit in the event of a change of provider;
  (e) the conditions, including fees, imposed by the provider for the use of the provided terminal device, without violating the right of the end users to use a terminal device of their choice in accordance with Article 3 (1) of Regulation (EU) 2015/2120;
  (f) for package services – the conditions for extension and termination of the contract, where applicable, the conditions for termination of the package or elements thereof;

(12) prices of the provided services and, as far as applicable, the respective prices for activation of the electronic communications service, as well as for all recurring or consumption-related fees;
(13) for Internet access services and for public interpersonal communication services:
  (a) detailed information on the specific tariff plan or plans under the contract: types of services offered, including, where applicable, information on their volume (megabytes, minutes, messages) and others) for the specified billing period, as well as for the price of the additional units of communication services;
  (b) in the case of a selected tariff plan or plans with a predetermined volume of services, the possibility for consumers to transfer any unused volume from the previous billing period to the next billing period, when such an option is included in the contract;
  (c) mechanisms to ensure transparency of invoicing and monitoring the level of consumption;
  (d) tariff information for each number or service to which special price conditions apply;
  (e) for package services and packages that include both services and terminal equipment, the prices of the individual elements in the package, insofar as they are also marketed separately;
  (f) conditions, including charges, for service, maintenance, and customer service;
  (g) the means to obtain up-to-date information on all applicable tariffs and maintenance fees.

The above information shall be provided by the undertaking in a clear and comprehensible manner on a tangible medium within the meaning of the Consumer Protection Act or, when the provision of a tangible medium is not possible, in a document provided by the undertaking which is easy to download. The undertaking explicitly draws the user's attention to the existence of this document and to the fact that it is important for the document to be downloaded for the purposes of documentation, future references, and unaltered reproduction.

The above information shall not be subject to change, unless the parties agree in writing for this before concluding the contract. The information shall be an integral part of the contracts concluded by the undertakings providing public electronic communications services, other than machine-to-machine transmission services, and the consumers, with a view to certifying identity between them and the terms of the contract at the moment of its conclusion. The undertakings must elaborate and publish a price list of services where the prices of the offered services are indicated, as well as price packages or tariffs, and conditions for their use. Finally, the Commission may issue mandatory guidelines to the undertakings with regard to the provision of the terms and conditions and their drafting in a clear and complete form, easily accessible for the end users.

Articles 228, 229, and 229a of the ECA regulate the moment of entry into force of the contract with the undertaking (within seven days after conclusion, unless the consumer has explicitly expressed their wish for the contract to enter into force immediately) as well as the duration and termination of the contract. Article 230 requires undertakings to publish the general terms and any corresponding amendments thereof on their websites and to make them available in their business premises not less than 1month before their entry into force. In addition to the general terms of the contracts with end users pursuant to Article 231a, undertakings must publish on their websites or provide free access to additional information.

Such information must contain, among other things, prices, quality of services, types of services offered, etc. Additionally, in case of amendments in the general conditions pursuant to Article 230(3), end users have the right to end their individual contract without sanctions for a period of one month after their entry into force, when amendments are on the initiative of the undertaking. It may be understood that, if amendments or supplementation of the general terms are in the exclusive interest of the end user or are of an administrative nature and do not adversely affect the end user, or are directly imposed by applicable law, EU law or a competent authority, such right is not applicable. Amendments and supplements may be initiated by either by the undertakings or also by the CRC itself for the purposes of protecting end users' interests. Additionally, the CRC can elaborate model general terms between undertakings and end users which are published on the website of the CRC (Article 234).

Article 237 provides that in case of force majeure, undertakings must take all necessary measures to ensure the fullest possible availability of publicly available telephone services, provided over public communications networks, and access to the Internet services in the event of a catastrophic network breakdown or in cases of force majeure. Undertakings shall secure uninterrupted access to emergency call services as well and uninterrupted transmission of warnings for the population.

Undertakings are liable for non-fulfilment of obligations laid down in Chapter 14 of the ECA. Therefore, end users are entitled to submit signed complaints to the CRC detailing every circumstance in relation to the non-performance of undertakings' duties. End users permanently residing in another Member State, recipients of services provided by undertakings established on the territory of Bulgaria are also entitled to file in complaints. The CRC checks the information in the complaint, requires a written statement from the undertaking and delivers judgment as well as any guidelines to the undertaking for elimination of the infringement.

§4. General Protection of Consumers in E-commerce and with Respect to Sale of Electronic Devices

I. General

284. There is no Consumer Code established in Bulgaria, hence the legal norms regulating the protection of consumers' interests are dispersed in a large number of laws and secondary normative acts. Due to its complexity and taxonomy, a primary importance is to be accorded to the Consumer Protection Act. Other acts important for the protection of consumers are the Products' Technical Requirements Act,[590] the Tourism Act,[591] the Insurance Code (IC),[592] the Penal Code,[593] etc. For the sake of completeness, it is worth mentioning that the consumer protection legislation was supplemented in 2021 with the adoption of a new the Provision of Digital Content and Digital Services and Sale of Goods Act (PDCDSSGA).[594] The PDCDSSGA transposes in Bulgarian legislation Directive (EU) 2019/770 of the European Parliament and of the Council of 20 May 2019 on certain aspects concerning contracts for the supply of digital content and digital services (Directive 2019/770)[595] and Directive (EU) 2019/771 of the European Parliament and of the Council of 20 May 2019 on certain aspects concerning contracts for the sale of goods, amending Regulation (EU) 2017/2394 and Directive 2009/22/EC, and repealing Directive 1999/44/EC (Directive 2019/771).[596] PDCDSSGA regulates the requirements for contracts for: 1. the provision of digital content and digital services concluded between traders and consumers, and in particular the requirements for the conformity of digital content or digital service, the means of protecting consumers from non-provision or non-compliance with digital content or digital service, the terms and conditions for the use of these remedies, and the terms and conditions for modifying digital content or the digital service; sale of goods concluded between traders and consumers, and in particular the requirements concerning the conformity of the goods, the means of protection of consumers in case of non-conformity, the terms and conditions for the use of these means of protection and the commercial guarantees.[597] The PDCDSSGA creates obligations mostly for traders that provide goods, digital content, and digital services to consumers.[598] In line with Directive 2019/770 and Directive 2019/771, the PDCDSSGA defines the said key terms as follows: (1) 'good' is (a) any tangible movable items; water, gas, and electricity are to be considered as goods within the meaning of the law where they are put up for sale in a limited volume or a set quantity; (b) any tangible movable items that incorporate or are interconnected with digital content or a digital service in such a way that the absence of that digital content or digital service would prevent the goods from performing their functions ('goods with digital elements' – examples of the latter are smart home appliances, smart watches[599]); (2) 'digital content' means data which are produced and supplied in digital form – examples of such are computer programs, audio and video files, e-books, as well as digital content that is provided on

590. SG, issue 86 of 1 Oct. 1999.
591. SG, issue 30 of 26 Mar. 2013.
592. SG, issue 102 of 29 Dec. 2015.
593. SG, issue 26 of 2 Apr. 1968.
594. SG, issue 23 of 19 Mar. 2021, in force of 1 Jan. 2022. The act applies to contracts for the sale of goods concluded after 1 Jan. 2022 and to contracts for the provision of digital content and digital services, regardless of the date of their conclusion.
595. OJ L 136, 22.5.2019, pp. 1–27.
596. OJ L 136, 22.5.2019, pp. 28–50.
597. PDCDSSGA, Art. 1.
598. R. Makshutova, What's new in the new Digital Goods and Services Act?, https://www.manager.bg/komentari/kakvo-novo-v-noviya-zakon-za-oblaganeto-na-cifrovite-stoki-i-uslugi?amp, accessed 28 Dec. 2021.
599. *Ibid.*

physical media, such as CDs, DVDs, USB devices, and memory cards;[600] (3) 'digital service' means a service that allows: (a) the consumer to create, process, store data in digital form or to have access thereto; or (b) the sharing of or any other interaction with data in digital form uploaded or created by the consumer or other users of that service.[601] Examples of the latter are file hosting and social media services.[602] The purpose of the PDCDSSGA is not to create entirely new rules, but rather to create special rules for digital products by taking into account their particularities which however are based on the solid foundations of consumer protection laws and principles.[603] From that perspective, the PDCDSSGA is lex specialis in terms of the ConsPA. The PDCDSSGA introduces the requirement for conformity of the digital content or digital service, understood as both subjective and objective requirements for conformity. The subjective requirements for conformity encompass conformity of the digital content or digital service with certain contractual requirements related e.g., to their contractual description, quantity, quality, functionality, compatibility, interoperability, and other characteristics, to being fit for certain purposes, to being supplied with contractually required accessories, instructions on installation, and customer assistance; to being updated as stipulated in the contract, etc. The objective requirements for conformity encompass conformity with the purposes for which digital content or digital services of the same type would normally be used, quantity, qualities, and performance features, the reasonable expectations of the consumer, with being supplied along with any accessories and instructions in line with which the consumer may reasonably expect to receive, with trial version or preview of the digital content or digital service, made available by the trader before the conclusion of the contract, etc.[604] The PDCDSSGA contains rules regarding the non-conformity with the above requirements and the trader's liability in that respect,[605] the means for protection of the consumers provided with digital content or digital service (the right to reclamation, to request price reduction or to terminate the contract),[606] the rights of the trader to modify the digital content or digital service beyond what is necessary to maintain the compliance of the digital content or digital service with the objective and individual requirements for conformity and to claim damages against the person or persons responsible for non-provision or non-compliance of digital content or digital services where the damages are due to an act or omission by a person in previous links of the chain of transactions (right of redress).[607] With regard to the sale of goods, the

600. *Ibid.*
601. PDCDSSGA, § 6, items 18, 3, 1 and 2 of the Additional Provisions.
602. R. Makshutova, What's new in the new Digital Goods and Services Act?, https://www.manager.bg/komentari/kakvo-novo-v-noviya-zakon-za-oblaganeto-na-cifrovite-stoki-i-uslugi?amp, accessed 28 Dec. 2021.
603. *Ibid.*
604. PDCDSSGA, Arts 9–11.
605. PDCDSSGA, Arts 12–15.
606. PDCDSSGA, Ch. 2, s. III and Ch. 4.
607. PDCDSSGA, Ch. 2, s. IV.

PDCDSSGA also introduces rules on individual and objective requirements for conformity,[608] on the non-conformity with the said requirements and the seller's liability in that respect,[609] on the means for protection of the consumers who buy goods such as the right of reclamation (to request repair or replacement of the sold goods), to request price reduction or to terminate the contract as well as on the right of the seller to claim damages against the person or persons responsible for non-compliance of the goods where the damages are due to an act or omission by a person in previous links of the chain of transactions, including omitting to provide updates to goods with digital elements (right of redress),[610] on commercial guarantees,[611] on ADR means for resolving consumer disputes,[612] etc.

The Consumer Protection Act introduces the important elements of the legal achievements in this area. The right of the independent consumer protection organizations to participate in the protection of the consumers' rights is guaranteed by law. The law respects the interests of independent consumer protection organizations to take a stand in the process of elaborating consumer protection legislation and to submit complaints to the administration on the part of consumers with the purpose of protecting their individual and collective interests.

The act introduces in Bulgarian legislation the European directives on misleading advertising,[613] liability for defective products,[614] contracts negotiated away from business premises,[615] common safety of products,[616] unfair terms in consumer contracts,[617] distance contracts,[618] indication of the prices of products offered to consumers,[619] contracts for temporary use of real estate,[620] sale of consumer goods and

608. PDCDSSGA, Ch. 3, Arts 26–28.
609. PDCDSSGA, Arts 29–32.
610. PDCDSSGA, Ch. 3, s. III and Ch. 4.
611. PDCDSSGA, Ch. 3, s. IV.
612. PDCDSSGA, Ch. 5.
613. Directive 2006/114/EC of the European Parliament and Council Directive dealing with Comparative Advertising repealing Directive 97/55/EC, Directive 2005/29/EC, and Directive 84/450/EEC.
614. Council Directive 85/374/EEC of 25 July 1985 on the approximation of the laws, regulations, and administrative provisions of the Member States concerning liability for defective products, OJ, L 210, 7 Aug. 1985, as amended by Directive 1999/34/EC.
615. Council Directive 85/577/EEC of 20 Dec. 1985 to protect the consumer in respect of contracts negotiated away from business premises, OJ, L 372, 31 Dec. 1985 and later repealed by Directive 2011/83/EU of the European Parliament and of the Council of 25 October 2011 on consumer rights, amending Council Directive 93/13/EEC and Directive 1999/44/EC of the European Parliament and of the Council and repealing Council Directive 85/577/EEC and Directive 97/7/EC of the European Parliament and of the Council Text with EEA relevance, OJ, L 304, 22 Nov. 2011, pp. 64–88.
616. Directive 2001/95/EC of the European Parliament and the Council from 3 Dec. 2001 on common safety of products, OJ, L 11, 15 Jan. 2002, as amended by Regulation (EC) No 765/2008 and Regulation (EC) No 596/2009.
617. Council Directive 93/13/EEC of 5 Apr. 1993 on unfair terms in consumer contracts, OJ, L 095, 21 Apr. 1993, as amended by Directive 2011/83/EU.
618. *See* Part IV, Ch. 1, §3 *supra.*
619. Directive 98/6/EC of the European Parliament and of the Council of 16 Feb. 1998 on consumer protection in the indication of the prices of products offered to consumers, OJ, L 080, 18 Mar. 1998.
620. Directive 2008/122/EC on the protection of consumers in respect of certain aspects of timeshare, long-term holiday product, resale and exchange contracts, replacing Directive 94/47/EC, OJ, L 280, 29 Oct. 1994.

associated guarantees,[621] injunctions for the protection of consumers' interests,[622] and the Unfair Commercial Practices Directive.[623,624]

285. Consumer Protection Act defines the following consumer protection bodies:

(1) the Minister of Economy;
(2) the Consumer Protection Commission;
(3) the National Council for Consumer Protection;
(4) consumer associations;
(5) reconciliation commissions for non-court settlement of consumer disputes;
(6) consumer protection units with the communities' administration.

The Minister of Economy is responsible for the elaboration and execution of a consumer protection policy and for the creation of consumer protection legislation. The Consumer Protection Commission at the Ministry of Economy is responsible for implementing consumer protection legislation. The Consumer Protection Commission is empowered to take actions and issue acts regarding infractions of consumer protection legislation, to analyse clauses of contracts offered to consumers, to initiate lawsuits for voiding unequal clauses in contracts offered to consumers, to initiate lawsuits for the prohibition of misleading advertising; and to ensure the observance of the Ordinance No. 3.[625]

In cases of infringement of consumer protection legislation, these supervisory bodies are entitled to impose administrative sanctions on economic subjects.

286. As a whole, neither the Consumer Protection Act, nor other consumer acts can release consumers from responsibility for their own actions. The act protects the sensible consumer, the one that has researched the market and has chosen a visibly reliable trader, who has taken due care to verify the quality of the chosen product before purchase and has procured the documents needed for establishing the content of the deal. The Consumer Protection Act lays down the main rights of consumers protected by law:

(1) right of information on goods and services;

---

621. Directive 1999/44/EC of the European Parliament and of the Council of 25 May 1999 on certain aspects of the sale of consumer goods and associated guarantees, OJ, L 171, 7 July 1999, as amended by Directive 2011/83/EU.

622. Directive 98/27/EC of the European Parliament and of the Council on injunctions for the protection of consumers' interests, OJ, L 166, 11 June 1998, codified by Directive 2009/22/EC, later repealed by Directive 2009/22/EC of the European Parliament and of the Council of 23 April 2009 on injunctions for the protection of consumers' interests (Codified version) OJ, L 110, 1 May 2009, pp. 30–36.

623. Directive 2005/29/EC of the European Parliament and of the Council of 11 May 2005 concerning unfair business-to-consumer commercial practices in the internal market and amending Directives 84/450/EEC, 97/7/EC, 98/27/EC and 2002/65/EC and Regulation (EC) No. 2006/2004 (Unfair Commercial Practices Directive).

624. Consumer Protection Act, Art. 13a of the Transitional and Final Provisions.

625. *See* Part IV, Ch. 2, para. 245 *supra*.

(2) right of protection against the risks of acquiring goods and services that could endanger their life, health, or property;
(3) right of protection of their economic interests when acquiring goods or services, unfair commercial practices and methods of sale, unfair contract terms;
(4) right of compensation for damages caused by defective goods;
(5) access to court and special non-court procedures for consumer protection;
(6) right of education on questions concerning their protection;
(7) right of association with the purpose of protecting consumers' interests;
(8) right of representation before state authorities taking decisions on matters that concern them.[626]

II. Ways of Protecting Consumers

287. Consumers participate in the economy by acquiring from the market various goods and services for the satisfaction of their needs and desires. It is necessary to protect the consumer as economically unequal and commercially inexperienced through adequate legislation adopted in compliance with the numerous international trends and European requirements.

This section contains a general overview of the ways of protecting consumers without scrutinizing the legislation related to the topic, since it falls out of the scope of this work.

A. Right of Withdrawal

288. An important means of protection of the economic interest of the consumer is the legal regulation of some risky commercial practices. The Consumer Protection Act envisages possibilities of unilateral withdrawal from a contract in the cases of:

(1) contracts concluded outside business premises (e.g., in the home of the consumer);
(2) distance contracts concluded by using means of distance communication (letters, catalogues, telephone, electronic mail, fax, etc.).

In such cases, the trader is obliged to inform the consumer in writing about his or her right of withdrawal. The withdrawal can be effected within fourteen days of the date of conclusion of the contract/accepting the goods/services (for certain types of sale contracts) and, if the consumer has not been notified about his or her right of withdrawal – within a year and fourteen days, and if the consumer was notified within one year as of conclusion of the contract – within fourteen days of the date of their notification (Articles 47(1), i. 8, 50, and 41, Consumer Protection Act).

626. Consumer Protection Act, Art. 1(2).

B. General Terms Contracts

289. In cases of concluding contracts under the so-called general terms, the general civil legislation gives an opportunity to adopt individual clauses that override the general ones. Still, in many cases, the consumer is pressed by the circumstances and has to accept clauses that are blatantly unfair. Such unequal clauses included in consumers' contracts are proclaimed void by the Consumer Protection Act unless they are individually negotiated. The Consumer Protection Act contains a list of clauses that are considered void in all cases.

C. Unfair Commercial Practices

290. A crucial way of protecting consumers in general as well as users of electronic services is the regulation of unfair commercial practices that harm consumers' financial interests. Such regulation increases consumers' confidence in the commercial sector and fosters business. Consequently, Bulgaria has implemented the Directive on Unfair Commercial Practices[627] in Bulgarian legislation through the Consumer Protection Act, Chapter 4 'Trade Practices and Means of Sale', section 4. The provisions laid down in Chapter 4 (pursuant to the Directive) guarantee the overall protection of consumers from the unfair practices of unscrupulous traders not regulated by existing sector normative acts (distance sales, sales 'from door to door', consumer credits, etc.).

627. *See* Part IV, Ch. 4, para. 284 *supra*.

Part V. Non-contractual Liability

291. Originating in Roman law, two types of liability are recognized – contractual and tortious (delictual), currently applicable to TSPs.

A dividing line between the two types of liability may be seen in the rules that establish duties, and thus give rise to corresponding subjective rights (so-called primary rules).[628] From this point of view, the duty not to cause damage established in tort law is always directed to everyone, while contractual duties are usually directed towards the other contractual party.[629] Furthermore, entering into a contractual relationship always depends on the free will of the parties, while everyone is subject to tortious duties regardless of whether they are willing to be bound by them or not.[630]

Another difference may be identified with respect to the rules giving rise to liability when the established duties, in tort or in contract, are breached (these are referred to as 'secondary rules'). First, contractual liability usually arises when there has been non-performance of valid obligations, either undertaken in contract or which have arisen under a unilateral transaction. Tort liability arises only when the duty not to cause damage present as a general primary rule is infringed[631] or when such an exposure is explicitly envisaged in particular primary rules.[632] Second, the sanctions, remedies, and possibilities for specific performance are much broader if contractual obligations are not fulfilled. Another divergence lies in the nature of the interest to be protected by engaging liability in contract and in tort. In tort, the interest of the damaged person is to have their *patrimonium* restored to the degree it would have been, had there been no tort committed, that is, to be restored in *status quo ante*.[633] In this respect, tortious liability aims at satisfying negative interest.[634] Contractual liability, on the other hand, shields the creditor's positive interest – the

628. W. Van Gerven, J. Lever & P. Larouche, *Cases, Materials and Text on National, Supranational and International Tort Law* 32 (Oxford and Portland Oregon: Hart Publishing, 2000).
629. This concept gives rise to classification of subjective rights in absolute and relative. *See* Pavlova M., *Civil Law*, 175; *see also ibid.*, 63–67; *see also* the famous case of the Italian Corte di Cassazione Luigi Meroni, 26 Jan. 1971, No. 174, Foro it. 1971-I-245.
630. A. Dugdale, M. Jones & M. Simpson, *Clerk & Lindsell on Torts* (15th ed., London. Sweet and Maxwell, 1982), at paras 1–5.
631. *See* Bulgarian OCA, Art. 45; *see* German Civil Code (or BGB), Art. 823, Juris BMJ 'German Civil Code' www.gesetze-im-internet.de/englisch_bgb/englisch_bgb.html; *see* French Civil Code, Art. 1383, www.legifrance.gouv.fr/affichCode.do?cidTexte=LEGITEXT000006070721 &dateTexte=20091211, 26 Nov. 2009.
632. The criminal codes list comprehensively cases of tortious behaviour that might give grounds for civil liability. In civil codes or laws, there are also sometimes explicitly listed cases of non-contractual liability. *See* Bulgarian OCA, Arts 12, 21(2) and 88(1); French Civil Code, Arts 384–386; German Civil Code, Arts 833–838.
633. P. Howing, *Positive and Negative Interest in Law* 104–113 (Deventer: Kluwer, 1992).

creditor should be placed in the position he or she would have expected to have been in, had the contract been performed fully, accurately, and without delay.[635]

The behaviour of the debtor, and the tortfeasor respectively, under both types of liability could be either action or omission. However, usually tort liability results from the active behaviour of a party, while non-fulfilment of contractual obligations is usually caused by omission.[636]

In some cases of contractual liability (e.g., when damages are agreed beforehand), the value of the actual damage caused may be less than the sum due under the contract.[637] In contrast to tort liability, the damages in some cases of contractual liability are not necessarily an element of the liability corpus.[638]

In contractual law, instruments exist to contractually extend or limit the liability. There is no such possibility in tort.

Finally, further differences may also be identified in the liability for the conduct of others, in respect of such issues as discharge from liability in circumstances of contributive fault, the regime of liability due to default, and prescription rules that are not subject of the analysis in the present work.[639]

---

634. T. Konov, *Grounds for Civil Liability*, 30–34; *see also* T. Weir (ed.), *Complex Liabilities*, in *International Encyclopaedia of Comparative Law*, vol. 11, Chs 125–126 (R. David et al. ed., Tübingen: Mohr, 1976).
635. A. Kalaydjiev, *Law on Obligations. General Part* 339 (Sofia: SIBI, 2001); *see also* W. Van Gerven et al., *Cases, Materials and Text on Tort Law*, 33; *see also* A. Borrows, *Remedies for Torts and Breach of Contract*, 17 (2nd ed., Oxford: Oxford University Press, 2005). As guiding the Principles of European Contract Law (PECL), Art. 9:502 establishes that 'the general measure of damages is such sum as will put the aggrieved party as nearly as possible into the position in which it would have been if the contract had been duly performed. Such damages cover the loss which the aggrieved party has suffered and the gain of which it has been deprived', 'Principles of European Contract Law', www.cisg.law.pace.edu/cisg/text/textef. html. The Principles are not binding but are basic and considered 'First Draft' of the future European Civil Code. *See* 'Short Survey of the Principles of European Contract Law: Introduction to the Principles of European Contract Law Prepared by The Commission on European Contract Law', http://frontpage.cbs.dk/law/commission_on_european_contract_law/survey_pecl.htm.
636. *Ibid.*, 341.
637. PECL, Art. 9:509(1) states that 'where the contract provides that a party who fails to perform is to pay a specified sum to the aggrieved party for such non-performance, the aggrieved party shall be awarded that sum irrespective of its actual loss'.
638. A. Kalaydjiev, *Law and Obligations*, 339.
639. For thorough analysis of the differences between the tortious and contractual liability, *see ibid.*, 338–346.

Chapter 1. Essence of Non-contractual Liability

292. Legal traditions interpret the essence of non-contractual liability through the concepts of unlawfulness and fault. These issues are treated differently throughout Europe. The Bulgarian legal system approach reveals its own *differentia specifica.*

For many centuries, liability in continental civil law was based on the wrongfulness concept.[640] Wrongfulness as a notion is considered to comprise two elements: 'objective' (unlawfulness)[641] and 'subjective' (fault).[642]

Under most European civil law jurisdictions, the two notions are considered to be separate elements of liability. However, fault in a strict sense plays a minor role in most jurisdictions, insofar as it is generally assessed under objective criteria and the types of fault can only increase the burden of liability.[643]

293. In Bulgarian legal theory, unlawfulness is a basic element of civil liability. It refers to the assessment of whether the behaviour of the alleged tortfeasor or debtor-in-fault has deviated from the standard of behaviour required by law. This standard is commonly referred to as 'duty of due care'.[644]

For centuries, the doctrine has seen culpability (in the sense of personal responsibility for reprehensible behaviour) as the essence of fault in civil law. In the course of the twentieth century, this concept changed, and the 'objective' theory has spread throughout almost all legal systems.[645] It provides an objective criterion – the fault should be understood as acting wrongfully, that is, in a course of conduct, whether by act or omission, in a way that is in breach of the duties expected by society from an average citizen carrying out the same activity under the same circumstances as the person whose conduct is assessed.[646] In this respect, fault in civil liability recedes from fault in criminal law, where the rule *nulla poena sine culpa* proves to be the main principle.

---

640. W. Van Gerven et al., *Cases, Materials and Text on Tort Law*, 352.
641. In Bulgarian – *'противоправност'*, in German – '*Rechtswidrigkeit*', in French – '*illiceité*'.
642. In many countries, culpability (*'виновност'*, '*culpabilité*', '*Vershulden*') is considered to be one of the elements rather than fault (*'вина'*, '*faute*', '*Fehler*') itself. In practice, there is no difference in the substance of the concept. In most of the systems, fault is referred to as negligence regardless of whether the person has acted intentionally or not.
643. W. Van Gerven et al., *Cases, Materials and Text on Tort Law*, 353. After thorough comparative research, authors find that under English law, the tort of negligence does not seem to distinguish between these two elements since wrongfulness (breach of duty) is assessed under an essentially objective standard; nevertheless, subjective factors, such as bad or evil motive, may play a role under certain torts. However, even in a legal system such as German law where culpability is still expressly mentioned as an autonomous element in addition to the condition of unlawfulness (German Civil Code, Art. 823(1) and (2)), culpability retains only limited significance at least according to the prevailing conduct theory.
644. PECL, Art. 1:201(1), 'The good faith and fair dealing': 'Each party must act in accordance with good faith and fair dealing.'
645. H. Kotz & K. Zweigert, *An Introduction to Comparative Law* 688–690 (Oxford: Clarendon Press, 1987).
646. W. Van Gerven et al., *Cases, Materials and Text on Tort Law*, 330.

For this reason, it is sometimes considered that fault in civil law is actually that very unlawful behaviour.[647] Thus, unlawful conduct is enough and fault is not a precondition for civil liability to arise.[648]

294. However, in Bulgaria, as in most of the jurisdictions within the EU, fault is envisaged explicitly as an element of the civil liability corpus both for contracts and torts.[649] The same approach is taken by the drafters of the Principles of European Tort Law (PETL).[650]

What is fault under the contemporary civil law doctrine?

Clarification of the notion of fault in civil law is related to the clarification of another notion – 'due care', that is, it is closely connected to unlawfulness as an element of liability.

As discussed, Bulgarian law and most national laws establish as a general model for the conduct of the debtor, both in contractual relations and tort, the duty of care of a 'reasonable person' in the same circumstances.[651] Since the circumstances will differ, the duty of care also differs.[652] In any case, it will be assessed *in abstracto*, as an objective criterion, not connected to the behaviour of a particular person, but rather to the normal, expected, and usual behaviour of people in similar circumstances.[653]

The objective approach to fault also provides an appropriate means to attach liability to legal entities both in contract and tort. A legal entity cannot be regarded, in formal terms, as having mental activity, whether one is talking about tort or contract. That is why legal persons cannot act wilfully when they fail to fulfil contractual obligations or commit a tort. As negligence does not amount to fault in the strict

647. A. Kalaydjiev, *Law and Obligations*, 371.
648. W. Van Gerven et al., *Cases, Materials and Text on Tort Law*, 332.
649. Article 45(2) of the OCA (*see* Part I, Ch. 5, 124), provides that 'In cases of tort the fault is presumed unless otherwise proved.' The OCA, Art. 82 provides that 'If the debtor has acted wilfully, s/he will be liable for all direct and immediate damages.' The German Civil Code, Art. 823 provides that 'a person who, wilfully or negligently, unlawfully injures the life, body, health, freedom, property or other right of another is bound to compensate him/her for any damage arising thereof' and 'the same obligation is placed upon a person who infringes a statute intended for the protection of others. If, according to the provisions of the statute, an infringement of this is possible even without fault, the duty to make compensation arises only in the event of fault'. In English law, the basic rule is often said to be that contractual liability is strict. In *Raineri v. Miles*, 1981, AC 1050, in his famous speech, Lord Edmund-Davies states that 'In relation to a claim for damages for breach of contract, it is, in general, immaterial why the defendant failed to fulfil his obligations and certainly to defence to plead that s/he had done his best.' *See* H. Beale et al., *Cases, Materials and Text on Contract Law* 665 (Oxford and Portland, Oregon: Hart Publishing, 2002).
650. PETL, Art. 1:101(2) reads that 'Damage may be attributed in particular to the person: (a) whose conduct constituting fault has caused it'; PETL, Art. 4:101 reads that 'A person is liable on the basis of fault for intentional or negligent violation of the required standard of conduct.' European Group on Tort Law, 'Principles of European Tort Law', www.egtl.org/principles/text.htm.
651. This notion varies from jurisdiction to jurisdiction; e.g., the Bulgarian law uses the term duty of care of 'the good master' ('добрия стопанин')
652. PECL, under Art. 1:302, reasonableness is to be judged by what persons acting in good faith and in the same situation as the parties would consider to be reasonable. In particular, in assessing what is reasonable the nature and purpose of the contract, the circumstances of the case, and the usages and practices of the trades or professions involved should be taken into account.
653. A. Kalaydjiev, *Law and Obligations*, 366.

sense of the word, but rather unlawful behaviour that falls beneath an acceptable level of care, legal entities would be liable for their negligent misconduct both in contract and tort.[654]

In different cases, the duty of care will have different substance. The duty of care of a trader, for example, is different from that of an ordinary citizen.[655] Thus, the duty of a TSP differs from the duty of the average trader or information technology service provider.

The tortfeasor can neither evade liability by proving lack of knowledge or personal skills; nor financial or intellectual potential. The qualified TSP, for example, cannot say in its defence that it failed to keep the directory of the certificates up-to-date due to lack of knowledge or financial means.[656] Because the model is abstract, it requires a certain level of knowledge, ability, and skills on the part of the members of the business sector to which the debtor belongs.[657] Otherwise, the model would not be applicable. Even though the standard may be particularized by law,[658] the average standard will always be assessed by court.

The law can deviate from this general model by imposing higher or lower standards of care on different market groups.[659]

The law may allow further contractual deviation from the standard of care – the so-called *favor debitoris*.[660] The framework for such deviations should lie, of course, within certain statutory limits, and will not always prove to be possible.[661] Bulgarian law restrains, for example, qualified TSPs from relying on contractual clauses giving exemption from liability. The restraint of such clauses applies in respect not only to intentional (*dolus*) or grossly negligent (*cupla lata*) misconduct,

---

654. *Ibid.*, 371.
655. CA, Art. 302.
656. eIDAS (Art. 24(2), i. b) II provides that the qualified TSP must employ staff and, if applicable, subcontractors who possess the necessary expertise, reliability, experience, and qualifications and who have received appropriate training regarding security and personal data protection rules and shall apply administrative and management procedures which correspond to European or international standards;. eIDAS (Art. 24(2), i. c) envisages that with regard to the risk of liability for damages in accordance with Art. 13, maintain sufficient financial resources and/or obtain appropriate liability insurance, in accordance with national law.
657. A. Kalaydjiev, *Law and Obligations*, 371.
658. For example, E-eIDAS establishes statutory standard of care by enlisting the duties of the TSPs (Arts 19 and 24).
659. For example, under Art. 65 of the Bulgarian Inheritance Act, the inheritor who has accepted the heritage under inventory list, shall take due care for the property as he would have taken for his own property; i.e., he shall be liable for *culpa levis in concreto*.
660. OCA, Art. 94 allows the parties to contractually agree on reducing the liability of the debtor, but not for malice (*dolus*) or gross negligence (*culpa lata*). The German Civil Code, Art. 442 reads that in contract the debtor *may not be released beforehand from responsibility for wilful conduct*. German Civil Code, Art. 443 provides that an agreement whereby the obligation of warranty of title imposed upon the seller by Arts 433–437 and 439–442, is released or limited is void, if the seller *fraudulently* conceals the defect. Similarly, Art. 637 of the German Civil Code establishes a rule that an agreement, whereby the obligation of the contractor as to responsibility for a defect in the work is released or limited, is void if the contractor *fraudulently* conceals the defect.
661. eIDAS, Art. 13(2) (3) and (4) reads that TSPs may impose limitations on the use of the services they provide, given that they duly inform their customers in advance thereof and where those limitations are recognizable to third parties, TSPs shall not be liable for damages arising from the use of services exceeding the indicated limitations.

but also to any kind of negligence (*culpa levissima in abstracto*). It is worth noting that general Bulgarian civil law otherwise allows this.[662]

The debtor/tortfeasor would be considered at fault if he or she has failed to act with due care, regardless of his or her personal subjective attitude towards the reprehensible behaviour or the consequences thereof. In other words, negligence in civil law should not be considered in terms of fault in the subjective sense.[663]

295. Despite the fact that the fault is assessed *in abstracto* as non-performance of the statutory or contractual duties in contrast to the expected due care of the 'average person', the types of fault are sometimes relevant for gauging the extent of the debtor's/tortfeasor's liability.

When speaking of types of fault, the criteria for classification are based mostly on the subjective attitude of the person, that is, the psychological position a person has towards his or her own reprehensible conduct. In such a sense, fault has two elements – intellectual and volitional. The intellectual element reveals the consciousness of the person in respect of the reprehensible conduct, and the volitional element reveals the attitude towards the detrimental consequences.

In this respect, the intentional fault is the intention of the person not only to pursue the course of conduct that breaches the standard of due care, but also to bring about the detrimental consequences.[664]

Negligence means that the person does not foresee the consequences of his or her behaviour as a result of failing to act with due care with which he or she was supposed to act. Some legal systems provide differentiation in view of the consequences of negligence and gross negligence (the negligent behaviour that the most negligent debtor would exhibit).

The other classifications of fault that exist do not seem to be of interest for this research.

The type of fault may play a role, often to increase the burden of liability for the harmful consequences of the wrongful conduct or to deprive the exemption clauses of their effect.[665] In view of the type of fault of the service providers, the legal regime in some countries, and particularly in Bulgaria, might also bring about such an effect.[666]

662. EDETSA, Art. 29, and OCA, Art. 94.
663. A. Kalaydjiev, *Law and Obligations*, 371.
664. T. Konov, *The Notion Unlawfulness in the Area of Delicts under the Bulgarian Civil Law*, 79 (Book 1) *Almanac of Sofia University* 155 (1986).
665. W. Van Gerven et al., *Cases, Materials and Text on Tort Law*, 32.
666. EDETSA, Art. 29 in connection with eIDAS, Art. 13 and with OCA, Art. 82: it could be deducted, for example, that should TSPs have proved to have acted with malice (intentionally), they will be liable for all foreseeable and unforeseeable direct and immediate damages, while for negligence, they could be held liable only for foreseeable damages.

Chapter 2. Liability of Network Operators

296. Under Bulgarian law, network operators may be subjects of civil, administrative, and criminal liability. Since civil and criminal liabilities apply to all persons, and no particular rules could be found to address the liability of network operators specifically, some aspects of their administrative liability will be analysed herein below.[667] The analysed rules will outline the specific liability regime of the network operators.

§1. Liability for Damages Caused During Construction Works

297. Particular rules regulating tort liability of network operators could be found to compensate the damages caused during the course of construction of networks.

The TRA[668] regulates to some extent the liability of the persons involved in the process of construction, *inter alia* construction of networks. The act rules that especially appointed and qualified person should supervise the construction work. This person shall have the functions to guarantee the safety of the construction works and to prevent any damages that might be caused to third parties (both personally and to their properties) as a result from construction works. It is also provided that the persons who exercise construction supervision are responsible for the damages caused due to the infringement of technical construction rules, the normative and the approved projects jointly with the constructor.[669]

298. A particular liability is introduced for network operators in respect to damages caused during the course of network construction or installation to already existing technical infrastructure. Special liability rules envisage that the network operator shall bear the burden to compensate such damage, or any expenses and costs for change of the location of existing facilities, where such are deemed necessary.[670]

§2. Administrative Liability

299. As far as the administrative control under the ECA[671] is concerned, it should be taken into account that there are several groups of administrative infringements, which could give rise to administrative liability. These may result in imposing sanctions such as fines or deprivation of licences.

---

667. *See* Part V, Ch. 2, para. 304 *infra*.
668. SG, issue 1 of 2 Jan. 2001.
669. TRA, Art. 168(1), i. 5 and Art. 168(7).
670. TRA, Arts 73, 82 and 87(4).
671. *See* Part I, Ch. 1, para. 39 *supra*.

The first group of infringements relates to:

(1) developing and exploring public electronic communications networks without a respective licence;
(2) using such networks for the purposes of exploring an individually assigned scarce resource subject to licensing;
(3) providing electronic communications services without proper notification submitted to the CRC when the law requires it.

The sanction that could be imposed is a fine, which may vary from BGN 5,000 to BGN 50,000. (ca EUR 2,500 to ca EUR 25,000). The fine for the infringement of the conditions of a licence can be up to BGN 100,000 (ca EUR 50,000). Some infringements may lead to sanctions where providing of access to or interconnection of networks is not performed in accordance to the statutory order. The administrative sanction will be a fine, which may be up to BGN 15,000 (ca EUR 7,500). In cases of a repeated infringement, the operator may be deprived of the right to provide the relevant electronic communications related to the infringement for a period of one year. The fine for an operator providing public electronic communications networks and/or services, who violates any of the General Requirements of the Regulatory Framework of the ECA and/or any specific obligations, can be up to BGN 15,000 (ca EUR 7,500).[672]

300. The second group of administrative infringements concerns the confidentiality of electronic communications, the provisions regarding the obligatory assistance of network operators for the purposes of national security and the preservation of public order, as well as infringements to the statutory duties for personal data protection in the communications sector. The fine envisaged may vary between BGN 1,000 and 100,000 (e.g., in cases of major public interest – such as of threatening national security) (ca 500 EUR and ca 50,000 EUR).[673]

301. Under Article 330 of the ECA, a fine for putting into operation a radio facility, which is not in compliance with the provisions set forth by the law, ranges between BGN 5,000 and 15,000. (ca EUR 2,500 and ca EUR 7,500).

302. Behaviour that could give rise to administrative liability is:

(1) the non-provision, late provision, or provision of an inaccurate information or documentation to the CRC by the network operator;
(2) the obstruction of the control functions of CRC;
(3) not acting in compliance with an effective decision of the CRC or not performing a temporary obligation imposed by an effective decision. The fine that may be imposed vary from BGN 500 to BGN 1,000 000 (ca EUR 500 and ca EUR 500,000). The amount range is wide, but it should be taken into

672. ECA, Arts 324–326.
673. ECA, Art. 327.

consideration that some of the infringements can be committed by operators with SMP and thus the negative effect to the society could be substantial.[674]

303. Specific fines are introduced for other infringements such as infringements of obligations related to:

(1) performance of protected services;
(2) provision of roaming service not in accordance with the regulations of EU law, etc.[675]

304. It should be taken into consideration that Bulgarian law established two terms pertaining to administrative liabilities – fines and financial sanctions. The term 'fine' is used to address a monetary administrative sanction to natural persons, while the term financial sanctions is used for monetary administrative sanction to legal entities.

674. ECA, Art. 331.
675. ECA, Arts 334a–334b.

Chapter 3. Liability of Service Providers

§1. Liability of Trust Service Providers

305. In view of establishing trust in electronic signatures and other trust services, eIDAS and EDETSA[676] provide specific rules for the liability of TSPs to the signature owner and to all third parties for damages caused by the non-fulfilment of the statutory requirements for their activities and duties.[677]

According to Article 29 of EDETSA in connection with Article 13 of eIDAS, the TSP bears responsibility for damages caused intentionally or due to negligence of a natural or legal person due to non-fulfilment of obligations. Article 13(1) of eIDAS stipulates that TSPs shall be liable for damage caused intentionally or negligently to any natural or legal person due to a failure to comply with the obligations under the regulation (e.g., the security requirements envisaged in Article 19 of eIDAS, the requirements applicable to qualified TSPs envisaged in Article 24 of eIDAS such as maintenance of sufficient financial resources, usage of trustworthy systems, employment of qualified personnel, etc.). The regulation contains rules allocating the burden of proof in case of damage claims against TSPs. The burden of proving intention or negligence of a non-qualified TSP shall lie with the natural or legal person claiming the damage, whereas the intention or negligence of a qualified TSP shall be presumed unless that qualified TSP proves that the damage occurred without its intention or negligence. Article 13(2) of eIDAS contains rule about the possible limitation of liability of the TSPs. According to the said rule, where TSPs duly inform their customers in advance of the limitations on the use of the services they provide and where those limitations are recognizable to third parties, TSPs shall not be liable for damages arising from the use of services exceeding the indicated limitations. The rule is imperative.

In respect to the types of fault within the limits of the liability exposure under general Bulgarian civil law and the laws in many other jurisdictions, exemption of liability can be agreed upon in a contract between the parties. Releasing of liability cannot be agreed for wilful misconduct or gross negligence.[678]

eIDAS clarifies that the above rules shall be applied in accordance with national rules on liability (Article 13(3)). When speaking of liability, maintaining insurance or available resources, which enable them to perform their activities and cover the damages caused by non-fulfilment of their obligations is mandatory for the TSPs (eIDAS, Article 24(2), i. c)).

Another issue of interest seems to be the approach of the Bulgarian legislator to explicitly establish a binding value of the Certification Practice Statement (CPS) and the Certificate Policy (CP) employed by the TSP. Under Bulgarian Law, the CPS and the CP jointly constitute general terms binding the TSP and the owner on contractual grounds. Therefore, any acts, omissions, or failures to comply with the

676. *See* Introduction, Ch. 5, para. 33 *supra*.
677. For thorough analysis on the transposition of Art. 29 of EDESA (now EDETSA) *see* G. Dimitrov, *Liability of Certification Service Providers*.
678. *See* especially the provision of Art. 94 of OCA.

provisions of the CPS and the CP would engage the liability of the TSP on a common civil liability grounds. The general rules could be found in the CA and the OCA.[679]

In respect to the relying party, under Bulgarian law, the CPS/CP is not binding. Therefore, any acts or omissions or failures to comply with the CPS/CP could entail the liability of the TSP on general tort grounds only by using the CPS/CP as a measure and criterion for the due care of the TSP to act. It should be proved that the negligent behaviour of the TSP in discrepancy with the prescriptions of the CPS/CP has caused the damage to the relying party.[680]

The signature owner shall always be liable to the TSP when he/she provides untrue data or fails to provide the data required.

§2. Liability of Information Society Service Providers

I. Overview

306. The E-commerce Act[681] transposes in Bulgarian legislation European Directive 2000/31/EC, known as the E-commerce Directive.[682] It created the basic legal framework for electronic commerce in the EU, removing obstacles to cross-border online services and providing legal certainty to business and citizens alike.

The E-commerce Directive specifies certain instructions to the traders, regarding information that they need to provide to consumers, along with each online sale.

The objective of the E-commerce Act is to create a legal framework to ensure the free movement of information society services, and at the same time, to establish a minimum set of rules to protect the consumers in contractual matters, particularly in respect to the provision of information society services.[683] To achieve this objective, the act imposes certain obligations on the Information Society Service Providers (ISSPs).[684] Infringement of these obligations might cause damages and thus, might attract their liability.

679. *See* especially the provision of Art. 16 of OCA.
680. Communication from the Commission COM (97) 503: Ensuring security and trust in electronic communication, 'Towards a European Framework for Digital Signatures and Encryption', www.swiss.ai.mit.edu/6805/articles/crypto/eu-october-8-97.html, s. 3.2.
681. *See* Part IV, Ch. 1, para. 213 *supra.*
682. *Ibid.*
683. In this respect, the provisions of the Directive are without prejudice to other analysed directives establishing rules for protection of consumers that might affect the TSPs liability. Recital (11) explicitly envisages, that the Directive is without prejudice to the level of protection for, in particular, consumer interests, as established by Community acts; among others, Directive 93/13/EEC on unfair terms in consumer contracts (Directive on Consumer Contracts) and the Directive on Distance Contracts; those Directives also apply in their entirety to information society services; that same Community *acquis*, which is fully applicable to information society services. Thus the Directive complements information requirements established by the above-mentioned Directives and, in particular, the Directive on Distance Contracts.
684. F. Groshieide & K. Boele-Woelki, *European Private Law (1999/2000)*, E-Commerce Issue, Molengrafica 11 (2000).

II. Obligations

307. One of the main statutory duties of the ISSP[685] is to render easily, directly, and permanently accessible the following minimum information to the recipients of the service and competent authorities:

(1) name;
(2) address of establishment;
(3) all details, including electronic mail address, which allow fast and direct communication with the ISSP;
(4) where the ISSP is registered in a commercial or similar public register, the commercial register in which the service provider is entered and its registration number, or equivalent means of identification in that register;
(5) where the activity is subject to an authorization scheme, the details of the relevant supervisory authority.

308. In addition, if trust services refer to prices, the ISSP should indicate them clearly and unambiguously and, in particular, the ISSP should indicate whether they are inclusive of tax and further costs.

Furthermore, commercial communications should comply with the following minimum conditions:

(1) the commercial communication shall be clearly identifiable as such;
(2) the natural or legal entity on whose behalf the commercial communication is made shall be clearly identifiable;
(3) promotional offers such as discounts, premiums, and gifts when permitted in the state where the ISSP is established, shall be clearly identifiable as such, and the conditions which are to be met to qualify for them shall be easily accessible and be presented clearly and unambiguously.

When contracts for provision of trust services are to be concluded electronically,[686] the ISSP should include the following information:

(1) the different stages in the course of contract formation;
(2) whether or not the concluded contract will be filed and whether it will be accessible;
(3) the expedients for correcting handling errors;
(4) the language options for the conclusion of the contract.

---

685. R. Weigenek, *E-Commerce: A Guide to the Law of Electronic Business*, 19 (3rd ed., London: Butterworths Lexis Nexis 2002).
686. Groshieide & Boele-Woelki, *European Private Law (1999/2000)*, 20.

III. Legal Consequences

A. Legal Consequences with Respect to Non-provision of General Information

309. At first glance, it might appear that the non-fulfilment of any of the obligations established for provision of general information would lead to invoking the ISSP's civil liability. Non-fulfilment of obligation for provision of information about the address or the details of the ISSP, for example, would hardly cause direct damages to the recipient of the service and thus would substantiate liability. Even if we assume that the lack of such information would mislead the recipient and she or he would enter into a contractual relationship, nullity of the contract due to infringement of such obligation seems to be an extremely harsh sanction.

It is true that such provisions are set forth for the protection of the interests of the recipients of information society services and hence peculiarities of the relationships were taken into consideration while drafting the Bulgarian Act.[687] Thus, those peculiarities crystallize in mandatory rules when it comes to the protection of consumers, that is, of the economically and knowledgably weaker party to negotiate.

There is a view that the E-commerce Act has left the consequences of non-fulfilment of general information requirements in the civil sphere.[688]

Therefore, the legal consequences in view of the civil relationships and thus the possibility for liability exposure would depend on the general rules in respect to the:

(1) grounds for nullity of the contract;
(2) grounds for voidance of the contract;
(3) grounds for pre-contractual liability;
(4) level of mandatory weight of the general information requirements in view of consumer protection;
(5) general consumer protection rules;
(6) general tort grounds.

The consequences and the liability would differ with each case.

310. Under the E-commerce Act, infringement of parts of general information requirements would lead to nullity of the contract, or to voidance, or to pre-contractual liability, or to contractual liability. For example, non-provision of complete information on the correct prices (Article 4(2) of the E-commerce Act) might lead to the nullity of the contract, as this would mean that no agreement reached on

---

687. Recitals (7) and (11) of the Directive.

688. The argument stems out of Art. 18(1) of the E-commerce Directive. It provides that Member States shall ensure that court actions available under national law concerning information society services activities allow for the rapid adoption of measures, including interim measures, designed to terminate any alleged infringement, and to prevent any further impairment of involved interests. At the same time, Art. 20 rules that Member States shall determine the sanctions applicable to infringements of national provisions adopted pursuant to this Directive and shall take all measures necessary to ensure that they are enforced. The sanctions they provide for shall be effective, proportionate, and dissuasive.

an essential element of the contract.[689] Any damages that have occurred as a result of entering into such a contract should be repaired – the ISSP would be held liable for all direct damages.[690]

At the same time, the lack of adequate information or misrepresentations that has caused the recipient to be misled (Article 4(1) of the E-commerce Act) and thus has made him or her express his or her will on entering into a contract, would not be considered a ground for nullity but rather for voidance of the contract.[691]

Declaring voidance is a subjective right of the person and whether to exercise it or not would depend on the person.[692] Should a person do so, he or she will be entitled to damages.[693]

In both cases above, the nature of the liability invoked would be pre-contractual.[694] Parties never enter into a contract (a nugatory contract is not considered a contract at all) or let alone a void contract (after declaring it void, the contract is considered not to be concluded at all – all consequences are obliterated with reverse effect).[695]

311. Should the infringement of the general information requirements fall beyond the scope of the nullity or voidance grounds, the contract will be valid. However, in such a case, any damage that might occur due to the non-fulfilment of the obligation should give a right for compensation on contractual grounds. The pre-contractual obligations would migrate into contractual liability.[696]

Where there are statutory provisions that might substitute the will of the parties, but the latter is either missing or deviating from mandatory rules, the statutory provisions would apply.[697] For example, Article 67(2) of the Bulgarian VAT Act[698] provides that should no reference in the contract exist on whether the price agreed incurs VAT (i.e., obligation under Article 5(2) of the Directive), the price should be considered VAT inclusive. In such respect, the contract would not be considered void due to the lack of an agreement on its essential element – a statutory irrefutable presumption exists to protect the interests of the contractual party.

312. It becomes obvious that the liability exposure of the ISSP due to non-provision of general information should be evaluated only on a case-by-case basis taking into consideration the seriousness of the breach and the type of general information that has not been provided.

---

689. Article 26(1) of the OCA. Also M. Pavlova, *General Civil Law*, 102 and 151.
690. Article 12 of the OCA. Also A. Kalaydjiev, *Law on Obligations*, 354.
691. Article 27(1) of the Bulgarian OCA: 'It could be declared void a contract concluded due to mistake, fraud, or under threat.' Also, M. Pavlova, *General Civil Law*, 166, et seq. *See* Art. 4(107) of the Principles of the European Contract Law, Art. 1116 of the French Civil Code and §123 of BGB.
692. OCA, Art. 28.
693. A. Kalaydjiev, *Law on Obligations*, 339.
694. OCA, Art. 1: When entering into a contract and during the course of negotiations the parties should proceed in bona fide. Some authors find that the pre-contractual liability is a type of tort liability in cases when it leads to non-entering into the contract or entering into a void contract.
695. M. Pavlova, *General Civil Law*, 126.
696. A. Kalaydjiev, *Law on Obligations*, 101.
697. Article 26(4) of the OCA. M. Pavlova, *General Civil Law*, 131.
698. SG, issue 63 of 4 Aug. 2006.

The possibility of ISSPs to manage their liability by placing clauses on releasing of liability due to non-provision of this information would be restricted because of the mandatory nature of the national rules *vis-à-vis* the civil relationship. Under Bulgarian law, deviation is not possible.

B. Legal Consequences with Respect to Non-provision of Information Before Entering into Electronic Contracts

313. In addition to the general information requirements, Article 8 of the E-commerce Act establishes specific requirements for provision of information that should be communicated to the recipients of the information society services when entering into electronic contracts prior to placing orders.

Parties may not deviate from the statutory rule by agreeing otherwise on releasing of responsibility and thus, on managing liability exposure unless they are not consumers. The provision of Article 12 explicitly restricts such a possibility.

The specific information that should be provided is as follows:

(1) the different technical steps the recipient should follow to conclude the contract;
(2) whether or not the concluded contract will be filed by the service provider and whether it will be accessible;
(3) the technical means for identifying and correcting input errors prior to placing the order;
(4) the languages options for the conclusion of the contract.

Further, except when otherwise agreed by parties who are not consumers, the service provider shall indicate any relevant codes of conduct to which the provider subscribes and information on how those codes can be consulted electronically. The ISSP will also have the obligation to make available the contract terms and general conditions provided to the recipient in a way that allows the recipient to store and reproduce them.

Therefore, the ISSP may not manage its liability by introducing clauses releasing them of responsibility due to non-distribution of such information. This would only be possible when the contractual party is not a consumer.

The analysis of the provision of Article 8 in relation to Article 12 shows that the mandatory level of the rule is of the highest density. While introduced for protection of consumers, any lack of information provision prior to placing the order would lead to nullity of the contract.[699] Invalidity of the contract may undoubtedly constitute grounds for invoking the ISSP's liability.

699. A. Lodder, H. Kaspersen, *eDirectives. Guide to European Union Law on E-commerce* 79 (The Netherlands: Kluwer Law International, 2002).

IV. Liability of Intermediaries

314. Chapter 4 of the E-commerce Act regulates the liability of ISSPs as intermediaries to information. Thus, the act protects users by keeping providers responsible in case of non-fulfilment of certain obligations. It should be noted that the obligations imposed on ISSPs cover the cases where the information society services are provided free of charge as well.

First, in case the information society service consists of the provision of access to or transmission through an electronic communication network pursuant to Article 13 of the E-commerce Act, the providers will not be liable for the content of the transmitted information or for the activity of the recipient of the service provided that they:

(1) do not initiate the transmission of the information;
(2) do not select the receiver of the transmission; and
(3) do not select or modify the information transmitted.[700]

The provision of such service shall include the automatic, intermediate, and transient storage of the information carried out for the sole purpose of transmission in the electronic communications network. In case the information is stored for a period longer than is reasonably necessary for the transmission or one of the above prerequisites is not met, the provider shall be legally responsible.

Similarly, pursuant to Article 14 where an information society service consists in the provision of automatic search of information, the service provider will not be liable for the content of the retrieved information provided that service:

(1) does not initiate the transmission of the retrieved information;
(2) does not select the recipient of the retrieved information; and
(3) does not select or modify the retrieved information.

Additionally, in case the information society service consists of the transmission in a communication network of information provided by the recipient of the service according to Article 15, the service provider will not be liable for the automatic, intermediate, and temporary storage of this information performed for the sole purpose of making more effective the information's onward transmission to other recipients of the service upon their request (caching),[701] provided that:

(1) the provider does not modify the information;
(2) the provider complies with the requirements regarding access to the information;
(3) the provider complies with the generally accepted and widely recognized rules regarding information updates;

---

700. This provision implements Art. 12 'Mere conduit' of the E-commerce Directive.
701. This rule transposes Art. 13 'Caching' of the E-commerce Directive.

(4) the provider does not interfere with the lawful use of technology, widely recognized, to obtain data on the use of the information;
(5) the provider acts expeditiously to remove or to disable access to the information it has stored upon obtaining actual knowledge of the fact that:
   (a) the information at the initial source of the transmission has been removed from the network or access to it has been disabled; or
   (b) a competent state body has ordered such removal.

Moreover, where an information society service consists in the storage of information provided by a recipient of the service pursuant to Article 16,[702] the service provider will not be liable for the information stored at the request of a recipient of the service, if:

(1) the provider does not have actual knowledge of illegal activity or information and, as regards claims for damages, is not aware of facts or circumstances from which the illegal activity or information is obvious; or
(2) the provider, upon becoming aware of that, acts expeditiously to remove or to disable access to the information.

However, the provider will be liable in case of becoming aware of the unlawful nature of the information, or in case of being notified by a competent state body of the unlawful nature of the recipient's activity, the service provider has failed to act expeditiously to remove or to disable access to the information; nevertheless that does not release the service provider from the legal obligation to preserve the information.

In addition, upon request of a competent state body, in accordance with law, the service provider shall submit any information regarding the recipient of the service and the activity thereof. Furthermore, the above-mentioned provisions shall also apply in those cases where a service provider provides access to other persons' information by way of a hyperlink.

Finally, service providers are exempted from general obligation to monitor the information that they transmit or store, or from the obligation actively to seek facts or circumstances indicating illegal activity.[703] However, this is without prejudice to obligations to promptly inform about alleged illegal content or activity or disable access to such content.

315. For the sake of completeness, it must be acknowledged that the above rules regarding 'safe harbour' of ISSPs in terms of their liability for the content processed by them in the course of provision of their services were affected by the latest EU legislation on copyright protection. In particular, Directive (EU) 2019/790 with its Article17 contains specific obligations for the so-called online content-sharing service providers (OCSSP) – a provider of an information society service of which the main or one of the main purposes is to store and give the public access

702. This provision implements Art. 14 'Hosting' of the E-commerce Directive.
703. This provision implements Art. 15 'No general obligation to monitor' of the E-commerce Directive.

to a large amount of copyright-protected works or other protected subject matter uploaded by its users, which it organizes and promotes for profit-making purposes (Article 2(6) of Directive (EU) 2019/790). Certain types of providers are explicitly excluded from this definition, namely providers of services, such as not-for-profit online encyclopedias, not-for-profit educational and scientific repositories, open source software-developing and-sharing platforms, providers of electronic communications services as defined in Directive (EU) 2018/1972, online marketplaces, business-to-business cloud services and cloud services that allow users to upload content for their own use. By virtue of Article 17(1) of Directive (EU) 2019/790, when OCSSP gives the public access to copyright-protected works or other protected subject matter uploaded by its users, this constitutes performance of an act of communication to the public or an act of making available to the public for the purposes of the Directive. Hence, OCSSPs should be obliged to obtain an authorization from the right holders referred to in Article 3(1) and (2) of Directive 2001/29/EC, for instance by concluding a licensing agreement, in order to communicate to the public or make available to the public works or other subject matter. That authorization shall also cover acts carried out by users of the services falling within the scope of Article 3 of Directive 2001/29/EC when they are not acting on a commercial basis or where their activity does not generate significant revenues (Article17(2)). Article 17(3) explicitly clarifies that when an OCSSP performs an act of communication to the public or an act of making available to the public under the conditions laid down in this Directive, the limitation of liability established in Article 14(1) of E-commerce Directive shall not apply to the situations covered by the said Article 17. Article 17(4) describes the cumulative preconditions that must be present for OCSSP to be exempted from liability if no authorization was granted, namely the OCSSP should have:

(1) made best efforts to obtain an authorization, and
(2) made, in accordance with high industry standards of professional diligence, best efforts to ensure the unavailability of specific works and other subject matter for which the right holders have provided the service providers with the relevant and necessary information; and
(3) in any event acted expeditiously, upon receiving a sufficiently substantiated notice from the right holders, to disable access to, or to remove from their websites, the notified works or other subject matter, and made best efforts to prevent their future uploads in accordance with (2).

Directive 2019/790 (Article 17(6)) softens the above requirements for start-ups, namely for OCSSPs the services of which have been available to the public in the EU for less than three years and which have an annual turnover below EUR 10 million, the conditions under the liability regime set out in Article 17(4) are limited to (1) making best efforts to obtain an authorization and to (2) acting expeditiously, upon receiving a sufficiently substantiated notice, to disable access to the notified works or other subject matter or to remove those works or other subject matter from their websites. OCSSPs with average number of monthly unique visitors of exceeding 5 million, calculated on the basis of the previous calendar year, shall also demonstrate that they have made best efforts to prevent further uploads of the notified works and other subject matter for which the right holders have provided relevant and necessary information. The application of the above rules as per the Directive shall not lead to any general monitoring obligation (Article17(8)).

The said Article 17 was probably the most controversial provision in the new Copyright Directive (EU) 2019/790. It still remains unclear how these requirements will be met in practice, as this is a major shift in the existing liability regime of ISSPs in terms of illegal content.[704] As of the moment of drafting of the present analysis, the rules of Directive (EU) 2019/790 have not been transposed in Bulgarian legislation yet.[705]

§3. Liability of Intermediaries to Electronic Statements

316. Bulgarian legislation regulates the activity and thus the liability of a particular type of TSP, the so-called Intermediary to Electronic Statements (IES). The regulation could be found in Article 6 of EDETSA. The figure of the IES is borrowed from the UNCITRAL's Model Law.[706] Under EDETSA, the term 'intermediary' has a different meaning from the one adopted in other normative acts.[707]

The intermediary of an electronic statement is a person, who upon assignment by the principal (owner), signatory or addressee sends, receives, records, and/or stores electronic statements or performs other services, related to them, (Article 6(1) of EDETSA). Intermediaries are, for instance, e-mail services providers, mobile operators for messages sent via mobile phones (SMS), etc. As the interpretation of Article 6(1) leads us to the conclusion that all owners are also addressees of the electronic statements (because the addressee is the person 'receiving' the statement), then under EDETSA an intermediary is also a person who receives, records, and stores an electronic statement by mandate from the addressee.[708]

It is possible that an electronic statement be made without an intermediary, for example, when a person sends electronic messages via Skype or some other standardized protocol/method for direct connectivity between computer systems (peer-to-peer).

The intermediary may provide other services as well – formatting, translation, authentication, as well as provision of services related to the security of electronic statements. The intermediary may be a trader if they meet the requirements of Article 1 of the CA, but it is not obligatory. The intermediary is a person different

704. For a detailed commentary on Art. 17 of Directive 2019/790 *see* E. Rosati, *Copyright in the Digital Single Market: Article-by-Article Commentary to the Provisions of Directive 2019/790*, Oxford, Oxford University Press, 2021, pp. 301–359.

705. *See* Bill for Amendment and Supplement to the CRRA, published for public consultation on 15.09.2021, but not adopted yet by the National Assembly: https://www.strategy.bg/PublicConsultations/View.aspx?lang=bg-BG&Id=6348, accessed 1 Dec. 2021.

706. *See* Part IV, Ch. 1, para. 214 *supra*.

707. CA, Art. 49–51.

708. G. Dimitrov et al., *Electronic Document and Electronic Signature. Commentary*, 8.

from the signatory, the owner, and the addressee of the electronic statement. Still, there is no obstacle for the intermediary to be a signatory, an owner, or an addressee in other electronic statements.[709]

317. EDETSA introduces an obligatory minimum of imperative requirements necessary for the provision of services by the intermediary. First, the intermediary shall dispose of technical and technological equipment ensuring reliability of the systems used.[710] The intermediary shall have not only the necessary technical equipment, but also the respective technology.

Second, in order to be able to provide their services, the intermediary shall manage experienced and qualified staff with the necessary level of expertise.[711] The intermediary has the obligation to ensure conditions for the exact determination of the time and source of the transmitted electronic statement.[712] This is needed because the statement may have legal consequences. The latter rule is relative and is applicable while taking into consideration the requirements of the turnover and the accessible technical and technological means.[713] The intermediary is under the obligation to use reliable equipment and a technology, permitting that the information about the time and source of the electronic statements be stored for a period of one year.[714] The information may be recorded and stored in journals or log files, archived after a certain period of time. The law shall not be infringed if the information is recorded on one media and is afterwards transferred to another one – for example from the hard disk of a computer to an optic disk. The one-year term is a minimal one.[715]

318. The infringement of their obligations is a ground for engaging the intermediary's civil liability.[716] This liability may be contractual – to the owner and the addressee of the statement, or tort – for damages inflicted on third parties.[717]

709. *Ibid.*, 9.
710. EDETSA, Art. 6(2), i. 1.
711. EDETSA, Art. 6(2), i. 2.
712. EDETSA, Art. 6(2), i. 3.
713. Dimitrov et al., *Electronic Document and Electronic Signature. Legal Regime*, 8.
714. EDETSA, Art. 6(2), i. 4 and 5.
715. The non-registration of information, respectively its storage for a lesser period, is a crime under Art. 319f of the Penal Code. This rule is confusing having in mind the fact that learning the secret of the private key is not incriminated – an action with a much higher level of public risk.
716. EDETSA, Art. 6(3).
717. G. Dimitrov et al., *Electronic Document and Electronic Signature. Commentary*, 8.

Chapter 4. Product Liability

319. In general, product liability refers to the liability of parties for damage caused by a product. This liability can be based either on a contract or on tort depending on whether a contractual relationship between the parties has arisen. In most of cases, no direct contractual relationship between the manufacturer of a product and the end consumer exists. It should also be considered that basing product liability on contract law can lead to liability derogations or limitations. Nevertheless, tort law cannot adequately provide protection of users' interests as they should prove that the manufacturer caused the damage either wilfully or negligently. Therefore, the basic provisions of contract or tort law do not represent by themselves an adequate mechanism for protection of consumers' interests. Specific rules introducing strict liabilities in deviation to the general national liability rules are enacted on an EU law, and are transposed in national legislations.

320. The legal framework of product liability in the field of electronic commerce could be found in the E-commerce Directive[718] and Council Directive 85/374/EEC of 25 July 1985 on the approximation of the laws, regulations, and administrative provisions of the Member States concerning liability for defective products.[719] The national legislation is dispersed between different legislative acts – the Consumer Protection Act, some specific provisions of the Tourism Act, the Consumer Credit Act,[720] the Tobacco and Related Products Act,[721] and other acts.

321. First of all, it should be considered that Directive 85/374/EEC provides that 'the existing divergences may distort competition and affect the movement of goods within the common market and entail a differing degree of protection of the consumer against damage caused by a defective product to his/her health or property'. Therefore, the Directive prohibits Member States to maintain higher levels of protection than those established by the Directive itself. These principles are entailed in the Bulgarian Consumer Protection Act. The Directive applies to movables which have been industrially produced, as well as movables incorporated into another movable or into an immovable, and establishes the principle of objective liability or liability without fault of the producer in cases of damage caused by a defective product. There is joint liability if more than one person is responsible for the same damage.

Before the enactment of the Consumer Protection Act, the product liability was regulated by the Consumers Protection and Trade Rules Act,[722] which provided the legal definition of a 'defect' as 'a fault which does not provide the safety of the product or its fitness to serve upon what has been agreed or by its usual designation'. The new Consumer Protection Act does not reproduce this definition, but states that the product is defective when it does not meet the generally accepted

718. *See* Part IV, Ch. 1, para. 213 *supra*.
719. OJ, L210, 7 Aug. 1985, as amended by Directive 1999/34/EC.
720. SG, issue 18 of 05 Mar. 2010, in force as of 12 May 2010.
721. SG, issue 101 of 30 Nov. 1993.
722. SG, issue 30 of 2 Apr. 1999.

requirements for usual use.[723] At the same time, all circumstances related to the presentation of the product in relation to quality, quantity, name, kind, ingredients, durability, specific characteristics, usual and possible use, advertisement of the product, and the information presented about it should be considered. The moment of the product's entry into circulation is also relevant. At the same time, a product cannot be considered defective for the only reason that afterwards another product with better indices has been put in circulation.[724]

322. The range of the object scope of the Consumer Protection Act is marked within the definitions given for a 'product' and 'service'. 'Product' is defined as movable tangible property, with the exception of the items sold in case of compulsory execution or through other measures by bodies authorized by law, as well as items abandoned or confiscated in favour of the state, announced for sale by state bodies. Goods are also water, gas, and electricity, when offered for sale, packaged in a limited volume or in a certain quantity. 'Service' is defined as 'each material or intellectual activity which is performed in an independent manner, is designated for another person, and is not a main object of transfer of a possession over a belonging'.[725]

323. Thus, it can be concluded that the material scope of the act is focused on the compensation of damages based upon the sale and provision of movable goods and services. The law explicitly provides that electricity is a product. Article 130 of the Consumer Protection Act provides a wider definition of 'product': each movable belonging, no matter whether it is a part of another movable or immovable belonging, including agricultural and stock-breeding materials and products, which have not been processed through initial treatment or manufacturing.[726]

324. The success of claims for defective products can be guaranteed only in case that it is clear who the manufacturer is, or who the importer, dealer, or distributor of the definite product or service is.[727] When more than one manufacturer, respectively importers, dealers, or distributors are involved, their liability shall be joint.[728] The law treats as producers those who present themselves as such, for example, affixing their name, trade name, trademark, commercial name, etc. If the manufacturer or importer cannot be identified, liability is imposed on the distributors of the product.[729] For the purpose of identifying manufacturers, respectively other responsible persons, the Consumer Protection Act introduces the obligation for proper product labelling.[730]

---

723. Consumer Protection Act, Art. 132(1) and (2).
724. *Ibid.*
725. Consumer Protection Act, Additional Provisions, i. 13 and 14.
726. Consumer Protection Act, Art. 130(2).
727. Consumer Protection Act, Additional Provisions, i. 2–5.
728. Consumer Protection Act, Art. 130. (3) or (4) and Art. 135.
729. Consumer Protection Act, Art. 134.
730. Consumer Protection Act, Arts 9–12.

325. Distributors or dealers of the product can be released of liability if within a fourteen-day term they present information about the name and the address of the manufacturer, the importer, or the person who has supplied the product. At the same time, distributors or dealers cannot refer the injured person to a person outside the Republic of Bulgaria.[731]

326. As it is explicitly provided by the Consumer Protection Act, the manufacturer shall be subject to liability for the damages caused by their product, irrespective of whether they have a fault for or have caused the defect.[732] The manufacturer shall bear the liability for the defect even when the product is manufactured in accordance with all existing standards and good practice or its putting into circulation is a result of an admission issued by an administrative authority.[733]

327. The above-mentioned provisions should be interpreted in the sense that the liability of the manufacturer is related to any kind of fault, insofar as Article 137 of the Consumer Protection Act specifies several grounds upon which the manufacturer can be exempt from product liability. This liability should be defined as a kind of tort liability with limited possibilities for exemption.[734] The injured person should prove the damage, the defect, and the causality chain between the damage and the defect.[735]

328. The possibilities for exemption of product liability are explicitly provided in the act. Manufacturers cannot be held liable if they manage to prove that they have not put the product into circulation, or in case that after taking into account all circumstances, it can prove possible that the defect that caused the damage had not existed when the manufacturer put the product into circulation, or the defect has arisen later. The manufacturers can also benefit from exemption of liability if they successfully prove that they have not produced the product with a sale purpose or any other distribution purpose, that the defect appearance is due to compliance of the product with statutory requirements determined by state authorities, or that the state of scientific and technical knowledge at the time when they have put the product into circulation was not such that allowed the existence of the defect to be detected.[736]

Manufacturer of a component shall not be subject to product liability if they prove that the defect of the component is due to the development or the design of the product, which this component is a part of, or to instructions given by manufacturers.[737]

329. Manufacturers can also be exempt from liability or their liability exposure can be limited when the damage is caused simultaneously by the defective product

731. Consumer Protection Act, Art. 134.
732. Consumer Protection Act, Art. 133(1).
733. *Ibid.*, Art. 137.
734. A. Kalaydjiev, *Law on Obligations*, 308.
735. Consumer Protection Act, Art. 136.
736. Consumer Protection Act, Art. 137.
737. *Ibid.*

and by actions of the injured person or a person for whom the injured person is responsible. Nevertheless, the manufacturer's liability cannot be limited when the damage is caused simultaneously by the defective product and by an action or an omission of a third person.[738]

330. Liability under the Consumer Protection Act only covers damages caused by death or physical injury. In case of damage to property other than the defective product itself, it is required that its value is higher than BGN 1,000 (ca EUR 500) in cases when the product had been designated for personal use and had been used by the injured person by designation. The act explicitly provides that non-material damages caused by the defective product can be compensated under the general liability regime of the OCA.[739] They stipulate that non-material damages are compensated by court evaluation *ex aequo et bono.*[740]

331. In order to protect consumers' interests at the highest level, the Consumer Protection Act explicitly prohibits contractually excluding or limiting the liability set out in the act's provisions. Hence, any such limitation or exemption clause shall be considered null.[741]

332. As far as the prescription terms for any claims based on product liability are concerned, it should be noted that the rights of the injured person shall expire in a ten-year term upon the date of distribution of the product that has caused the damage except in cases when in the meantime the injured person has filed a claim against the manufacturer. The claim for compensation from damages caused by a defect of a product can be filed in three-year term as from the date the claimant has become aware or should have become aware of the damage, the defect, or the identity of the manufacturer.[742]

333. The provisions of the Consumer Protection Act do not deprive the injured person of their compensation right as far as it is provided by other law. Thus, consumers' interests are adequately and sufficiently guaranteed.[743]

738. Consumer Protection Act, Art. 138.
739. *See* in particular the provisions of Art. 45 and the following of OCA.
740. OCA, Art. 52.
741. Consumer Protection Act, Art. 139.
742. Consumer Protection Act, Arts 140–141.
743. Consumer Protection Act, Art. 142.

Part VI. Privacy Protection

Chapter 1. Regulatory Framework on Personal Data Protection

334. 'The regulatory framework on personal data protection that applies in Bulgaria can be divided into three main groups of legal acts: (1) legal acts of the EU which apply to the Republic of Bulgaria by virtue of its membership in the EU; (2) national legislation of Bulgaria; and (3) acts of the international law which were ratified by the Republic of Bulgaria or are otherwise applicable by virtue of its participation in international organization and by virtue of the mechanisms of international law. The first group includes: the Treaty on the Functioning of the EU;[744] the Charter of Fundamental Rights of the EU;[745] Regulation (EU) 2016/679 of the European Parliament and of the Council of 27 April 2016 on the protection of natural persons with regard to the processing of personal data and on the free movement of such data, and repealing Directive 95/46/EC (GDPR/Regulation 2016/679);[746] Directive (EU) 2016/680 of the European Parliament and of the Council of 27 April 2016 on the protection of natural persons with regard to the processing of personal data by competent authorities for the purposes of the prevention, investigation, detection or prosecution of criminal offences or the execution of criminal penalties, and on the free movement of such data, and repealing Council Framework Decision 2008/977/JHA (Law Enforcement Directive/Directive 2016/680).[747] The key national acts in the area of privacy are: the Constitution of the Republic of Bulgaria (the Constitution);[748] the PDPA;[749] the Rules of Procedure of the CPDP and its Administration.[750] Special rules on data protection can be found in numerous legal acts such as the ECA,[751] the Health Act,[752] the Ministry of Interior Act,[753] the Act

744. OJ, C 326, 26 Oct. 2012, pp. 47–390. *See* in particular Art. 16 (ex Article 286 TEC).
745. OJ, C 326, 26 Oct. 2012, pp. 391–407. *See* in particular Arts 7–8.
746. OJ, L 119, 4 May 2016, pp. 1–88.
747. OJ, L 119, 4 May 2016, pp. 89–131.
748. SG, issue 56 of 13 July 1991, in force as of 13 July 1991; last amendment SG, issue 100 of 18 Dec. 2015.
749. SG, issue 1 of 4. Jan. 2002, in force as of 1 Jan. 2002; last amended SG, issue 93 of 26 Nov. 2019 with Decision No. 8 of 15 Nov. 2019 of the Constitutional Court of the Republic of Bulgaria under constitutional case No. 4/2019.
750. SG, issue 60 of 30 July 2019, in force as of 30 July 2019; last amended SG, issue 52 of 9 June 2020, in force as of 9 June 2020.
751. *See* Part I, Ch. 1, para. 34 *supra.*
752. SG, issue 70 of 10 Aug. 2004, in force as of 1 Jan. 2005; last amended SG, issue 21 of 12 Mar. 2021, in force as of 12 Mar. 2021.
753. SG, issue 53 of 27 June 2014; last amended SG, issue 20 of 9 Mar. 2021.

on the State Agency of National Security (ASANS),[754] and others. From the third ground, worth mentioning are Convention for the Protection of Individuals with regard to Automatic Processing of Personal Data (ETS No. 108)[755] and Convention for the Protection of Human Rights and Fundamental Freedoms (ECHR).[756]

335. The Constitution does not explicitly envisage the right to personal data protection. Nonetheless, in the part dedicated to the fundamental rights of the citizens, there are some provisions that are relevant to the right to data protection seen as part of the general notion of the right to privacy. Article 32 of the Constitution stipulates that the private life of the citizens is inviolable. Everyone has the right to protection against unlawful interference with their private and family life and against any damage to their honour, dignity and reputation. No one may be monitored, photographed, filmed, recorded, or subjected to other similar actions without their knowledge or despite their explicit disagreement, except in the cases provided by law. Article 34 proclaims that the freedom and secrecy of correspondence and other communications are inviolable. Exceptions to this rule shall be allowed only with the permission of the judiciary where this is necessary for the detection or prevention of serious crimes. Until 2002, there was no explicit legislation regarding personal data protection in Bulgaria.[757] In the course of Bulgaria' accession to the EU, in 2002 the PDPA – the first Bulgarian data protection act was adopted. The PDPA also established a special data protection supervisory authority – the CPDP. The PDPA implemented in the national legislation of Bulgaria the requirements of the old EU Data Protection Directive 95/46.[758] In the area of protecting the privacy and the personal data within the electronic communications, in 2003 the TA[759] was adopted which was based on Directive 97/66/EC of the European Parliament and of the Council of 15 December 1997 concerning the processing of personal data and the protection of privacy in the telecommunications sector.[760] The currently in force ECA[761] further supplements and frames the rules on privacy in the area of electronic communications.

336. In 2016, probably the largest reform in the sector of privacy up to date took place. In consisted of the adoption of three key legislative acts, namely the GDPR and two directives – the Law Enforcement Directive and Directive 2016/681. The GDPR is in general based on the old Data Protection Directive 95/46, but further

---

754. SG, issue 109 of 20 Dec. 2007, in force as of 1 Jan. 2008; last amended SG, issue 51 of 05 June 2020.
755. https://www.coe.int/en/web/conventions/full-list?module=treaty-detail&treatynum=108, accessed 13 Dec. 2021.
756. https://www.echr.coe.int/documents/convention_eng.pdf, accessed 13 Dec. 2021. *See* in particular Art. 8.
757. G. Dimitrov, *Information and Communication Technologies Law – Administrative Law and Technological Aspects Vol II* (Law and Internet Foundation 2014), p. 164.
758. Directive 95/46/EC of the European Parliament and of the Council of 24 Oct. 1995 on the protection of individuals with regard to the processing of personal data and on the free movement of such data, OJ, L 281, 23.11.1995, pp. 31–50.
759. *See* Part I, Ch. I, para. 34 *supra.*
760. OJ, L 24, 30 Jan. 1998.
761. SG, issue 41 of 22 May 2007.

develops the legal framework given the technological development that took place in the period 1995-2016 providing for new or substantially broadening the scope of existing data subjects' rights, for new obligations of data controllers and data processors, for procedures for coordination between the competent data protection supervisory authorities, and for high amount of sanctions for violations, reaching for the most severe sanctions to the highest amount to EUR 20 million or 4% of the total worldwide annual turnover of the preceding financial year, whichever is higher. Given the large number of changes, a transitional period of two years was granted to the data controllers, processors, and public authorities to adapt their data processing operations to the new requirements. Hence, GDPR applied effectively as of 25 May 2018. In February 2019, the PDPA was amended[762] for three main reasons related to the GDPR[763]: (1) to remove texts contradicting GDPR; (2) to resolve certain administrative matters such as formally appointing data protection authorities under GDPR for Bulgaria, and (3) to implement national rules in the areas where GDPR explicitly permits that.[764] Finally, the amendments to the PDPA were also necessary to transpose the requirements of the Law Enforcement Directive and a result, new Chapter 8 Rules for the Protection of Natural Persons with regard to the Processing of Personal Data by Competent Authorities for the Purposes of Prevention, Investigation, Detection or Prosecution of Criminal Offenses or the Execution of Criminal Penalties, Including Protection against Threats to Public Order and Security and Their Prevention' was created. As of 2021, the above set of acts determines the main legal framework in Bulgaria devoted to privacy and data protection.

762. SG, issue 17 of 26 Feb. 2019.

763. M. Zahariev, 'The Amendments in the Personal Data Protection Act following GDPR – Key Aspects', *TITA Taxes Magazine*, Issue 114 (Apr. 2019), https://assets.website-files.com/5fed988aacad01db88e78ec3/619b605ea807c683f777d41b_97-amendments-in-bulgarian-personal-data-protecion-legislation-key-changes-848.pdf accessed 16 Dec. 2021.

764. *See* in particular Ch. IX Provisions relating to specific processing situations.

Chapter 2. Main Rules of the GDPR

§1. Key Concepts of the Personal Data Protection Regime

337. GDPR applies to the processing of personal data wholly or partly by automated means and to the processing other than by automated means of personal data which form part of a filing system or are intended to form part of a filing system[765] with certain exceptions explicitly envisaged in Article 2(2) and (3). The key concepts of the data protection regime such as personal data, processing, data controller, data processors, etc. are defined in the GDPR. 'Personal data' is defined as 'any information relating to an identified or identifiable natural person ("data subject"); an identifiable natural person is one who can be identified, directly or indirectly, in particular by reference to an identifier such as a name, an identification number, location data, an online identifier or to one or more factors specific to the physical, physiological, genetic, mental, economic, cultural or social identity of that natural person'.[766] Processing means any set of operations that can be performed on personal data, irrespective of whether by automated or non-automated means. GDPR provides certain examples of such operations such as collection, recording, organization, structuring, storage, adaptation or alteration, retrieval, consultation, use, disclosure by transmission, dissemination or otherwise making available, alignment or combination, restriction, erasure or destruction.[767] However, any other operation not mentioned in this listing that can possibly be performed on personal data should be considered processing as well. 'Filing system' means 'any structured set of personal data which are accessible according to specific criteria, whether centralized, decentralized or dispersed on a functional or geographical basis'.[768] 'Data controller' or 'controller' is 'the natural or legal person, public authority, agency or other body which, alone or jointly with others, determines the purposes and means of the processing of personal data; where the purposes and means of such processing are determined by Union or Member State law, the controller or the specific criteria for its nomination may be provided for by Union or Member State law'.[769] The legal doctrine sees in this definition two criteria for determining who acts as a data controller – organizational – related to the legal form of the respective controller, and the more important one: functional – related to determining the means and purposes of the processing.[770] The CPDP has issued several opinions to clarify this concept in specific contexts and situations. According to the CPDP, 'without being implied as an absolute rule, it can be assumed that companies that provide services under strict and comprehensive legislation, on the basis of a licence or similar individual

765. GDPR, Art. 2(1).
766. GDPR, Art. 4(1).
767. GDPR, Art. 4(2).
768. GDPR, Art. 4(6).
769. GDPR, Art. 4(7).
770. D. Toshkova-Nikolova & N. Feti, *Personal Data Protection*, Sofia, IK Trud I Pravo, 2019, pp. 75–80.

permit from the state and under the control of explicitly designated public authorities, would not in principle be considered as processors of personal data and as independent controllers'.[771] Typical examples of controllers are employers, public authorities when exercising their public powers, banks, insures, couriers, telecoms, medical institutions, etc. 'Processor' according to the GDPR means 'a natural or legal person, public authority, agency or other body which processes personal data on behalf of the controller'. Its main characteristic is that it conducts the processing *on behalf* of the controller, i.e., according to the CPDP, the legal consequences of the processing arise directly in the legal sphere of the controller.[772] Typical examples of processors are cloud service providers, collocation service providers, for Bulgaria – accountants and accounting firms. GDPR also introduces a new figure – joint controllers, namely two or more controllers which jointly determine the purposes and means of processing. The main consequence of the presence of this figure is that the joint controllers shall in a transparent manner determine their respective responsibilities for compliance with the obligations under the GDPR, in particular as regards the exercising of the rights of the data subject and their respective duties to provide the information referred to in Articles 13 and 14 of GDPR, by an arrangement between them unless, the respective responsibilities of the controllers are determined by EU or Member State law to which the controllers are subject. The arrangement (i) may designate a contact point for data subjects, (ii) duly reflect the respective roles and relationships of the joint controllers towards the data subjects and its essence shall be made available to the data subjects. In any case, the data subject may exercise his or her rights under this regulation in respect of and against each of the controllers.[773] The European Data Protection Board has issued guidelines on the concepts of controller and processor under the GDPR.[774] In certain cases, GDPR extends its territorial scope to more than just processing operations conducted in the context of EU establishments (establishment criterion). Also, it applies to the processing of personal data of data subjects who are in the EU by a controller or processor not established in the EU, where the processing activities are related to (a) the offering of goods or services, irrespective of whether a payment of the data subject is required, to such data subjects in the EU; or (b) the monitoring of their behaviour as far as their behaviour takes place within the EU (targeting criterion).[775] Such controllers/processors have obligation to appoint a representative – a natural or legal person established in the EU who, designated by the

---

771. Opinion of the CPDP regarding a request received from Speedy AD on issues related to the application of Regulation (EU) 2106/679, Reg. No. НДМСПО -17-604/20.06.2018, https://www.cpdp.bg/index.php?p=element_view&aid=2118, accessed 15 Dec. 2021.
772. Opinion of the CPDP on issues related to the determination of the qualities 'controller' and 'processor of personal data' in the relationship between insurance companies and medical institutions, Reg. No. НДМСПО -01-1174/10.12.2018, https://www.cpdp.bg/index.php?p=element_view&aid=2150, accessed 15 Dec. 2021.
773. GDPR, Art. 26.
774. EDPB, Guidelines 07/2020 on the concepts of controller and processor in the GDPR, https://edpb.europa.eu/our-work-tools/documents/public-consultations/2020/guidelines-072020-concepts-controller-and_en, accessed 15 Dec. 2021.
775. GDPR, Art. 3(2). For more detailed analysis on this provision *see* also EDPB, Guidelines 3/2018 on the territorial scope of the GDPR (Article 3) – version adopted after public consultation, https://edpb.europa.eu/our-work-tools/our-documents/guidelines/guidelines-32018

controller/processor in writing pursuant to Article 27 of the GDPR, represents the controller/processor with regard to their respective obligations under the GDPR. The representative shall be mandated by the controller/processor to be addressed in addition to or instead of the controller/the processor by, in particular, supervisory authorities and data subjects, on all issues related to processing, for the purposes of ensuring compliance with the GDPR.[776] Data subject is the natural person to whom the personal data refers. The supervisory authority is an independent public authority which is established by a Member State pursuant to Article 51 of the GDPR. In Bulgaria, two main public authorities are designated as supervising authorities: the CPDP[777] and the Inspectorate to the Supreme Judicial Council (the Inspectorate), the latter acting with regard to the processing activities conducted by the court in the performance of its functions as a body of the judiciary, and the prosecutor's office and the investigative bodies in the performance of their functions as bodies of the judiciary for the purposes of preventing, investigating, detecting or prosecuting crimes or serving sentences– the Inspectorate to the Supreme Judicial Council[778] (the Inspectorate).[779] This opportunity to introduce a special data protection supervisory authority for the processing activities performed by the judiciary is in line with Recital 20 of GDPR, according to which 'The competence of the supervisory authorities should not cover the processing of personal data when courts are acting in their judicial capacity, in order to safeguard the independence of the judiciary in the performance of its judicial tasks, including decision-making. It should be possible to entrust supervision of such data processing operations to specific bodies within the judicial system of the Member State, which should, in particular ensure compliance with the rules of this regulation, enhance awareness among members of the judiciary of their obligations under this regulation and handle complaints in relation to such data processing operations.'[780] In this sense is also the rule of Article 55(3) of GDPR which stipulates that supervisory authorities shall not be competent to supervise processing operations of courts acting in their judicial capacity. The judiciary authorities have inherent dualism when performing data processing operations – when they act as bodies of the judiciary and exercise their powers to resolve disputes, in which case they shall be under the supervision of the Inspectorate, and where they act as 'ordinary' controllers – e.g., as employers, assignors under public procurements, when they manage court buildings and establish access control or CCTV surveillance, etc. In the latter scenario they are under the supervision of the CPDP.[781]

-territorial-scope-gdpr-article-3-version_en, accessed 15 Dec. 2021.

776. GDPR, Art. 4(17) in connection with Art. 27.
777. Website: https://www.cpdp.bg/en/index.php?p=home&aid=0, accessed 14 Dec. 2021.
778. Website: http://www.inspectoratvss.bg/en, accessed 14 Dec. 2021.
779. PDPA, Arts 17–21.
780. More about the necessity to ensure the independence of the judiciary when performing data processing operations can be found in M. Zahariev, 'GDPR Issues in Commercial Arbitration and How to Mitigate Them', Kluwer Arbitration Blog, 7 Sep 2020, http://arbitrationblog.kluwerarbitration.com/2019/09/07/gdpr-issues-in-commercial-arbitration-and-how-to-mitigate-them, accessed 14 Dec. 2021.
781. Opinion of the CPDP on the application of Regulation (EU) 2016/679 (General Data Protection Regulation) in the judiciary, Reg. No. НДМСПО -17-865/12.10.2018, https://www.cpdp.bg/?p=element_view&aid=2135, accessed 15 Dec. 2021.

338. The GDPR introduces several key requirements that shall apply to the data processing operations – the principles related to the processing of personal data. In the doctrine, they are defined as rules which, although formulated in a general way, create direct obligations to the controllers of personal data – a kind of a criterion for due care in data processing.[782] They are also defined as the most essential and key requirements aimed at guaranteeing the right to protection of personal data[783] and seven basic principles which, due to their fundamental nature, should be observed throughout the 'life cycle' of data – from their creation to their erasure or destruction of their media.[784] The principles go beyond the traditional notion of a legal principle, permeate the entire legal regime for data protection and embody its spirit, and non-compliance leads to legal liability for controllers. The principles reveal the signs of legal norms. The conclusion that the principles have established themselves as a kind of standard for personal data protection is justified.[785] The principles are defined in Article 5 of the GDPR and are as follows:

(1) Lawfulness, fairness, and transparency – requirement to process the personal data in compliance with the law, in a fair manner, i.e., not contradicting to the reasonable expectations of the data subjects and not engaging in excessive data processing operations, and to duly inform the individuals about the processing of their data in compliance with Articles 12–14 of GDPR.

(2) Purpose limitation – requirement to collect for specified, explicit, and legitimate purposes and not further processed in a manner that is incompatible with those purposes with certain exceptions for archiving purposes in the public interest, scientific or historical research purposes or statistical purposes.

(3) Data minimization – requirement that the data is adequate, relevant, and limited to what is necessary in relation to the purposes for which they are processed.

(4) Accuracy – requirement that the personal data is accurate and, where necessary, kept up to date. In addition, GDPR requires that every reasonable step must be taken to ensure that personal data that are inaccurate, having regard to the purposes for which they are processed, are erased or rectified without delay.

(5) Storage limitation – the requirement to store the personal data for specific periods or at least, to determine criteria for the retention of the data, in line with the purposes pursued and the applicable legislation, including to the extent that the data may be necessary to protect the controller's rights and legitimate interests before the state courts or other competent authorities.

(6) Integrity and confidentiality – the requirement to implement appropriate security measures for the data processing.

(7) Accountability – the requirement to keep appropriate documentation so that controllers are able at any time to prove they comply with all the above requirements, as they have the burden to demonstrate compliance therewith.

---

782. G. Dimitrov, *Information and Communication Technologies Law – Administrative Law and Technological Aspects Vol II* (Law and Internet Foundation 2014), p. 176.
783. D. Krusteva & A. Alexandrov, Handbook Protection of Personal Data – Mission Possible. First edition, Sofia, Rezon Bulgaria OOD, 2018, p. 38.
784. D. Toshkova-Nikolova & N. Feti, *Personal Data Protection*, Sofia, IK Trud I Pravo, 2019, p. 89.
785. M. Zahariev, 'Principles of Personal Data Processing – Nature and Significance as a Standard for Personal Data Protection', in *Collection Knowledge Society and 21st Century Humanism*, Sofia, Za Bukvite O Pismeneh, 2020, p. 463.

§2. LEGAL GROUNDS FOR PROCESSING OF PERSONAL DATA

339. The GDPR differentiates three main groups of personal data and hence, three different legal regimes for personal data processing can be distinguished. First, a category of personal data to the processing of which no general rules apply can be distinguished. It can be called 'ordinary' personal data, although the latter is not a term officially adopted by the GDPR. This category encompasses a very broad category of information that enables the identification of individuals such as names, contact details, PIN, ID documents details, financial information such as incomes, salary, taxes and social security contributions, and many other. This category is not exhaustively defined in the GDPR. To the contrary, the other two groups of personal data are exhaustively defined and as a result, any personal data not falling within the scope of these two other groups falls under the general notion of 'ordinary' personal data. Second, the so-called special categories of personal data or sensitive personal data are envisaged in Article 9(1) of GDPR. The GDPR follows an objective approach, defining strictly what is considered 'sensitive' irrespective of the individual perceptions and expectations and the level of tolerance each person may have towards interferences in their private sphere. The categories of data enlisted as sensitive are strongly influenced by the non-discrimination laws and the necessity to react to the modern technological advancements in order to ensure appropriate level of privacy and data protection. Therefore, as sensitive data are enlisted personal data revealing racial or ethnic origin, political opinions, religious or philosophical beliefs, or trade union membership, and the processing of genetic data, biometric data for the purpose of uniquely identifying a natural person, data concerning health or data concerning a natural person's sex life or sexual orientation. These categories are defined as 'sensitive' under the data protection laws and should not be confused with the term 'sensitive' data used in the payment services legislation, which usually refers to payment credentials. The final third group also falls under special regime but is not considered 'sensitive' data within the meaning of the GDPR. It is envisaged in Article 10 of the Regulation 2016/679 and includes personal data relating to criminal convictions and offences or related security measures.

340. In order to lawfully process an 'ordinary' personal data, there must be a legal ground for the processing under Article 6. This could be one of the following conditions:

(1) Consent – any freely given, specific, informed, and unambiguous indication of the data subject's wishes by which he or she, by a statement or by a clear affirmative action, signifies agreement to the processing of personal data relating to him or her.[786] The consent must be actively given, hence, silence, pre-ticked boxes or lack of active behaviour cannot be considered valid consent. The consent can be withdrawn at any time. Special rules were introduced with regard to giving consent on behalf of children in relation to information society services – if the child is under the age of 16, the child must be given or authorized by the holder of parental responsibility over the child. Member States may provide by law for a lower age

786. GDPR, Art. 3(11).

for those purposes provided that such lower age is not below the age of 13. In Bulgaria the age is set at 14.[787] Due to the requirement to be freely given, consent is not suitable in cases of clear imbalance of power such as employer-employee relationship (at least for the core processing activities related to the employment), citizen-public authority, etc.[788] Despite these peculiarities, the notion of consent was broadly misunderstood in Bulgaria and many controllers required only consent from data subjects – via special declarations, via clauses in contracts, etc. As a result, the CPDP issued guidance where it stipulated that consent is only one of the possible legal grounds for the processing, that it does not enjoy hierarchical supremacy in comparison to the other grounds for data processing and this it is not suitable for specific data processing operations and contexts. The CPDP even provided an exemplary list where consent was not suitable legal ground for the processing.[789] Gradually, the business and the public authorities are adapting their practices to the latter guidance, but still consent is broadly and frequently requested in cases where other legal ground is more suitable – contract, legal obligation, legitimate interest, etc.

(2) Necessity to perform a contract to which the data subject is a party or taking steps prior to contract conclusion upon request of the data subject – the peculiarity here is that the contract must be concluded with the data subject whose data is being processed and this processing must be necessary[790] for the contract performance (e.g., for delivery, for payment, etc.). Any type of contract can be used here if it is concluded with the data subject such as sales contracts, service contracts, donation contracts, employment contracts, etc. Also, data processing in the context of pre-contractual relations can be based on this legal ground – e.g., for preparation of offers, for credibility assessments prior to granting bank loans, for negotiations, for assessing CVs or conducting interviews during recruitments, etc.

(3) Legal obligation – it must be imposed on the controller by virtue of the EU or the Member State law to which the controller is subject.[791] Here the controller does not have any room for manoeuvre and should perform the processing, otherwise would violate the respective legislation applicable to it – e.g., processing for tax, accounting purposes, for compliance with employment and social security obligations, for responding to requests from public authorities, etc.

(4) Vital interests of the data subject or of another person – this condition enables the processing in situations of life and death, i.e., where severe consequences for the life and/or health of a given person could arise if the processing does not take place. It has limited practical application in the business context. Example of this legal ground is maintaining lists of emergency contact of employees and establishing contact with them in case of accidents or similar emergencies.

---

787. *See* Part VI, Ch. 3, § 1, para. 353 *infra*.
788. EDPB, Guidelines 05/2020 on consent under Regulation 2016/679, https://edpb.europa.eu/sites/default/files/files/file1/edpb_guidelines_202005_consent_en.pdf, pp. 8–9, accessed 15 Dec. 2021.
789. Practical guidelines of the CPDP in which cases consent is not required for personal data processing, https://www.cpdp.bg/index.php?p=element&aid=1163, accessed 15 Dec. 2021.
790. *See* EDPB, Guidelines 2/2019 on the processing of personal data under Art. 6(1)(b) GDPR in the context of the provision of online services to data subjects, https://edpb.europa.eu/sites/default/files/consultation/edpb_draft_guidelines-art_6-1-b-final_public_consultation_version_en.pdf, pp.7–11, accessed 15 Dec.
791. GDPR, Art. 6(3).

(5) Task carried out in the public interest/exercise of official authority – two legal grounds are envisaged here. The official authority is vested to public authorities by virtue of the EU or Member State law, and they can perform the processing in order to exercise their public powers – e.g., for exercising controlling powers, for imposing sanctions or corrective measures, etc. The public interest is a concept not defined in the GDPR of the PDPA. The CPDP in its practice defines it as 'an abstract legal, political, philosophical, and socio-economic category, the content of which depends both on the state of society at a particular historical moment and on the individual interests of individual members of society'.[792] In order to mitigate potential abuses of this legal ground, every data controller intending to base its processing on it should undergo a prior consultation procedure with the CPDP.[793]

(6) Legitimate interest – it could be either of the controller itself of a third party such as controller's employees, managers, contractors, business partners, entities from the same corporate group, even in theory the data subject him/herself. In order to be able to rely on this legal ground, this legitimate interest should override the interests or fundamental rights and freedoms of the data subject. The supervisory authorities and the legal doctrine define in that respect the necessity to conduct a balancing test to assess whose interests are overriding. There are certain cases in which the legitimate interest is evidently overriding and no such test is necessary – e.g., for the establishment, exercise or defence of legal claims.[794] Public authorities cannot rely on this legal ground for the data processing activities related to the performance of their tasks.

341. Article 9 stipulates the conditions for processing of sensitive data. In principle, processing of such data is prohibited. However, there are several exceptions from this rule aiming to ensure the normal performance of a number of activities such as ensuring health and safety conditions at work, performance of political, trade union or religious activity, ensuring the possibility to process sensitive data in the healthcare sector, etc. Hence, sensitive data can be processed if:

(1) the data subject has given explicit consent to the processing of those personal data for one or more specified purposes, except where EU or Member State law provide that the prohibition for processing of sensitive data may not be lifted by the data subject;

(2) processing is necessary for the purposes of carrying out the obligations and exercising specific rights of the controller or of the data subject in the field of employment and social security and social protection law insofar as it is authorized by EU or Member State law or a collective agreement pursuant to Member State law providing for appropriate safeguards for the fundamental rights and the interests of the data subject;

792. Opinion of the CPDP on issues related to the introduction of video surveillance in kindergartens (nurseries and kindergartens), as well as in schools, Reg. No. П- 5375/2017, https://www.cpdp.bg/index.php?p=element_view&aid=2106, accessed 15 Dec. 2021.

793. PDPA, Art. 12(2) in connection with GDPR, Art. 36(5).

794. *See* Art. 21(1) of GDPR. This is also reaffirmed in Decision No. 3354 of 15 Mar. 2021 of the SAC under administrative case No. 10154/2020.

(3) processing is necessary to protect the vital interests of the data subject or of another natural person where the data subject is physically or legally incapable of giving consent;

(4) processing is carried out in the course of its legitimate activities with appropriate safeguards by a foundation, association or any other not-for-profit body with a political, philosophical, religious or trade union aim and on condition that the processing relates solely to the members or to former members of the body or to persons who have regular contact with it in connection with its purposes and that the personal data are not disclosed outside that body without the consent of the data subjects;

(5) processing relates to personal data which are manifestly made public by the data subject;

(6) processing is necessary for the establishment, exercise or defence of legal claims or whenever courts are acting in their judicial capacity;

(7) processing is necessary for reasons of substantial public interest, on the basis of EU or Member State law which shall be proportionate to the aim pursued, respect the essence of the right to data protection and provide for suitable and specific measures to safeguard the fundamental rights and the interests of the data subject;

(8) processing is necessary for the purposes of preventive or occupational medicine, for the assessment of the working capacity of the employee, medical diagnosis, the provision of health or social care or treatment or the management of health or social care systems and services on the basis of EU or Member State law or pursuant to contract with a health professional and subject to the obligation for professional secrecy;

(9) processing is necessary for reasons of public interest in the area of public health, such as protecting against serious cross-border threats to health or ensuring high standards of quality and safety of healthcare and of medicinal products or medical devices, on the basis of EU or Member State law which provides for suitable and specific measures to safeguard the rights and freedoms of the data subject, in particular professional secrecy;

(10) processing is necessary for archiving purposes in the public interest, scientific or historical research purposes or statistical purposes in accordance with Article 89(1) of the GDPR based on EU or Member State law which shall be proportionate to the aim pursued, respect the essence of the right to data protection and provide for suitable and specific measures to safeguard the fundamental rights and the interests of the data subject.

342. Member States may maintain or introduce further conditions, including limitations, with regard to the processing of genetic data, biometric data or data concerning health. By virtue of that rule, Article 107 and 454 in connection with § 7(3) of the Additional Provisions of the Bulgarian IC[795] enable the processing of health data in the context of establishing the insurance event and the damages caused by it and of conclusion of life insurance. In the context of the COVID-19 pandemic, especially topical became the problems related to the admissibility of processing of health data of the employees – such as results of COVID-19 testing, vaccination status, etc. for the purposes of tackling the pandemic and adhering to the anti-epidemic measures. The CPDP has issued several opinions in that respect.[796] In general, private data controllers should adhere to what is prescribed in the anti-epidemic legislation and should not engage in uncharacteristic activities such as tracing epidemic chains, collecting tests results, etc. – these should remain in the competence of the health authorities.[797]

343. Article 10 of GDPR lays down the conditions for processing of personal data relating to criminal convictions and offences or related security measures. The said provision contains a reference to Article 6(1) of the GDPR, i.e., to the legal conditions for processing of 'ordinary' personal data under the general legal regime. However, Article 10 further stipulates that such processing shall be carried out only under the control of official authority or when the processing is authorized by EU or Member State law providing for appropriate safeguards for the rights and freedoms of data subjects. Any comprehensive register of criminal convictions shall be kept only under the control of official authority. This rule, read in the light of the Bulgarian employment law legislation, limits the cases where employers can request criminal conviction certificates – this can be done only for positions for which there is a legal recruitment for the employee to be non-convicted. Thus, the widespread practice in Bulgaria to request such for practically any position during recruitment contradicts Article 10 of the GDPR. This was reaffirmed by the CPDP in a recent opinion, according to which criminal convictions in employment contest can be requested only on the basis of legal obligation (Article 6(1)(c) of the GDPR).[798]

795. SG, issue 102 of 29 Dec. 2015, in force as of 1 Jan. 2016, last amended SG, issue 21 of 12 Mar. 2021.

796. *See* e.g., Opinion of the CPDP on the processing of personal health data and the level of information of employees in case of infection with COVID-19, Reg. No. ПНМД -17-114/2020, https://www.cpdp.bg/?p=element_view&aid=2263, accessed 15 Dec. 2021, Opinion of the CPDP on the processing of data on vaccination status, Reg. No. ПНМД -01-93/2021, https://www.cpdp.bg/?p=element_view&aid=2287, accessed 15 Dec.2021 and others.

797. M. Zahariev, 'On the admissibility of certain personal data processing operations by the employer in the context of the COVID-19 pandemic', *TITA Taxes Magazine*, Issue 128 (May 2020), https://www.tita.bg/free/commercial-law/685, accessed 15 Dec. 2021.

798. Opinion of the CPDP on the requirement to present a criminal record when appointing non-reporting positions, Reg. No. ПНМД – 01 – 5/16.01.2020, https://www.cpdp.bg/?p=element_view&aid=2255, accessed 15 Dec. 2021.

§3. Data Subjects' Rights and Main Regulatory Obligations of Data Controllers and Processors

344. The GDPR proclaims that natural persons should have control over their own personal data (Recital 7). In that respect, on the basis of the solid foundations of Directive 95/46, the GDPR further supplements the set of data subjects' rights – either by broadening the scope of existing rights (e.g., the right to erasure) or by providing for brand new rights (e.g., the right to data portability). As a result, data subjects have the right to receive detailed information about the processing of their data in clear and plain language (often done in practice via privacy policies, privacy notices or similar documents), right of access, right to rectification, right to erasure, restriction of processing, and to data portability, provided that specific conditions laid in the GDPR are met, right to object against processing based on task carried out in the public interest/exercise of official authority or legitimate interest, right not to be subject to a decision based solely on automated processing, including profiling,[799] which produces legal effects concerning him or her or similarly significantly affects him or her.[800] Last, it must be noted that some of the rights cannot be freely exercised at any time, but rather need to meet certain conditions laid down by the Regulation 2016/679.[801] The GDPR also sets certain exceptions where the exercising of the rights can be refused by the controller[802] and also provides for the possibility to restrict their application.[803] The data subjects also have the right to withdraw their consent without affecting the lawfulness of processing based on consent before its withdrawal and to lodge a complaint with a data protection supervisory authority, if they believe the processing of their personal data violates the applicable data protection rules.[804]

345. In order to foster accountability and compliance with the high data protection standards set by the EU, the GDPR imposes a detailed list of obligations on the controllers and processors.[805] Controllers need to implement appropriate technical and organizational measures to ensure and to be able to demonstrate that processing is performed in accordance with the GDPR, to adhere to the privacy by design and default standards for all their processing operations, to arrange appropriately their relations with joint controllers or data processors via DPAs, if entering into relations with such, to notify the data protection supervisory authorities within 72 hours of personal data breaches (and to be notified by the processor without undue delay

799. More about the notion of 'profiling' *see* M. Zahariev, 'The evolution of EU data protection law on automated data profiling', *Privacy in Germany PinG* 02.2017, pp. 73–79.
800. GDPR, Arts 12–22.
801. GDPR, Art. 17(1).
802. GDPR, Art. 17(3).
803. GDPR, Art. 23.
804. GDPR, Arts 7(3) and 77.
805. More about good practices for compliance with the GDPR requirements such as control methodologies, appointing of data protection officer, CCTV and training programmes in the field of personal data protection can be found in V. Tselkov et al., *Data Protection – Principles and Practices.* Sofia, Za Bukvite O Pismeneh, 2019, pp. 145–283.

after becoming aware of a personal data breach) and in certain cases – to communicate such with the data subjects, to conduct prior data protection impact assessment where a type of processing in particular using new technologies, and taking into account the nature, scope, context, and purposes of the processing, is likely to result in a high risk to the rights and freedoms of natural persons and if further necessary – to conduct prior consultation with the supervisory authority to further restrict the risks of the processing.[806] Both controller and processor need to appoint representative in the EU if the GDPR applies to them by virtue of the targeting criterion, to keep records of processing activities, to cooperate with the supervisory authority, to apply appropriate security measures on the basis of risk-based approach, in certain cases – to appoint data protection officer (DPO).[807]

346. The GDPR also introduces the possibility to voluntarily adhere to codes of conduct – a tool that takes into account of the specific features of the various processing sectors and the specific needs of micro, small, and medium-sized enterprises and certification and needs to be approved by competent supervisory authority.[808] As of today, in Bulgaria there are no approved codes of conduct.[809] Also, the GDPR regulates the certification mechanisms – the possibility to obtain from a third independent party (certification body) that processing operations of controllers/processors comply with the GDPR.[810] In Bulgaria it is the CPDP which grants accreditation to the certification bodies. However, sub-legislative amendments are expected to make this mechanism working for Bulgaria.[811]

§4. Transfers of Personal Data Outside EU

347. The technologies enable the free movement of personal data and the transborder data flow in an unprecedented manner. To address this issue, following the approach adopted in Directive 95/46, the GDPR contains special rules regarding the transfers of personal data outside EU. They are envisaged in Chapter V of the GDPR 'Transfers of personal data to third countries or international organizations'. According to the general principle for transfers,[812] the special rules for transfers to a third country or to an international organization shall be applied in order to ensure that the level of protection of natural persons guaranteed by the GDPR is not undermined. As a result, the GDPR contains a list of alternative instruments for transfer that follow certain internal hierarchy – if the first is present, then it is sufficient to justify the transfer, if not – the exporting party must check whether the second mechanism is present and so on. First, the GDPR introduces the so-called adequacy concept – the possibility for the EC to decide that the third country, a territory or

806. GDPR, Arts 24, 25, 26, 28, 33–36.
807. GDPR, Arts 27, 30, 31, 32, 37–40.
808. GDPR, Arts 40–41.
809. CPDP, https://www.cpdp.bg/?p=pages&aid=60, accessed 15 Dec. 2021.
810. GDPR, Arts 42–43.
811. PDPA, Art. 14.
812. GDPR, Art. 44.

one or more specified sectors within that third country, or the international organization in question ensures an adequate level of protection. Such a transfer shall not require any specific authorization. The EC has so far recognized Andorra, Argentina, Canada (commercial organizations), Faroe Islands, Guernsey, Israel, Isle of Man, Japan, Jersey, New Zealand, the Republic of Korea, Switzerland, the United Kingdom under the GDPR and the Law Enforcement Directive, and Uruguay as providing adequate protection.[813] If no such decision has been made, a transfer may be possible by virtue of the so-called appropriate safeguards (with or without permission of the supervisory authority). The most common ones include the SCC and the Binding Corporate Rules. The latest developments in the area of international transfers, namely the invalidation of the Privacy Shield mechanism by the CJEU in the Schrems II case[814] and the potential question mark that was put over the SCCs and other similar instruments for transfers to countries such as USA, Russia, China, etc. who have strongly developed law enforcement and intelligence services led to several initiatives. First, the EDPB adopted guidance on ensuring compliance for data transfers following the Schrems II case.[815] Later in 2021, the EC adopted new SCCs for international transfer of personal data.[816] It remains to be seen whether the new SCCs will respond to the need of the business for reliable instruments that enable predictable data flow between EU-USA and other third countries. If no appropriate safeguards are present, the derogations for specific situations under Article 49 of the GDPR may be used (such as explicit consent, necessity to perform a contract, necessity for the establishment, exercise or defence of legal claims, etc.). The last exception is in case where a transfer could not be based on any of the mentioned instruments. Then, a transfer to a third country or an international organization may take place only if the transfer (1) is not repetitive, (2) concerns only a limited number of data subjects, (3) is necessary for the purposes of compelling legitimate interests pursued by the controller which are not overridden by the interests or rights and freedoms of the data subject, and (4) the controller has assessed all the circumstances surrounding the data transfer and has on the basis of that assessment provided suitable safeguards with regard to the protection of personal data. The controller shall inform (5) the supervisory authority of the transfer and (6) the data subject of the transfer and on the compelling legitimate interests pursued.[817]

813. *See* https://ec.europa.eu/info/law/law-topic/data-protection/international-dimension-data-protection/adequacy-decisions_en, accessed 17 Dec. 2021.
814. CJEU, https://curia.europa.eu/juris/liste.jsf?num=C-311/18, accessed 15 Dec. 2021.
815. EDPB, Recommendations 01/2020 on measures that supplement transfer tools to ensure compliance with the EU level of protection of personal data, https://edpb.europa.eu/our-work-tools/our-documents/recommendations/recommendations-012020-measures-supplement-transfer_en, accessed 15 Dec. 2021.
816. *See* https://ec.europa.eu/info/law/law-topic/data-protection/international-dimension-data-protection/standard-contractual-clauses-scc/standard-contractual-clauses-international-transfers_en, accessed 15 Dec. 2021.
817. GDPR, Art. 49(1), second paragraph.

§5. SUPERVISION, LIABILITY AND REMEDIES FOR PROTECTION

348. The GDPR contains rules aimed at ensuring appropriate control for compliance with the requirements of the data protection laws. It envisages the creation of independent data protection supervisory authorities[818] with wide range of tasks[819] and powers,[820] including to conduct audits and where necessary – to impose sanctions for violations of the GDPR. The one-stop-shop mechanism is introduced via the figure of leading supervisory authority,[821] enabling more predictability and less administrative burden for the business which now needs to interact only with the lead supervisory authority in case of cross-border processing. The GDPR contains a complex set of rules on how the competent authority is to be determined, but the interactions on the matter need to be conducted by the authorities ex officio, including with the assistance of the EDPB. Special rules on international cooperation are also introduced.[822] At European level, the EDPB board is established as a successor of the Article 29 Working Party under Directive 95/46 with the main task to ensure the consistent application of the Regulation 2016/679 and with detailed list of powers, including with the possibility to issue guidelines, recommendations, and best practices on certain matters.[823]

349. With regard to the remedies, liability, and penalties, the GDPR introduces the right to lodge a complaint with a supervisory authority, to an effective judicial remedy against a supervisory authority and to an effective judicial remedy against a controller or processor, including the right to seek compensation for material and non-material damages from controller/processor under the national rules.[824] There are administrative sanctions (fines) for its violations, divided into two main groups in terms of the maximum amount of the sanctions – more severe violations (e.g., of the principles for data processing, of the legal grounds and the rights of the data subjects, of the rules for data transfers in third countries, as well as for failure to comply with certain acts issued by the supervisory authority or otherwise to cooperate with it, etc.), reaching up to 20,000,000 EUR, or in the case of an undertaking, up to 4 % of the total worldwide annual turnover of the preceding financial year, whichever is higher, and less severe (e.g., for breaching the main obligations of controllers/processors under Articles 8, 11, 25 to 39 and 42 and 43 of GDPR) reaching up to 10,000,000 EUR, or in the case of an undertaking, up to 2 % of the total worldwide annual turnover of the preceding financial year, whichever is higher. There is a wide range of criteria for assessing the severity of the violation and for determining the amount of the sanction.[825]

818. GDPR, Art. 55
819. GDPR, Art. 57.
820. GDPR Art. 58.
821. GDPR, Art. 56.
822. GDPR, Arts 60–67.
823. GDPR, Art. 70.
824. GDPR, Arts 77–79 and Art. 82.
825. GDPR, Art. 83.

Chapter 3. Special National Rules for Personal Data Protection

§1. Special Personal Data Protection Rules Supplementing the General Data Protection Regime under the GDPR

350. The 2019 amendments in the PDPA supplemented the GDPR in the areas where the Regulation 2016/679 permitted that. Below is a summary of the key changes introduced with the PDPA at a national level that are relevant for the general data protection regime under the GDPR.

351. First, amendments were made with regard to the limitation period of the right to lodge a complaint with the supervisory authority. Data subjects are entitled to file their complaint with the competent authority within six months of becoming aware of the violation, but no later than two years from the date of the violation. For violations that took place in the transitional period between the effective date of GDPR (25 May 2018) and the date of entry into force of the amendments in the PDPA (2 March 2019) the periods for filing the complaint remain the same as those before the changes – one year of becoming aware of the violation but no longer than five years from the date of the violation.[826]

352. Second, national penalties for sanctions under the PDPA were also introduced. For example, sanctions up to the maximum amounts under the GDPR for incompliance with the rules for processing of personal data for journalistic purposes, special rules for processing in the employment context and processing of personal data for archiving purposes in the public interest, scientific or historical research purposes or statistical purposes were introduced.[827] There are sanctions for infringements of the rules for obtaining consent from children under the age of 14 reaching EUR 10,000,000/2 % of the total worldwide annual turnover of the preceding financial year for undertakings, whichever is higher. The PDPA sets a general penalty of up to BGN 5,000 (approx. EUR 2,550) for 'other infringements', i.e., for all infringements for which no higher penalty is provisioned by the GDPR or national legislation.[828]

353. Third, the PDPA provided for certain special rules.[829] The most important ones are summarized below: where personal data is provided by the data subject to a controller or processor without a legal basis under GDPR or contrary to the GDPR principles, within one month of becoming aware thereof, the controller/processor shall return the data, and if this is not possible or would require disproportionate

826. R. Makshutova & M. Zahariev, 'GDPR Implementation Series – Bulgaria', *European Data Protection Law Review*, 3/2020, p. 426.
827. *Ibid.*
828. *Ibid.*
829. PDPA, Arts 25a–25n (in Bulgarian Arts 25a–25o). For a more detailed analysis of these rules *see* also R. Makshutova & M. Zahariev, 'GDPR Implementation Series – Bulgaria', *European Data Protection Law Review*, 3/2020, pp. 426–429.

efforts, it shall erase or destroy the data. Erasure and destruction have to be documented.[830] Controllers/processors need to notify the CPDP in case they appoint a DPO. This obligation is fulfilled via a special form approved by the CPDP.[831] The processing of data of a person under the age of 14 based on consent, including in cases of direct provision of information society services, is lawful only when the consent is given by the parent exercising parental rights or by the guardian of the person. The controller/processor may process personal data of deceased persons only if there is a legal basis for that. In such cases, the controller/processor shall take appropriate measures to prevent the unfavourable impairment of the rights and freedoms of others or the public interest. The controller is obliged to provide upon request access to the personal data of a deceased person, including a copy of it, to their heirs or other persons who have legal interest. If a controller or processor conducts large-scale processing of personal data and large-scale surveillance of publicly accessible areas, it has to adopt and apply rules concerning this processing with specific content prescribed by the PDPA. A controller or processor may copy an identity document, a driving licence or a residence document only if this is provided for by law. Free public access to information containing the national identifiers used for Bulgarian citizens or foreigners is prohibited, unless a law provides otherwise. The controllers providing electronic services shall take appropriate technical and organizational measures that prevent these identifiers PNF from being the only means of identifying the user when providing remote access to the service. There are also special rules for processing of personal data for journalistic purposes, as well as academic, artistic or literary expression which are aimed to balance the freedom of expression and the right to seek and disseminate information and the right to privacy. Special rules are applicable in employment context – employers have obligations to adopt internal rules if they engage in certain specific data processing operations such as (1) using a reporting system for violations (i.e., a whistleblowing system); (2) restrictions on the use of in-house resources; (3) introduction of systems for access control, control over the working time and the labour discipline. The retention period for personal data of participants collected in job recruitment procedures should be determined by each data controller, but it may not exceed (six) months unless the applicants have given their consent for a longer retention period. After the expiration of that period, the employer has to delete or destroy the stored personal data, unless a special law stipulates otherwise. Within the said six-month term the employer should return to non-elected candidates original documents or notarized copies of documents certifying the applicant's physical and mental fitness, the required qualification degree and work experience. The PDPA also contains rules for processing of personal data for humanitarian purposes by public authorities or humanitarian organizations, for archiving and statistical purposes as well as processing in the event of disasters.

830. PDPA, Art. 25a.
831. *See* Notification to the CPDP for appointment of a Data Protection Officer, https://www.cpdp.bg/?p=sub_rubric&aid=227, accessed 15 Dec. 2021.

§2. Special Personal Data Protection Rules in the Telecommunications Sector

354. The right to personal data protection and the right to privacy in the telecommunications sector have their solid foundations on constitutional level. The Constitution of the Republic of Bulgaria[832] proclaims the inviolability of the freedom and confidentiality of correspondence and all other communications. Exceptions towards the provision shall be allowed only upon a permission of the judicial authorities for the purpose of discovering or preventing serious crimes.[833]

According to the court practice, confidentiality of correspondence in the sense of Article 34(1) of the Constitution means that the information contained in the correspondence shall remain familiar to the sender and the person it was designated for until the moment one of them decides otherwise.[834]

355. On the basis of the constitutional protection and in line with the European legal framework *acquis'* 2002 for electronic communications, the ECA contains specific rules with regard to privacy and data protection in the telecommunications sector. The ECA reinforces the constitutional principle of confidentiality of communications. A special Chapter 15 is present in the ECA devoted to the privacy and data protection entitled 'Electronic communication network and services security, confidentiality of communications and protection of user data'. Undertakings providing public electronic communications networks or services shall take appropriate and proportionate technical and organizational risk management measures for the security of networks and services providing a level of security commensurate with the assessed risk. These measures, including encryption, where appropriate, shall be aimed at preventing and minimizing the impact of security incidents on users and other networks and services.[835] There are also special rules for notification to the competent authorities for security incidents.[836]

Sections II and III, of Chapter 15 of the ECA – 'Confidentiality of Communications' and 'Protection of User Data' – contain only the special regulation on the personal data protection for the purposes of provision of electronic communication services.

356. Section II of Chapter 15 of the ECA, 'Confidentiality of Communications', directly regulates electronic communications privacy matters.

Article 245 obliges undertakings providing public electronic communications networks and/or services not to disclose and distribute communications and related

832. *See* Introduction, Chs 1, 3.
833. Bulgarian Constitution, Art. 34.
834. *See* Decision No. 7982 of 22 Dec. 2000 of the SAC under administrative case No. 3351/2000.
835. ECA, Art. 243.
836. ECA, Arts 243b–244.

traffic data, information about user's location, and data required for end user's identification when they have become known to them in the course of provision of electronic communications networks and/or services. This obligation shall also apply to the employees of the undertakings who have access or could obtain access to such communications and information.

In order to protect the confidentiality of messages and related traffic data, according to Article 246 of the ECA listening, recording, storing or other types of interception or tracking of messages by persons other than the sender and recipient of the message shall be prohibited without the express consent of the sender and recipient, except when provided by law. This prohibition does not apply to undertakings providing electronic communications networks and/or services, when: (1) storage is necessary for technical reasons or is an essential part of the provision of the service; (2) an inspection of the technical parameters of the service shall be carried out by authorized persons under the ECA. In such cases undertakings providing public electronic communications networks and/or services shall be obliged to delete the stored messages immediately after the grounds for their storage have ceased to exist. These limitations do not apply to recording of messages and related traffic data and under the following conditions: (1) the recording is necessary and provided by law in order to prove the conclusion of commercial transactions, and (2) the sender and recipient of the messages are notified in advance of the recording, purposes and time for storage, as well as for the right to refuse it. The recorded messages and the related traffic data shall be stored for a period not longer than the period in which they may be used in accordance with the purposes described above.[837]

357. Section III of Chapter 15 of the ECA introduces special rules for protecting the privacy of the users in the telecommunications sector. These rules are *lex specialis* and shall apply with priority in comparison with the general rules under GDPR, and the latter only applies for matters unregulated in the ECA.[838] The supervision for compliance with these rules is vested in the CPDP.[839] ECA contains special rules for processing of data of the end users such as traffic data, data necessary to prepare detailed bills, and detailed information on the services used together with primary accounting document and location data.[840] The data minimization principle is envisaged in Article 249 of ECA, according to which undertakings providing public electronic communications services may not require from an end user more data than those under Article 248(2), item 2, letter 'a' of the ECA for the provision of the services, unless otherwise provided by law or the service cannot be provided without the presence of other required data. Retaining and processing traffic data for billing purposes and to assist certain law enforcement authorities to investigate serious crime, as well as to assist the competent authorities in case of disasters are also regulated by the ECA.[841] ECA contains certain provisions on who may process traffic data within the undertakings (only authorized officials), on the possibility to process

837. ECA, Arts 245–247.
838. ECA, Art. 249(5).
839. ECA, Art. 262.
840. ECA, Art. 248.
841. ECA, Arts 249, 250–251i.

location data, etc.[842] Rules on notification to the CPDP in case of data breach are also introduced with the latest amendments in the ECA.[843] Following the 2021 amendments to the ECA, a new rule[844] provides that where a terminal device is also provided when concluding a contract, undertakings providing public electronic communications services shall have the right to request from other undertakings providing public electronic communications services information on the existence of unpaid end-user obligations to them. The requested undertakings shall provide the requested information under strict conditions. The CRC and the CPDP recently issued an instruction on the conditions, methodology, and deadlines for the provision of information between undertakings providing public electronic communications services on the existence of due debts by the end user.[845] The instruction stipulates the specific rules and procedures for handling such data.

§3. Special Personal Data Protection Rules in the Law Enforcement Sector

358. The data protection regulations in the law enforcement sector need to balance two contradicting forces – the right to privacy and data protection and the necessity to ensure high standard for protecting the fundamental rights of the individuals whose data is being processed in the context of prevention, investigation, detection or prosecution of criminal offences or the execution of criminal penalties, on the one hand, and enhanced public powers of the competent authorities, on the other. The legal framework in that sector is explicitly excluded from the material scope of the GDPR[846] and as a result is governed by the Law Enforcement Directive, also part of the EU data protection reform package from 2016. It is transposed in a special Chapter 8 of the PDPA 'Rules for the Protection of Individuals in Relation to the Processing of Personal Data by Competent Authorities for the Purposes of Prevention, Investigation, Detection or Prosecution of Criminal Offenses or the Execution of Criminal Penalties, including Protection Against Threats to Public Order and Security and Their Prevention'. These rules resemble the above-mentioned balance. They follow in general the rules of the GDPR, but have certain peculiarities. First, the processing for the mentioned purposes ('Law Enforcement Purposes') shall be conducted only by competent authorities – authorities with explicit powers in that area. If these authorities process personal data for other purposes, the rules of the GDPR shall apply. Personal data collected for Law Enforcement Purposes shall not be processed for other purposes unless the EU or Bulgarian law envisage otherwise. Controller is the competent authority or the relevant administrative structure of which this authority is a part, which independently or jointly with other authorities determines the purposes and means of processing personal data (unless otherwise provided by law). Hence, by virtue of explicit rules in the

842. ECA, Arts 252–254.
843. ECA, Arts 261c–261e.
844. ECA, Arts 249(3)
845. SG, issue 109 of 21 Dec. 2021.
846. GDPR, Art. 2(1)(d).

respective legislation, controller is the Minister of Interior, the Director of the Customs Agency the Chairman of State Agency National Security (SANS). With regard to the judiciary, the Judiciary Power Act lacks specific provision on the matter. In the doctrine it is correctly stipulated that in the absence of such rules, data controllers should be considered the respective legal entities – courts, prosecution offices, etc. and not the single judges, prosecutors, investigators, etc.[847]

359. Given the enhanced public powers, special rules in this area are present: transparency is not envisaged as data protection principle, consent or contract that are typical for the private law are not suitable legal grounds for data processing. The processing of personal data shall be lawful when it is necessary for the exercise of powers by a competent authority for Law Enforcement Purposes and is provided for in the EU or Bulgarian law, in which the purposes of the processing and the categories of personal data to be processed are determined.[848] The processing of sensitive data is permitted when absolutely necessary, there are appropriate guarantees for the rights and freedoms of the data subject and it is provided for in the law of the EU or in the legislation of the Republic of Bulgaria.[849] Alternatively, sensitive data may be processed where absolutely necessary, provided that there are appropriate safeguards for the rights and freedoms of the data subject and: 1. the processing is for the protection of the vital interests of the data subject or another natural person; or 2. if the processing concerns for data that have been made manifestly public by the data subject. Controller, where applicable and as far as possible, shall make a clear distinction between personal data of different categories of data subjects, such as: (a) persons with regard to whom there are serious grounds for believing that they have committed or are about to commit a criminal offence; (b) persons convicted of a criminal offence; (c) victims of a criminal offence or persons with regard to whom certain facts give rise to reasons for believing that he or she could be the victim of a criminal offence; and (d) other parties to a criminal offence, such as persons who might be called on to testify in investigations in connection with criminal offences or subsequent criminal proceedings, persons who can provide information on criminal offences, or contacts or associates of one of the persons referred to in points (a) and (b).[850] Instead of specific retention periods, the competent authorities may establish periodic checks for the necessity of retaining respective data,[851] there are possibilities for the data subjects to exercise indirectly their rights before the controllers – via the CPDP or the Inspectorate,[852] etc.[853]

---

847. N. Feti & D. Toshkova-Nikolova, *Application of the Personal Data Protection, Methods, recommendations and Practical Steps*, Sofia, IK Trud I Pravo, 2020, p. 486.
848. PDPA, Art. 49.
849. PDPA, Art. 51.
850. PDPA, Art. 47 and Law Enforcement Directive, Art. 6.
851. PDPA, Art. 46.
852. PDPA, Art. 57.
853. *See* more about the topic N. Feti & D. Toshkova-Nikolova, *Application of the Personal Data Protection, Methods, recommendations and Practical Steps*, Sofia, IK Trud I Pravo, 2020, pp. 484–524.

§4. Special Personal Data Protection Rules for Usage of Passenger Name Records for Countering Serious Crime and Terrorism

360. The special regulation in the area of processing passenger name records (PNR) stems from an EU Directive (EU) 2016/681 of the European Parliament and of the Council of 27 April 2016 on the use of PNR data for the prevention, detection, investigation, and prosecution of terrorist offences and serious crime (PNR Directive)[854] which was part of the data protection reform package adopted in 2016. The PNR Directive is transposed in Chapter 6a of the ASANS. The PNR Directive defines a special category of personal data, the PNR, as record of each passenger's travel requirements which contains information necessary to enable reservations to be processed and controlled by the booking and participating air carriers for each journey booked by or on behalf of any person, whether it is contained in reservation systems, departure control systems used to check passengers onto flights, or equivalent systems providing the same functionalities.[855] By virtue of the PNR Directive, each Member State shall establish or designate an authority competent for the prevention, detection, investigation or prosecution of terrorist offences and of serious crime or a branch of such an authority, to act as its passenger information unit (PIU). The National PIU for Bulgaria is a special unit within the SANS.[856] The PIU shall be responsible for: (a) collecting PNR data from air carriers, storing, and processing those data and transferring those data or the result of processing them to the competent authorities entitled to request or receive PNR data or the result of processing those data from the PIU in order to examine that information further or to take appropriate action for the purposes of preventing, detecting, investigating, and prosecuting terrorist offences or serious crime; and for (b) exchanging both PNR data and the result of processing those data with the PIUs of other Member States and with Europol in accordance with Articles 9 and 10 of the PNR Directive.[857] The National PIU under Article 11a ASANS receives and processes PNR data of the passengers in the Republic of Bulgaria, transported by air, and data of the crew of the aircraft.[858] These data are processed only for the purposes of the prevention, detection, investigation, and prosecution of exhaustively listed serious crimes and terrorist offences.[859] Air carriers are obliged at their own expense, independently or through an authorized service provider to transmit to the National PIU PNR data of passengers and crew data for all flights to, in or from the Republic of Bulgaria.[860] The PNR Directive and ASANS regulate the possibility to exchange data between competent authorities (mainly in case of coincidences according to predefined criteria and by comparison with information funds) in order to counter serious crime and terrorism. Data controller for the PNR processing conducted in Bulgaria is the

854. OJ, L 119, 4 May 2016, p. 132–149.
855. PNR Directive, Art. 3(5).
856. ASANS, Art. 11a.
857. PNR Directive, Art. 4.
858. ASANS, Art. 42a(1).
859. ASANS, Art. 42a(2).
860. ASANS, Art. 42b.

head of the National PIU.[861] The control over the protection of the rights of individuals in the processing of PNR data and in the access to such data is exercised by the CPDP. Outside of these cases, the control over the fulfilment of the obligations of the air carriers under Chapter 6a of the ASANS is carried out by the National PIU.[862]

861. ASANS, Art. 42m (in Bulgarian Art. 42Н)).
862. ASANS, Art 42n (in Bulgarian Art. 42o).

Part VII. Computer-Related Crime

Chapter 1. Legal Developments

361. The legal framework of computer crimes in Bulgaria could be found in one legislative act – the Bulgarian CC[863] since Bulgaria is following the codification legal technique of systematizing rules on crimes. The legislator stays close to legal traditions in regulating the *corpora delicti* of different crimes and has thus chosen a twofold approach.

First, all crimes falling within the qualification of special cybercrimes (or cyber-crimes per se) are systematized together in a single purposefully created Chapter IX-a called 'Cybercrime'. These crimes have a special object – information technologies and computer data.

Second, the *corpora* of otherwise traditional crimes performed by means of information and communication technologies are classified within traditional crimes. Thus, computer fraud[864] is regulated within the classic *corpus* of fraud, the infringement of secrecy of correspondence for electronically sent communications is placed with the traditional violation of the inviolability of correspondence,[865] destroying or damaging property of another by unauthorized access to a computer system is in the Destruction and Endamagement section,[866] and untrue statements in digitally sent communications – where the general false documentation is regulated,[867] etc. The *corpora* of crimes against intellectual property related to the use of information technologies,[868] as well the dissemination of pornographic materials, including child pornography via Internet are considered computer crimes as well.[869]

362. The legal framework of computer crimes was introduced by the amendments of the CC of September 2002.[870] After several unsuccessful attempts to amend the unclear and largely contradictory initial rules,[871] the act for amendments

863. *See* Part II, Ch. 2, para. 130 *supra*.
864. CC, Art. 212a.
865. CC, Art. 171(1), i. 3 and 171(3).
866. CC, Art. 216(3).
867. CC, Art. 313(1) and 313(3).
868. CC, Art. 172a.
869. CC, Art. 159.
870. Criminal Code Amendment Act, SG, issue 92 of 27 Sept. 2002.
871. *See* Criminal Code Amendment Act introduced to the National Assembly on 19 July 2001, No. 154-01-24, Criminal Code Amendment Act introduced to the National Assembly by the Council of Ministers on 19 Apr. 2002, No. 202-01-22, Criminal Code Amendment Act introduced to the National

of the provisions on computer crimes was successfully passed in April 2007, and thus after some subsequent changes in 2017, the CC has reached its present state. By these amendments, a considerable revision took place for most of the norms related to computer crimes. A major part of the discrepancies existing up to that moment were removed. New legal definitions were introduced, and compliance between the legally defined terms and the ones used for formulating the *corpus* of each crime was achieved.

363. A number of legal definitions related to computer crimes were introduced in Article 93.

An 'information system' shall be each separate device or combination of interrelated or similar devices which in execution of a certain program provides or one of the elements of which provides automatic data processing, as well as computer data stored, processed, extracted or transmitted by such device or group of devices for the purpose of operating this data and use, protection and maintaining them.[872]

A 'computer data' shall be considered each presentation of facts, information, or terms in a form susceptible to processing in information systems including program which is able to make an information system perform a certain function.[873]

'Computer and information services provider' is introduced as a term, but it cannot be found in any of the *corpora* of the crimes regulated by the CC. It refers to every legal or natural person that provides an opportunity for communication via an information system or that processes or stores computer data for this communication service or for its users.[874]

Another term of importance for most traditional cybercrimes is the 'computer network' – a combination of interconnected information systems or devices that provides an opportunity for exchange of computer data.[875]

The 'computer program' is a sequence of machine instructions that can make an information system to perform given functions. Before the 2007 amendment, this term was used in parallel with another identical term – 'software'.[876]

A term that was previously used to define one of the main *corpora* of computer crimes per se – 'computer virus' was also introduced with the 2007 amendments. It refers to a computer program distributed automatically and without the will or without the knowledge of the users of the information systems and is designed for setting information systems or computer networks in conditions undesired by their users or for making them achieve undesired results.[877]

For the purposes of criminalizing different aspects of pornography, in particular, creation, distribution, and holding materials revealing child pornography, a special term was introduced. A 'pornographic material' shall be made in any way, obscene,

Assembly by the Council of Ministers on 5 Jan. 2005, No. 502-01-5, Criminal Code Amendment Act introduced to the National Assembly by the Council of Ministers on 22 Mar. 2006, No. 602-01-15.

872. CC, Art. 93, i. 21.
873. CC, Art. 93, i. 22.
874. CC, Art. 93, i. 23.
875. CC, Art. 93, i. 25.
876. CC, Art. 93, i. 26.
877. CC, Art. 93, i. 27.

unacceptable or incompliant with public morality material, the content of which presents overt sexual behaviour. Such is considered a behaviour that presents actual or simulated fornication, sexual intercourses between persons of the same or opposite sex, sodomy, masturbation, sexual sadism or masochism, or lascivious demonstration of one's reproductive organs.[878]

The 2017 changes did not substantially affect the existing rules, rather made some small refinements. These changes were aimed mainly at enhancing the sanctions for the violations, providing the imprisonment and the monetary penalties as cumulative sanctions, increasing the maximum years of imprisonment (for the crimes it was envisaged) and providing for imprisonment (for the crimes for which only monetary penalty was envisaged). These changes reflect the legislator's understanding of the increased public hazard of this type of crimes and its desire to act preventively on this type of criminal activity.

878. CC, Art. 93, i. 28.

Chapter 2. Application of Substantive Criminal Law in the Area of ICT

§1. Computer Crimes Per Se

I. Accomplishing Access to an Information System or Part Thereof Without Right

A. *Main* Corpora Delicti

364. Article 319a(1) of the CC regulates the following *corpora delicti* based on the nature of the committed act: accomplishing access to an information system of part thereof without permission.

The crime impacts the public relations related to privacy of information in a digital form and its protection against its disclosure, dissemination, or any other unauthorized use.

365. The crime is characterized by a specific object of encroachment – an information system or part thereof within the meaning of Article 93, i.21 of the CC.[879] The scope of application of the regulation is restricted because the access should be established to an information system. This way all the hypotheses in which establishing access to data that is not in a certain computer system and are stored on a media are excluded. For example, a smart card is not an information system within the meaning of Article 93, i.21 of the CC and the access to the data on it, e.g., data for creating an electronic signature, will not be an indictable act under Article 319a(1) of the CC. Actually, in most cases access to computer data stored on another media can be accomplished only after this media is plugged in the information system; therefore, at the moment of encroachment, the data will be in the system. The amendments in this provision, namely abolishing the requirement for the data to which an access has been established to be in the computer system, were made in order to avoid difficulties in interpretation and application of this rule. As a result, establishing mere access to the information system or part thereof is incriminated, irrespective of where and how the data is stored.[880]

366. The executive act of the crime is defined as accessing.

According to the Explanatory Report on the Convention on Cybercrime,[881] 'accessing' means penetrating in a certain computer system or in a part of it, including through another computer system when the two systems are connected to each other via public telecommunications networks or are in a common network (e.g., local network or Internet). The access to the system is the broader concept and

879. *See* Part VII, Ch. 1, para. 363 *supra*.
880. *See* D. Markov, *Legal Regulation of the Computer Crimes under the Bulgarian Law*, in *Electronic Document and Electronic Signatures. Commentary* 2004 Sofia, Ciela - Soft and Publishing, p. 375 (G. Dimitrov et al.).
881. Explanatory Report on the Convention on Cybercrime, Council of Europe, ETS No. 185, http://conventions.coe.int/treaty/en/reports/html/185.htm, 8 Nov. 2001.

means presence of certain information in a foreign system. The simple sending of a message or a file via electronic mail from one computer system to another, as well as sending an SMS to a mobile phone, cannot be qualified as a crime under Article 319a(1) of the CC. The executive act of the access without permission finds expression in access to computer data, that is, presence of such information in a foreign computer system, which enables the offender to find out or to affect in a certain way the data in it. Access to certain data is each provision of an opportunity for disclosing, copying, changing, or affecting the data in any other way. The unauthorized access often rests on the basis of other computer crimes with a higher level of public danger.

The incrimination of the unauthorized access as an individual crime complies with the provision of Article 2 of the Convention on Cybercrime[882] that allows parties to announce as a crime under their internal law the very illegal access to the whole computer system or to a part of it without the necessity for another criminal result.

367. Article 319a(1) of the CC determines a comparatively broad scope of the crime of accessing. Along these lines, the Convention on Cybercrime explicitly provides an opportunity for the parties to limit the scope of application of criminal repression, as they project additional requirements for the indictability of the act, for example, the offence in breach of security measures with the intention of taking computer data or with other criminal intention, as well as in relation to a computer system connected to another computer system. Bulgarian law adopts a broad approach and does not envisage such restrictions by which it considerably expands the regulative scope of application. This is reasonable, as far as this way the information systems and the computer data stored therein are protected against the broadest possible range against violations. An exception from the scope of application of this rule are only the cases under Article 9(2) of the CC, when due to its insignificance the act is not of public danger or its level of public danger is obviously insignificant.

Under the main *corpora delicti*, the executive act can be accomplished only by its mere performance.

The executive act should be committed without permission when such is required. The old version of the text used the term ‘unregulated access’ which was closer to the term ‘illegal access’ used by the Convention on Cybercrime defined in the Explanatory Report on it as access ‘without right’.[883]

The need for permission can ensue both from the regulation of an enactment and under other applicable rules and procedures. The act, however, should be indictable when under an enactment the person having granted the permission does not have the right to grant access to the computer to third parties, for example due to enhanced security requirements of the particular computer system. Examples of such enhanced security requirements are the systems for issuing and managing the certificates for qualified electronic signatures. One of the requirements for the TSPs

882. Convention on Cybercrime, Council of Europe, ETS No. 185 http://conventions.coe.int/Treaty/EN/Treaties/html/185.htm, 23 Nov. 2003.

883. Explanatory Report to the Convention on Cybercrime, i. 38.

issuing certificates for qualified electronic signatures is to provide reliable security to the systems for issuing and managing certificates. In accordance with Article 19 and 24 of eIDAS, the qualified TSPs should implement appropriate technical and organizational measures to manage the risks posed to the security of the trust services they provide and access should be granted only to duly authorized officials in compliance with their duties. The access to these systems by persons who are not employees of the TSP should be prohibited.

The act will not be indictable in respect to open systems designed for free (unrestricted) access. For example, such systems are websites on the Internet. The keeping of a publicly accessible Internet website reveals the agreement of its owner to provide access to this website to an unrestricted number of users from the global network. According to the Explanatory Report on the Convention on Cybercrime,[884] the application of standard technical means incorporated in protocols and programs used on a massive scale taken alone cannot be qualified as illegal access because the circumstance that the user has decided to use these protocols and programs means that they have tacitly agreed with the application of these means.

368. A crime will not be present also when the act is committed by a person who exercises their legal powers, for example, when conducting an inspection by a competent supervisory body. In this case, the act is lawful, regardless of the presence or lack of permission or consent by the person administrating or using the computer.

The moment the court assesses the presence or lack of permission should be the moment of the performance of the executive act. The subsequent obtaining of a permission has no relation to the indictability of the act, but can be considered an extenuating circumstance, and in certain cases – a circumstance excluding criminal liability due to insignificance of the act within the meaning of Article 9(2) of the CC.

Accessing is regulated as a formal crime (crime of simple perpetration) – presence of a certain act with the respective data is enough to qualify this act as use. For the indictability of the act, it is enough that the person has accomplished access to a certain information system or part thereof. The crime is completed by the actual commitment of the executive act without the need for another result.[885]

Incriminated are cases of significance, i.e., which are not minor. Minor case is one in which the committed crime, in view of the absence or insignificance of the harmful consequences or in view of other mitigating circumstances, represents a lower degree of public danger in comparison with the ordinary cases of a crime of the respective type (CC, Article 93, i. 9).

Each liable person can be subject to criminal liability. The person should have acted with malice aforethought while committing the crime. The perpetrator realizes that for committing the respective actions, permission is required, and that she or he has not obtained such, but yet deliberately copies, uses, or accomplishes access to the computer data.

884. Explanatory Report to the Convention on Cybercrime, i. 48.

885. *See* D. Doncheva, *Computer Crimes under Chapter Nine 'a' of the CC, Legal Thought*, No. 2, 2003. According to the author, the crime is productive, as the result consists of accessing and revealing the information in the computer.

The punishment is imprisonment for up to two years, which is more severe in comparison to the older regime, which provided only for monetary sanction, namely for a fine up to BGN 3,000.

B. *Qualified* Corpora Delicti

369. The CC regulates several qualified *corpora* of accomplishing access to an information system or part thereof without permission. Qualifying circumstances are the object of the crime (data for creating electronic signature, information that is considered state, or other secrets protected by law), the subject (two or more persons, or one person in case of repetition), and the criminal result (gravity of consequences).

When formulating the qualified *corpora*, the CC uses only classic qualifying circumstances, without taking into account the specific nature of computer crimes. They do not take into consideration the model qualifying circumstances proposed by the Convention on cybercrime such as violating security measures, criminal intention, or violation related to the computer system. It is indisputable in the theory that these circumstances also enhance the act's public danger level as at the same time they reflect some specific particularities of this type of act. For example, the public danger level of an act committed by overcoming special security measures very often will be the same as or even higher than that of an act committed for the second time. The significance of these circumstances can be judged also from the opportunity provided in Article 2 of the Convention on Cybercrime for the parties not to incriminate in their internal law the cases of illegal access in general but *only* those in which the above-mentioned qualified circumstances are present. However, in the current version of Article 319a of the CC the presence of any of these circumstances will be judged only when the punishment is individualized.

1. Qualified *Corpora Delicti* in Relation to the Subject of the Crime

370. The CC makes provisions for two qualified *corpora* with a view of the subject of the crime – when the act is committed by two or more persons who have arranged in advance the commitment of such an act[886] and when it is committed for the second time.[887]

Article 319a(2) of the CC introduces provisions for a graver punishment (imprisonment for up to two years and a fine of up to BGN 3,000) for the cases when the act is committed by two or more persons who have arranged in advance the commitment of such an act.

Article 319a(3) of the CC makes provision for a qualified *corpus* if the act is committed for the second time. The provided punishment is imprisonment for up to

886. CC, Art. 319a(2).
887. CC, Art. 319a(3).

three years and a fine of up to BGN 5,000.[888] According to case law, 'crimes identical by type within the meaning of Article 28 of the CC are the crimes by which are performed one and the same or different *corpora delicti* of one and the same crime, including when it is considered privileged'.[889] This means that repetition is present when the perpetrator has committed a crime under the *corpora delicti* under Article 319a of the CC before he or she has been sentenced with an effective sentence on any other crime under the same article.

2. Qualified *Corpora Delicti* in Relation to the Object of the Crime

371. The qualified *corpora* in relation to the object of the crime are provided for in Article 319a(3) and (4) of the CC.

Under Article 319a(3) of the CC, the special object of the crime is the electronic signature-creation data,[890] and the provided punishment is imprisonment for up to three years and a fine up to BGN 5,000.

The qualified *corpora delicti* with an object electronic signature-creation data was introduced by the CC Amendment Act of May 2007.[891] The amendment was imposed with a view of the more widespread use of electronic signature and hence – the high level of public danger of the violations against the secret of this data, which did not comply with the punishment provided under the main *corpus* which before the 2017 amendments used to be a fine of up to BGN 3,000.

372. Under Article 319a(4) of the CC, the special object of the crime is information that is proclaimed a state secret[892] or another confidential information protected by law, and the punishment is imprisonment for one to three years, if the perpetrator is not subject to a graver punishment.

With regards to other confidential information protected by law, such regulations can be found with respect to:

---

888. Within the meaning of Art. 28(1) of the CC, the crime is committed for the second time, if the perpetrator has committed it after being sentenced with an effective sentence for another similar crime.

889. Decree No. 2 of 27–29 Apr. 1970 70 Plenum of the High General Assembly of the Supreme Court, i. 1.

890. In accordance with Art. 3(13) of eIDAS, 'electronic signature creation data' means unique data which is used by the signatory to create an electronic signature. Depending on the type of electronic signature, the data for its creation is different. With the basic electronic signatures, this is each piece of information (symmetric or asymmetric keys, pseudo-random numbers, unique information objects, etc.) used for the creation of the signature. With respect to qualified electronic signatures, the signature-creation data is the so-called private key – one of a pair of keys used in an asymmetric cryptosystem for electronic signature creation.

891. SG, issue 38 of 11 May 2007.

892. The state secret is legally defined in the Protection of Classified Information Act (PCIA), in which also the order determines the procedures for accessing such information. In accordance with Art. 25 of PCIA, a state secret is the information defined in the list under Appendix No. 1, the unregulated access to which would cause danger to or would harm the interests of the Republic of Bulgaria related to the national security, defence, foreign policy, or the protection of the order established by the Constitution.

- the insurance secret under Articles 149 and 150 of the IC;[893]
- the social insurance secret under Article 109(2) of the Social Security Code (SIC);[894]
- the industrial and trade secret under section 1, i. 9 of the Additional Provisions to the CPA;[895]
- the bank secret under Article 62(2) of the CIA;[896]
- the different types of professional secret under Article 20 of the Private Executive Magistrates Act,[897] Article 26 of the Notaries and Notary Activity Act,[898] Article 11 of the Independent Financial Audit Act,[899] etc.

373. The crime should be committed with malice aforethought – the perpetrator had realized that the information in relation to which he or she committed the respective act was confidential but acted regardless.

The qualified *corpus* under Article 319a(4) of the CC has a subsidiary nature. It applies only in cases when the perpetrator is not subject to a heavier punishment. Heavier punishments are provided, for example, for espionage (disclosing or gathering information that is a state secret with the purpose of disclosing it to a foreign state or organization).

3. Qualified Corpus Delicti in Relation to the Criminal Result

374. The criminal result is a qualifying circumstance under Article 319a(5) of the CC. This is the only *corpus delicti* under Chapter IX of the CC, under which a grave crime within the meaning of Article 93, i. 7 of the CC is present, as the provided punishment is imprisonment for a period ranging between one and eight years.

The specificity of this case comes from the presence of two qualifying circumstances. One of these is the criminal result which is defined by law as appearance of grave consequences. Furthermore, however, the regulation explicitly states that it applies only in relation to acts under Article 319a(4) of the CC, that is, the presence of the special object is also required – information that is proclaimed by law as a state secret or as another secret.

The appearance of grave consequences should be a direct and immediate result of the executive act. Qualifying the consequences as grave shall be done in court in every concrete case. As far as the qualified *corpus delicti* deals only with violations against information that is proclaimed by law as a state or another secret, when judging the graveness of the consequences, the court shall be guided by the level of endangering or impairing interests related to the respective secret.

---

893. SG, issue 102 of 29 Dec. 2015.
894. SG, issue 110 of 17 Dec. 1999.
895. *See* Part I, Ch. 1, para. 41 *supra.*
896. *See* Part IV, Ch. 3, para. 258 *supra.*
897. SG, issue 43 of 20 May 2005.
898. SG, issue 104 of 6 Dec. 1996.
899. SG, issue 95 of 29 Nov. 2016.

II. Criminal Violations Against Information Systems or Data

A. *Main* Corpora Delicti

375. A direct object of criminal encroachments against information systems and computer data are public relations securing the inviolability of these systems and data and their protection against illegal damaging.

The crime must be committed in respect to a special object – an information system within the meaning of Article 93, i. 21 of the CC, or computerized data within the meaning of Article 93, i. 22 of the CC.[900]

376. The executive act can be adding, copying, using, changing, transferring, deleting, damaging, degrading, hiding and erasing or suspending the access to.[901] Adding computer data is considered by the theory as introducing new program data in a computer (information) system that have not existed before the act. Such introducing can be done through the computer peripheral devices (e.g., by the keyboard) as well as by their transferring from a portable media (compact disc, flash memory) or remotely by using another computer (information) system.[902]

Copying means reproducing the data, i.e., making exact copies thereof and extracting them somewhere – in an information system and/or portable media. 'Using' presupposes such activity with the data, aimed at accomplishing or achieving something, i.e. some purpose defined by the perpetrator, although it is not necessary to achieve the aimed result in order to commit the said *corpora delicti*. Changing data means qualitative or quantitative modification of already existing data. The modification usually leads to a change in the system's functioning and/or the data integrity.

Transferring data means 'moving' the data from one system to another or to a portable media.

Deletion means eliminating the access of the users to the respective data. In most cases, deletion does not mean a complete erasure of the data from the information system. When data is merely deleted, the information indicating its location on the hard disc or on the other storage device is erased. This information is used by the operating system for the construction of the computer's directory structure. When this information is erased, the respective data becomes invisible to the operating system. It exists but the operation system does not know where to find it. By recovering this information, which can be done by special programs, the deleted data can be recovered.

In contrast, erasing means a complete obliteration of the data from the information system. In case of erasing, the whole information is obliterated and the respective data cannot be recovered by any means. Usually completely erasing certain information from the computer appears when recording of new data onto the existing data takes place. The operating system regularly records new information on the

900. *See* also Part VII, Ch. 3, para. 433 *infra*.
901. D. Doncheva, *Computer Crimes under Chapter IX 'a' of the CC*.
902. D. Markov, *Legal Regulation of the Computer Crimes under the Bulgarian Law, Electronic Document and Electronic Signatures. Commentary, ibid.*, 385 (G. Dimitrov et al.).

data for which the information about its location has been erased. This means that the longer period of time has passed from the deletion of certain data, the more likely it is for the operating system to record other data on its place so that data is completely erased. Certain forms of the act can be committed by using the physical qualities of the storage devices, for example, intensive electromagnetic fields, mechanical or chemical interventions by liquids, acids, abrasive materials, etc.

Damaging and degrading are acts aimed at worsening the status of the data (its completeness, quality, accuracy, etc.). Hiding/suspending the access to the data are acts aimed at making the data unavailable to the respective operational system (e.g., either it is not readable or the access to it cannot be established), whereas the data still remains present therein, i.e., is not formally deleted/erased.

All forms of the act reveal its productive nature – there should be a result present: an added, changed, deleted, erased or otherwise affected computer data.

The act must be executed without the permission of the person who uses or administrates the information system. The case should be of significance similarly to the crime under Article 319a. In accordance with Article 93, i. 9 of the CC, a minor case shall be the case when either with a view of the insignificance of the harmful effects, or with a view of other extenuating circumstances, has a lower level of public danger compared to the usual cases of crime of such a type. Whether the case is insignificant is subject to the court's assessment in each particular case.

377. The subject of the crime can be each criminally liable person except for the persons administering or using the information system. The crime should be committed with malice aforethought. The perpetrator is aware that she or he does not have the required permission but nevertheless adds, changes, deletes, erases or has other unlawful activity among the ones described above towards the data.

The punishment provided under the main *corpus* is imprisonment for up to two years and a fine up to BGN 3,000.

B. Qualified Corpora Delicti

378. The CC provides for several qualified *corpora delicti* in Article 319b(2)-(5) and Article 319c. The qualifying circumstances are the criminal result (infliction of considerable damages or occurrence of other grave consequences), the criminal purpose (for material benefit or hindering the fulfilment of an obligation), the means to commit the crime and the criminal result (through a computer program, password, access code or other data for access to an information system or to a part of it, intended to affect more than one information system, and considerable damages or occurrence of other grave consequences have occurred) and the perpetrator (the crime has been committed by a person acting on behalf of or in execution of a decision of an organized criminal group) / the object of the crime (information that by virtue of a law must be provided electronically/on an electronic or other carrier or information system part of the critical infrastructure).

1. Qualified *Corpora Delicti* in Relation to the Criminal Result

379. The criminal result is a qualifying circumstance as per Article 319b(2) of the CC. The law indicates two possible results – infliction of considerable damages or causing other grave consequences. The stipulated graver punishment is imprisonment for up to three years and a penalty of up to BGN 5,000.

According to case law, considerable damages cover only property damages. They constitute the reduction of the property (reduction of the assets or increase of the liabilities) of a certain person. There are two criteria to determine whether the damages are ordinary or considerable – the absolute value of the damage and its relative value compared to the value of the whole property. According to case law, if the relative value of the damage is significant and in its absolute value, it is insignificant, there shall be no considerable damage within the meaning of the law. And when the absolute value of the damage is significant, but compared to the value of the damaged *patrimonium* it is insignificant, then a considerable damage should be present.[903] Considerable property damages means mainly that the damages are considerable in their absolute value, that is, the monetary equivalent of the caused damages is significant.[904]

As for the occurrence of other grave consequences, such shall be interpreted as infliction of non-material damages since material damages are covered by the term 'considerable damages'. Whether these consequences are grave is a factual matter and shall be subject to assessment by the court on a case-by-case basis.

The two possible results are indicated alternatively. In any case, it is necessary to have a cause-effect relationship between criminal result and executive act.

2. Qualified *Corpora Delicti* in Relation to the Means to Commit the Crime and the Criminal Result

380. The means to commit the crime and the criminal result are qualifying circumstances as per Article 319b(4) of the CC. With regard to the result, the law contains a reference to the two possible results analysed above – infliction of considerable damages or causing other grave consequences.[905] The means to commit the crime are through a computer programme, password, access code or other data for access to an information system or to a part of it, intended to affect more than one information system. The qualifying circumstances regarding the means are that the result must be cumulatively present. The stipulated graver punishment is imprisonment from one to four years and a penalty of up to BGN 6,000.

---

903. *See* Interpretative Ruling No. 6 of 15 Nov. 1973 of the General Part of the CC as per interpretative criminal case No. 2, 1973.
904. *See* Interpretative Ruling No. 2 of 9 Aug. 1993 of the General Part of the CC as per interpretative criminal case No. 2, 1993.
905. *See* Part VII, Ch. 2, para. 387 *supra.*

3. Qualified *Corpora Delicti* in Relation to the Perpetrator or the Object of the Crime

381. The perpetrator of the crime is a qualifying consequence as per Article 319b(5), i. 1 of the CC – if this is a person acting by order or in execution of a decision of an organized criminal group (OCG). OCG is defined by Article 93, i. 20 of the CC as structured permanent association of three or more persons in order to commit concerted in the country or abroad crimes punishable by imprisonment for more than three years. The association is structured and without a formal distribution of functions between the participants, duration of participation or developed structure. The object of the crime is a qualifying consequence as per Article 319b(5), i. 2 of the CC and is determined as information system that is part of the critical infrastructure.[906] The punishment is imprisonment from five to eight years and a penalty of up to BGN 10,000.

382. The object of the crime is a qualifying consequence as per Article 319c(1) of the CC and is determined as information that is given by virtue of the law electronically or on an electronic or other carrier. The punishment is imprisonment for up to three years and a penalty of up to BGN 3,000.

Presence of an explicit legal provision to stipulate an obligation to present specific information, as well as a possibility for this information to be presented electronically or on an electronic, or other media, is sufficient to trigger the criminal liability under Article 319c(1). The applicable field of the provision covers two groups of cases. In the first case, the law stipulates an obligation for the information to be presented only electronically or on a special medium. In the second case, a scenario is feasible whereby the law may stipulate that the information should be submitted electronically or on a media (as an alternative to paper submission). The interpretation of the provision in the sense that the information is presented only in an electronic form or on a special media would narrow its applicable field.

As for the various types of media, Article 319c(1) of CC provides for one type of media (electronic), and it is explicitly noted that the provision will also apply to information that could be presented on any other media.

Article 319c(1) of the CC neither contains limitations on the person who could present the respective information, nor to whom it must be presented. In particular, no requirements are present indicating that this information should be presented by

906. The term is defined by Art. 2(a) of Council Directive 2008/114/EC of 8 December 2008 on the Identification and Designation of European Critical Infrastructures and the Assessment of the Need to Improve Their Protection as 'an asset, system or part thereof located in Member States which is essential for the maintenance of vital societal functions, health, safety, security, economic or social well-being of people, and the disruption or destruction of which would have a significant impact in a Member State as a result of the failure to maintain those functions'. OJ, L 345, 23 Dec. 2008, pp. 75–82. The Defense and the Armed Forces of the Republic of Bulgaria Act (SG, issue 35 of 12 May 2009 r., in force as of 12 May 2009) defines the critical infrastructure as 'a system of facilities, services and information systems, the shutdown, malfunction or destruction of which would have a serious negative impact on the health and safety of the population, the environment, the national economy or the effective functioning of state governance' – § 1., i. 18 of the Additional Provisions.

or to a state body. The presence of a legal provision establishing an obligation for presenting specific information electronically would be enough to trigger the liability rule.

4. Qualified *Corpora Delicti* in Relation to the Special Purpose of the Perpetrator

383. The CC stipulates two qualified *corpora delicti* with a view to the special purpose of the perpetrator – material benefit (Article 319b(3) or to frustrate the execution of an obligation Article 319c(2)).

Article 319b(3) of the CC rules that when the special purpose of the perpetrator is a property benefit, the punishment should be imprisonment from one to three years and a penalty of up to BGN 5,000. This is the so-called self-interest purpose. The perpetrator seeks to achieve favourable changes in its property or in the property of a third party. The actual achievement of the purpose is of no significance for the indictability of the act, but it would be assessed upon the individualization of the punishment.

In Article 319c(2) of the CC, the special purpose of the perpetrator is expressed as hindering the execution of an obligation and the stipulated punishment is imprisonment from one to three years and a penalty of up to BGN 5,000.

The text of Article 319c(2) of the CC applies only in relation to acts under Article 319c(1) of the CC, that is, it is necessary for the special object of the crime to be cumulatively available – information that is presented by virtue of a law electronically or on an electronic, or other carrier. Usually the presentation of this information is related to the rise of an obligation for a specific person. For example, the references and declarations under tax and customs legislation are the basis for the rise of specific tax or customs obligations.

'Hindering' means creation of obstacles for the fulfilment of the obligation. It is not necessary for an obligation to exist, for the perpetrator to strive to hinder it[907] The type and the density of the obligation are of no significance. The qualifying circumstance is only the intent of the perpetrator to hinder the execution of the obligation. The realization of this purpose is of no significance to the indictability of the act. The actual frustration of the execution of the obligation, however, may be assessed by the court when ruling on the punishment.

III. Loading of Computer Viruses and Other Malicious Programs

A. *Main* Corpora Delicti

384. Article 319d of the CC establishes two main *corpora delicti*, which differ in the means of committing the crime – a computer virus under Article 319d(1) and

907. *See* M. Kopcheva *Computer Crimes* 95 (Sofia: Sibi, 2006). According to the author, the obligation is foreign, i.e., it does not pertain to the perpetrator of the crime.

a computer program, which is designed to disrupt the activity of an information system or a computer network or to gather, erase, delete, change, or copy computer data without permission when such permission is required (Article 319d(2)).[908]

The direct object of the crime is the social relations securing a normal functioning of information systems and computer networks and the privacy of computer data.

The loading of a malicious program that is not a virus in a computer system or network was criminalized with the amendments of the CC of May 2007. The new text of Article 319d(2) of the CC comes as a response to the criticism regarding the former legal framework, which excluded from its applicable field various harmful or malicious programs that are not computer viruses. The reasons for the proposed amendments even indicated that compared to computer viruses, the loading of other malicious programs presents the same, or even a higher level of public hazard.

Article 319d(2) mentions a computer program that is designed to disrupt the activity of an information system or a computer network or to gather, erase, delete, change, or copy computer data without permission, when such permission is required. In particular, these are programs that are not distributed automatically (they are not self-replicating). All programs that are distributed automatically and have the indicated designation fall within the scope of the definition of computer virus under Article 93, i. 27 of the CC and their loading will be qualified as introduction of a computer virus under Article 319d(1).

The purpose of a malicious computer program is formulated as a 'violation of the operation of an information system or a computer network' or 'gathering, erasing, deleting, changing or copying of computer data without permission, when such permission is required'. The disturbance of the activity of an information system or a computer network means changes in the functioning of the system or the network such as slowing down of the performance speed affecting the results of programs and other undesired results. Gathering of computer data without permission is present when the perpetrator gets access to specific data, to which he or she has no right to access by virtue of law or by will of the person who operates or administers an information system or resources thereof. Erasure is the complete removal of specific data from the information system or network. Deletion is the destruction of the information indicating the location of the data. Compared to erased data, deleted data can be restored in some cases. Changing computer data means introduction of a change in already existing data. Copying is related to the creation of one or more copies of the data on the same or on other media.

385. The executive act is defined in the CC as 'loading': loading constitutes execution of the virus or other malicious program in a specific information system or network. The loading of the virus can happen in all manners, in which computer data can be introduced into the computer (system) – from direct execution through peripheral system devices (the devices for reading of information stored on external drives) to remote execution (through networks).

---

908. *See* D. Markov, *Legal Regulation of the Computer Crimes under the Bulgarian Law*, in *Electronic Document and Electronic Signatures. Commentary*, 391 (G. Dimitrov et al.).

The crime is considered committed when a result is present – appearance of the virus or the malicious program in a specific information system or network.[909]

In contrast to Article 319d(1) of the CC criminalizing the loading of a computer virus, Article 319d(2) concerning other malicious programs, is of subsidiary nature and applies only if the act does not constitute a grave crime. For example, if while using the loaded program, the perpetrator has copied electronic signature-creation data or information constituting a state secret, the act will be qualified under Article 319a(3) or Article 319a(4) of the CC, respectively.

386. The subject of the crime under both main *corpora delicti* may be any person liable under criminal law. The perpetrator should act with malice aforethought. The person aims to load the computer virus or other malicious program in a specific information system of network. The malice as an element of the crime is of great significance for triggering the liability under this provision. The loading of computer viruses affects the information systems since they have the ability to self-replicate. The act shall be indictable only when the perpetrator is aware that the code he or she is loading into a computer/system constitutes a computer virus and nevertheless he or she aims to load it. There will be no crime if the person is not aware that the program or the data contain a virus or other malicious program. The same applies to the cases when due to the activation of the virus the system automatically introduces the virus in other information systems or computer networks or sends it via e-mail.

The punishment stipulated by the CC for the loading of a computer virus or another malicious program is imprisonment for up to three years and a penalty of an amount of up to BGN 3,000.

B. *Qualified* Corpora Delicti

387. Article 319d(3) of the CC envisages two qualified *corpora delicti* of the loading of a computer virus or other malicious program. In the first case, the emphasis is put on the criminal result indicated in the law as the occurrence of considerable damages. The exclusion of the occurrence of other grave consequences from the criminal result is an omission of the legislator. Thus, the non-material damages are groundlessly excluded from the qualifying circumstances.

In the second case, the act is qualified when it is performed repeatedly. The special quality of the subject of the crime is the qualifying circumstance. Within the meaning of Article 28(1) of the CC, the crime is performed repeatedly if the perpetrator has performed it after being sentenced with an effective verdict for such a crime. Under case law similar in type of crimes are 'those which implement the same or different *corpora delicti* of the same crime including when it is qualified or

909. *See* Doncheva, *Computer Crimes under Chapter Nine 'a' of the CC*. The crime is completed when the virus reaches a specific computer or information network, regardless of whether it is activated or neutralized by a special antivirus program.

privileged', repeatability will also be present when the perpetrator introduces a computer virus after being sentenced with an effective verdict for loading of another malicious computer program and vice versa.[910]

Under both qualified *corpora delicti*, the stipulated punishment is imprisonment for up to five years and a penalty of up to BGN 3,000.

IV. Distribution of Passwords and Access Codes for Computer Systems or Data

A. *Main Corpus Delicti*

388. Immediate object of the crime are the social relations providing the confidentiality and privacy of information in electronic form.

The crime is characterized by a special object – computer programs, passwords, access codes or other similar access data to an information system or part thereof. With the amendments of May 2007, the provision of Article 319e(1) of the CC was changed from a terminological point of view. According to the old wording, the object of the crime was defined as 'computer or system passwords'. The current wording is broad to cover different types of data that can be used to establish access to information systems or parts thereof – passwords, access codes or other data used for access, as well as computer programs.

The executive act of the crime is creation, procurement for the perpetrator or for somebody else, importing or otherwise distribution. The legislator encompasses different types of criminal activity aimed at the respective passwords or access codes. The executive act may be performed only by an action. The passwords can be created, procured, imported or otherwise distributed electronically, as well as by other ways including on paper. Whether the act has been performed free of charge or against payment is of no significance to the indictability of the act.[911]

The performance of the act should be done with special purpose, i.e., should be aimed at achieving a special result – committing one of the enlisted crimes, namely crimes under Article 171(3), Article 319a, Article 319b, Article 319c or Article 319dd.

For the indictability of the act, it is of no significance whether the perpetrator has become aware of the respective passwords or access codes legally. The perpetrator should have acted with malice aforethought while willing to perform the executive act (the distribution) and thus to achieve the criminal purpose (to commit one of the exhaustively enlisted crimes).

The stipulated punishment under the main *corpus delicti* is imprisonment for up to two years.

---

910. *See* Part VII, Ch. 2, para. 387 *supra*.

911. *See* M. Kopcheva, *Computer Crimes*, 64. According to the author, Art. 319e(1) of the CC applies only to free distribution since the law stipulates a qualified *corpus delicti* when the act has been performed with self-interest (Art. 319e(2)). However, it is possible that the perpetrator has received some kind of benefit without having a self-interest objective in the moment of performing the act, or that he/she has had the objective to gain some kind of benefit and that objective has been realized.

B. Qualified Corpora Delicti

389. Article 319e(2) and (3) of the CC regulate several qualified *corpora delicti*. The first hypothesis covers the cases where a criminal result has been achieved – due to the unlawful act, personal data, or classified information or some other secret protected by law should have been made available to third parties Personal information is defined in GDPR,[912] which also regulates the rules of processing of such information and the rules for access thereto. According to Article 4, i. 1 of GDPR, personal data should be any information relating to an identified or identifiable natural person ('data subject'); an identifiable natural person is one who can be identified, directly or indirectly, in particular by reference to an identifier such as a name, an identification number, location data, an online identifier or to one or more factors specific to the physical, physiological, genetic, mental, economic, cultural or social identity of that natural person.

Other types of information covered by the *corpus delicti* are those constituting classified information or other secret protected by law.[913]

The indictable act under Article 319e(2) of the CC will be present when a causal relationship between the executive act and the criminal result is proved. The causal relationship is an element of the crime and means that the disclosure of personal data or information constituting classified information or other secrets protected by law must be a direct and immediate consequence of the distribution of the passwords or the access codes.[914] The provision of Article 319e(2) of the CC is of subsidiary nature. To fall under the scope of Article 319e(2), the unlawful act should not constitute more severe crime such as espionage and other crimes against the republic.

The second and third hypotheses encompass all cases where the unlawful activities conducted with the passwords or the access codes are committed for material benefit or by a person acting by order or in execution of a decision of an OCG. The last hypothesis encompasses all cases where considerable damages have been inflicted or other grave consequences have occurred with the act.[915] Thus, the property damages, as well as the non-material damages constitute an indictable result.

The penalty for each of the above qualified *corpora delicti* is imprisonment for up to five years.

---

912. *See* Part VI, Ch. 5, para. 337 *supra*.

913. *See* for the types of classified information – state secret, official secret and foreign-classified information Art. 25, Art. 26 and Art. 27 of the Protection of Classified Information Act, SG issue 45 of 30 Apr. 2002; correction SG, issue 5 of 17 Jan. 2003.

914. *See* D. Markov, *Legal Regulation of the Computer Crimes under the Bulgarian Law*, in *Electronic Document and Electronic Signatures. Commentary*, 395 (G. Dimitrov et al.).

915. *See* Part VII, Ch. 2, para. 387 *supra*.

V. Crimes Related to EDETSA

390. Some acts are criminalized by Article 319f of the CC when the social relations related to the normal sending, receiving, writing, and recording of electronic communications might lead to public hazard. These social relations are regulated by EDETSA.[916]

The executive act under this rule is the violation of the obligation to store data on the time and source of transmitted electronic communications for a term of one year.

391. The executive act may be performed through an action (destruction of the respective information) or inaction (wilful failure to undertake the necessary measures to store the respective information while knowing that this might damage third parties).

The crime under Article 319f of the CC is characterized by a special subject. This is a person acting as an intermediary to electronic communications within the meaning of Article 6(1) of EDETSA.[917]

When the intermediary is a legal entity, the subject of the crime will be the natural person – the executive director, the employee of the provider, or other person, who according to internal rules, is responsible for storing the indicated information but deliberately fails doing so.[918]

The law stipulates that the executive act shall be performed during the course of delivery of information services. The scope of the activity on delivering information services can be derived from the term 'provider of computerized information services' as defined in Article 93, i. 23 of the CC. Within the meaning of this definition, the delivery of information services will constitute the offering of the possibility to users to communicate through an information system or the processing or storing computer data for this communication service or for the users.[919]

392. Under Article 319f, the perpetrator should have acted with malice aforethought. The perpetrator is aware that she or he is bound to store the indicated information for the specified term, but nevertheless she or he violates this obligation.

The provision of Article 319f of the CC is of subsidiary nature. It applies only in cases when the perpetrator is not subject to a graver punishment.

The stipulated punishment is a penalty of up to BGN 5,000. Besides that, Article 6(3) of EDETSA also stipulates liability for damages resulting from the non-execution of the obligation to store information.

916. *See* Introduction, Ch. 5, para. 33 *supra.*
917. *See* Part IV, Ch. 1, para. 216 *supra.*
918. *See* D. Markov, *Legal Regulation of the Computer Crimes under the Bulgarian Law*, in *Electronic Document and Electronic Signatures. Commentary*, 397 (G. Dimitrov et al.).
919. *See* Part VII, Ch. I, para. 363 *supra.*

§2. COMPUTER-RELATED CRIMES

I. Computer Fraud

A. Main Corpus Delicti under Article 212a(1) of the CC

393. Under Bulgarian legal theory, the computer fraud is qualified as a crime against the property. It is placed systematically in section 4 'Fraud' of Chapter 5 'Crimes against Property' of the special part of the CC.

The rules of the CC protect the public relations securing privacy and normal exercising of property rights, on one hand, and those guaranteeing the security of computer data, on the other.

The computer fraud under Article 212a(1) of CC is characterized by a special object of encroachment – computerized data within the meaning of Article 93, i. 22 of the CC.[920] The material media, on which the data is stored, can also be the object of computer fraud. These can be magnetic and optical discs, storage devices in computer systems, and other media.[921]

394. The executive act of the crime consists of two related elements. The first element is indicated in the law as deceiving or maintaining deceit and means bringing a false knowledge of facts and circumstances of the objective reality which motivate the deceived person in acting or failing to do so. Deceiving constitutes an initial creation of incorrect knowledge of given facts and circumstances, while the maintaining of a deceit is expressed in the confirmation of incorrect awareness initially created without the participation of the perpetrator.

The second element consists of several executive acts – introducing, changing, deleting, or erasing computer data or using of another person's electronic signature.

The introduction, changing, deleting, and erasing of computer data are the same executive acts as in criminal encroachments upon computer programs and data under Article 319b of the CC regardless of the terminological difference between the two provisions (Article 212(1) of CC uses the terms 'introduces', 'amends', and 'erases', while Article 319b(1) of the CC uses the terms 'adds', 'changes', and 'destroys').[922]

A use of another person's electronic signature means a use of a specific electronic signature by any person other than its author. The use itself is expressed in the creation of a signature by using the data, to which, under eIDAS and EDETSA, only the signatory can have access.

The second element of the executive act is a manner or means for reaching of the main purpose of the crime – deceiving or maintaining a deceit.[923]

---

920. *See* Part VII, Ch. 1, para. 363 *supra*.
921. *See* A. Stoynov, 'Computer Fraud', *Modern Law*, No. 4, 2002. According to the author, the object of computer fraud is also the person influenced by the perpetrator as well as the property in the factual possession of the deceived person.
922. *See* Part VII, Ch. 2, para. 376 *supra*.
923. *See* D. Markov, *Legal Regulation of the Computer Crimes under the Bulgarian Law*, in *Electronic Document and Electronic Signatures. Commentary*, 399 (G. Dimitrov et al.).

395. Computer fraud under Article 212a(1) of the CC is an effective crime. The criminal results are two. The first one is the change in the computer data and second one – the occurrence of damages for the deceived person or other persons.[924]

The crime shall be present if the perpetrator acts with malice aforethought. The perpetrator performs an encroachment knowing that he or she rises or maintains a deceit in relation to the deceived person. Besides that, the law requires the presence of a special purpose – the perpetrator aims to achieve benefit for him- or herself or for somebody else.[925]

The stipulated punishment under the main *corpus delicti* of computer fraud under Article 212a(1) of the CC is imprisonment from one to six years and a penalty of up to BGN 6,000.

B. Main Corpus Delicti under Article 212a(2) of the CC

396. The CC introduces another crime by its Article 212a(2), which differs from the one under Article 212a(1).[926]

First, there is a difference in the executive act. Unlike the main *corpus* of the computer fraud Article 212a(2) of the CC provides that the introduction, changing, deleting, or erasing of computer data is done without rising or maintaining of deceit. The perpetrator acts so by manipulating data to create positive consequences for him- or herself. For example, the perpetrator changes the data in the electronic property register so that he or she would become an owner of a given real estate.

The crime under Article 212a(2) is also effective, but the result covers only the occurred change in the computer data. The indictability of the act does not depend on the occurrence of damages for the deceived person or for other persons.

397. Similar to the main *corpus* of the computer fraud, the crime under Article 212a(2) shall be present when the perpetrator has acted deliberately, but with a different purpose – to acquire something, which he or she does not possess. If the perpetrator aims for the benefit of a third party, the act will not be indictable under Article 212a(2) but under Article 319b of the CC.[927]

The stipulated punishment under the main *corpus delicti* of computer fraud under Article 212a(2) is the same as under Article 212a(1) – imprisonment from one to six years and a penalty of up to BGN 6,000.

---

924. *See* A. Stoynov, 'Computer Fraud'. According to the author the harm from computer fraud may be either only property damages, or a combination of property and moral damages.
925. *See* Part VII, Ch. 2, para. 385 *supra.*
926. For more detailed information on relations between *corpora delicti see* the analysis of Art. 212a(1) and (2) of the CC, as well as on the relations between computer fraud and other types of fraud, *see* A. Stoynov, 'Computer Fraud'.
927. *See* Part VII, Ch. 2, para. 385 *supra.*

II. Crimes Against Intellectual Property

398. Infringements of intellectual property rights were criminalized for the first time with the amendments of the CC of 1995.[928] These texts remained almost unchanged until 2006 when the legal framework of crimes against intellectual property was substantially changed.[929]

At present, the main problem the protection of copyrights faced by the society is the illegal distribution of objects of intellectual property using modern information technologies.

The main provision related to crimes against intellectual property that can be considered belonging to the family of computer crimes is Article 172a of the CC.

A. *Main Corpus Delicti under Article 172a(1) of the CC*

399. Article 172a(1) of the CC criminalizes the illegal use of copyright.

The immediate target of this crime are the social relations existing around a normal exercising of copyright and related rights, as well as the conditions and the statutory order of exercising those rights.

Under the analysed rule, the object of the crime is defined as 'an object of copyright or a related right, including copies thereof'. The punishment is imprisonment for up to five years and a penalty of up to BGN 5,000.

400. The objects of copyright are legally defined in the CRRA.[930] According to Article 3(1) of the CRRA as such shall be considered any work of literature, art, and science, which is a result of a creative activity and is expressed in any manner and any objective form whatsoever. In addition to this definition, the law lists in a non-exhaustive manner the most widespread objects of copyright, such as literary works, including works of scientific and technical literature, music and theatrical works, movies, works of art, and so on.

According to Article 72 of CRRA, the rights related to the copyright include the rights of actors over their plays, of the producers of music over their records, of the producers of the initial record of a movie over the original and the copies obtained as a result from this record, and of the radio and television organizations over their broadcasts.

A copy of an object of copyright is each individual piece of it stored in any objective form.

The object of the crime is another person's object of copyright or related right, that is, the perpetrator is not the holder of the respective right.

928. Criminal Code Amendment Act, SG, issue 50 of 1 Jun. 1995.
929. *Ibid.*, issue 5 of 12 Sep. 2006.
930. *See* Part II, Ch. 1, para. 121 *supra.*

401. The illegal result can be achieved by various executive acts; that is why, the legislator has chosen to list in a non-exhaustive manner some of most common ones: recording, reproduction, distribution, broadcasting, transmission, and others.[931]

Reproduction and distribution are legally defined in the CRRA. According to paragraph 2, i. 3 of the Additional Provisions of the CRRA, 'reproduction of a work' shall be the direct or indirect duplication in one or more copies of the work in whatever manner and form, temporary or permanent, including its recording in electronic form on an electronic carrier. According to i. 4 to paragraph 2 of the Additional Provisions of the CRRA, 'distribution of a work' is the sale, exchange, granting, leasing, storing in commercial quantities, and offering for sale or leasing of originals or copies of the work.

The legal definitions under the CRRA can be used for clarification of the contents of the remaining listed executive acts of the crime under Article 172a(1) of the CC. Thus, for example, on the grounds of paragraph 2, i. 7 of the Additional Provisions of the CRRA, which gives definition of the term 'audio recording', the contents of the executive act recording can be defined as fixing on a permanent tangible media of an object of copyright in a manner allowing for its perception, reproduction, consecutive recording, broadcasting wirelessly, or through a cable or some other technical device.

The term 'broadcasting of a work wirelessly' is defined in paragraph 2, i. 5 of the Additional Provisions of the CRRA. It covers each broadcasting on the radio or television using ground-based infrastructure, as well as its inclusion into an uninterrupted communication network to a satellite and back to Earth through signals carrying programmes under the control and responsibility of the broadcasting organization with a view to being received whether directly and individually by the audience or indirectly by an organization other than the broadcasting one.

As far as the last indicated form of the executive act transmitting is concerned, its content is similar to that of broadcasting with the difference that instead of wirelessly it is implemented through a cable or other carrier.

Besides these explicitly indicated cases, the executive act of the crime under Article 172a(1) of the CC is also present upon each 'use in any other manner' of the respective copyright without the consent of the copyright holder. Thus, the legislator is trying to cover larger scope of encroachments upon the objects of copyright and related rights. An important element of the *corpus* of the crime is the lack of consent of the copyright holder where such is required by law. The cases in which this consent is required, the order for its obtaining and the term of its operation are regulated in detail in the CRRA.

The stipulated punishment for the acts under Article 172a(1) of the CC is imprisonment for up to five years and a penalty of up to BGN 5,000.

---

931. Upon the approval of the changes in the CC, it was discussed whether to add two more acts (importing and exporting) to the exemplary listing, but this proposal was rejected.

B. Main Corpus Delicti under Article 172a(2) of the CC

402. Article 172a(2) of the CC criminalizes the illegal holding of media containing another person's objects of copyright or related rights or a mould for reproduction of such media. Such acts were criminalized for the first time with the amendments to the CC in 2006.

Most of the terms pertaining to this crime were officially defined by the Act on Administrative Regulation of Production and Trading with Optical Discs, Moulds and Other Objects of Copyright and Related Rights.[932] According to the Additional Provisions of this law, 'other media' (besides optical discs) are all permanent material media on which objects of copyright and related rights are stored and which allow for these objects to be brought to the attention of the public by suitable means. 'Optical discs'[933] are media on which information can be stored in an electronic form readable by means of an optical mechanism that employs a laser or other high-frequency light source, where this category includes CD, CD-DA, CD-I, CD-P, CD-ROM, CD-R, CD-RW, CD-WO, DVD, DVD-RAM, DVD-ROM, LD, MD, VCD, CVD, SVCD and SACD. In practice, a wide range of material media exist nowadays, which could contain objects of copyright or related rights. These include portable media, such as magnetic discs and diskettes, optical discs, external memory (USB flash memory), various types of memory cards for mobile phones, and so on, as well as media that are parts of other devices, such as the hard disks, the integrated memory chips of mobile phones, etc.

The Act on Administrative Regulation of Production of Optical Discs and Moulds defines the term 'mould' or 'matrix'[934] as the prototype of an optical disc containing information from which limited copies of optical discs can be produced using a special technology.

403. The executive act is holding the media, which means exercising factual possession of the respective material media or moulds used for their reproduction. The holding should be exercised without the consent required by law.

Mere holding of material media would not always constitute a crime. The law reads that the value of these media should be substantial. According to case law, such will be the cases when the monetary value of the object of the crime exceeds the minimum salary in the country seventy times.[935]

404. The crime should be committed deliberately – the perpetrator is aware that she or he does not have the consent for holding the respective material media or mould required by law but holds copies of the copyrighted material regardless.[936]

---

932. SG, issue 74 of 13 Sep. 2005. The title of the act has been changed to Act on Administrative Regulation of Production of Optical Discs and Moulds (SG 26/2020).
933. *Ibid.*, Additional Provisions, para. 1, i. 2.
934. *Ibid.*, s. 1, i. 3.
935. *See* Interpretative Ruling No. 1 of 30 Oct. 1998 of the general part of the CC as per interpretative criminal case No. 1/98.
936. Upon the acceptance of the changes in the CC, it was discussed as an element of the subjective side of the crime under Art. 172a(2) of the CC whether to add a special objective of the perpetrator defined as 'commercial'. Such an objective is not present in either of the other provisions of the

The punishment stipulated for committing a crime under Article 172a(2) of the CC is imprisonment for two to five years and a penalty of BGN 2,000 to BGN 5,000.

C. *Qualified* Corpora Delicti

405. The qualified *corpora delicti* of the crimes against intellectual property are envisaged in Article 172a(3) and (4) of the CC. The qualifying circumstances are the subject of the crime and the criminal result, and for the act under Article 172a(2) of the CC – the graveness of the act. After the amendments of 2006, all qualified *corpora delicti* of the infringements of copyright and related rights are now qualified as grave crimes within the meaning of Article 93, i. 7 of the CC.

1. Qualified *Corpora Delicti* in Relation to the Subject

406. The CC stipulates only one qualified *corpus* of the crimes under Article 172a(1) and (2) of the CC – when the act is performed repeatedly (Article 172a(3) of the CC).[937] The stipulated punishment is imprisonment for one to six years and a penalty of BGN 3,000 to BGN 10,000.

Re-offence will always be present when the perpetrator has committed a crime envisaged by one of the first two paragraphs of Article 172a of the CC, after she or he has been sentenced for other crime under the same paragraph regardless. For example, if a person is sentenced with an effective verdict for illegal recording of copyrighted object and subsequently is accused of distribution of copies of such object, the act will be qualified as recommitted.

2. Qualified *Corpora Delicti* in Relation to the Criminal Result

407. The crimes under Article 172a(1) and (2) of the CC are more severely punishable (imprisonment from one to six years and a penalty from BGN 3,000 to BGN 10,000) when considerable harmful consequences have been caused by the act. The harmful consequences cover material and non-material damages. The consequences must be a direct and immediate result of the act. Whether they are considerable will be decided on a case-by-case basis by the court, which must take into consideration the amount of the damages suffered by the copyright holder.

CC and therefore was removed from the final draft passed by the Parliament. For analysis and criticism of this proposal, *see* 'E-Bulgaria 2006 Report' 82 (Sofia: Applied Studies and Communications Foundation, 2006).

937. For more detailed information on the acts committed under conditions of repeatability, *see* Part VII, Ch. 2, 379.

3. Other Qualified *Corpora Delicti*

408. According to Article 172a(4) of the CC, the crime is more severely punishable (imprisonment from two to eight years and a penalty from BGN 10,000 to BGN 50,000) when damages of particularly high value have been caused. According to case law, such shall be present when the monetary value of the object of the crime exceeds the established minimum salary 140 times.[938]

D. Insignificant Cases

409. According to Article 172a(5) of the CC, the perpetrator is penalized for insignificant cases under the administrative procedure of the CRRA. The administrative penalties have a stipulated range of BGN 2,000 to BGN 20,000.

According to Article 93, i. 9 of the CC, an insignificant case is present when the committed crime with a view to the lack or the insignificance of the harmful consequences or with a view to other mitigating circumstances reveals lower level of public hazard compared to common crimes of the respective type. The rules imposing administrative punishments for insignificant cases of intellectual property infringements nowadays are more frequently applied in view of the increased number of cases of illegal distribution of copyrighted objects over the Internet. In practice, it is impossible, unjust, and unnecessary to sanction every single violation of copyrights using the slow, clumsy, and expensive mechanism for realization of criminal liability.

E. Confiscation of the Subject Matter of the Crime in Favour of the State

410. Article 172a(6) of the CC stipulates confiscation in favour of the state and the destruction of the subject matter of the crime regardless of whose property it is.

In its new wording, the law brings up a few questions with a view of the scope of the term 'subject matter of the crime'.

As per Article 172a(1) of the CC, a subject matter of the crime is the copyrighted object or a copy thereof. Such could be confiscated only when it is materialized on a certain medium. In practice, what can be confiscated is the media itself – magnetic or optical disc, diskette, magnetic tape, and so on. The same applies to the copies.

Under Article 172a(2) of the CC, the subject matter of the crime is a material media containing copyrighted object or moulds for reproduction of such media. When the media is a part of a larger device, for example, a hard disk or a memory card being part of a computer, the media itself must be subject to confiscation, not the whole device. It is still disputable on how to proceed when the material media

938. *See* Interpretative Ruling No. 1 of 30 Oct. 1998 of the General Part of the CC as per interpretative criminal case No. 1/98.

cannot be physically separated from the respective device without damaging it. Such would be the case, for example, of devices with integrated memory (mobile phones, MP3 players, and others).

III. Crimes Related to Pornographic Materials

411. The crimes related to pornographic materials, just like the crimes against intellectual property are not typical computer crimes. Due to the wide penetration of information technologies, however, the distribution of such materials electronically becomes easier and practically at no cost. This form of distribution reveals a very high level of public hazard, because in contrast to the distribution on paper, the use of information technologies makes it possible for the materials to reach a practically unlimited number of persons including minors.

A. *Main* Corpora Delicti

412. The CC provides three main *corpora delicti* of crimes related to pornographic materials. They both do not make a difference whether computers or other information technologies have been used for the commitment of the act.

The first main *corpus* covers the creation, exposure, presentation, broadcasting, offering, sale, renting, or distribution in any other manner of pornographic materials (Article 159(1) of the CC).[939]

With the amendments to the CC from April 2007, a legal definition of the term 'pornographic material' (Article 93, i. 28 of the CC) was introduced for the first time in Bulgarian legislation. It proves to be a material which is indecent, unacceptable, or incompatible with public morals and expresses explicit sexual behaviour. The definition consists of two elements. First, it is about a material which represents an exposed sexual behaviour. Article 93, i. 28 of the CC gives examples of such cases – real or simulated fornication, sexual intercourse between persons of the same or different sex, sodomy, masturbation, sexual sadism or masochism, or lascivious showing of sexual organs. The listing is exemplary and in every concrete case, the court must assess whether a specific action is explicit sexual behaviour or not. The second element of the definition contains the public assessment of this material, namely that it is indecent, unacceptable, or incompatible with public morality. Case law determines when a specific material is indecent, unacceptable, or incompatible with public morality. What is of significance in this case is the fact that the two elements of the definition must be present at the same time in order for a certain material to be qualified as pornographic. If certain material represents exposed sexual behaviour, but in its nature, it is not indecent, unacceptable, or incompatible with public morals, it will not be categorized as pornographic. Examples of such materials are various textbooks for educational purposes, science literature, works of art,

---

939. M. Kopcheva, *Computer Crimes*, 120–123.

and others. When a material is indecent, unacceptable, or incompatible with public morals, but it does not represent an exposed sexual behaviour, it will not be categorized as pornographic either.

The main *corpus delicti* of the crime under Article 159(1) of the CC is formulated in a technologically neutral manner and covers the creation and dissemination of pornographic materials in any manner whatsoever. The listing of the various ways of distribution is exemplary, and the provision shall apply in relation to any other act that can be categorized as dissemination, that is, as bringing the contents of the respective materials to the attention of third parties. The applicable field of the provision covers the dissemination of pornographic materials on paper (newspapers, magazines, posters, calendars, and so on), as well as on an electronic media (CDs, videotapes, DVDs, and others) or online (websites, multimedia communications through mobile phones, and others). Neither the material carrier, nor the manner of dissemination of the materials is of significance to the indictability of the act. The stipulated punishment is imprisonment for up to one year and a penalty from BGN 1,000 to BGN 3,000.

The second main *corpus delicti* includes the acts of holding or obtaining for oneself or for somebody else through an information or communication technology or in any other manner of pornographic materials, the creation of which involves a person of age under 18 or one who looks under 18.[940] Despite the explicit indication of the information or communication technology as a possible means of the crime, this main *corpus* also covers all possible acts that can be qualified as holding or obtaining.[941] Holding means exercising factual possession over the respective pornographic material, while obtaining means of the act of acquiring the material. Whether the perpetrator holds or obtains the pornographic material for him- or herself or for somebody else is of no significance to the indictability of the act. The moment of creating the material is of utmost importance. Whether a person looks like a minor (under 18 years of age) is a factual matter and shall be assessed by the court on a case-by-case basis. The media of the pornographic materials is of no significance to the indictability of the act. The explicit indication of the information or communication technology as an exemplary media to store the material seems to be an attempt to emphasize on the public hazard of the act. The act will be considered a crime upon holding or obtaining the said materials on any media whatsoever (paper, optical disks, magnetic discs, flash memory, etc.). The punishment stipulated for this crime is deprivation of liberty of up to one year or a fine of up to BGN 2,000.

The third main *corpus delicti* includes the act of establishing access to pornographic material used by a person under the age of 18 or a person who appears to be under the age of 18. This should be done through information or communication technology and knowingly, i.e., the perpetrator was aware and desired to establish access. Hence, if somebody by accident accesses such material – e.g., by clicking on links in fishing emails that leads to websites with such pornographic content, the crime would not be considered committed due to lack of malice. The punishment

940. CC, Art. 159(6).
941. *See* Part VII, Ch. 1, para. 363 *supra*.

stipulated for this crime is the same as for the crime under Article 159(6) of the CC – deprivation of liberty of up to one year or a fine of up to BGN 2,000.

B. *Qualified* Corpora Delicti

413. The CC stipulates qualified *corpora delicti* only in relation to the crime under Article 159(1) of the CC. Qualifying circumstances are the specific manner of committing the crime (dissemination through information or communication technology), the object of the crime (a person who has not reached 16 years of age), the means of the crime (pornographic material, the creation of which involves a person under the age of 18 or who looks under 18 or a person who does not understand the nature and the significance of what has been done), the perpetrator (by two or more persons), and other elements depending on the circumstances (performed repeatedly or act committed by order or in execution of a decision of an organized criminal group).

The qualified *corpus delicti* that is closest to computer crimes is the dissemination of pornographic materials through the Internet (Article 159(2) of the CC). The stipulated graver punishment for this crime is imprisonment for up to two years and a penalty from BGN 1,000 to BGN 3,000.

414. The manner of dissemination of the pornographic materials is defined by the expression 'through information or communication technology'. This wording of the provision is not precise and may lead to groundless widening of the applicable field of the norm to acts that reveal lower level of public hazard. The meaning of the text is to sanction those acts, which lead to the dissemination of pornographic materials to an unlimited number of persons. Such dissemination includes mainly publishing of materials on publicly accessible websites on the Internet or via other technology. Lower, but still high level of public hazard is revealed by the accessing of pornographic materials that are stored in the perpetrator's computer system via peer-to-peer communication technologies by an unlimited number of persons.

Proving the type of fault of these acts is of utmost importance for the successful application of the analysed rules. The crime shall be present if the perpetrator has acted with malice aforethought; therefore, she or he must have been aware that the material is pornographic and still disseminates it purposefully. For example, if a person publishes pornographic materials on an Internet site, she or he is the one who should be held liable since she or he is aware of the nature of the materials and still publishes it. The employees of the information society service provider who develop a given website shall not be liable unless they maintain the website and were aware of its contents.

415. The *corpus delicti* under Article 159(3) of the CC is qualified with a view to the object of the crime and covers the hypotheses when the pornographic material is exposed, presented, sold, rented, or in any other manner disseminated to a person of age under 16. The stipulated punishment is imprisonment for up to three years and a penalty of up to BGN 5,000. The *corpus delicti* does not reveal specific features with a view to the use of computers or other information technologies. The executive acts are the same as per the main *corpus delicti* under Article 159(1) of the CC and cover distribution of the material on an electronic media or electronically, but as well as in any other way.

Under Article 159(4), the qualifying circumstances are the means of the crime (pornographic material the creation of which involves a person of age under 18 or a person who looks under 18 or a person who does not understand the nature and the significance of what has been done), the perpetrator (if committed by two or more persons) where the act is performed repeatedly and the punishment is imprisonment for up to six years, and a penalty of up to BGN 8,000. Under Article 159(5), the act is more severely punishable when it is committed upon the assignment or in execution of a decision of an organized criminal group. The punishment is imprisonment from two to eight years and a penalty of up to BGN 10,000. The court may still decide on confiscating the whole or part of the property of the perpetrator. Both qualified *corpora* do not explicitly envisage any elements which could qualify them as computer crimes, but still they are applicable to cases when pornographic materials are disseminated through the Internet.

In all the above cases of the main and qualified *corpus delicti* the court may also impose the sanctions' deprivation of the right to hold a certain state or public position or deprivation of the right to exercise a certain profession or activity (Article 37, i. 6 and i. 7 of the CC), depending on the role, function, and capacity of the perpetrator.[942]

C. Confiscation of the Object of the Crime in Favour of the State

416. According to Article 159(9) of the CC, the object of the crime should be confiscated in favour of the state and if it is missing or expropriated, its equivalence shall be adjudicated. The correct determination of the object of the crime is of great significance to the practical application of the provision.

§3. Crimes Committed by Electronic Means

I. Computer Crimes Against the Confidentiality of Correspondence

A. Main Corpora Delicti

417. The immediate target of the crimes against confidentiality of correspondence is the public relations providing the privacy and confidentiality of correspondence as a whole and in particular of the one transmitted electronically.[943]

942. Article 159(8) of the CC.
943. A. Stoyanov, *Paragraph Criminal Law. Special Part. Crimes Against Human Rights* 205 et seq. (Sofia: Siela, 1997).

Article 171(1), i. 3 of the CC introduces two crimes that differ in respect to the executive act. The first one relates to illegal learning of the contents of other persons' messages sent electronically and the second one – to diverting such messages from reaching their recipients.[944]

In contrast to traditional crimes against privacy of correspondence that have two objects – the information itself, on one hand, and the media of this information, on the other hand (e.g., a letter, a telegram, etc.) – crimes against electronic correspondence reveal public danger with the mere access to the electronic message, since learning its contents can be made without a physical access to the material media.

418. The executive act under the first main *corpus delicti* is formulated as learning, i.e., bringing the contents of the message to the attention of the perpetrator. The perpetrator may learn someone else's message by gaining access to the information (computer) system of the sender, of the recipient or of an intermediary who stores or transmits the message. The message would not have been addressed to the perpetrator. The crime is effective – the perpetrator should have obtained new knowledge of the contents of the message.[945]

Under the second main *corpus delicti*, the executive act consists of diverting the message from its recipient. The diverting of the message means impeding its receiving by the recipient to whom it is addressed.

419. The perpetrator should have acted with malice aforethought to be subject to criminal liability. The perpetrator should have been aware that the message has not been addressed to him or her and despite that he or she has learned its contents or has hindered its delivery to the recipient.

The punishment stipulated under Article 171(1), i. 3 of the CC is imprisonment for up to one year or a penalty from BGN 100 to BGN 300.

B. *Qualified* Corpora Delicti

420. The CC stipulates four qualified *corpora delicti* of encroachments against the confidentiality of correspondence when it is implemented electronically. The qualifying circumstances are the subjects who could commit the crime (an official), the means of the crime (special technical devices), the object of the crime (computer data transmitted within one or more information systems, including electromagnetic emissions from an information system), the criminal purpose (self-interest purpose), and the criminal result (infliction of considerable damages).

---

944. D. Markov, *Legal Regulation of the Computer Crimes under the Bulgarian Law,* in *Electronic Document and Electronic Signatures. Commentary*, 401 (G. Dimitrov et al.).

945. M Kopcheva., Computer Crimes, 55. According to the author, the crime is formal under both main corpora delicti.

1. Qualified *Corpora Delicti* with a View to the Subject Who Could Commit the Crime

421. The act is qualified with a view to the subject who could commit the crime when the person is an official who has abused his or her professional capacity.[946] The stipulated punishment is imprisonment for up to two years, and the court may also rule for the deprivation of the right to occupy a specific state or public position.

By virtue of Article 93, i. 1 of the CC, an official is a person to whom it is assigned to fulfil against remuneration or free of charge, temporarily or permanently: (a) a job in a state establishment, with exception of those carrying out activity of material performance and (b) managerial job or a job related to keeping or management of another's property in a state enterprise, cooperation, public organization, other corporate body, or with a sole entrepreneur, as well as of private public notary and assistant public notary, private bailiff, and deputy private bailiff. A crime under Article 171(2) of the CC shall be present where the official has abused his or her professional capacity, that is, has acted during the course of exercising his or her official duties to gain access to a message that is not addressed to him or her.[947]

2. Qualified Corpora with a View to the Means of the Crime

422. The crime shall reveal graver consequences when special technical means are used for its commitment.[948] In such cases, the punishment shall be imprisonment for up to two years. This rule should be applied only in relation to establishing access to or learning the contents of a message, but not in relation to hindering the delivery of a message to its recipient.

The *corpus* reveals that the message must be sent through a computer network or other communication device.[949]

The crime must also have been committed by using special technical devices.[950] These are devices used for the implementation of specific technical activities. When the message is sent through a computer network, these technical devices could be either hardware tools or software program for sniffing, cracking encryptions, or similar which may deliver the desired result of reading the message contents.

946. CC, Art. 171(2).
947. *See* A. Stoyanov, *Paragraph Criminal Law. Special Part. Crimes Against Human Rights*, 36.
948. CC, Art. 171(3). *See also* M. Kopcheva, *Computer Crimes*, 56–59; according to the author the text of Art. 171(3) of the CC regulates a different main *corpus delicti* of a crime against the confidentiality of correspondence.
949. *See* Part VII, Ch. 1, para. 363 *supra*.
950. *See* A. Stoynov, *Paragraph Criminal Law. Special Part. Crimes Against Property* 33 (Sofia: Ciela, 2008).

3. Qualified *Corpora Delicti* with a View to the Object of the Crime

423. With the amendments to the CC from 2017, a new qualified *corpora delicti* of encroachments against the confidentiality of correspondence was added. The qualifying circumstance is the object of the crime (computer data transmitted within one or more information systems, including electromagnetic emissions from an information system). This *corpora delicti* is regulated by Article 171(4) of the CC, and the stipulated punishment is imprisonment for up to two years.

4. Qualified *Corpora Delicti* with a View to the Criminal Purpose and the Criminal Result

424. With the amendments to the CC from May 2007, two more qualified *corpora delicti* of encroachments against the confidentiality of correspondence were added. The qualifying circumstances are the criminal purpose (self-interest purpose) and the criminal result (infliction of considerable damages).[951] Both *corpora delicti* were regulated by Article 171(4) of the CC, now after the 2017 amendments – under Article 171(5) of the CC, and the stipulated punishment is imprisonment for up to three years and a penalty of up to BGN 5,000. The particular issue about this provision is that it applies only in relation to Article 171(3) and (4) of the CC, that is, it concerns only the cases of illegal learning of a message sent by phone, telegraph, through a computer network, or other communication device by using special technical devices or when the object of the crime is computer data transmitted within one or more information systems, including electromagnetic emissions from an information system.

II. Destruction and Damaging of Foreign Property

425. The destruction and damaging of foreign property by gaining illegal access to an information system is provided for in Article 216(3) of the CC.

The executive act of the crime includes two elements. The first one is the gaining of illegal access to an information system, which is of significance to an enterprise, institution, legal entity, or natural person. The information system is defined in Article 93, i. 21 of the CC. Whether a specific information system is of significance to the enumerated entities is a factual matter which shall be assessed by the court on a case-by-case basis. For this assessment, the court should consider the properties of the system itself, as well as the information and data stored in it. Illegal access is any access which is not justified by law (by a normative act, provision from internal rules or procedures, private legal transaction and others).[952]

The second element of the executive act is the same as under the main *corpus delicti* under Article 216(1) of the CC – destroying and damaging foreign property.

---

951. *See* Part VII, Ch. 1, para. 363 *supra*.
952. *See* D. Markov, *Legal Regulation of the Computer Crimes under the Bulgarian Law*, in *Electronic Document and Electronic Signatures. Commentary*, 404 (G. Dimitrov et al.).

It should be taken into consideration that the crime under Article 216(3) will be present when functional relationship exists between the two acts where the gaining of illegal access is the means for the destruction of the foreign property.

426. According to Article 216(5) of CC, the act is more severely punishable (imprisonment for up to ten years and the court may also rule on deprivation of the right to occupy a specific state position or to exercise a specific profession or activity), if a specific criminal result is present (inflicted considerable damages or other grave consequences), if it has been committed by a subject having particular functions (a person engaged in security, an employee at an organization performing security or insurance activity, a person acting by order of such organization or pretending to be acting by such order, a person from the members of the Ministry of Interior or a person who pretends to be such a member, a person who acts upon assignment or in execution of a decision of an organized criminal group or organization or a group, which uses force to strike fear to conclude transactions or gain benefits) or if it is aimed at a special object (related to the destruction or damaging of elements from a communication network).

When the act is of lower significance, the punishment is imprisonment for up to six months or a penalty from BGN 100 to BGN 300,[953] and when it has been committed carelessly, the punishment is imprisonment for up to two years or a penalty from BGN 100 to BGN 300 (Article 216, (6) of the CC).[954]

III. False Documenting

427. With the amendments to the CC from 2002, the electronically sent message was added to the *corpora delicti* of false documenting under Article 313(1) and (3) of the CC as the object of the crime. The rules of the CC criminalize the confirmation of an untruth or the concealment of a truth in various types of documents, and the only relation to computer crimes is the possibility of these documents to be submitted electronically.[955]

The amendments in the *corpora delicti* of false documenting were unnecessary. By virtue of Article 3, (2) of EDETSA, the electronically sent message will be equalized to a paper document within the meaning of the CC if it complies with the requirements for an electronic document containing electronic statement under EDETSA (in connection with the provisions of eIDAS on electronic documents). Thus, the act will fall within the scope of Article 313 of the CC even before the amendments.[956]

953. CC, Art. 216(4).
954. CC, Art. 216(6).
955. *See* M. Kopcheva, *Computer Crimes*, 125–127.
956. D. Markov, *Legal Regulation of the Computer Crimes under the Bulgarian Law*, in *Electronic Document and Electronic Signatures. Commentary*, 405 (G. Dimitrov et al.).

Chapter 3. Application of Criminal Procedure Law in the Area of ICT

§1. Search and Seizure of Stored Computer Data

428. Special rules for search and seizure of stored computer data could be identified in the Criminal Procedure Code. Upon request of the court or the pretrial bodies, all institutions, legal entities, officials, and citizens shall be obliged to preserve and hand over all objects, papers, computerized information data, and other data that may be of significance to the case.[957] The old version of the provision provided for obligation to provide also traffic data,[958] but with the amendments from 2015 it was replaced with the more generic 'other data'.

429. In a pretrial procedure, search and seizure shall be performed only upon an authorization by a judge from the respective first instance court or a judge from the first instance court in the area in which the action is taken upon the prosecutor's request. In emergency cases, where this is the only possible way to collect and keep evidence, pretrial bodies may perform physical examination without such authorization. The record of the investigative action shall be submitted for approval by the supervising prosecutor to the judge forthwith, but not later than 24 hours thereafter. In the judicial procedure, search and seizure shall be performed following a decision of the court which is reviewing the case.[959]

430. Searches and seizures shall be conducted in the presence of certifying witnesses and of the person who uses the premises, or of an adult member of the person's family. Where the person who uses the premises or a member of his or her family cannot attend, the search and seizure shall be performed in the presence of the house manager or of a representative of the municipality or mayor's office. Searches and seizures in premises used by state and/or municipal authorities shall be performed in the presence of their representative. Searches and seizures in premises used by legal entities shall be performed in the presence of a representative thereof. Where no representative of the legal person may be present, the search and seizure shall be carried out in the presence of a representative of the municipality or mayoralty. Searches and seizures in premises of foreign missions and of missions of international organizations or in dwellings of their employees who enjoy immunity with respect to the criminal jurisdiction of the Republic of Bulgaria shall be conducted with the consent of the head of mission and in the presence of a prosecutor and a representative of the Ministry of Foreign Affairs. Where searches and seizures concern computerized information systems and software, these shall be

957. Criminal Procedure Code, Art. 159.
958. According to the Additional Provisions, para. 1, i. 2 of the Criminal Procedure Code, 'Traffic Data' included all data concerning communications passing through a computer system as an element of a communications chain and containing data on the origin, location, route, time, date, size, and length of the connection or the main service. This provision was repealed with the amendments from 2015.
959. Criminal Procedure Code, Art. 161.

conducted in the presence of an expert – technical assistant.[960] Article 163 makes clear that seizure of computerized data shall be carried out through record on paper or another carrier.

§2. INTERCEPTION

431. Retention and seizure of correspondence shall be allowed only where this is necessary for disclosure or prevention of serious crimes. In a pretrial procedure, such shall be performed upon the request of the prosecutor with the authorization of a judge from the respective first instance court or a judge from the court in the area of which the action is taken, and in judicial procedure search and seizure of correspondence shall be performed by a decision of the court which is reviewing the case.[961]

432. With the amendments from 2015, a new provision – Article 165(3) – was introduced in the Criminal Procedure Code. According to it, in emergency cases, when this is the only opportunity to collect and preserve evidence in the investigation of crimes under Article 108a and Article 354a of the CC, the bodies of the pretrial proceedings may detain undelivered correspondence without the abovementioned court authorization. The supervising prosecutor shall immediately, but not later than 24 hours, present to the judge of the respective court the protocol for the performed action together with a motivated written request for seizure of the detained correspondence. The seizure shall be carried out with the written motivated permission of the judge, who shall rule immediately, but not later than 24 hours. In case of refusal, the judge shall also rule on the retained correspondence. This rule applies only in case of investigation of specific crimes, namely terrorism (Article 108a of the CC) and manufacturing, processing, acquiring or holding narcotic substances or their analogues for the purpose of distribution, or distributing narcotic substances or their analogues (Article 354a of the CC).

433. The Criminal Procedure Code entitles pretrial bodies to use the following special intelligence means: technical means – electronic and mechanical devices and substances that serve to document operations of the controlled persons and sites, as well as operational techniques – observation, interception, shadowing, penetration, marking and verification of correspondence and computerized information, controlled delivery, trusted transaction, and investigation through an officer under cover. They shall be used where this is required for the investigation of serious offences of intent where the relevant circumstances cannot be established in any other way or this would be accompanied by exceptional difficulties. Computer information service providers shall be under the obligation to provide assistance to the court and pretrial bodies in the collection and recording of computerized data through the use of special technical devices only when this is required for the purposes of detecting such crimes. The authorization for use of special intelligence

960. Criminal Procedure Code, Art. 162.
961. Criminal Procedure Code, Art. 165.

means shall be given in advance by the Chairperson of the respective District Court or by a Deputy Chairperson explicitly authorized thereby. They shall rule immediately following receipt of a request in a written and well-justified order. Special rules are included for the competent court to grant authorization for usage of special intelligence means for investigation of crimes committed by judges, prosecutors, investigators, chairmen of courts, etc.[962] The term for application of special intelligence means may not exceed two months and only in one specific hypothesis envisaged in the Special Intelligence Means Act[963] could be for up to twenty days – with regard to objects to establish the identity of (i) persons for whom data have been received and there is reason to assume that they are preparing, committing or have committed a serious intentional crime by those listed under Article 3(1) from the act or (ii) persons for whose actions data have been obtained and there is reason to believe that they are used by the persons under (i), without being aware of the criminal nature of the activity.[964] It is important that the indictment and the sentence may not be based only on data obtained from special intelligence means or on these data only and on testimony of witnesses whose identities are kept secret.[965]

§3. Jurisdiction

434. Articles 3–6 of the CC set out the principles that govern the objectives and scope of the CC. As a rule, Bulgarian Courts are competent, if the crime was committed on the territory of the Republic of Bulgaria. The crime is considered committed, when the act is carried out as well as where the effects of the crime take place. The crime would also be committed on the territory of the Republic of Bulgaria when only part of the act or only the effects of the crime take place on Bulgarian territory. Moreover, Bulgarian courts are competent if the crime was committed on the territory of the Republic of Bulgaria irrespective of the nationality of the offender, Bulgarian or other.[966]

435. Bulgarian Courts have jurisdiction over crimes committed outside the Bulgarian territory when:

(1) the crime is committed by Bulgarian citizens abroad;
(2) foreigners have committed crime of general nature abroad affecting the interests of the Republic of Bulgaria or of a Bulgarian citizen;
(3) foreigners have committed crime abroad against world peace and humanity, thus affecting the interests of another country or foreign citizens;
(4) crimes committed by foreigners abroad wherever stipulated by an international agreement party to which is the Republic of Bulgaria.[967]

962. Criminal Procedure Code, Art. 174(5) and (6).
963. SG, issue 95 of 21 Oct. 1997.
964. Criminal Procedure Code, Arts 172–175.
965. Criminal Procedure Code, Art. 177 and Art. 124.
966. A. Stoynov, *Criminal Law*, *General Part* 103 (Sofia: Ciela Publishing 2007).
967. CC, Arts 4–6.

§4. Extradition and Judicial Cooperation

436. Extradition procedures are governed by the Extradition and European Arrest Warrant Act(EEAW).[968] Evidently, extradition shall be admitted only if the act constitutes a criminal offence as per Bulgarian legislation and as per the legislation of the applying country, and for this offence imprisonment penalty or measure requiring detention for at least one year unless a more severe penalty is stipulated.[969]

A request for extradition of a person, who has committed an offence judicable before a Bulgarian court, shall be made by the Chief Prosecutor for an accused or sentenced person with an enforced sentence and by the Minister of Justice for a defendant upon a proposal of the respective court.[970]

437. Bulgarian law provides sufficient guarantees to ensure the cooperation between jurisdictions. Some of the basic conventions to which the Republic of Bulgaria is a party are the European Convention on Mutual Assistance in Criminal Matters[971] ratified by Bulgaria on 27 April 1994, the European Convention on the Transfer of Procedure in Criminal Cases[972] and the Council of Europe Convention on the International Validity of Criminal Judgments,[973] both ratified on 28 January 2004. On 1 April 2005, Bulgaria ratified the Council of Europe Convention on Cybercrime[974] which is the first international treaty for crimes performed through the Internet and other computer networks. As regards cooperation at EU level, contact points for cooperation with the European Judicial Network (EJN)[975] have been established. The EJN is providing support to Bulgaria in its building of effective judicial cooperation.[976]

§5. Electronic Evidence

438. The current legal provisions concerning evidence are general and abstract, and there is no legislative distinction between evidence obtained by means of an analogue device and evidence from a digital device. However, generally the evidentiary rules do not exclude the use of analogue evidence such as video-recorded and

968. SG, issue 46 of 3 June 2005.
969. EEAW, Art. 5.
970. EEAW, Art. 23.
971. European Convention on Mutual Assistance in Criminal Matters, Council of Europe, Strasbourg, 20 Apr. 1959, http://conventions.coe.int/Treaty/EN/Treaties/Html/030.htm.
972. European Convention on the Transfer of Proceedings in Criminal Matters, Council of Europe, Strasbourg, 15 May 1972, http://conventions.coe.int/treaty/EN/Treaties/Html/073.htm.
973. European Convention on the International Validity of Criminal Judgments, Council of Europe, Hague, 28 May 1970, http://conventions.coe.int/Treaty/EN/Treaties/Html/070.htm.
974. *See* Part VII, Ch. 2, para. 375, *supra*.
975. European Judicial Network, www.ejn-crimjust.europa.eu.
976. Ministry of Interior of the Republic of Bulgaria, http://eu.mvr.bg/en/Areas/Judicial_coop/default.htm.

tape-recorded evidence. Furthermore, special procedural provisions exist concerning the collection of digital data as evidence.[977] The Criminal Procedure Code has laid down detailed rules as to the use of electronic evidence in criminal procedure. However, current legislation does not stipulate special rules concerning the admissibility of electronic evidence, and as a result, the general rules presently apply. In circumstances where the electronic evidence is related to the subject of proof and is collected in compliance with the law, it is admissible and is enclosed with the trial materials.[978]

977. G. Dimitrov & D. Krusteva, *Electronic Evidence in Bulgaria*, in *International Electronic Evidence*, Ch. 6, 105–125 (St. Mason ed., London: British Institute of International and Comparative Law 2008).
978. *Ibid.*, 108–109.

Part VIII. Conclusion

439. The legal framework of the information and communication technologies in Bulgaria is very dynamic. The legislator strives against the necessity to keep up with the necessity of protecting the lawful interest of people while relations emerge, develop, and come to an end in a virtual world where constantly emerging technologies are used. At the same time, lawmakers aim at preserving the main principle of the law – to regulate relations between people for a relatively long period of time. Is the long-lasting and bureaucratic legislative process adapted to face the challenges of the quickly developing information technologies? Is it capable of bringing long-term life of the legal norms by keeping technological neutrality? The present work shows that in Bulgaria, like in other jurisdictions, this proves to be very difficult. Laws are amended frequently, and by the time when the amendments come into force, new regulations are already necessary. The legislations cannot keep up with the new realities of the cyberspace.

The difficulties are far more challenging since the freedom of movement of people, goods, and money should be preserved as a main principle in the internal market of the EU. Therefore, legal protection shall be harmonized on a supranational level as well. In that regard, evident is the tendency for the past ten years within the EU to harmonize key areas of law related to the usage of ICT such as e-documents, e-signatures, and other trust services (via eIDAS), the data protection (via the GDPR and Directives 2016/680 and 2016/681), the copyright protection in the digital single market (Directives 2019/789 and 2019/790), and many more. The relations between people in cyberspace definitely demand new approaches, principles, and rules in setting legal regulations both on national and supranational level.

Selected Bibliography

§1. Books

Beale, H., et al. *Cases, Materials and Text on Contract Law*. Oxford and Portland, OR: Hart Publishing, 2002.

Borrows, A. *Remedies for Torts and Breach of Contract*. 2nd ed. Oxford: Oxford University Press, 2005.

Cholakov, R. *Law of Radio and Television Organizations in Bulgaria*. Sofia: Ciela – Soft and Publishing, 2000.

Cruquenaire. *Internet: la proplématique des noms de domaine*. Ing.-Cons., 1997.

Dimitrov, G., et al. *Commercial Register Act. Commentary*. Sofia: Centre for Study of the Democracy, 2007.

Dimitrov, G., et al. *Electronic Document and Electronic Signature. Legal Regime*. Sofia: Ciela Publishing/CSD, 2004.

Dimitrov, G. & D. Krusteva. 'Electronic Evidence in Bulgaria', in *International Electronic Evidence*, edited by St. Mason. London: British Institute of International and Comparative Law, 2008, Chapter 6.

Dimitrov, G. *Information and Communication Technologies Law – Administrative Law and Technological Aspects Vol II* (Law and Internet Foundation 2014).

Dimitrov, G. *Liability of Certification Service Providers*. Saarbruecken: VDM Verlag Dr Mueller, 2008.

Dugdale, A., M. Jones & M. Simpson. *Clerk & Lindsell on Torts*. 15th ed. London: Sweet and Maxwell, 1982.

Feti, N. & D. Toshkova-Nikolova, *Application of the Personal Data Protection, Methods, recommendations and Practical Steps*, Sofia, IK Trud I Pravo, 2020.

Gerdjikov, O. *Comment on the Commercial Act*, Book 1. Sofia: Sofi-R, 2007.

Van Gerven, W., J. Lever & P. Larouche. *Cases, Materials and Text on National, Supranational and International Tort Law*. Oxford and Portland, Oregon: Hart Publishing, 2000.

Howing, P. *Positive and Negative Interest in Law*. Deventer: Kluwer, 1992.

Kalaydjiev, A. *Law on Obligations. General Part*. Sofia: SIBI, 2001.

Kamenova, Tsv. *Copyright: International and National*. Sofia: ILS – BAS, 1999.

Kaspersen, H. & A. Lodder. *eDirectives. Guide to European Union Law on E-commerce*. The Netherlands: Kluwer Law International, 2002.

Konov, T. *Grounds for Civil Liability*. Sofia: University Publishing House 'St. Kliment Ohridski', 1995.

Kopcheva, M. *Computer Crimes*. Sofia: SIBI, 2006.

Kotz, H. & K. Zweigert. *An Introduction to Comparative Law*. Oxford: Clarendon Press, 1987.
Krusteva, D. & A. Alexandrov, Handbook Protection of Personal Data – Mission Possible. First edition, Sofia, Rezon Bulgaria OOD, 2018.
Pavlova, M. *General Civil Law*. Sofia: Sofi-R, 1997.
Rosati, E. *Copyright in the Digital Single Market: Article-by-Article Commentary to the Provisions of Directive 2019/790*, Oxford, Oxford University Press, 2021.
Stoyanov, A. *Paragraph Criminal Law. Special Part. Crimes against Human Rights*. Sofia: Ciela, 1997.
Stoynov, A. *Criminal Law, General Part*. Sofia: Ciela, 2008.
Toshkova-Nikolova, D. & N., Feti, *Personal Data Protection*, Sofia, IK Trud I Pravo, 2019.
Tselkov, V., D. Petkov, G. Sredkov & P. Georgiev. *Data Protection – Principles and Practices*. Sofia, Za Bukvite O Pismeneh, 2019.
Viefhues, M. *Kennzeichenrecht in: Hoeren, Thomas, Sieber, Ulrich*. München: Handbuch Multimedia-Recht, 1999.
Weigenek, R. *E-commerce: A Guide to the Law of Electronic Business*. 3rd ed. London: Butterworths Lexis Nexis, 2002.
Weir, T. (ed.). 'Complex Liabilities', in *International Encyclopaedia of Comparative Law*, edited by R. David et al. Vol. 11. Tübingen: Mohr, 1976, Chapter 12.
De Otaola Zamora, J. 'Monograph Spain in Cyber Law', in *International Encyclopedia of Law*, edited by R. Blanpain. Suppl. 4. The Hague: Kluwer Law International, 2004.

§2. Articles

Apostolova, R. 'Protection of the Distribution of Movies and Entertainment Software on the Internet'. *Ownership and Law Magazine* 6 (2002): 64.
Bubert, I. & M. Buening. *Domain Name Issues – European Jurisdiction*. ESPRIT Project 27028, Electronic Commerce Legal Issues Platform (2000).
Dimitrov, G. 'Bulgaria Adopts Revolutionary E-Governance Act'. *I-Ways Journal of E-Government Policy and Regulation* 31 (2008): 149.
Dimitrov, G. 'Legal Nature and Protection of Domains'. *Market and Law Magazine* (2002): 69.
Doncheva, D. 'Computer Crimes under Chapter Nine "A" of the CC'. *Legal Thought*, No. 2 (2003).
'E-Bulgaria 2006 Report'. Sofia: Applied Studies and Communications Foundation, 2006.
Groshieide, F. & K. Boele-Woelki. 'European Private Law (1999/2000)'.
E-Commerce Issue, Molengrafica (2000): 11.
Hourigan, P. 'Domain Names and Trade Marks: Disputes from an Australian Perspective', in *Going Digital: Legal Issues for Electronic Commerce, Multimedia and the Internet*, edited by C. Cifuentes, et al. New South Wales: Prospect Media, 1998.
Konov, T. 'The Notion Unlawfulness in the Area of Delicts under the Bulgarian Civil Law'. *Almanac of Sofia University 1986* 79(Book 1) (1986): 155.
Krivachka, M. & M. Markov. 'New Conditions in the Public Procurement Act'. *Labour and Law* (2006): 169–176.

Lipton, J. 'What's in a (Domain) Name? Web Addresses as Loan Collateral'. *The Journal of Information, Law and Technology* 2 (1999).

Makshutova, R. & M., Zahariev, 'GDPR Implementation Series – Bulgaria', *European Data Protection Law Review,* 3/2020.

Slavinski, A. 'The Broadband Market in Bulgaria'. BASSCOM. Paper given at the SFERA Annual Conference, Brussels, 2008.

Stoynov, A. 'Computer Fraud'. *Modern Law* 4 (2002).

Yee, K. 'Location.location.location: A Snapshot of Internet Addresses as Evolving Property'. *The Journal of Information, Law and Technology* 1 (1997).

Zahariev, M. 'Principles of Personal Data Processing – Nature and Significance as a Standard for Personal Data Protection', in Collection *Knowledge Society and 21st Century Humanism*, Sofia, Za Bukvite O Pismeneh, 2020.

Zahariev, 'The evolution of EU data protection law on automated data profiling', *Privacy in Germany PinG* 02.2017.

Zahariev, M. 'Protection of trademark against bad faith registration of domain name', *Computerworld*, 14 Feb. 2017.

§3. Online Publications

Berger, K. & J. Bick. *New Jersey Law Journal,* www.law.com/jsp/cc/PubArticleCC.jsp?id=120243387879618, 18 September 2009.

'Broadband: Gap between Best and Worst Performing Countries in Europe', www.nieuwsbank.nl/en/2008/11/28/v018.htm, 28 November 2008.

'Broadband: Gap between Best and Worst Performing Countries in Europe', www.nieuwsbank.nl/en/2008/11/28/v018.htm, 28 November 2008, 1.

Bulgaria 2011 Telecommunications market and regulatory developments. http://ec.europa.eu/digital-agenda/sites/digital-agenda/files/BG_Country_Chapter_17th_Report_0.pdf, accessed 16 September 2013.

CBN Pannoff, Stoytcheff & Co. 'National ICT Forum Bulgaria 2009', www. cbn-bulgaria.com/index_eng.htm.

CJEU, https://curia.europa.eu/juris/liste.jsf?num=C-311/18, accessed 15 Dec. 2021.

Commission of the European Communities. 'Progress Report on the Single European Electronic Communications Market (13th Report)' (COM(2008)153). http://ec. europa.eu/information_society/policy/ecomm/library/communications_reports/annualreports/13th/index_en.htm, 19 March 2008.

Convention on the Grant of European Patents, www.epo.org/patents/law/legal-texts/html/epc/1973/e/ma1.html, 5 October 1973.

Coordination Council for Information Society. 'National Broadband Programme of the Republic of Bulgaria', www.broadband-europe.eu/Pages/StrategyDetail.aspx?-ItemID=28, December 2008.

Coordination Council for Information Society, 'National Broadband Programme of the Republic of Bulgaria', www.broadband-europe.eu/Pages/StrategyDetail.aspx?ItemID=28, December 2008.

CPC, CRC. 'Rules for Collaboration and Coordination between CPC and CRC', www.crc.bg/files/_bg/PRAVILA_26.02.2008.pdf, 26 February 2008.

CPC. Who are the types of conciliation committees, https://kzp.bg/koi-sa-vidovete-pomiritelni-komisii, accessed 03 Oct. 2021.

CRC. 'Annual Report 2008', www.crc.bg/section.php?id=593&lang=bg.

CRC. 'Annual Report 2007', www.crc.bg/section.php?id=44&lang=en.
CRC. 'Annual Report 2020', https://crc.bg/files/AR_CRC_2020_22.06.2021.pdf, accessed 09 Dec. 2021.
CRC. 'Decisions from the first round of identifications, analysis and evaluation of the relevant electronic communications markets': https://crc.bg/bg/rubriki/221/okonchatelni-reshenija-prieti-ot-krs-v-rezultat-ot-pyrvija-kryg-opredeljane-analiz-i-ocenka-na-syotvetnite-pazari-na-elektronni-syobshtenija, accessed 26 Dec. 2021.
CRC. 'Decisions from the second round of identifications, analysis and evaluation of the relevant electronic communications markets': https://crc.bg/bg/rubriki/220/okonchatelni-reshenija-prieti-ot-krs-v-rezultat-ot-vtori-kryg-opredeljane-analiz-i-ocenka-na-syotvetnite-pazari-na-elektronni-syobshtenija, accessed 26 Dec. 2021
CRC. 'Decisions from the third round of identifications, analysis and evaluation of the relevant electronic communications markets': https://crc.bg/bg/rubriki/219/okonchatelni-reshenija-prieti-ot-krs-v-rezultat-ot-treti-kryg-opredeljane-analiz-i-ocenka-na-syotvetnite-pazari-na-elektronni-syobshtenija, accessed 26 Dec. 2021.
CRC. 'Decisions from the fourth round of identifications, analysis and evaluation of the relevant electronic communications markets': https://crc.bg/bg/rubriki/618/okonchatelni-resheniq-prieti-ot-krs-v-rezultat-ot-chetvyrti-kryg-na-opredelqne-analiz-i-ocenka-na-syotvetnite-pazari-na-elektronni-syobshteniq, accessed 26 Dec. 2021.
CRC. ' List of Radio Equipment using Frequency Bands Harmonised throughout the EU and Electronic Communications Terminal Equipment', www.crc.bg/files/_en/LIST_of_radio_equipment1.pdf, 20 December 2007.
CRC. 'Methodology for Measuring Intermodulation Products of type "A1" during the Operation of Closely Situated VHF-FM Radio Broadcasting Stations (in conformity with i. 2.5 of Appendix 1 to the Technical Requirements for Electronic Communications Networks of Broadcasting Services and Related Equipment)', www.crc.bg/section.php?id=124&lang=en.
CRC. 'National Numbering Plan'. Annex to Decision No. 873, www.crc.bg/files/bg/n8.htm, 4 June 2007.
CRC Annual Report 2012. http://www.crc.bg/files/_bg/I._Sustoyanie,_razvitie_i_perspektivi_na_pazara_na_elektronnite_suobshteniq_GD2012.pdf.
CRC 'Annual Report': http://www.crc.bg/files/_bg/I%D0%86_Elektronni_syobshtitelni_mreji_i_uslugi_CRC_GD_2012.pdf, 2012, accessed 16 September 2013.
CRC 'Annual Report': http://www.crc.bg/files/_bg/I%D0%86_Elektronni_syobshtitelni_mreji_i_uslugi_CRC_GD_2012.pdf, 2012, accessed 16 September 2013.
CRC 'Annual Report': http://www.crc.bg/files/_bg/I%D0%86_Elektronni_syobshtitelni_mreji_i_uslugi_CRC_GD_2012.pdf, 2012, accessed 16 September 2013.
CRC 'Annual Report': http://www.crc.bg/files/_bg/I%D0%86_Elektronni_syobshtitelni_mreji_i_uslugi_CRC_GD_2012.pdf, 2012, accessed 16 September 2013.
CRC. 'Annual Report'. http://www.crc.bg/files/_bg/I_GD2011.pdf, 2011, accessed 16 September 2013.
Creative Commons International, Bulgaria. http://creativecommons.org/international/bg/.

Doctorow, C. 'Shrinkwrap Licences: "An Epidemic of Lawsuits Waiting to Happen"', www.informationweek.com/news/management/showArticle.jhtml?article ID= 197003052, 3 February 2007.
EC, Adequacy decisions, https://ec.europa.eu/info/law/law-topic/data-protection/international-dimension-data-protection/adequacy-decisions_en, accessed 17 Dec. 2021.
EC, 'Progress Report on the Single European Electronic Communications Market' (13th Report), http://ec.europa.eu/information_society/policy/ecomm/library/communications_reports/annualreports/13th/index_en.htm, 87, accessed 16 September 2013.
EC, Standard contractual clauses for international transfers, https://ec.europa.eu/info/law/law-topic/data-protection/international-dimension-data-protection/standard-contractual-clauses-scc/standard-contractual-clauses-international-transfers_en, accessed 15 Dec. 2021.
Economist Intelligence Unit – IT industry competitiveness index 2011, http://globalindex11.bsa.org/, accessed 16 September 2013.
EDPB, Guidelines 3/2018 on the territorial scope of the GDPR (Article 3) – version adopted after public consultation, https://edpb.europa.eu/our-work-tools/our-documents/guidelines/guidelines-32018-territorial-scope-gdpr-article-3-version_en, accessed 15 Dec. 2021.
EDPB, Guidelines 2/2019 on the processing of personal data under Article 6(1)(b) GDPR in the context of the provision of online services to data subjects, https://edpb.europa.eu/sites/default/files/consultation/edpb_draft_guidelines-art_6-1-b-final_public_consultation_version_en.pdf, accessed 15 Dec. 2021.
EDPB, Guidelines 05/2020 on consent under Regulation 2016/679, https://edpb.europa.eu/sites/default/files/files/file1/edpb_guidelines_202005_consent_en.pdf, accessed 15 Dec. 2021.
EDPB, Guidelines 07/2020 on the concepts of controller and processor in the GDPR, https://edpb.europa.eu/our-work-tools/documents/public-consultations/2020/guidelines-072020-concepts-controller-and_en, accessed 15 Dec. 2021.
EDPB, Recommendations 01/2020 on measures that supplement transfer tools to ensure compliance with the EU level of protection of personal data, https://edpb.europa.eu/our-work-tools/our-documents/recommendations/recommendations-012020-measures-supplement-transfer_en, accessed 15 Dec. 2021.
'E-Government Factsheets: e-Government in Bulgaria', www.epractice.eu/en/document/288402, 2009.
'E-government Factsheets: E-government in Bulgaria'. http://www.epractice.eu/files/eGovernmentBulgaria.pdf, 2011, 1, accessed 1 October 2013.
'E-government Factsheets: E-government in Bulgaria'. http://www.epractice.eu/files/eGovernmentBulgaria.pdf, 2011, 1, accessed 1 October 2013.
European Commission, 'EU: i2010 – Annual Information Society Report 2008'. www.epractice.eu/en/library/292889#at, 16 April 2008.
European Group on Tort Law, 'Principles of European Tort Law', www.egtl.org/principles/text.htm.
European Commission, 'EU: i2010 – Annual Information Society Report 2008', www. epractice.eu/en/library/292889#at, 16 April 2008, 13.

Selected Bibliography

European Commission, BULGARIA 2011: Telecommunication Market and Regulatory Developments, http://ec.europa.eu/digital-agenda/sites/digital-agenda/files/BG_Country_Chapter_17th_Report_0.pdf, 2012, accessed 16 September 2013.

European Commission, BULGARIA 2011: Telecommunication Market and Regulatory Developments, http://ec.europa.eu/digital-agenda/sites/digital-agenda/files/BG_Country_Chapter_17th_Report_0.pdf, 2012, accessed 16 September 2013.

EUROSTAT, http://epp.eurostat.ec.europa.eu/portal/page/portal/eurostat/home, 23 Feb. 2009.

European Judicial Network, www.ejn-crimjust.europa.eu/.

Explanatory Report on the Convention on Cybercrime, Council of Europe, ETS No. 185. http://conventions.coe.int/treaty/en/reports/html/185.htm, 8 November 2001.

Finkelstein, T. & D.C. Wyatt. 'Shrinkwrap Licences: Consequences of Breaking the Seal'. *St. John's Law Review*. http://findarticles.com/p/articles/mi_qa3735/is_199710/ai_n8778077/.

Global E-Government Development Reports and Survey by the UN Public administration programme; http://unpan3.un.org/egovkb/datacenter/CountryView.aspx?reg=EUROPE%20~%20Eastern%20Europe, 2012, accessed 1 October 2013.

'GNU General Public License', www.gnu.org/licences/gpl.html.

Halbert, D. 'The Open Source Alternative: Shrink-Wrap, Open Source and Copyright'. *Murdoch University Electronic Journal of Law.* www.murdoch.edu.au/elaw/issues/v10n4/halbert104_text.html, December 2003.

ICANN, Reserved Domain Names, http://res-dom.iana.org.

IMENA.BG EAD 'TERMS AND CONDITIONS FOR DOMAIN NAME REGISTRATION AND SUPPORT IN THE Бг ZONE' https://www.imena.bg/tld_user_nam/app.pl?action_key=ac_c1p3d1_to_general_terms&frame_key=fr_c1p3_main_frame&lang=en 2018, accessed 17 Oct. 2021.

Internet portal for anti-corruption, www.anticorruption.bg/.

Internet portal for e-government in Bulgaria, www.egov.bg/.

Makshutova, R. What's new in the new Digital Goods and Services Act?, https://www.manager.bg/komentari/kakvo-novo-v-noviya-zakon-za-oblaganeto-na-cifrovite-stoki-i-uslugi?amp, accessed 28 Dec. 2021.

Ministry of Economy, List of ADR bodies for resolution of consumer disputes on Bulgarian territory, https://www.mi.government.bg/files/useruploads/files/zashtita_na_potrebitelite/spisuk_adr_2018.pdf, accessed 03 Oct. 2021.

Ministry of Interior of the Republic of Bulgaria. http://eu.mvr.bg/en/Areas/Judicial_coop/default.htm.

Kunkel JD, R. 'Recent Developments in Shrinkwrap, Clickwrap and Browsewrap Licences in the United States'. *Murdoch University Electronic Journal of Law*. Vol. 9, www.murdoch.edu.au/elaw/issues/v9n3/kunkel93_text.html#Shrinkwrap%20Licence%20Cases_T, September 2002.

Ministry of State Administration and Administrative Reform, www.mdaar.government.bg/press.php.

Ministry of State Administration and Administrative Reform, 'Draft Report on the State of the Administration'. http://law.uni-sofia.bg/Kat/T/IP/T/EP/DocLib/Доклад%20на%20състоянието%20на%20администрацията%20през%202007%20г.pdf, 2007.

National Concession Register, https://nkr.government.bg/Information/GetPage/09cdd63b-386a-4851-9564-51aa10de24d3, accessed 03 Oct. 2021.

National Statistical Institute, 'AVERAGE LIFE EXPECTANCY OF THE POPULATION DURING THE PERIOD 2018 – 2020', https://www.nsi.bg/sites/default/files/files/pressreleases/LifeExpectancy_2018-2020_106QOF0.pdf, 2020, accessed 9 Dec. 2021.

National Statistical Institute, 'Birth rate by statistical regions, districts and places of residence', https://www.nsi.bg/bg/content/2968/коефициент-на-раждаемост-по-статистически-райони-области-и-местоживеене, 2020, accessed 9 Dec. 2021.

National Statistical Institute, 'Births by place of residence, statistical regions, districts and sex', https://www.nsi.bg/bg/content/2956/раждания-по-местоживеене-статистически-райони-области-и-пол, 2020, accessed 9 Dec. 2021.

National Statistical Institute, 'Creation and dissemination of information and creative products; telecommunications', https://www.nsi.bg/bg/content/7697/брой-на-предприятията, accessed 18 Jan. 2021.

National Statistical Institute, 'Employed persons and employment rates – national level; statistical regions; areas', https://www.nsi.bg/bg/content/4009/заети-лица-и-коефициенти-на-заетост-национално-ниво -статистически-райони-области, 2020, accessed 9 Dec. 2021.

National Statistical Institute, 'Employees in enterprises that use the Internet', https://nsi.bg/bg/content/2854/заети-лица-в-предприятията-които-използват-интернет, accessed 18 Jan. 2022.

National Statistical Institute, 'Enrolled students, levels breakdown, according to The International Standard Classification of Education (ISCE)-97, latest data', http://www.nsi.bg/otrasal.php?otr=23&a1=2226&a2=2228#cont, 2013.

National Statistical Institute, 'Enterprises Internet Access', https://nsi.bg/bg/content/2848/предприятия-с-достъп-до-интернет, accessed 9 Dec. 2021.

National Statistical Institute, 'Enterprises selling goods and services on the Internet', https://nsi.bg/bg/content/2872/предприятия-които-продават-стоки-и-услуги-по-интернет, accessed 10 Dec. 2021.

National Statistical Institute, 'Enterprises that have a website', https://nsi.bg/bg/content/2856/предприятия-които-имат-уебсайт, accessed 18 Jan. 2022.

National Statistical Institute, 'Enterprises that use CRM', https://nsi.bg/bg/content/content/2887/предприятия-които-използват-софтуер-за-управление-на-информацията-за-клиенти-crm, accessed 10 Dec. 2021.

National Statistical Institute, 'Enterprises that use ERP', https://nsi.bg/bg/content/2885/предприятия-които-използват-софтуер-за-управление-на-ресурсите-erp, accessed 10 Dec. 2021.

National Statistical Institute, 'Household Internet access', https://www.nsi.bg/bg/content/2808/достъп-на-домакинствата-до-интернет, 2021, accessed 18 Jan. 2022.

National Statistical Institute, 'People who use the Internet regularly', https://nsi.bg/bg/content/2814/лица-регулярно-използващи-интернет, accessed 10 Dec. 2021.

Selected Bibliography

National Statistical Institute, 'People who have purchased goods and services online for personal use in the last 12 months', https://nsi.bg/bg/content/2831/лица-които-са-купували-стоки-и-услуги-по-интернет-за-лични-цели-през-последните-12-месеца, accessed 18 Jan. 2022.

National Statistical Institute, 'People who have never used the Internet', www.nsi.bg/bg/content/2828/лица-които-никога-не-са-използвали-интернет, 2021, accessed 18 Jan. 2022.

National Statistical Institute, 'People using the Internet for the purpose of interaction with public institutions', https://nsi.bg/bg/content/2824/лица-използващи-accessed 10 Dec. 2021.

National Statistical Institute, 'Population and Demographic Processes in 2012', http://www.nsi.bg/EPDOCS/Population2012_IZXIDOM.pdf, 2013.

National Statistical Institute, 'Population by districts, municipalities, place of residence and sex', https://www.nsi.bg/bg/content/2975/население-по-области-общини-местоживеене-и-пол, 2020, accessed 9 Dec. 2021.

National Statistical Institute, 'Population under, in and over working age by districts, municipalities and place of residence', https://www.nsi.bg/bg/content/13038/население-под-във-и-над-трудоспособна-възраст-по-области-общини-и-местоживеене, 2020, accessed 9 Dec. 2021.

National Statistical Institute, 'Preliminary estimation of the population of Bulgaria as of 7 September 2021', https://www.nsi.bg/sites/default/files/files/pressreleases/Census2021_predvaritelna_ocenka.pdf, 2022, accessed 18 Jan. 2022.

National Statistical Institute, 'Turnover by sectors and by groups according to the number of persons employed in them for 2019', https://www.nsi.bg/bg/content/7699/Оборот, accessed 18 Jan. 2021.

National Statistical Institute, http://www.nsi.bg/otrasal.php?otr=70&a1=2461&a2=2462&a3=2467#cont, 2011, accessed 1 October 2013.

National Statistical Institute, http://www.nsi.bg/otrasal.php?otr=17&a1=2422&a2=2423&a3=2426#cont, 2012, accessed 16 September 2013.

National Statistical Institute, http://www.nsi.bg/otrasal.php?otr=17&a1=2405&a2=2406&a3=2407#cont, 2012, accessed 16 September 2013.

National Statistical Institute, Information Society data, http://www.nsi.bg/otrasal.php?otr=17&a1=2422&a2=2432&a3=2434#cont, 2012, accessed 16 September 2013.

National Statistical Institute, Information Society data, http://www.nsi.bg/otrasal.php?otr=17&a1=2422&a2=2436&a3=2439#cont, 2012, accessed 16 September 2013.

National Statistical Institute, Information Society data, http://www.nsi.bg/otrasal.php?otr=17&a1=2422&a2=2432&a3=2434#cont, 2012, accessed 16 September 2013.

National Statistical Institute, Information Society data, http://www.nsi.bg/otrasal.php?otr=17&a1=2422&a2=2436&a3=2439#cont, 2012, accessed 16 September 2013.

National Statistical Institute, Information Society data, http://www.nsi.bg/otrasal.php?otr=17&a1=2422&a2=2436&a3=2496#cont, 2012, accessed 16 September 2013.

National Statistical Institute, Information Society data, http://www.nsi.bg/otrasal.php?otr=17&a1=2422&a2=2436&a3=2496#cont, 2012, accessed 16 September 2013.

National Statistical Institute, 'Students according to degree classification, citizenship, form of education, and gender in academic year 2012/2013, latest data', http://www.nsi.bg/otrasal.php?otr=23&a1=782&a2=783&a3=784#cont, 2013.

National Statistical Institute, 'STUDENTS IN EDUCATIONAL QUALIFICATION, CITIZENSHIP, FORM OF EDUCATION AND SEX, IN HIGHER EDUCATION INSTITUTIONS IN THE FORM OF OWNERSHIP, DURING THE SCHOOL YEAR 2020/2021', https://www.nsi.bg/bg/content/3390/студенти-по-образователно-квалификационна-степен-гражданство-форма-на-обучение-и-пол-във-висшите-училища-по-форма-на-собственост, 2020, accessed 9 Dec. 2021.

National Statistical Institute, 'The Education in the Republic of Bulgaria during the school year 2020/2021', https://www.nsi.bg/sites/default/files/files/pressreleases/Education2020_8POU0B1.pdf, 2020, accessed 9 Dec. 2021.

National Statistical Institute: Final Census 2011: http://www.nsi.bg/EPDOCS/Census2011final.pdf, accessed 16 September 2013. Data to be taken with caution due to high number of blank responses.

National Statistical Institute: Final Census 2011: http://www.nsi.bg/EPDOCS/Census2011final.pdf, accessed 16 September 2013. Data to be taken with caution due to high number of blank responses.

National Statistical Institute: Statistical data 2012: http://www.nsi.bg/EPDOCS/Population2012_IZXIDOM.pdf, data as of 31 December 2012, accessed 16 September 2013.

'Network Service'. http://en.wikipedia.org/wiki/Network_service.

Notification to the CPDP for appointment of a Data Protection Officer, https://www.cpdp.bg/?p=sub_rubric&aid=227, accessed 15 Dec. 2021.

Opinion of the CPDP on issues related to the determination of the qualities "controller" and "processor of personal data" in the relationship between insurance companies and medical institutions, Reg. No. НДМСПО -01-1174/10.12.2018, https://www.cpdp.bg/index.php?p=element_view&aid=2150, accessed 15 Dec. 2021.

Opinion of the CPDP on issues related to the introduction of video surveillance in kindergartens (nurseries and kindergartens), as well as in schools, Reg. No. П – 5375/2017, https://www.cpdp.bg/index.php?p=element_view&aid=2106, accessed 15 Dec. 2021.

Opinion of the CPDP on the application of Regulation (EU) 2016/679 (General Data Protection Regulation) in the judiciary, Reg. No. НДМСПО -17-865/12.10.2018, https://www.cpdp.bg/?p=element_view&aid=2135, accessed 15 Dec. 2021.

Opinion of the CPDP on the processing of personal health data and the level of information of employees in case of infection with COVID-19, Reg. No. ПНМД -17-114/2020, https://www.cpdp.bg/?p=element_view&aid=2263, accessed 15 Dec. 2021.

Opinion of the CPDP on the processing of data on vaccination status, Reg. No. ПНМД -01-93/2021, https://www.cpdp.bg/?p=element_view&aid=2287, accessed 15 Dec. 2021.

Selected Bibliography

Opinion of the CPDP on the requirement to present a criminal record when appointing non-reporting positions, Reg. No. ПНМД – 01 – 5/16.01.2020, https://www.cpdp.bg/?p=element_view&aid=2255, accessed 15 Dec. 2021.

Opinion of the CPDP regarding a request received from Speedy AD on issues related to the application of Regulation (EU) 2106/679, Reg. No. НДМСПО -17-604/20.06.2018, https://www.cpdp.bg/index.php?p=element_view&aid=2118, accessed 15 Dec. 2021.

Practical guidelines of the CPDP in which cases consent is not required for personal data processing, https://www.cpdp.bg/index.php?p=element&aid=1163, accessed 15 Dec. 2021.

'Principles of European Contract Law', www.cisg.law.pace.edu/cisg/text/textef.html.

Rambarran, I. *Are Browse-Wrap Agreements All They Are Wrapped Up to Be?*. http://law.bepress.com/expresso/eps/1885/, 25 November 2006.

Register.BG Ltd, 'Terms and Conditions for Domain Name Registration and Support in the BG Zone and the Sub-zones' https://www.register.bg/user/static/rules/bg/index.html, 2011, accessed 16 Sep. 2013, latest version available at: https://www.register.bg/tld_user_reg/documents/en/terms_and_conditions-v4.9.pdf, accessed 12 Dec. 2021.

Registry Agency. Internet portal for e-registration, www.brra.bg/.

'Short Survey of the Principles of European Contract Law: Introduction to the Principles of European Contract Law Prepared by the Commission on European Contract Law'. http://frontpage.cbs.dk/law/commission_on_european_contract_ law/survey_pecl.htm.

Updated Strategy for the Development of E-Governance in the Republic of Bulgaria 2019 – 2025, https://e-gov.bg/wps/wcm/connect/e-gov.bg-18083/1506d64e-0f16-4954-ba0b-dfd77ae58184/Стратегия+за+развитие+на+електронното+управление+ 2019-2025.pdf?MOD=AJPERES&CVID=nyx-ndJ&useDefaultText=0&useDefaultDesc=0, accessed 10 Dec. 2021.

Wassenaar Arrangement. 'Wassenaar Lists of Dual-use Goods and Technology and Munitions List', www.wassenaar.org/controllists/index.html, December 2005.

'White Paper of the e-government in Bulgaria', www.jnn-marketing.com/index. php?p=egovernmentbg, 2005.

World Bank, 'Achieving Intelligent Growth', http://www-wds.worldbank.org/external/default/WDSContentServer/WDSP/IB/2012/06/13/000333037_20120613234638/Rendered/PDF/662630ESW0P07800B00PUBLIC0BULGARIAN.pdf, 2012, accessed 16 September 2013.

World Bank, 'Achieving Intelligent Growth', http://www-wds.worldbank.org/external/default/WDSContentServer/WDSP/IB/2012/06/13/000333037_20120613234638/Rendered/PDF/662630ESW0P07800B00PUBLIC0BULGARIAN.pdf, 2012, accessed 16 September 2013.

World Bank, 'Accelerating Bulgaria's Convergence: The Challenge of Rising Productivity', Report No. 38570, http://siteresources.worldbank.org/INTBULGARIA/Resources/ABCReport_ Volume_2.pdf, http://siteresources.worldbank.org/INTBULGARIA/Resources/ABCreport_ volume_1.pdf, accessed 16 September 2013.

Wikipedia. 'BSD Licences'. http://en.wikipedia.org/wiki/BSD_licences.

Wikipedia. 'Browse Wrap'. http://en.wikipedia.org/wiki/Browse_wrap.
Wikipedia. 'Facility Management'. http://en.wikipedia.org/wiki/Facility_management.
Wikipedia. 'GNU General Public License'. http://en.wikipedia.org/wiki/GNU_General_Public_License.
Wikipedia. 'Shareware'. http://en.wikipedia.org/wiki/Shareware.
Wikipedia. 'Shrink Wrap Contract'. http://en.wikipedia.org/wiki/Shrink_wrap_ contract.
Wikipedia. 'Turnkey'. http://en.wikipedia.org/wiki/Turnkey.
World Bank. 'Accelerating Bulgaria's Convergence: The Challenge of Rising Productivity'. Report No. 38570. http://siteresources.worldbank.org/INTBULGARIA/Resources/ABCReport_Volume_2.pdf, http://siteresources.world-bank.org/INTBULGARIA/Resources/ABCreport_volume_1.pdf, July 2007.
US Legal Definitions. 'Contractual Maintenance Agreement'. http://definitions.uslegal.com/c/contractual-maintenance-agreement.
Zahariev, M. & D., Krusteva, 'The Legal Nature of Domain Names' *TITA Taxes Magazine* Issue 132 (September 2020), https://www.tita.bg/free/commercial-law/706?fbclid=IwAR0xEfA--qWa7hS_SWL20NXMYGGa3b7HDmPg-qewzh4ly_wJzm9BhXNHrOA, accessed 16 Dec. 2021.
Zahariev, M. 'GDPR Issues in Commercial Arbitration and How to Mitigate Them', Kluwer Arbitration Blog, 7 Sep 2020, http://arbitrationblog.kluwerarbitration.com/2019/09/07/gdpr-issues-in-commercial-arbitration-and-how-to-mitigate-them/, accessed 14 Dec. 2021.
Zahariev, M. 'On the admissibility of certain personal data processing operations by the employer in the context of the COVID-19 pandemic', *TITA Taxes Magazine*, Issue 128 (May 2020), https://www.tita.bg/free/commercial-law/685, accessed 15 Dec. 2021.
Zahariev, M. 'The Amendments in the Personal Data Protection Act following GDPR – Key Aspects', *TITA Taxes Magazine*, Issue 114 (April 2019), https://assets.website-files.com/5fed988aacad01db88e78ec3/619b605ea807c683f777d41b_97-amendments-in-bulgarian-personal-data-protecion-legislation-key-changes-848.pdf accessed 16 Dec. 2021.

Index

The numbers given are paragraph numbers.

Index

Index

www.ingramcontent.com/pod-product-compliance
Ingram Content Group UK Ltd.
Pitfield, Milton Keynes, MK11 3LW, UK
UKHW020134290926
15471UKWH00003B/476

9 789403 54955